THE APPLICATION OF THE EUROPEAN
CONVENTION ON HUMAN RIGHTS

THE APPLICATION OF THE EUROPEAN CONVENTION ON HUMAN RIGHTS

BY

J. E. S. FAWCETT

CLARENDON PRESS · OXFORD

1987

Oxford University Press, Walton Street, Oxford OX2 6DP

Oxford New York Toronto
Delhi Bombay Calcutta Madras Karachi
Petaling Jaya Singapore Hong Kong Tokyo
Nairobi Dar es Salaam Cape Town
Melbourne Auckland

and associated companies in
Beirut Berlin Ibadan Nicosia

Oxford is a trade mark of Oxford University Press

Published in the United States
by Oxford University Press, New York

First edition 1969
Second edition 1987

British Library Cataloguing in Publication Data
Fawcett, J. E. S.
The application of the European Convention
on Human Rights. —2nd ed.
1. European Convention on Human Rights
2. Civil rights (International law)
I. Title
341.4'81 K3240.4
ISBN 0-19-825510-1
ISBN 0-19-825509-8 (pbk)

Library of Congress Cataloging in Publication Data
Fawcett, J. E. S. (James Edmund Sandford), 1913–
The application of the European Convention on Human Rights.
Bibliography: p.
Includes index.
1. Civil rights—Europe. I. Convention for the
Protection of Human Rights and Fundamental Freedoms
(1950) II. Title.
KJC5132.F39 1987 341.4'81 86-23774
ISBN 0-19-825510-1
ISBN 0-19-825509-8 (pbk.)

Typeset by Joshua Associates Limited, Oxford
Printed in Great Britain
at the University Printing House, Oxford
by David Stanford
Printer to the University

ΤΩΙ ΠΑΤΡΙ
ΜΝΗΜΗΣ
ΧΑΡΙΝ

PREFACE

THE purpose of this second edition is to update the survey of the application of the Convention, describing the reports and decisions of its appointed organs, Article by Article and Clause by Clause, from 1968 to the end of 1982; some information is included where material has become available since then.

The method used has been to set out the provisions of the Convention and the First, Fourth and Sixth Protocols, with references to the *travaux preparatoires* that appear useful; to describe the issues raised in leading or typical applications brought under the Convention; and to elucidate the reasoning in the decisions of the Convention organs upon them.

Given the vast expansion of human rights since 1968, the survey has to be confined to the Convention, and there is no attempt to discuss legal or political doctrine; and while books and articles were referred to in relevant contexts, to offer a bibliography is no longer practicable. I have only to add that, if at some points I oppose or favour an interpretation of a Convention provision, the views are my own.

In preparing this survey I owe much to the Secretariat of the Commission in reference to source material, and in article discussion of many Convention issues.

J. E. S. FAWCETT

1986

CONTENTS

ABBREVIATIONS AND TERMS

A.C.	Appeal Cases (House of Lords; Judicial Committee of the Privy Council).	United Kingdom
A.D.	Annual Digest of Public International Law Cases	
A.E.R.	All England Law Reports	England
A.I.R.	All India Law Reports	India
Althing	Parliament	Iceland
Amtsgericht	District Court	Federal Republic of Germany
Arios Pagos	Supreme Court	Greece
B.I.I.C.L.	British Institute of International and Comparative Law	
Bundesgerichtshof (BGH)	Federal Supreme Court	Federal Republic of Germany
Bundestag	Federal Parliament	Federal Republic of Germany
Bundesverfassungs-gericht	(BverfG.) Federal Constitutional Court	Federal Republic of Germany
B.Y.I.L.	*British Yearbook of International Law*	England
C.E.D.H.	European Court of Human Rights: Reports	
Ch.	Chancery Division Reports	United Kingdom
C.I.A.	US Central Intelligence Agency	
C.L.B.	Commonwealth Law Bulletin	
C.M.	Committee of Ministers of the Council of Europe	
Cmd., Cmnd.	Command Papers	United Kingdom
Commission	The European Commission of Human Rights	
Corte di Cassazione	Supreme Court	Italy
Cour de Cassation	Supreme Court	Belgium: Luxembourg
the Court	European Court of Human Rights	
C.P.R.	Civil and Political Rights Covenant	
Cr. App. R.	Criminal Appeal Reports	England
Doc.	Council of Europe Document	

D.R.	Commission decisions and reports (July 1975–)	
Ermittlungsrichter	Investigating judge	Federal Republic of Germany
GA	UN General Assembly	
Folketing	Parliament	Denmark
Grundgesetz	Constitution; basic law	Federal Republic of Germany
Hoge Raad	Supreme Court	Netherlands
House of Lords	Supreme Court	United Kingdom
Höyesterett	Supreme Court	Norway
I.C.L.Q.	*International and Comparative Law Quarterly*	
I.C.J.	International Court of Justice	
I.L.R.	International Law Reports	
Journal of I.C.J.	*Journal of International Commission of Jurists*	
Judgment	of European Court of Human Rights	
Juge d'instruction	Investigating judge	Belgium; Luxembourg
Landgericht	Regional Court	Federal Republic of Germany
Landesgericht		Austria
Nationalrat	Federal Parliament	Austria
Nederlands Jurisprudentie	Law reports	Netherlands
N.J.W.	Neue Juristische Wochenschrift (Law reports and articles)	Federal Repubic of Germany
Oberlandesgericht (OLG)	Regional Appeal Court	Federal Republic of Germany: Austria
Oberster Gerichtshof (OGH)	Supreme Court	Austria
Oberverwaltungsgericht	Administrative Appeal Court	Federal Republic of Germany
P. or P.D.	Probate Division Reports	England
P.C.	Privy Council	United Kingdom
Recueil (numbered) *Recueil* (1959)–	Series of publications of Commission decisions	
S.L.T.	Scottish Law Times	
Staatsanwalt	Public Prosecutor	Federal Republic of Germany: Austria
Storting	Parliament	Norway
Strafprozessordnung (SPO)	Code of Criminal Procedure	Federal Republic of Germany: Austria
T.P.	Travaux préparatoires, vols. I–V	

Untersuchungshaft	Detention on remand	Federal Republic of Germany: Austria
Untersuchungsrichter	Investigating judge	Austria
U.N.T.S.	United Nations Treaty Series	
U.S.	United States Supreme Court Reports	
Verfassungsgericht	Constitutional Court	Austria
Yearbook	*Yearbook of the European Convention On Human Rights* (1958–)	

Applications brought to the Commission and dealt with by it are described, as far as possible, by their registered number, and the name of the applicant and the respondent state. The registered numbers follow a continuous numerical order with indication of the year.

CONVENTION

FOR THE PROTECTION OF HUMAN RIGHTS AND FUNDAMENTAL FREEDOMS

CONVENTION

DE SAUVEGARDE DES DROITS DE L'HOMME ET DES LIBERTÉS FONDAMENTALES

THE Governments signatory hereto, being Members of the Council of Europe,

Considering the Universal Declaration of Human Rights proclaimed by the General Assembly of the United Nations on 10th December 1948;

Considering that this Declaration aims at securing the universal and effective recognition and observance of the Rights therein declared;

Considering that the aim of the Council of Europe is the achievement of greater unity between its Members and that one of the methods by which that aim is to be pursued is the maintenance and further realisation of Human Rights and Fundamental Freedoms;

Reaffirming their profound belief in those Fundamental Freedoms which are the foundation of justice and peace in the world and are best maintained on the one hand by an effective political democracy and on the other by a common understanding and observance of the Human Rights upon which they depend;

Being resolved, as the Governments of European countries which are like-minded and have a common heritage of political traditions, ideals, freedom and the rule of law, to take the first steps for the collective enforcement of certain of the Rights stated in the Universal Declaration;

Have agreed as follows:

Les Gouvernements signataires, Membres du Conseil de l'Europe,

Considérant la Déclaration Universelle des droits de l'homme, proclamée par l'Assemblée Générale des Nations Unies le 10 décembre 1948;

Considérant que cette Déclaration tend à assurer la reconnaissance et l'application universelles et effectives des droits qui y sont énoncés;

Considérant que le but du Conseil de l'Europe est de réaliser une union plus étroite entre ses Membres, et que l'un des moyens d'atteindre ce but est la sauvegarde et le développement des Droits de l'homme et des libertés fondamentales;

Réaffirmant leur profond attachement à ces libertés fondamentales qui constituent les assises mêmes de la justice et de la paix dans le monde et dont le maintien repose essentiellement sur un régime politique véritablement démocratique, d'une part, et, d'autre part, sur une conception commune et un commun respect des Droits de l'homme dont ils se réclament;

Résolus, en tant que gouvernements d'États européens animés d'un même esprit et possédant un patrimoine commun d'idéal et de traditions politiques, de respect de la liberté et de prééminence du droit, à prendre les premières mesures propres à assurer la garantie collective de certains des droits énoncés dans la Déclaration Universelle;

Sont convenus de ce qui suit:

ARTICLE 1

The High Contracting Parties shall secure to everyone within their jurisdiction the rights and freedoms defined in Section I of this Convention.

Les Hautes Parties Contractantes reconnaissent à toute personne relevant de leur juridiction les droits et libertés définis au Titre I de la présente Convention.

shall secure to/reconnaissant à

The contracting states have assumed two basic obligations. The Commission has described the first:

in accordance with the general principles of international law,[1] borne out by the spirit of the Convention as well as by the preparatory work, the Contracting Parties have undertaken, without prejudice to the provisions of Article 64 ... to ensure that their domestic body of law is compatible with the Convention, and if need be to make any necessary adjustments to this end, since the Convention is binding on all the authorities of the Contracting Parties, including the legislative authorities.[2]

The second basic obligation is to remedy any breach of the provisions of Section I, if and when it occurs. This is restated, in the particular context of Article 5(5) and generally in Article 13, as an express obligation, and conversely in Article 26 as an implied right, of contracting States.

That the provisions of Section I should have domestic effect, as a direct protection of the rights and freedoms of individuals in their territories, is made plain by the character of these provisions, the terms of Articles 57 and 64, and the history of Article I itself. The terms of Article 57 clearly imply that the domestic law of a contracting State must be such as to 'ensure the effective implementation' of Convention provisions.

The exclusion in Article 64 of reservations of a general character also implies that acceptance of the Convention was not a mere

---

[1] See *Exchange of Greek and Turkish Populations* [1925] P.C.I.J.: Ser. B, No. 10 at 20, 21, '... a State which has contracted valid international obligations is bound to make in its legislation such modifications as may be necessary to ensure the fulfilment of the obligations undertaken'.

[2] 214/56: 2 *Yearbook* 234.

undertaking to bring law and practice into conformity with the provisions of Section I, as convenient and over time. Further the words 'shall
undertake to ensure/s'engageront à assurer' in the original draft were
replaced by the present words,[1] which speak from entry into force.

But there are several possible ways in which the provisions of
Section I may have domestic effect. They may, by a constitutional
rule, become part of domestic law on ratification; or the national
legislature may incorporate the Convention, in whole or in part, into
domestic law either in the Act approving it or by a separate enactment;
or a contracting State might, on ratification of the Convention, have
taken the position that its law and practice were already such as to be
consistent with, or even wider than,[2] the provisions of Section I.

The Convention has left it to each contracting State to secure in its
own way domestic efficacy for the provisions of Section I. A requirement that a contracting State must incorporate those provisions in
terms into its domestic law[3] is not clearly evidenced either by the
terms of the Convention itself, or the preparatory work, or the
subsequent practice of the parties. Articles 5 (5) and 13, it is true, point
towards incorporation of Section I into domestic law, but they do not
necessitate it, and are, as will be seen later, difficult to interpret with
any certainty on this point. Further, a proposal to include a clause
imposing a requirement of legislative incorporation was rejected by
the Conference of Senior Officials[4] in these terms:

7. *Solemn declaration by which the internal laws of the High Contracting Parties shall
give full effect to the provisions of the Convention.*

The Conference considered unanimously that it was useless to insert into
the Convention a provision of this kind. Indeed, in the absence of any
provision to the contrary, every signatory State is presumed to give full effect
to the provisions of the Convention from the moment the State has given its
adherence.

If the solemn declaration was to be an undertaking to incorporate
Convention provisions into domestic law by legislation, and this is not
certain, then in describing it as useless—perhaps a not very apt

---

[1] *T.P.* I. 223.

[2] Compare Article 60.

[3] For an examination of the issue see H. Golsong, 'Die europäische Konvention
etc.', *Jahrbuch des öffent. Rechts* [1961] 123, 128; T. Buergenthal, *Effect of the Convention on
the Internal Law of Member States, B.I.I.C.L.*, International Law Series No. 5, 79, 80–3.

[4] *T.P.* III. 649. Compare also the initial Recommendation of the Consultative
Assembly to the Committee of Ministers (8.9.1949): *T.P.* I. 224.

translation of 'inutile'—the Senior Officials may have meant either that it was not practicable or that it was unnecessary.

In their practice, subsequent to the conclusion of the Convention, some countries have incorporated Convention provisions by legislation and some have not. We have then to ask in what senses a provision of the Convention can become part of domestic law, what its place is as such in the internal hierarchy of law, and what differences there are between countries that have incorporated Convention provisions into domestic law and those that have not.

First, where provisions of the Convention have become part of domestic law either as a direct constitutional effect of its ratification, or by legislative enactment, which rights and freedoms are directly enforceable at the instance of individuals, and which require and call for enabling legislation? Chief Justice Marshall in an often-cited judgment in *Foster* v. *Neilson* (1829) distinguished between treaty provisions that are, and those that are not, 'self-executing':

Our Constitution declares a treaty to be the law of the land. It is, consequently, to be regarded in courts of justice as equivalent to an act of the legislature, whenever it operates of itself without the aid of any legislative provision. But when the terms of the stipulation import a contract, when either of the parties engages to perform a particular act, the treaty addresses itself to the political, not the judicial department, and the legislature must execute the contract before it can become a rule for the Court.

It appears then that a provision of the Convention would be 'self-executing' in the above sense, if it could be invoked, either by an individual or the State itself,[1] and applied by judicial or administrative authority, in the framework of domestic law and procedure as it stood at the entry into force of the Convention. However, some provisions of the Conventions would on examination be found to be, and some not to be, 'self-executing', and it would be therefore incorrect to speak of the Convention, or even Section I, as being 'self-executing' as a whole.

The second question concerns the status in domestic law of provisions of the Convention, which have been incorporated and are 'self-executing'. Can they rank as constitutional law, overriding any

---

[1] Viz. in justification of restrictions imposed under the second paragraphs of Articles 8–11. For an analysis of the notion of 'self-executing' in terms of the Convention see M. Sørensen, 'Obligations of a State party to a treaty in respect of municipal law', *Vienna Colloquium* (October 1965) H/Coll. (65) 11 at 15–20.

legislation past or future, which is inconsistent with them,[1] or do they operate in the same way as ordinary legislative enactments, invalidating existing law or legislation inconsistent with them, but themselves vulnerable to subsequent enactments, on the principle *lex posterior derogat legi priori*?[2]

Finally, two differences must be noticed between the position of the Convention in a country where its provisions are in one way or another part of its domestic law and the position in a country where they are not. First, if Convention provisions cannot be directly invoked or enforced at the instance of individuals, and if the country has not accepted the right of individual petition under Article 25, there is no way open to them in which the assumption that domestic law is consistent with the provisions of the Convention can be tested or controlled. Secondly, before an application can be made to the Commission under a Convention provision, which forms part of domestic law, that provision must be expressly invoked, as far as it is procedurally possible, in the national courts, so that they may have an opportunity under the domestic remedies rule to pass upon the alleged breach of the Convention.

In fourteen of the countries, parties to the Convention, its provisions have become in various ways part of domestic law, either constitutionally as treaty provisions or by legislative enactment, while in the other seven countries the Convention does not have this formal status.[3] But it would be rash to draw too simple conclusions from these differences, for the legal reorganization and implementation of Convention provisions is in practice a matter of degree, though the substantive obligations are accepted in all the Convention countries.[4] So in the United Kingdom it has come to be the practice of the courts to take Convention provisions into account as guidelines to statutory

[1] In Federal States the provisions of the Convention may have the status of a Federal law, setting limits to the legislation of political subdivisions of the Federation, but itself subject to the *lex posterior* rule.

[2] The question whether the Convention embodies applicable principles of public policy or *ordre public* will be considered under Article 19.

[3] The Convention countries, all members of the Council of Europe, are the following, the seven countries mentioned being those in italic; Austria, Belgium, Cyprus, *Denmark*, France, Federal Republic of Germany, Greece, *Iceland*, *Ireland*, Italy, Liechtenstein, Luxembourg, *Malta*, Netherlands, *Norway*, Portugal, Spain, *Sweden*, Switzerland, Turkey, *United Kingdom*.

[4] An authoritative and detailed account of the domestic role of the Convention is given in A. Drzemczewski, *European Human Rights Convention in Domestic Law* (Oxford, 1982).

interpretation or even to fill gaps in the common law. In *Waddington* v. *Miah* (1974) 1 W.L.R. 683 Lord Reid stressed the presumption that Parliament does not enact legislation contrary to the Convention; and in *R.* v. *Secretary of State for Home Affairs, ex pte Bhajan Singh* [1975] 3 W.L.R. 225 the Master of the Rolls observed that:

> The courts can and should take the Convention into account. They should take it into account whenever interpreting a statute, which affects the rights and liberties of the individual. It is to be assumed that the Crown, in taking its part in legislation, would do nothing which was in conflict with treaties.

Again in *Gleaves* v. *Deakin and others* [1979] 2 A.E.R. 497 the scope of criminal law on defamatory libel was found in the House of Lords to be inconsistent with Article 10 of the Convention, and call for change.

A similar approach to the Convention is made by the European Court of Justice. In the judgment summarizing earlier decisions,[1] it said that:

> ... fundamental rights form an integral part of the general principles of law; that in safeguarding those rights the Court is bound to draw inspiration from constitutional traditions common to the member States ... and that similarly international treaties for the protection of human rights, on which the member States have collaborated, or of which they are signatories, can supply guidelines, which should be found within the framework of Community law.

The presumably deliberate use of the term 'signatories' stresses further that such treaties do not depend on ratification and entry into force to express general principles to be accepted.

A brief review will now be made of the position of the Convention in the domestic law of the participating countries. Ratification of the Convention include the First and Fourth Protocols, unless otherwise stated.

Austria. The Convention was approved for ratification by the Nationalrat in July 1958, and was duly ratified and published[2] with effect from 3 September 1958, reservations being made to Article 5 and to Article 1 of the Protocol.

---

[1] *Hauer* v. *Land Rheinland Pfalz* [1979] E.C.R. 3727.

[2] Bundesgesetzblatt, Nr. 210/1958 (24.9.1958), under Austrian Staatsgrundgesetz, Article 50. Publication was a mandatory condition of the incorporation of its provisions into domestic law.

The precise domestic effect has been a matter of dispute,[1] as to whether the Convention has the status of a constitutional law in Austria, so that its provisions would take precedence over all legislation inconsistent with them, whether prior or subsequent, and whether its provisions were 'self-executing', so as not to require further legislation. As regards the first point the procedure followed by the Nationalrat was not wholly clear. Its president had, for purposes of counting the quorum and the size of the voting majority, proceeded on the assumption that the Nationalrat was enacting a constitutional law: but the Convention was not expressly designated as such by the Nationalrat in giving its approval.[2] As to the second point, the Austrian Federal Government introduced a Bill on 23 September 1959,[3] to amend and add to a number of existing constitutional provisions, 'in order to complete the rights and freedoms guaranteed; in Austria, as required by the Convention. In explaining the reasons for the Bill, the Government stated[4] that: 'From this date [3 September 1958] the Convention and the Protocol thereto place upon the Austrian legislator the duty to bring domestic legislation into conformity with the provisions of the Convention, in so far as the said legislation does not conform . . . and does not guarantee more extensive rights than those resulting from the Convention and Protocol thereto.' It added that 'It is moreover essential that there should be an express domestic law making it quite clear what is legal and what is not to those who are subject to it . . .' This appears to assume that at least some of the Convention provisions were not 'self-executing'.

Both issues came before the Verfassungsgericht. It took the view that as a consequence of the approval of the Convention by the Nationalrat[5] and its publication in the official gazette, it became a part of domestic law and was 'equivalent to a Federal law', but that the

---

[1] See V. Leibscher, 'Austria and the European Convention', *Journal of I.C.J.* (1963), 282–93, and T. Buergenthal, 'Domestic status of the European Convention of Human Rights', 13 *Buffalo Law Review* (1964) 359, for discussion and references to the Austrian literature on the matter.

[2] Bundesverfassungsgesetz (1929), Article 44 (1), requires for the enactment of constitutional law, or for the approval under Article 42 (1) of a treaty modifying constitutional law, the presence of at least one-half of the Nationalrat and a two-thirds majority in favour, and the express designation of the enactment as a 'constitutional law'.

[3] For text see 2 *Yearbook* 528–40. This Bill came into force in that year.

[4] Ibid. 532, 534.

[5] The court referred to Article 50 (1) which provides that all political treaties, and other treaties containing provisions modifying existing law, require the approval of the

content of the Convention must be examined in order to decide whether it contained any rule of law that was immediately applicable, or merely constituted obligations upon the legislature to adapt existing legislation to the Convention, in so far as it did not already conform thereto, and not to promulgate in future any law that would be in conflict with the Convention. The court then proceeded to find that Article 6 was not 'self-executing'.[1] When contrasted with the elaborate rules of domestic law on criminal and civil procedure, the provisions of Article 6 were too imprecise to form a body of law immediately applicable, but rather constituted principles for a programme of legislation.

In a later decision,[2] the court was concerned in Article 5 with paragraphs I (c) and (3), and pointed out that certain questions were left unresolved, such as, what would be a reasonable period within which an accused person should be brought to trial, and what should be the conditions of release on bail or other security, including in particular the amount of bail. The court no doubt had in mind the condition set out at the head of Article 5 (1), 'in accordance with a procedure prescribed by law/selon les voies légales', words which plainly called for legislation in so far as the questions posed by the court were not already answered in terms of Austrian law.[3] The court concluded that, although the provisions of Article 5 had the status of a Federal law and were subsequent to the Finanzstrafgesetz (26.6.1958) under § 85 of which the appellant had been detained, they were not 'self-executing' and could not therefore prevail, under the *lex posterior* rule, over earlier enactments which were: 'A provision that is not self-executing, and one that is, are not mutually exclusive, and for that reason a non-self-executing cannot modify a self-executing one.' Further § 85 was not covered by the Austrian reservation to Article 5.

In the same decision the Verfassungsgericht expressly denied any constitutional status to the Convention, on the grounds that it had not been expressly designated a constitutional law by the Nationalrat, that the terms of approval nowhere stated that the Convention modified the Constitution, and that its content alone could not confer that status.

Nationalrat for their validity; for denial of domestic effect to a treaty not so approved see *Pokorny* v. *Republic of Austria* [1952] Austria, Oberster Gerichtshof: 19 *I.L.R.* 461.

[1] B 469/59/12 (27.6.1960): translated in 3 *Yearbook* 616–23.
[2] 14.10.1961: translated in 4 *Yearbook* 614–17. See also Oberster Gerichtshof, 29.1.1963: *Österr. Juristen-Zeitung* [1963] 327.
[3] See below under Article 5 (3) for a fuller discussion of the issues.

These problems were in part resolved when on 4 March 1964 the Convention was accorded the status of constitutional law in Austria.[1] However, the question whether a particular provision of the Convention is to be applied as 'self-executing' remains: so, although the Verfassungsgericht had observed that, if Article 5 was a constitutional provision, and could be so interpreted that detention under Finanz-strafgesetz § 85 did not fall within one of the exceptions permitted in Article 5 (1) a—f, it would have to be declared unconstitutional. But the elevation of the Convention to constitutional status by the amendment of 5 March 1964 would not, it appears, in itself alter the decision of the court that Article 5 was not in terms 'self-executing'.[2]

Belgium. The Convention as ratified for Belgium on 14 June 1955, a law approving it having received the assent of both Houses.[3] It appears that it has in consequence the same domestic effect as any legislative enactment, no less and no more. It can and has been directly invoked in the Belgian courts[4] and Articles 6 and 9 at least have been treated as 'self-executing'. Prior legislation will be construed as far as possible to avoid conflict with provisions of the Convention,[5] but in case of conflict the provisions of the Convention would it is believed prevail.

Cyprus. Cyprus ratified the Convention on 6 October 1962. The extension of the Convention to Cyprus by the United Kingdom under Article 63 did not have the effect, by any rule of succession, of continuing it in force in Cyprus after independence in 1960. Under the Treaty concerning the Establishment of the Republic, it had undertaken to observe the principles of the Convention,[6] and these

[1] Bundesgesetzblatt, Nr. 59/1964, Article II. 2. 7 designated the Convention as having been 'approved' in the sense of Bundesverfassungsgesetz (1929), Articles 50 (2) and 44 (1). Soon after the Oberster Gerichtshof named Article 5 of the Convention among the constitutional provisions protecting personal liberty in Austria: *Österr. Juristen-Zeitung* [1964] 578.

[2] See G. Kunst, *Österr. Juristen-Zeitung* [1964] 197 for a discussion of the new law.

[3] *Constitution*, Article 68 (2): 'Les traités de commerce et ceux qui pourraient grever l'État ou lier individuellement les Belges n'ont d'effet qu'après avoir reçu l'assentiment des Chambres'.

[4] See under Articles 6, 9, and 10 below.

[5] *Cymerman* v. *Office National de l'Emploi* [1962] in 5 *Yearbook* 364, 366, a decision confirmed on appeal: *Journal des Tribunaux* (1963) 285.

[6] Article 5 of the Treaty: Cmnd. 1093 (1960) at 14. It stipulates that 'the Republic of Cyprus shall secure to everyone within its jurisdiction human rights and fundamental freedoms comparable to those set out in Section I . . . and the Protocol'. Article 5 of the Treaty has the status of constitutional law in Cyprus.

principles were in fact set out, elaborated and added to, in the Constitution.[1] Since the provisions of the Convention have not been incorporated as such into the law of Cyprus, even by reference, the fact that some of the Articles of Part II of the Constitution are cast in identical or almost identical language with that of corresponding Articles of the Convention,[2] does not mean that the Convention can be directly invoked in the courts of Cyprus. This was made clear in a decision of the Supreme Constitutional Court on the question of whether a Cypriot citizen might be lawfully detained for purpose of extradition.[3] The Constitution, Article 11 (2) modelled very closely on Article 5 (1) of the Convention, permits '. . . the arrest or detention . . . of an alien against whom action is being taken with a view to deportation or extradition'. The court held that the detention complained of was unconstitutional, and it pointed out that there was a critical difference between Article 11 (2) f and the otherwise identical language of Article 5 (1) f of the Convention, in that in the latter the word 'person' appeared in place of 'alien'. But it was not suggested that Article 5 (1) f had any standing before the court.

Denmark. The Convention was ratified for Denmark on 13 April 1953, but in Denmark, as in the other Scandinavian countries,

la ratification, même avec l'approbation parlementaire, ne produit en principe aucun effet juridique au niveau du droit interne . . . Il faut que le traité soit transformé en droit national par un acte visant cet effect.[4]

Ratification was approved by the Folketing by a resolution as distinct from a law, but the provisions of the Convention were not incorporated into Danish law by further legislation.

Federal Republic of Germany. The Bundestag approved the Convention in the form of an enactment under Grundgesetz, Article 59 (2), so that it acquired the force in Germany of a Federal Law (Bundesgesetz),[5] and it was ratified by Germany on 5 December 1952. It is not disputed that, as Federal Law, its provisions prevail over all laws enacted by the

---

[1] Part II, Fundamental Rights and Liberties, Articles 6–35.
[2] Compare Articles 8 with 3, and 10 with 4, respectively.
[3] *Attorney General* v. *Afamis* [1961] I Reports of S.C.C. 121.
[4] M. Sørensen, 'Principes de droit international public', *Recueil des Cours* [1960] 111, 118.
[5] Grundgesetz (June 1953), Article 19 (1).

Länder, invalidate any prior Federal Laws inconsistent with it, except of course the Grundgesetz itself, and may be directly invoked in the ordinary Germany courts.[1] As will be seen under particular Articles below, the German courts have not been too rigorous in requiring a provision of the Convention to be 'self-executing' in order that it may be applied.

Suggestions have been made[2] that the Convention, since it amplifies the general foundation of human rights in the Grundgesetz, must be treated as having become part of it; or, alternatively, that, in so far as it embodies 'general rules of international law', it is supreme law, under Grundgesetz, Article 25.[3] The first suggestion has been rejected by the German courts. The Bundesverfassungsgericht has declared that the Convention may not be invoked, by way of constitutional appeal before it, as a standard by which the validity of legislation may be tested.[4] The second suggestion poses the more difficult question of the content of 'the general rules of international law'. Grundgesetz, Article 25, makes no distinction between customary and conventional international law, so that 'the general rules' must include customary rules. But while it might be said that at least those provisions of the Convention which may not be derogated from in any circumstances[5] are 'general rules of international law', it is difficult to see how the Convention could be regarded as more than declaratory of those rules; in other words, those rules would take precedence under Grundgesetz, Article 25, by virtue, not of the Convention, but of their general acceptance, so that the provisions of the Convention would not as such be incorporated into German law by that Article. The Oberverwaltungsgericht, Münster, denied the Convention any such incorporation under Grundgesetz, Article 25,

---

[1] The Convention has 'den Rang eines einfachen Bundesgesetzes': Oberlandesgericht, Bremen [1960] N.J.W. 1265–6: 3 Yearbook 634.

[2] For references and discussion see T. Buergenthal, op. cit. in footnote 7, 367–8. For the principle that legislation, at least if enacted after the Convention, should be interpreted according to its principles, see Oberlandesgericht, Köln (11.6.1963), [1963] N.J.W. 1749.

[3] 'Die allgemeinen Regeln des Völkerrechts sind Bestandteil des Bundesrechts. Sie gehen den Gesetzen vor und erzeugen Rechte und Pflichten unmittelbar für die Bewohner des Bundesgebietes.'

[4] 14.1.60: 3 Yearbook 628. See also Oberverwaltungsgericht, Münster [1955]: 2 Yearbook 572. For decisions to the same effect in Bavaria and Rheinland-Pfalz see W. Morvay, 'Rechtsprechung nationaler Gerichte zur MRK', Zeitschrift für ausländisches öffent. Recht u. Völkerr. [January 1961] 89, 105.

[5] See under Article 15 below.

and did not attempt to distinguish between Convention provisions, saying:

... the Convention cannot be regarded as a codification of general rules of international law, since the basic rights set forth therein are not recognised in most parts of the world, as is proved by the failure of the attempts of the United Nations to conclude a similar Convention.[1]

While the conclusion of the court as regards the relation of the Convention to Grundgesetz, Article 25, seems irreproachable, the reasoning is open to question. The failure of the United Nations up to that time to bring the Draft Covenants to completion was due to disagreement rather over the measurements of implementation than over the rights embodied in the Covenants, many of which have won wide recognition and observation, and therefore may be regarded as general principles of law, forming part of international law, regardless of the entry into force of the Covenants.

France. The Convention and the First and Fourth Protocols were ratified on 3 May 1975 following authorization by the National Assembly and the Senate on 31 December 1973.

By virtue of Article 55[2] of the Constitution, the directly applicable provisions rank as a higher law in relation to both prior and subsequent legislation in conflict with them. France has made declarations under Articles 25 and 46.

Greece. The Convention was ratified on 28 March 1953, having received parliamentary assent embodied in a law.[3] The Council of State and the *Arios Pagos*[4] have both affirmed that, in accordance with the Constitution (January 1952), Article 32,[5] the Convention has consequently become a part of domestic law. However, political conflicts in Greece have sometimes led the courts, when Convention provisions were invoked before them, to have recourse to Article 15.

[1] 2 *Yearbook* 580.
[2] 'Treaties or agreements duly ratified or approved shall, upon their publication have an authority superior to that of laws, subject, for each agreement or treaty, to its application by the other party.'
[3] 2329/1953: Official Journal I, No. 68 (3 March 1953).
[4] Decisions 724/1954, and 386/155: 2 *Yearbook* 606, respectively.
[5] '... les traités de commerce et tous autres traités portant concessions sur lesquelles, en vertu d'autres dispositions de la présente Constitution, il ne peut être statué que par une loi, ou qui grevent individuellement les Hellènes, n'ont pas de force qu'avec l'assentiment de la Chambre'. (Translation by Professor Kyriacopoulos.)

It was interrupted by the withdrawal of Greece from the Council of Europe, and its denunciation of the Convention, in 1970, following the *Greek Case*, to be reviewed below. Greece renewed its ratification of the Convention and the First Protocol in July 1974. Greece adopted a new constitution in June 1975, which in Article 28(1) stated that:

The general rules of international law as well as international treaties, duly ratified by the legislature and entered into force in accordance with their provisions, form an integral part of Greek domestic law and are superior to any contrary legal provision.

and Article 100 provided for the establishment of a Constitutional Court to determine the applicablity of international law rules, given domestic status under Article 28(1).

Iceland. The Constitution (1944), Article 21, assigns the treaty-making power to the President, but he may not without the consent of the Althing conclude treaties which 'entail renouncement of or servitude on territory or territorial waters or if they imply constitutional changes'. Whether that consent, if given, would itself make the treaty effective in domestic law would perhaps depend on whether it was cast in the form of a Bill, a resolution, or an address to the President (Constitution, Article 38); and whether acceptance of the Convention could imply constitutional changes is not entirely clear. At any rate a number of the principles of Section I are to be found expressed in the Constitution, in particular in Articles 63–75. However, the Convention, ratified on 29 June 1953, has not been given the force of domestic law in Iceland by consent of the Althing, and its provisions cannot be invoked in the courts.[1]

Ireland. The Constitution (1937) is more explicit than many on the conclusion and domestic implementation of treaties. Article 29 provides that:

5.1°. Every international agreement to which the State becomes a party shall be laid before the Dail Eireann.

6.   No international agreement shall be part of the domestic[2] law of the State save as may be determined by the Oireachtas.

---

[1] *A. Olafsson* v. *Ministry of Finance* [1960] Reykjavik Town Court: 3 *Yearbook* 646. See also under Article 1 of the Protocol for the issue in this case before the Commission: 511/59.

[2] Article 15 (1) 2°: 'The Oireachtas [National Parliament] shall consist of the

The Convention was ratified by Ireland on 25 February 1953, but in the words of the Supreme Court:

The Oireachtas has not determined that the Convention . . . is to be part of the domestic law of the State, and accordingly this court cannot give effect to the Convention if it be contrary to the domestic law or purports to grant rights or impose obligations additional to those of domestic law.[1]

The Supreme Court also rejected two further arguments for giving domestic effect to the provisions of the Convention: that the State, having accepted the Convention, should be estopped from exercising powers not authorized by the Convention; and that the court should so construe the statute in issue, *Offences against the State (Amendment) Act 1940*, as not to violate general rules of international law, which, the appellant argued, Articles 5 and 6 of the Convention constituted. The Supreme Court predicated its answer on a clear separation of international law and municipal law. While such an estoppel might operate as between the High Contracting Parties to the Convention, a domestic court administering domestic law could not take account of it; and domestic law, at least in statutory form, must further prevail over any general rules of international law inconsistent with it.

Italy. Law 848/1955, Article 1, authorized[2] the ratification of the Convention, which took place on 27 October 1955, and Article 2 concludes:

È fatto obbligo a chiunque spetti di osservarla e di farla osservare come legge dello Stato.[3]

The French text of the Convention and the first Protocol follow. It appears then that the Convention falls within the class described by the Corte di Cassazione:

President and two Houses, viz: a House of Representatives to be called Dail Eireann and a Senate to be called Seanad Eireann.' The Oireachtas has 'sole and exclusive powers of making laws for the State'.

[1] *O'Laighleis* v. *O'Sullivan and Minister of Justice* [1957] Irish Reports 93: 2 *Yearbook* 624. For further proceedings by the plaintiff, Lawless, before the Commission and Court under the Convention, see under Article 15 below.

[2] Constitution (1948), Article 80: 'Le Camere autorizzano con legge [en vertu d'une loi] la ratifica dei trattati internazionali che sono di natura politica, o prevedono arbitrati o regolamenti giudiziari, o importano variazioni del territorio od oneri alle finanze o modificazioni di leggi.'

[3] *Gazzetta Ufficiale No. 221* (4.8.1955), 3372.

We must remember that in Italy the adaptation of internal law to the conventional rules of international law is made—as a general rule—by means of an executive order which may be in the form of a law or decree providing that a certain international treaty or convention is fully operative.[1]

Nevertheless, the problem of which provisions are 'self-executing' must still arise, though the courts do not yet appear to have met it. Further, the constitutionality of the Convention could, as regards provisions found to be 'self-executing', be determined by the Constitutional Court.

Liechtenstein. The Convention, but not the First or Fourth Protocol, was ratified on 8 September 1982, and the approval of the Diet for that purpose appears to give it the status of domestic law.[2]

Luxembourg. The Convention was ratified with the approval of the legislature, on 3 September 1953, thus in fact serving to bring it into force internationally. Subject to the condition that they are found to be 'self-executing', the provisions of the Convention form part of the domestic law of Luxembourg, prevailing, it appears, over both prior and subsequent legislation, where that is found to be inconsistent with them.[3]

Malta. The position is broadly similar to that in Cyprus. The provisions of the Convention have not been incorporated in domestic law, but are closely reflected in provisions of the Constitution of 1964.

Netherlands. The Convention was approved by law of 28 July 1954, and ratified on 31 August 1954. The controlling provisions of the Constitution (1887, as amended to 1963) are, in addition to Article 61 under which the Convention was approved by enactment of a law:

Article 65. Provisions of international agreements which by their terms can bind everyone (*naar haar inhoud een jeder kunnen verbinden*) shall have such binding force after being published.

Article 66. Legislation in force in the Kingdom shall not be applied if its application would be incompatible with provisions of international agree-

---

[1] *Combes des Lestrade* v. *Ministry of Finance* [1955] 22 I.L.R. 882, 884.

[2] 21 *Yearbook* (1969) supplementary volume.

[3] See Luxembourg court decisions cited by T. Buergenthal, op. cit., n. 7 at 378–9. For the view of one Luxembourg tribunal: 4 *Yearbook* 622 that, for alleged breaches of the Convention, recourse must be had not to national courts but to the Commission, see under Article 19, below. See also Pescatore, *Conclusion et effets des traités* (1964) 106.

ments which bind everyone and have entered into force either before or after such legislation.

It is clear then that the provisions of the Convention, which satisfy the conditions of Article 65 of the Constitution, prevail over legislative enactments in the Netherlands, whether prior or subsequent to its ratification. So

all Netherlands laws must be examined for their compatibility with the Convention.[1]

But the condition prescribed by Article 65 is that the Convention shall be 'self-executing', so:

As the Court of Appeal has said, Article 13 [of the Convention] merely imposes upon the contracting States the obligation to organise their legislation in such a way that in the cases defined by the Article effective remedies will exist. The Court of Appeal rightly decided that Article 13, according to its nature, cannot directly be applied by the Courts and therefore under Article 66 of the Constitution, does not belong to those provisions of international agreements that are binding upon everyone and by which municipal legislation shall be judged.[2]

The relation between the Convention and the Netherlands Constitution itself is not so clear. On the one hand, Article 60 (4) of the Constitution declares that the courts shall not pronounce on the constitutionality of international agreements (*grondwettigheid van overeenkomsten*); on the other hand, Article 63 provides that:

When the development of the international legal order (*rechtsorde*) so requires, provisions of the constitution may be derogated from by an international agreement ...

But, as might be expected, such an agreement must be enacted into law by a special increased majority of the two Chambers of the States General. The Convention was not enacted into law under Article 63 and therefore its provisions do not appear to be capable of derogation from the Constitution, even if found to be inconsistent,[3] nor, it is believed, could recourse be had here to the rule in Article 60 (4) since

---

[1] *Hoge Raad* (*Supreme Court*) [1960] Nederl. Jurisprud. No. 436 (1993): 3 *Yearbook* 650.
[2] *Hoge Raad* [1960] cited by T. Buergenthal, op. cit., n. 7 at 384. For further Netherlands court decisions, finding Article 9 'self-executing', see under that Article below. See also van Emde Boas, *European Yearbook* (1962) 226.
[3] See under Article 9 for Netherlands court decisions on this point.

its purpose is not to give the status of constitutional law to international agreements, but to assign the task, of determining whether an international agreement has or has not that status, to the legislature rather than the judiciary.

Norway. The Constitution does not distinguish very clearly between the conclusion and implementation of treaties. Article 26 (2) provides that:

> Treaties bearing on matters of special importance, and in any case such treaties as, according to the Constitution, necessitate a new law or a decision on the part of the Storting in order to be carried into effect, shall not be binding until the Storting has given its consent thereto.[1]

This clause covers in a single sentence a number of disparate issues of treaty practice and is not unambiguous, but it implies that a treaty, which would alter the law, cannot have domestic effect without legislation. The Convention, ratified by Norway on 15 January 1952, and the first Protocol, ratified on 18 December following, have not been enacted into Norwegian law. Nevertheless, when Article 4 of the Convention was invoked in the *Iversen Case*,[2] the Höyesterett neither confirmed nor denied the admissibility of a plea in the courts based on the Convention. Judge Hiorthöy giving the judgment of the court said:

> It seems hardly doubtful to me that the prohibition in the Convention against subjecting anyone to perform 'forced or compulsory labour' cannot reasonably be given such a wide construction that it includes instructions to perform public service of the kind in question here. ... Accordingly, as I cannot see that there is any contradiction between the Convention and the Norwegian Act in question, I need not enter into the question as to which of these shall prevail in the event of conflict.

The final words at least suggest that the learned judge had in mind other possible grounds than enactment into domestic law, on which a court might take notice of the Convention.

---

[1] Constitution, Article 75 (*g*), lists among the prerogatives of the Storting that 'to have communicated to them the treaties and agreements that the King, on behalf of the State has entered into with foreign powers ...'. No other provisions appear to relate directly to the making or implementation of treaties.

[2] *Public Prosecutor* v. *Iversen* [1961]: 6 *Yearbook* 286. See further under Article 4, below: 1468/62.

Portugal. The Convention was ratified on 9 November 1978, and under the new Constitution its provisions apply in municipal law: Article 8 (2), as was confirmed by the Lisbon Court of Appeal,[1] but whether these provisions prevail over a subsequent enactment of the legislature has not yet been determined.

Spain. The Convention, but not the First or Fourth Protocol, was ratified on 4 October 1979. Under the Constitution, which entered into force in December 1978, the provisions of the Constitution are part of the internal legal system: Article 96 (1).

Sweden. Though the oldest of the written constitutions of the contracting States, that of Sweden (1809, as amended) is more explicit than some later instruments. Article 12 (1) provides that:

> The King shall have power to enter into agreements with foreign powers after the council of state has been heard upon the subject. When such agreements deal with matters which are required under this instrument of government to be decided by the Riksdag either alone or with the King, or when though not dealing with such matters they are of major importance, they shall be laid before the Riksdag for approval; and such agreements shall contain a reservation making their validity dependent upon the Riksdag's sanction. (Peaslee, *Constitutions*.)

Again the assent to the conclusion of a treaty and the legislative action to implement it are dealt with, as it were, in one breath, but it is clear that, where the objects of the treaty involve changes in domestic law, legislation is necessary. Sweden ratified the Convention on 4 February 1952, and the first Protocol on 22 June 1959, but no legislation incorporating their provisions into domestic law followed.

Switzerland. The Convention was ratified on 28 November 1974, but not the First or Fourth Protocols. Approval of such a treaty by the Federal Assembly authorizes its ratification by the Federal Council, and it then becomes an integral part of Swiss law, having at least 'the rank of federal law'.[2]

Turkey. The Constitution (1945) threw no light on the domestic effect of Law 6366/1954[3] which authorized ratification of the Convention by

---

[1] Decision of 17.11.1978: see A. Drzemczewski, op. cit. at p. 155.
[2] According to the Swiss Government in its report under Article 57: CE/H/7 Q15(15.10.1976).   [3] 1 *Yearbook* 43.

Turkey. However, certain expressions in the Law itself suggest that its purpose and effect was to incorporate provisions of the Convention into domestic law: so Article 3 of the Law reads:

> Article 2 of the Protocol shall not affect the provisions of Law No. 430 of March 3, 1924 relating to the verification of education.

The new Constitution (1961), Article 65, contains detailed provisions on the ratification of international agreements, in particular:

> International treaties duly put into effect carry the force of law. No recourse to the Constitutional Court can be made as provided in Articles 149 and 151 with regard to these treaties.

Whether this provision speaks only from the entry into force of the new Constitution, or has a retroactive effect upon the Convention has not yet been determined.

United Kingdom. Ratified on 22 February 1951, the Convention has not been given statutory form, either directly or by reference, in the United Kingdom. Since the ratification of the Convention is plainly not an exercise by the Crown of its prerogative rights to conduct war and make peace,[1] and since its provisions have not been incorporated in a United Kingdom statute, they are not justiciable in any court of the United Kingdom.[2]

The variety of practice which is revealed among the contracting States for securing the domestic enforcement of the Convention hardly permits any general conclusions, but certain observations may be made on the formal relation of the Convention to domestic law. First, there is an assumption that domestic law conforms in each participating country to the provisions of Section I, and indeed many of these provisions are to be found expressed in one form or another in constitutional instruments in all the countries. On this assumption rest both the undertaking expressed in Article 1 and the attitude taken by several countries that specific legislation to incorporate Convention provisions is not necessary. Secondly, where these provisions

---

[1] Treaties concluded in the exercise of these rights are directly applicable in the courts, but the extent of this exception is itself disputed.

[2] See the *Parlement Belge* [1879] 4 P.D. 129, 154–5, confirmed on appeal on this point [1880] 5 P.D. 197: *Attorney General for Canada* v. *Att. Gen. for Ontario* [1937] A.C. 326 Privy Council; *Republic of Italy* v. *Hambros Bank* [1950] 1 A.E.R. 430. For United Kingdom memorandum, under Article 57 of the Convention, on the conformity with the Convention of its law and practice, see Doc. DH (66) 9 Add. 2.

are formally made part of domestic law, the extent of their incorporation is by no means always clear, and the courts are often circumspect in applying them directly, and may give great weight to the criterion of what is or is not 'self-executing'. Thirdly, whatever the formal relation of the Convention to domestic law of a participating country may be, ways have been suggested in which the provisions of Section I might be said to be applicable in that country otherwise than as part of the positive rules of domestic law; these ways will be considered under Article 19.

everyone/à toute personne

This marks the great departure taken by the Convention from traditional forms of the international protection of individuals, for its dispenses with nationality as a condition of protection. Each contrasting State undertakes to secure the rights and freedoms of Section I to everyone within its jurisdiction, whether he or she is an alien, a national of the State, or a stateless person, and regardless of civil status.

within their jurisdiction/relevant de leur juridiction

It is believed that the jurisdiction of a contracting State is for this purpose, the area or objects of its jurisdiction, as defined by its domestic law within the limits prescribed by international law, and by any declaration made by it under provisions of the Convention. So

à certains égards, les ressortissants d'un État contractant relèvent de sa juridiction même lorsqu'ils ont leur domicile ou leur résidence à l'étranger; . . . en particulier les représentants diplomatiques et consulaires de leur pays d'origine exercent à leur sujet une série de fonctions dont l'accomplissement, peut, le cas échéant, engager la responsabilité de ce pays sur le terrain de la Convention.[1]

Territorial extent. The Convention can be said to extend, for each contracting State, over the whole of its national territory,[2] with qualifications in the following cases.

The Federal Republic of Germany has declared that:

---

[1] 1611/62: *Recueil* (1965) i. But the Convention has been held not to guarantee any *right* of diplomatic protection for nationals abroad: 1828/63: *Recueil* (1964) ii.

[2] Greenland became part of metropolitan Denmark on 5 June 1953.

(a) The territory to which the Convention shall apply extends also to Western Berlin.

(b) The Protocol of the Convention ... signed at Paris on March 20, 1952, applies also to the Land Berlin with effect from February 13, 1957, the date on which the Protocol entered into force with respect to the Federal Republic of Germany.

The Commission has held itself competent to receive applications, and has received a number concerning acts or events in Land Berlin, but has also held that no application can be admissible regarding acts or events in East Berlin or the German Democratic Republic.[1] This is predicated on recognition of the German Democratic Republic as a State not party to the Convention.

The Netherlands has extended the Convention under Article 63 to the Netherlands Antilles with a reservation touching Article 6 (3) c, and the former is also at present covered by the Netherlands acceptance of the right of individual petition and the compulsory jurisdiction of the court.

The United Kingdom has also extended the Convention to the following territories[2] under Article 63, and its declarations of 14 January 1966, under Articles 25 and 46 has been extended to those in italics:

Bermuda	*Montserrat*
British Virgin Islands	*St. Helena*
Cayman Islands	*Seychelles*
Channel Islands	Swaziland
Falkland Islands	*Turks and Caicos*
Gibraltar	*Islands*
Isle of Man (Article 46)	*Windward Islands*
Leeward Islands	(Article 25)

It is an accepted principle of the Convention, that it ceases to apply to a territory, to which it has been extended under Article 63, when that territory attains independence, and so a contracting State is not responsible for subsequent actions of the government of that territory.[3] The reason for this is that participation in the Convention as of

---

[1] 448/59: 3 *Yearbook* 255; 1074/61: *Recueil* (1962) i. For the competence of the Bundesverfassungsgericht to receive constitutional appeals from Land Berlin see under Article 26 below.

[2] It may be noted that the total population of these territories is less than 3 million.

[3] 944/60: *Recueil* (1961) ii.,

right is confined to members of the Council of Europe, and therefore could not pass simply by way of succession to a State not a member.

The territorial extension of the Convention is distinct from the exercise of jurisdiction, as was recognized in the applications brought by Cyprus against Turkey,[1] in response to its invasion of Cyprus in September 1974. Cyprus claimed that breaches of many provisions of the Convention had been committed on a large scale by Turkish armed forces that had invaded the island. Among its objections to the admissibility of the applications, Turkey maintained that 'within their jurisdiction' comprises only acts done within the national territory of a contrasting State, unless jurisdiction had been extended to other territories under Article 63. The Commission did not accept this objection. It considered that the exercise of jurisdiction under Article 1 is in large part a matter of fact:

... authorised agents of a State, including diplomatic or consular agents and armed forces, not only remain within its jurisdiction when abroad but bring any other persons or property 'within the jurisdiction' of that State.... In so far as, by their acts or omissions they affect such persons or property, the responsibility of the State is engaged.

The competence of the Commission to examine the applications could not then be excluded on the grounds that Turkey 'has neither enlarged any part of Cyprus, nor ... established either military or civil government there'. Further,

The purpose of Article 63 is not only the territorial extension of the Convention but its adaptation to the measure of self-government attained in particular non-metropolitan territory and to the cultural and social differences in such territories; Article 63 (3) confirmed this interpretation. This does not mean that the territories to which Article 63 applies are not within the 'jurisdiction' within the meaning of Article 1.

Succession. Questions of responsibility under the Convention accruing by way of succession arose in the case of the Saarland, but did not have to be determined. The Saarland had, as an Associate Member of the Council of Europe, ratified the Convention on 14 January 1953. In 1954 certain claims for compensation were brought in the Saar courts, in respect of twenty-one houses demolished in 1939 as part of a town-planning scheme. The Saar courts administered German law as regards both substance and procedure, but were autonomous, being

[1] 6780/74 and 6350/75: 1 D.R. 125.

part neither of the French nor the German system of courts.[1] The claims were rejected for lack of proof of responsibility of the respondent township, and an application to the Saar Government for compensation was rejected. In an application to the Commission on 15 December 1956 it was alleged that the conduct of proceedings in the Saar courts and the refusal of compensation were not in accord with the Convention and Protocol respectively. On 1 January 1957 the Saarland was incorporated in the Federal Republic of Germany. Since the Saarland had not recognized the right of individual petition under Article 25, and since at the dates of the events complained of and of the application itself the Saarland was not within the jurisdiction of the Federal Republic, the application was inadmissible. However, in so far as the applicants were seeking compensation from the Federal Republic[2] on the ground that, as from 1 January 1957, it had assumed by succession the obligations of the Saarland under the Convention, the Commission found that it was open to them to raise this issue in the German courts under Grundgesetz, Article 19 (4), and rejected the application for non-exhaustion of domestic remedies.[3]

In so far as the applicants alleged a denial of justice in the Saarland courts and a refusal by its authorities to pay just compensation for property taken, the Federal Republic could not, it is believed, be held responsible as successor, unless it had assumed responsibility by agreement or through acts of its officials.[4] However, Article 65 (2) and (3) appear to be such an agreement. Since the effect of Article 65 (3) was that the Saarland ceased to be a contracting party as from 1 January 1957, but of Article 65 (2) that its Convention obligations for acts before that date were not extinguished, Germany might be held bound by them being itself a contracting State. But even if the obligations of the Saarland under Article 1 were transferred to Germany by succession, the further question would arise whether they were not transferred with the limitation that they could only be enforced against Germany, as they could have been against the

[1] See *Rendition of Suspected Criminal (Saar Territory) Case* [1955] Germany, Bverf G. 24 I.L.R. 512; and *Société Koehl et Cie* v. *Hildebrand* [1950] France, Cour d'Appe, Colmar: 17 I.L.R. 36.
[2] The application appears to have been treated as being in effect directed against the Federal Republic, though antedating the transfer of responsibility on 1 January 1957. The application was actually registered on 14 January: on this procedure, see under Article 25 below.
[3] 245/57: 1 *Yearbook* 182, 187.
[4] See *Robert E. Brown Claim* [1923] Nielsen Rep. 187.

Saarland, that is, at the instance of another contracting State under Article 24. Since the obligations under Section I and under Article 25 are distinct and independent of each other, and since no obligation existed for the Saarland under Article 25, it is difficult to see how Germany could have an obligation to answer individual petitions in respect of events in the Saarland before 1 January 1957.

Special courts. What is the responsibity of a contracting State under the Convention for the conduct of courts, which are functioning on its territory but are not part of its ordinary system of courts? The test appears to be, not how the court is composed, or in whose name it gives judgment, or what law it applies, or the place given to it in the domestic law of the territory where it sits, but the actual source in State authority of its exercise of jurisdiction.

So the Commission, in determining its competence to receive an application against the Federal Republic of Germany in respect of proceedings in the Oberstes Rückerstattungsgericht (Supreme Restitution Court), said that:

for the purposes of determining the responsibility of the Federal Republic in the present case, the Supreme Restitution Court must be regarded as an international tribunal with respect to whose procedure the Federal Republic had no powers of legislation or control; whereas also it is clear that, in general, a State does not have responsibility for the acts or omissions of an international tribunal merely by reason that it has its seat and exercises its functions on the territory of that State . . . accordingly, the Commission rejects the submissions of the Applicant in so far as they seek to attribute responsibility to the Federal Republic on the basis that the Supreme Restitution Court was a court within its jurisdiction or a court subject to its power of legislation and control . . .[1]

The Commission analysed the structure and functions of the Supreme Restitution Court in detail, pointing out that it was established by the international Convention on the Settlement of Matters arising out of the War and Occupation 1952, to be administered and controlled in the performance of its functions by a Presidential Council of nine justices drawn from each of the three Divisions of the Court; that the Federal Republic had no legislative power to regulate or modify the procedure of the court; and that the fact that the

---

[1] 235/56: 2 *Yearbook* 288. See also 743/60: *Recueil* (1961) i; and 2095/63: *Recueil* (1965) ii (Swedish membership of the Court does not engage the responsibility of Sweden under the Convention); 2213/64: *Recueil 20* (decision of appellate court covered by that of Supreme Restitution Court—incompatible *ratione personae*).

court had been established as an international tribunal to review, in matters of restitution, the decisions of courts of the Federal Republic, did not render the Federal Republic responsible for the conduct or results of that review since

the responsibility of a State can only go as far as its sovereignty: in the same measure as the latter is restricted, that is to say, as the State cannot act in a free and independent manner the liability of the State must also be restricted.[1]

So in an earlier application, concerning the U.S. Court of Restitution Appeals,[2] the Commission observed that its judgments delivered before the termination of the occupation:

émanent en fait non point de la juridiction de la République Fédérale d'Allemagne au sens de l'Article 1er de la Convention, mais de celle des États-Unis

and the Court

se trouvait placée en dehors de l'ordre juridictionnel de la République Fédérale et relevait entièrement de l'autorité du Gouvernement militaire, puis du Haut-Commissariat des États-Unis en Allemagne . . .[3]

the rights and freedoms defined in Section I/les droits et libertés définis au Titre 1

Shared jurisdiction. Where a Convention country shares jurisdiction with other States under an international agreement, the locality and individuals covered are not within its jurisdiction under Article 1. So the detention of Rudolf Hess in the Allied Military Prison in Berlin–Spandau could not be made the basis of an application by his wife against the United Kingdom.[4]

---

[1] *Salem Case: United States—Egypt* [1932]: A.D. 1931–2, No. 98. In citing passages from the arbitral award in this case the Commission observed that its reasoning applied 'with even greater force because in the present case, the Supreme Restitution Court is an international tribunal which pronounces its judgments in its own name whereas the Mixed Courts in Egypt formed part of the Egyptian judicial system and pronounced their judgments in the name of the King of Egypt': 2 *Yearbook* 298.

[2] Established by Law No. 59 of the U.S. Military Government.

[3] 182/56: 1 *Yearbook* 169. Some differences of opinion to be found in the German courts as to whether or not the 'Occupation' courts exercised German jurisdiction were resolved by the Bundesgerichtshof (Supreme Court) in the sense that they did not: see *Recidivist (Military Tribunal of Occupant) Case* [1951] 18 I.L.R. 618: compare *Madsen* v. *Kinsella* [1952] 343 U.S. 341: 19 I.L.R. 602, holding that the application of German law by U.S. courts in Germany 'springs from its express adoption by the U.S. Military Government' and did not imply that they exercised German jurisdiction.

[4] 6231/73 (U.K.): 2 D.R. 72.

Of greater significance is the relation of the European Communities to the Convention. In the first place the European Communities form an international organization, which is not itself a party to the Convention, though each of its member States is. Its accession to the Convention has been proposed and debated in recent years, though it is far from clear what the practical results would be: in particular, it could be asked whether applications could be brought under the Convention and, if so, how such a process would affect the jurisdiction of the European Court of Justice.

It has been asked whether the member States, when taking part in a decision of the Council of the Communities, are exercising their jurisdiction under Article 1 of the Convention, so that applications can be brought against any of them. An application[1] brought by the C.F.D.T. (Confédération Française-Démocratique de Travail) against the European Communities and its member States was declared inadmissible by the Commission on the grounds that it was outside the competence of the Commission *ratione personae*, the Communities not being party to the Convention, and the member States not exercising jurisdiction under Article 1 in the Council decision.

But jurisdiction of a contracting State may be exercisable in the territory of another State on the basis of a bilateral agreement, prescribing the jurisdiction and its form of exercise: for example, under a treaty of 1923 and subsequent agreements, Liechtenstein was made part of the customs zone of Switzerland, raising Convention issues for Switzerland in respect of the control of entry of individuals.[2]

The jurisdiction of the Commission. The competence of the Commission to deal with applications under the Convention depends on State jurisdiction in that the Commission has to ask: Is a Convention right or freedom involved in the application? Is the State responsible for the acts or events in issue? Are any time-limits prescribed in the Convention or is international law applicable? The Commission has sometimes described the answering of these questions as determinations, respectively *ratione materiae*, *ratione personae*, and *ratione temporis*. In short, they point to limits to the competence of the Commission inherent in the scope and purpose of the Convention or derived from international law. The Commission has many times rejected applications, which do not in fact invoke any right or freedom recognized in the Convention, sometimes acting expressly *ratione materiae*.

---

[1] 8030/77: 5 D.R. 231.
[2] 7289/75 and 7349/76: 9 D.R. 7.

The rejection of an application *ratione personae*, no State responsibility being capable of being demonstrated, became less easy over time, given that in all the Convention countries what is public and what is private, and what is or is not State participation in, for example, transport, energy, or health services. The Commission found that, in a system of compulsory education in State schools, the State can be held responsible for the conduct of school-teachers who administer corporal punishment.[1] Again, while an admitted solicitor in the United Kingdom is an 'officer of the Supreme Court', and is subject to disciplinary jurisdiction of the courts, and is 'responsible to the client by whom he is engaged, and is independent of any organ of government', the State can be held responsible for disciplinary action against him.[2] These are, of course, only casual examples of the problems that State activity now poses.

Inadmissibility *ratione temporis* will be described under Article 26.

An application may be withdrawn or struck off the list after it has been registered or admitted. The conditions of withdrawal are that it be at the request, or with the consent, of the applicant, and that there is, in the view of the Commission, no general interest to be served by retaining it.[3] An application may be struck off if it is found to be an abuse of the right of petition under Article 27 (2), or there is some change of circumstances in which no useful purpose is served by continuing with it.

The word 'defined' is not very apt. None of the rights and freedoms are defined in the strict sense, though some Articles state what certain rights or freedoms may or do not include. Articles 13, 14, and 17 speak more accurately of the rights and freedoms 'set forth/reconnus', Article 18 refers 'to the said/aux dits' rights, and the Preamble to the First Protocol to 'those already included/ceux qui figurent déjà'. The Commission has described the rights and freedoms as being 'limitatively listed',[4] and from an early stage has spoken of the Convention as 'guaranteeing' some rights and not others. The title of the Convention uses the term 'protection/sauvegarde', and the word 'guarantee' does not have a place in the Convention. While 'guarantee' and 'protection' are generally used interchangeably, their meaning is

---

[1] *Campbell* 7511/76 (U.K.) 12 D.R. 49.
[2] 6956/75 (U.K.) 8 D.R. 103.
[3] *Brückmann* 6242/73 (F.R.G.) 6 D.R. 57.
[4] 254/57: 1 *Yearbook* 152.

not perhaps identical, and there is a sense in which a contracting State may under the Convention be obliged to protect rights which it is not in terms bound to guarantee, that is to say, there may be rights which it is not bound to grant to individuals within its jursidiction, but if it does grant these rights, then they come under the protection of the Convention; for example, there is no provision of the Convention which obliges a contracting State to establish a form of appeal against conviction or sentence on a criminal charge, but if appeal is made available under domestic law then the standards of Article 6 must be observed in the appeal proceedings.

A further point is to be noticed in the use of the word 'guarantee'. To describe a right or freedom as 'guaranteed' might be taken as equivalent to saying that it was absolute and subject to no exception. As will be seen, only a limited number of Convention rights and freedoms are guaranteed in this sense; and, in general, where the Commission has described a right or freedom as 'guaranteed' or 'not guaranteed', it has simply meant that it is or is not included among those set out in Section I.

Inevitably many applications to the Commission are predicated upon claims of rights which are not included in Section I, and it would serve no useful purpose to enumerate here the many claims of rights that have been rejected for that reason, but an example can be given of the terms in which the Commission has declared such an application inadmissible:

> Le droit á une nationalité, qui a pour corollaire la possibilité pour un individu de se faire délivrer un passeport parles autorités de l'État dont il a la nationalité, ne figure pas en tant que tel parmi ces droits et libertés.[1]

The limitation to Section I is important. It means that only Articles 2–18 of the Convention may be invoked in applications to the Commission under Articles 24 and 25.

This survey of Article 1 must be completed by a general description of the derogations or restrictions which the Convention itself permits in respect of the rights and freedoms guaranteed.

The provisions of Section I fall, under this aspect, into three groups. In the first group are Articles 3 and 4 (1), containing the only Convention rights that can properly be described as fundamental in

---

[1] 862/60: *Recueil* (1961) ii, and compare 288/57: 1 *Yearbook* 209. See further under Article 27 (2) for the notion of applications that are incompatible with the Convention.

that there are no circumstances in which derogation from them can be justified. In the second group fall Articles 2 and 7 (1). No derogation is permitted from them even in time of war or national emergency, but the rights described are themselves circumscribed by particular exceptions, set out in Articles 2 (2), 15 (2), and 7 (2), respectively. The third group is formed by the remaining rights and freedoms set out in Section I. All are subject to possible derogation under Article 15; and some are subject either to particular exceptions or to restrictions, permitted by the Convention, in more or less common form, on various grounds of national or public policy.

These restrictions are permitted under the second paragraph of Articles 8, 9, 10, and 11; under Articles 16 and 17, and Article 1 of the Protocol. They may be briefly described under four heads: form, legality, necessity, and purpose.

The *form* of possible restrictions is variously described as 'interference/ingérence' in Articles 8 and 10; 'limitations/restrictions' in Article 9; 'formalities, restrictions, conditions or penalties/ formalités, conditions, restrictions ou sanctions' in Article 10; 'restrictions/restrictions' in Articles 11, 16, and 18; deprivation of possessions and 'control of the use/réglementation de l'usage' of property in Article 1 of the Protocol; and 'conditions/conditions' in Article 2. There do not appear to be substantive differences between these terms, which express in the various contexts the idea of limitation or restriction of the exercise of rights and freedoms.

The requirement of *legality* of the restrictions imposed is found throughout, since they must be prescribed by law or 'in accordance with the law/prévues par la loi' in Articles 8, 9, 10, and 11; or on 'conditions provided for by law/conditions prévues par la loi' in Article 1 of the Protocol. The unity of idea is marked in the French text by the use of 'prévues par la loi' throughout.

There is a further requirement of consistency with obigations arising under international law of derogations under Article 15, and of the taking of the property of aliens under Article 1 of the Protocol.

Finally, Article 18 contains the idea of 'détournement de pouvoir' in requiring that no restriction shall be imposed or applied for any purpose other than that for which it has been prescribed; that is to say, for the purposes prescribed in the Articles mentioned, as justifying derogations or restrictions.

The criterion of *necessity* is also general. Restrictions must be 'necessary in a democratic society/nécessaires dans une société démocratique' in Articles 8–11, or simply 'necessary/nécessaires' in Article 1 of the Protocol; and derogations must be 'strictly required by the exigencies of the situation/dans la mesure où la situation l'exige' in Article 15.

The prescribed *purposes*, which may be served by restrictions, are drawn from many fields of national and public policy. They are concerned with (*a*) *order*: 'national security/la sécurité nationale' in Articles 8, 10, and 11; 'territorial integrity/l'intégrité territoriale' in Article 10; 'public safety/la sécurité publique' in Articles 8–11; 'prevention of disorder or crime/la défense de l'ordre et la prévention des infractions pénales' in Articles 8, 10, and 11; 'the protection of public order/la protection de l'ordre' in Article 9; 'maintaining the authority and impartiality of the judiciary/pour garantir l'autorité et l'impartialité du pouvoir judiciaire' in Article 10; (*b*) *welfare*: 'the economic well-being of the country/le bien être économique du pays' in Article 8; 'the protection of health and morals/protection de la santé ou de la morale publique' in Articles 8–11; and (*c*) the *conflict of rights*: 'protection of the rights and freedoms of others/protection de droits et libertés d'autrui' (Articles 8, 9, and 11); and, in particular, 'preventing the disclosure of information received in confidence/pour empêcher la divulgation d'informations confidentielles' in Article 10.

Certain of these terms and concepts will be considered further under the Articles in which they occur, but three general observations may be made on them here. First, the English and French expressions are not always equivalent: for example, 'le pouvoir judiciaire' is wider in sense than 'the judiciary', and 'la morale publique' perhaps narrower than 'morals'. Secondly, the public purposes, which may justify restrictions under these various Articles, are not only numerous but large in range and sometimes difficult to define or distinguish: for example, 'public safety', 'public order', and 'disorder'. It follows that the controlling requirement that measures of restrictions must be 'necessary in a democratic society' has a very heavy burden to carry if the rights and freedoms guaranteed are not to be submerged in restrictions which the Convention permits. Here the third observation is in point, that a margin of appreciation of the necessity for particular derogations or restrictions has been accorded by Convention organs to the parliaments and governments of contracting States.[1]

---

[1] Compare a ministerial statement in the *United Kingdom* Parliament that the restrictions and derogations permitted under Articles 8–11 and 15 are 'political

It is not easy then for an applicant, invoking rights or freedoms under Section I, to overcome these various obstacles to the admissibility of his claim.

decisions and cannot in our view be decided upon legal grounds . . . they are not matters to be assessed by a court': Joint Under Secretary of State for Foreign Affairs—*Commons Debates*, vol. 607, col. 1555 (25.6.1959), explaining the refusal of the United Kingdom at that time to accept the jurisdiction of the Court under Article 46. For an analogous argument by counsel for the Belgian Government in *Case relating to Certain Aspects of the Laws on the Use of Languages in Education in Belgium* [1966] European Court H.R.: Doc. CDH/Misc. (66) 3 (22.11.1966) at 9–12.

SECTION I

ARTICLE 2

(1) Everyone's right to life shall be protected by law. No one shall be deprived of his life intentionally save in the execution of a sentence of a court following his conviction of a crime for which this penalty is provided by law.

(2) Deprivation of life shall not be regarded as inflicted in contravention of this Article when it results from the use of force which is no more than absolutely necessary:

- (a) in defence of any person from unlawful violence;
- (b) in order to effect a lawful arrest or to prevent the escape of a person lawfully detained;
- (c) in action lawfully taken for the purpose of quelling a riot or insurrection.

1. Le droit de toute personne à la vie est protégé par la loi. La mort ne peut être infligée à quiconque intentionnellement, sauf en exécution d'une sentence capitale prononcée par un tribunal au cas où le dèlit est puni de cette peine par la loi.

2. La mort n'est pas considérée comme infligée en violation de cet article dans les cas où elle résulterait d'un recours à la force rendu absolument nécessaire:

- (a) pour assurer la défense du toute personne contre la violence illégale;
- (b) pour effectuer une arrestation régulière ou pour empêcher l'évasion d'une personne régulièrement détenue;
- (c) pour réprimer, conformément à la loi, une émeute ou une insurrection.

This Article is broadly the text of a United Kingdom draft,[1] which, however, in addition to minor verbal differences, did not contain the first sentence of the final version, and had at the end of paragraph (2) (c) the words 'or for prohibiting entry to clearly defined places to which access is forbidden on grounds of nation security'. A later draft[2] added the first sentence, perhaps to bring the Article closer to Article 3 of the Universal Declaration, and omitted the words already quoted, so constituting the final version. A proposal to include a provision relating to genocide was rejected[3] as being more suitable for a Consultative Assembly resolution.[4] There is almost no reported discussion of the drafts.

everyone's right to life/le droit de toute personne à la vie

While it cannot be doubted that 'life' means at least the continuing life of a human being, and that it biologically begins at conception, there are difficult questions to be answered: Does 'everyone' include the unborn child, and if so, when does the right to life begin? Who may exercise the right to life of the unborn child? Again it must be asked whether the right to live necessarily entails the right not to live—the right to euthanasia.

The American Convention on Human Rights (1978) is alone among the international instruments in setting limits to *abortion*. Article 2 (1) states:

Everyone has the right to have his life respected. This right shall be protected by law and in general, from the moment of conception. No one shall be arbitrarily deprived 'of his life'.

Under this provision the unborn child is held to be a person, with a right to life from the moment of conception, though it is not absolute given the qualifying language of 'in general' and 'arbitrarily'. The U.S. Supreme Court has expressed a similar idea of the unborn child as a person, in saying that life here is 'something more than mere animal existence';[5] but it has left open the question when life begins, saying that:

---

[1] *T.P.* ii. 352.
[2] Presented at Conference of Senior Officials (14.6.1950): *T.P.* iii. 596.
[3] See now C.P.R. Covenant, Article 6 (2).
[4] *T.P.* iv. 905.
[5] *Muran* v. *Illinois* [1877] 33 U.S. 113, interpreting the Fifth Amendment to the U.S. Constitution 'No person . . . shall be deprived of life . . . without due process of law'.

with respect to the State's important and legitimate interest in potential life, the *compelling* point is viability.[1]

The Commission has not expressed any final opinion on whether, in the language of the Convention, 'everyone' covers the unborn child in Article 2 (1), but, in comparing the uses of the term in other provisions of the Convention, it has doubted it. Nevertheless, given that there is no express exclusion in Article 2 (1) of a right to life for the unborn child, a right to life to be accorded it must be derived from the contents of the Article read as a whole.[2] An application was brought against the United Kingdom[3] by a husband, who had been told by his wife that, being eight weeks pregnant, she intended to have an abortion. Two doctors had given certificates, authorizing the abortion under the Abortion Act (1967) S.1(1)a for the 'prevention' of injury to the physical or mental health of the mother'. The applicant sought an injunction in the Family Division of the High Court to prevent the abortion being carried out. The injunction was refused on the ground that an injunction can be granted only to restrain the infringement of a legal right: that in English law the foetus has no legal rights before birth, though it has a separate existence from its mother; and that the father, whether married or not to the mother, has no legal right to prevent her having an abortion, or to be consulted or informed about it, if the requirements of the Abortion Act (1967) are being complied with.

The Commission held that since Article 2 read as a whole did not declare the right to life of human beings to be absolute, but limited it in certain circumstances, there could be implied limitations to the right to life of the unborn child, in particular to secure the life and health of the mother. It said:

The 'life' of the foetus is intimately connected with and cannot be regarded in isolation of, the life of the pregnant woman. If Article 2 were held to cover the foetus and its protection under this Article were to be seen as absolute, an abortion would have to be considered as prohibited, even where the continuance of the pregnancy would involve a serious risk to the life of the

---

[1] *Roe* v. *Wade* [1973] 410 U.S. 113.

[2] The Austrian Constitutional Court made a similar approach and interpreted Article 2 as not according a right to life to the unborn child: Decision (11.10.1974). C.P.R. Covenant, Article 6 (5) provides that 'Sentence (of death) shall not be carried out on a pregnant woman'. In the U.K. the Sentence of Death (Expectant Mothers) Act (1931) has the same prohibition.

[3] 8416/79 (U.K.): D.R. 9.244.

pregnant woman. This would mean that the 'unborn life' of the foetus would be regarded as being of a higher value than the life of the pregnant woman.

It concluded, with a perhaps important though unexplained qualification as to the length of the pregnancy:

23 . . . [The Commission] finds that the authorisation by the United Kingdom authorities of the abortion complained of is compatible with Article 2 (1), first sentence, because if one assumes that this provision applied at the initial stage of the pregnancy the abortion is covered by an implied limitation protecting the life and health of the woman at that stage of the '*right to life*' of the foetus.

Sterilization. The Commission has said that 'an operation of this kind is felt, in certain circumstances, to involve a breach of the Convention in particular of Articles 2 and 3', but that it was acceptable under the Convention when carried out 'for medication reasons only' and with the consent of the woman.[1]

Euthanasia. The Commission has not had to consider the effect under Article 2 of the consent of an individual to life being terminated. There is a difference here between the giving of fatal drugs to sick persons, whose death was certain,[2] and causing or assisting death at the request or by persuasion of the individual.

Medical services. The protection of life obliges the State 'not only to refrain from taking life *intentionally*, but, further, to take appropriate steps to safeguard life'.[3] An applicant association claimed that there was evidence to show that many children suffered adverse reactions to vaccination in the United Kingdom, and that 15 per cent of those eventually die. The Commission found, on the evidence before it, that the 'nationwide programme of vaccination were a measure of protection against infectious diseases, that the number of 'adverse reactions' was 'miniscule compared with the millions of vaccinations given each year', and that the State had established 'a system of control and supervision' of vaccination and immunization, sufficient to meet its obligations to protect life.

---

[1] 1287/61.
[2] Found to be not contrary to Article 2: Verwaltungsgericht Bremen: N.J.W. [1960] 400.
[3] 7154/75: 14 D.R. 31.

Nuclear products. An application, protesting against nuclear tests and the disposal of radioactive waste in the sea, requested

qu'il soit interdit à la République Fédérale d'Allemagne de déverser les déchets atomiques dans la Mer du Nord et d'entreposer sur son territoire des matériaux atomiques et que de façon générale le réarmement atomique soit arrêté.

The Commission found the application to be manifestly ill founded, there being no appearance of a violation, on the facts presented, by the Federal Republic of either Article 2 or Article 3.[1]

protected by law/protégé par la loi

This is the kind of expression which provokes broad and sometimes extravagant constructions. It might be argued, for example, that failure to impose speed limits on the roads, or to enact safety legislation for industrial work, engaged the responsibility of a contracting State under Article 2 for accidental deaths on the road or in factories. But this argument ignores the fact that it is not life, but the right to life, which is to be protected by law. This is a legal concept which implies that no one may be deprived of his life save on conditions prescribed by law, those conditions being further defined in the rest of Article 2, so as to set limits to the taking of life by public authority, and to permit the State to declare killing in self-defence to be on certain conditions lawful. It could also reasonably be implied that the State must make the deliberate taking of life by individuals a punishable offence.[2] But the failure to prosecute such offences cannot be made the ground of an individual application to the Commission.[3] The question whether a contracting State is required by the first sentence of Article 2 to provide by law for the recovery of damages or for compensation for the estate of the deceased, in case of an unlawful killing, has not arisen for the Commission. In England a Criminal Injuries Compensation Board was established in 1964.

---

[1] 715/60: *Recueil* (1960) ii. The application appears to have been a roundabout way of challenging nuclear tests and the disposal of radioactive waste at sea, as practised in particular by the United States and United Kingdom, against which countries applications could not be brought *ratione personae*.

[2] In the United Nations debates on Article 6 of the First U.N. Covenant 'while the view was expressed that the article should concern itself only with protection of the individual from unwarranted actions by the State, the majority thought that States should be called upon to protect human life against unwarranted actions by public authorities as well as by private persons'.

[3] 809/60: *Recueil* (1962) i. But see also under Article 24 below.

sentence of a court/une sentence capitale prononcée par un tribunal

The word 'court' has presumably the same sense as in Article 5, under which it will be considered. The word 'capitale' appears otiose.

crime for which this penalty is provided by law/au cas où le délit es puni de cette peine par la loi

The death penalty has been abolished or its application greatly limited in all the contracting States.[1] The position may be briefly described.

The death penalty has been totally abolished in the Federal Republic of Germany, and it is reported that in Belgium 'there is a rigid tradition that, even if the sentence is pronounced, it is not carried out', a similar practice being followed in Luxembourg in peacetime.[2] However, in all the other contracting States certain offences committed in time of war are punishable with death, but no offences are punishable with death in peacetime in Austria,[3] Denmark, Ireland, Italy, Netherlands, Norway, or Sweden.

In Greece the death penalty is retained for voluntary homicide, brigandage, and treason; in Ireland for treason and murder of police officers, and in Turkey for certain aggravated forms of murder, treason, forming or directing a drug-traffic gang, and cumulation of offences involving life imprisonment.[4]

In Cyprus Article 7 of the Constitution, which is similar to Article 2 of the Convention, restricts the offences for which the death penalty may be provided by law to premeditated murder,[5] high treason, piracy *jure gentium*, and certain offences under military law.

In the United Kingdom the Murder (Abolition of Death Penalty) Act 1965 s. 1 (1) provides that 'no person shall suffer death for murder

---

[1] For a recent review see *The Death Penalty in European Countries* (Report of European Committee on Crime Problems: Council of Europe, 1962).

[2] Op. cit. in n. 14 at 61 and 71. The execution in 1948 of a man convicted of five murders appears to be the single exception.

[3] Certain ordinary crimes are, however, punishable with death when a state of emergency (*Standrecht*) has been proclaimed.

[4] For a decision of the Turkish Constitutional Court (1.7.1963) on the compatibility of the death penalty with 'fundamental rights and freedoms' see 6 *Yearbook* 820.

[5] See *The Republic* v. *Loftis* [1961] 1 Reports of Supreme Court, Cyprus 30 (a provision to the effect that any person convicted of murder shall be sentenced to death held unconstitutional in so far as it covered murder not premeditated). Premeditation here is not identical with the 'malice aforethought' of English law.

and a person convicted of murder shall . . . be sentenced to imprisonment for life',[1] the trial judge having power to recommend a minimum length of sentence to be served before conditional release. The Act applies to England, Wales, and Scotland, but not to Northern Ireland except in sentences imposed by courts martial. The Act is to expire on 31 July 1970, unless Parliament resolves otherwise. Certain offences remain punishable by death,[2] but it is doubtful whether sentence of death would be carried out for offences in time of peace.

It appears that in those countries where the death penalty is retained for certain offences the court may be able either to impose an alternative penalty prescribed by law, or, by invoking mitigating circumstances, to impose a sentence of imprisonment.[3]

No execution is now carried out in public in any of the contracting States.

shall not be regarded as inflicted in contravention of this Article/n'est pas considérée comme infligée en violation de cet Article

The Commission has not so far had to consider the extent of the exceptions. It may be observed that, read literally, they cover both acts of individuals and acts of public authority; for example, action to quell a riot or insurrection or, generally, to effect a lawful arrest or prevent escape from detention, while acts in self-defence or in defence of others will generally be acts of private individuals. In principle an act of a private individual cannot itself constitute a breach of the Convention, and from this it must follow that, in the administration of the Convention, the exceptions listed in this paragraph must be understood as being applicable only to acts of killing by persons exercising public authority.

But a problem arises under exception (b) in cases where an arrest may be effected in certain circumstances by an individual under

---

[1] If he is under eighteen, detention is ordered in such place and under such conditions as the Home Secretary may direct. See also First U.N. Covenant, Article 6 (5), prohibiting sentence of death on persons under eighteen.

[2] *High treason*: Treason Act 1814, s. 1; *piracy with violence endangering life*: Piracy Act 1837, s. 2; *firing the Queen's ships or arsenals*: Dockyards Protection Act 1772, s. 1, repealed in Scotland as regards death penalty in 1892 and certain offences by members of the armed forces in time of war.

[3] However, the death sentence is mandatory in Turkey for all offences for which that penalty is prescribed, and in Greece for participation in an attack upon the territorial integrity of the State.

domestic law. So, for example, in England a private individual must at common law use whatever force is necessary to capture the offender where a treason or violent felony is committeed in his presence. It would seem that the private individual is exercising public authority in effecting such an arrest, and that, if he kills the offender in the course of the arrest, using more force than necessary, the responsibility of the contracting State concerned will be engaged under Article 2.

The qualification 'lawfully' in exception (*c*) also raises a question of responsibility: is it sufficient that public order regulations permit killing by soldiers quelling a riot, or is the action still unlawful if the force used is excessive in the circumstances? An applicant, alleging that the killing of her husband by a soldier in the quelling of a riot in Belfast was felt not to have exhausted domestic remedies because she had taken this issue to the courts, whether the action by the soldier was excessive and therefore a criminal offence, unlawful under Article 2 (2)c.[1]

It may be observed that the defence of property does not appear among the exceptions.

absolutely necessary/absolument nécessaire

These words have in any case to carry a large burden. If the killing can be shown to be necessary simply to effect the arrest or prevent the escape, is it covered by the exception (*b*)? Or must it be necessary in the light of all the circumstances, including the gravity of the offence? The second criterion, hidden away perhaps in the word 'absolutely', seems to be the better for, as long ago as 1879, it was said by the Criminal Code Bill Commission in England:

> We take one great principle of the common law to be that, though it . . . permits the use of force to prevent crimes to preserve the public peace, and to bring offenders to justice, yet all this is subject to the restriction that the force used is necessary: that is, that the mischief sought to be prevented could not be prevented by less violent means; and that the mischief done by, or which might be reasonably anticipated from, the force used is not disproportionate to the injury or mischief which it is intented to prevent.[2]

The element of proportionality is missing from the Convention provision, but it may be supplied in a number of contracting States through the medium of Article 60.

---

[1] *Farrell* (U.K.) 6861/75 3 D.R. 147.
[2] Quoted by Kenny, *Outlines of Criminal Law*, ed. J. W. C. Turner (1952), 112.

ARTICLE 3

No one shall be subjected to torture or to inh
degrading treatment or punishment.

Nul ne peut être soumis à la torture ni à des peines ou traitements inhumains ou dégradants.

This rule is absolute in the sense that no derogation may be made
from it under Article 15. The text is, save for the omission of the word
'cruel' before 'inhuman', identical with that of Article 5 of the
Universal Declaration.[1]

inhuman treatment or punishment/des peines ou traite-ments inhumains

On a narrow view it might be said that the word 'inhuman'
characterizes primarily the doer rather than what is done and so must
be confined to treatment altogether outside the expected range of
human behaviour, or that it marks the enormity of the pain or suffering
inflicted. On a broader view 'inhuman treatment' could be taken to be
cruelty in any form, that is, the infliction of pain or suffering for its own
sake.

The preparatory work brings out, as an essential element, lack of
consent. Two proposals were made for additions to the original draft
texts. The first, by Mr. Cocks (United Kingdom), would have added to
Article 2 (1) of the Teitgen report:[2]

In particular no person shall be subjected to any form of mutilation or
sterilisation or to any form of torture or beating. Nor shall he be forced to take
drugs nor shall they be administered to him without his knowledge and
consent. Nor shall he be subjected to imprisonment with such an excess of
light, darkness, noise or silence, as to cause mental suffering.

This was withdrawn on the understanding that it would be incorporated instead in a draft Resolution to be submitted to the Consultative Assembly.[3] The second proposal by the United Kingdom member
of the Committee of Experts, was to add the sentence:

---

[1] Reproduced as the first sentence of First U.N. Covenant, Article 7, to which there
is added a provision concerning medical and scientific experimentation.

[2] Doc. 77: *T.P.* i. 105, 137.

[3] *T.P.* i. 137 (French version. The English version omits the reason for withdrawal).

No one shall be subjected to any form of physical mutilation or medical or scientific experimentation against his will.[1]

as an Article to the list of rights and freedoms in the same Article 2 (1). The proposal was not, as appears from later drafts, adopted; nor is the dropping of the word 'cruel' explained, though perhaps it was regarded as repetitive.

Inhuman treatment would then be the deliberate infliction of physical or mental pain or suffering, against the will of the victim, and, when forming part of criminal punishment, out of proportion to the offence. The reference, in the second amendment proposed by the United Kingdom, to medical or scientific experimentation raises the question how far free consent of the patient may be taken: will free consent always justify any form of experimentation, or is public policy to set a limit in the sense of Article 3.[2]

Lack of consent and disproportion have had judicial recognition as elements in cruelty or inhuman treatment. So the U.S. Supreme Court has spoken of cruelty as 'the wanton infliction of pain' though the majority found that, on the facts of the case before them, there was 'no purpose to inflict unnecessary pain'.[3]

Again it was argued before the Judicial Committee of the Privy Council that the mandatory death penalty, prescribed by Rhodesian law even for a *socius criminis* (accessory) in the crime of arson, was the kind of punishment which is 'out of relation to that which, in particular circumstances or in reference to an offence by a particular nature, is deserved' and was therefore inhuman treatment contrary to Rhodesian Constitution, 1961, s. 60 (1), which is, in terms, almost identical with Article 3 of the Convention.[4] It has also been held in Germany that 'inhuman treatment' in Article 3 is not to be understood only as 'grausam und vernichtend', spelling extermination, but as

---

[1] The language of Article 7 of the First U.N. Covenant now corresponds closely to this, and is a great improvement on the version of that Article in A/2929.

[2] For ten basic principles to be observed 'in order to satisfy moral, ethical and legal concepts' see in *re Brandt and others* [1947] U.S. Military Tribunal, Nuremberg, 14 *I.L.R.* 296, 298. See also David Daube, 'Transplantation: acceptability and the required legal sanctions', *CIBA Foundation Symposium on Ethics in Medical Progress, 1966*.

[3] *Louisiana, ex rel. Francis* v. *Resweber* [1947] 329 U.S. 459, interpreting the Eighth Amendment.

[4] *Runyowa* v. *The Queen* [1966] 1 A.E.R. 633. The Judicial Committee did not have to decide the question, since it found that the death penalty was not in itself 'inhuman treatment', and that s. 60 (3) of the Constitution expressly precluded the application of s. 60 (1) to any provision of law existing at the entry into force of the Constitution. The requirement of the death penalty in the instant case was such a provision.

treatment which is 'disproportionate, violating the personal rights of the individual'.[1]

In application to the Commission four forms of inhuman treatment or punishment have been alleged: torture, sterilization, ill treatment of prisoners serving sentence, and deportation of individuals to countries where they might expect severe punishment for earlier political activities.

The notions of Article 3 are not wholly separable. Torture is part of inhuman treatment, and either may be also degrading; and each of them may have the character of punishment. They will be reviewed, then, in terms of applications to the Commission under Article 3, in which the following stand out: the use of torture; forms of ill-treatment in detention; the conditions of psychiatric detention; and the control by Article 3 of extradition and deportation.

It must first be observed that allegations of breaches of Article 3 are inherently difficult to prove for reasons advanced by the Commission.[2] First, a victim or witnesses may hestitate to reveal all that has happened for fear of personal reprisals. Secondly, torture or ill-treatment by police or prison authorities or in the armed services may generally be committed without witnesses, and perhaps without knowledge or higher authority. Thirdly, all such public authorities have a collective reputation to defend, and this makes them reluctant to allow inquiries into the facts alleged, and still less to admit responsibility for them. Finally, physical traces of injury can become unrecognizable over time even for medical experts.

As a standard of proof, then, of allegations of breaches of Article 3, the Commission and the Court have both invoked proof beyond reasonable doubt, the Commission adding that this means 'not a doubt based on a merely theoretical possibility, or raised in order to avoid a disagreeable conclusion, but a doubt for which reasons can be given drawn from the facts'; and the Court explaining that proof may follow on this standard from 'the coexistence of sufficiently strong, clear and concordant inferences'.[3]

---

[1] Amtsgericht, Wiesbaden (25.1.1963): *N.J.W.* [1963] 967. See, however, *District Officer, Nicosia* v. *Hadriyiannis* [1961] Rep. Sup. Ct. Cyprus 79, where a mandatory penal provision was held unconstitutional as being disproportionate to the gravity of the offence [Constitution, Article 12 (5)], but not it seems 'inhuman treatment' [Constitution, Article 8].

[2] *Denmark et al.* v. *Greece* (3321–33232/67: 3344/67: 3344/67) Report (25.1.1976) 12 *Yearbook*.

[3] Ibid: 12 *Yearbook* 1968.

Further, there may be numerous allegations of ill-treatment in a particular or in a disturbed situation. The principle that it is *victims* that are the essential subjects of Convention applications was observed by the Commission in both the cases, concerning Greece and Northern Ireland,[1] just referred to. Faced with collective allegations of ill-treatment, the Commission would select a number of individuals or situations for specific investigation; so where written evidence was presented by the applicant government of 228 cases of ill-treatment in Northern Ireland, the Commission investigated a relatively small number of them, but in depth, examining the written evidence and the reactions to it of the respondent government, and hearing 100 witnesses.

Related to this is the notion of administrative practice, composed of a repetition of acts of ill-treatment and official tolerance of them. The Commission explained this notion in the Greek Case:

By *repetition of acts* is meant a substantial number of acts of torture or ill-treatment which are the expression of a general situation. . . . By *official tolerance* is meant that, though acts of torture or ill-treatment are plainly illegal, they are tolerated in the sense that the supervisors of those immediately responsible, though cognisant of such acts, take no action to punish them or prevent their repetition; or that higher authority, in face of numerous allegations, manifests indifference by refusing any adequate investigation of their truth or falsity, or that, in judicial proceedings, a fair hearing of such complaints is denied.[2]

The Commission went further, distinguishing, in this notion of administrative practice, its effect on the exhaustion of domestic remedies, its relation to the principle and extent of State responsibility for ill-treatment, and its intensification of ill-treatment when seen as a whole. That domestic remedies may be in effect reduced or eliminated by official tolerance as described is obvious, and the requirement of their exhaustion may then be inapplicable.

With regard to State responsibility for ill-treatment, the United Kingdom government maintained that, under the Convention, a State could be responsible only for: 'tolerance of ill-treatment that was found at the level of the executive authority, which was empowered to order or arrange the administration in which the ill-treatment had taken place.' The Commission did not accept this argument, saying that:

[1] *Ireland* v. *U.K.* (S310/71): Judgment (18.1.1978) 23.I.
[2] 12 *Yearbook* 195–6. See also *Donnelly* (U.K.) 5577–5583/73: 4 D.R. 4.

The responsibility of a State under the Convention may arise fc
organs, agents and servants. As in connection with responsibilit
national law generally, their rank is immaterial in the sense th;
their acts are *imputed* to the State . . . its existing obligation can be
by a person exercising an official function vested in him at any, ev
level, without express authorisation and even outside or against instructions.[1]

Evidence of an adminsitrative practice may also not only serve to
establish the truth of allegations of ill-treatment, but must then
necessarily intensify its gravity. We come now to the use of torture.

Torture. The U.N. General Assembly, in a Declaration on the
Protection of all Persons from Torture and other Cruel, Inhuman, or
Degrading Treatment or Punishment: Resolution 3452–xxx, said that:

Torture constitutes an aggravated and deliberate form of cruel, inhuman and
degrading treatment or punishment;

and the European Commission spoke of the term as being used to
describe

inhuman treatment, which has a purpose such as the obtaining of information
or confessions or the infliction of punishment, and it is generally an
aggravated form of inhuman treatment.

Whether some particular treatment of a person constitutes torture is
inevitably a matter of subjective opinion, but to describe it as an
aggravated form of inhuman treatment, suggests a higher level of
severity, rather than the factor of purpose, as separating it from other
forms of inhuman treatment. It is difficult to understand this, or the
reasoning of the Court in its judgment on the use of interrogation
methods by the security forces in Northern Ireland. Five methods of
pressure were used there: wall-standing, hooding, subjection to noise,
deprivation of sleep, and reduction of diet. The Commission considered that none of these techniques, with the possible exception of
wall-standing, lasting in one case for sixteen hours, could be said to
cause in itself sufficient pain and suffering to constitute torture.
Nevertheless, there could, in the view of the Commission, be a
combination of elements in the use of the techniques, which, given
their deliberate use for obtaining information, could make them
torture; these elements were the duration of a method used, its
repetition, and the application of all techniques to one person. The

[1] e.g. 8462/79: 20 D.R. 84.

Commission, on this approach, concluded that, in a number of individual cases, the combination of elements in the use of techniques constituted torture, and therefore inhuman treatment, which was also degrading. The majority of the Court however found the use of the five techniques in a number of cases to be inhuman and degrading treatment, but held at the same time that they did not cause suffering of an intensity and cruelty, such as to constitute torture.

Inhuman treatment is itself an extreme, its prohibition being absolute, and it is difficult to see how it can be aggravated or extended. To have found that the use of the five techniques, whatever their combination or direction, was not inhuman treatment, was a possible position: but to describe it as inhuman treatment, but still call for a higher level of severity, to make that inhuman treatment torture, is inexplicable.

The beating of the feet, *falanga* or *bastinado*, revealed in the Greek Case, was unquestionably inhuman treatment and torture, causing as it did excruciating pain and suffering, designed to break the will: it had the advantage for its users of causing no bone or muscular damage, and leaving only short-lived external marks.

Related is corporal punishment, used in respect of criminal offences, or as a disciplinary measure in schools. The first was brought to the Commission by an applicant, who had undergone birch strokes, ordered by a Juvenile Court in the Isle of Man.[1] The Commission considered that:

Birching as a punishment ordered by a Court and administered as provided for in the Isle of Man is an assault on human dignity, which humiliates and disgraces the offender without any redeeming social value . . . [Furthermore] other persons involved may be humilitated or disgraced by the whole procedure.

The Court agreed that the birching, while not instituting torture or inhuman punishment was nevertheless degrading, and contrary to Article 3.[2]

On corporal punishment in school, complaints have been raised of its actual use, and of the threat of its use. Caning of a girl, aged fourteen, by the headmistress, for eating potato crisps in class, had left three red weals across the buttocks; the pain and discomfort had lasted several days, and the marks left remained for about two months.

[1] *Tyrer* (U.K.) 5856/72. Judgment No. 26 (25.4.1978).
[2] Court Judgment (26.4.1978) m.26.

The application to the Commission ended in a settlement under Article 28 (b).[1]

Objections to the use of the tawse, or strapping device, as corporal punishment in the Scottish schools, were made in applications by the mothers of two boys, who had not in fact been strapped with a tawse.[2] The Commission and the Court both found no breach of Article 3, and the Court said:

Corporal punishment is traditional in Scottish schools and indeed appears to be favoured by a large majority of parents . . .[3] Of itself, this is not conclusive of the issue before the Court for the threat of a particular measure is not excluded from the category of 'degrading', within the meaning of Article 3, simply because the measure has been in use for a long time, or even meets with general approval. . . . However, particularly in view of the above-mentioned circumstances obtaining in Scotland, it is not established that pupils at a school, where such punishment is used, are, solely by reason of the risk of being subjected thereto, humiliated or debased in the eyes of others to the requisite degree at all.

As to the sons of the applicants being humiliated or debased in their own eyes, the Court, while recognizing this possibility, noted that

it has not been shown by means of medical certificates or otherwise that they suffered any adverse psychological or other effects.[4]

Ill-treatment of detainees. Article 3 is often invoked by detainees[5] on solitary confinement, length of detention, and disciplinary punishments.

Solitary confinement has to be considered in the light of its purpose, forms and effects.[6] A prisoner may be isolated to prevent escape or its planning, particularly where the prisoner has a record of acts dangerous to others; and so contacts with other prisoners, visits from outside, and his correspondence, may for some time be stopped. Solitary confinement may also be used in prisons as a disciplinary measure: for example, to prevent repetition of assault on prison officers, and as a punishment for disciplinary offences.[7] A detainee on

---

[1] 7907/77 (U.K.) H.D.R. 205.
[2] *Campbell/Cosans* (U.K.) 7511/76 and 7743/76. Judgment No. 48 (25.2.1982).
[3] Pack Committee Report (1977), based on an opinion survey.
[4] Court Judgment (25.2.1982) vol. 48 pp. 29, 30.
[5] This term may be used to cover generally persons in detention, including prisoners serving sentence, referred to as prisoners.
[6] '. . . its strictness, its duration, and the end pursued': 7854/77 12 D.R. 189.
[7] *Hilton* (U.K.) 5613/72 4 D.R. 177.

remand may be put in solitary confinement to prevent collusion or suppression of evidence: so solitary confinement had been ordered for ten days for an applicant, arrested on charges of theft and of carrying explosives and firearms. The competent court extended it twice to a total of 28 days, when the preliminary investigation, involving interrogations and interviews, was ended. The Commission considered that, in the circumstances, the solitary confinement has 'not caused him great physical or mental suffering with the aim of breaking down his resistance and extracting confessions from him'.[1]

Solitary confinement can range from virtual sensory isolation, confinement for the time being in a dark cell with only the occasional contacts with prison staff, through degrees of separation from other prisoners, from visitors including doctors and legal advisers, and from the outside world through radio and television.

The Commission has said that, in its effects, complete solitary isolation can destroy the personality: thus it constitutes a form of inhuman treatment which cannot be justified by the requirements of security.[2] How far solitary confinement approaches this limit in its effects is a matter of fact in each case,[3] and the Commission could look for some medical evidence. So where a prisoner had no contacts within the prison for six weeks except with prison officers, though not apparently denied visits from outside, he stated that as a result of this solitary confinement

... he was feeling 'very depressed', that he 'was having great difficulty sleeping at night' and that he had 'developed a facial twitching'.

But the Commission concluded:

without neglecting that also a relatively short segregation may have negative effects on a person's health, the Commission considers nevertheless that it would have been reasonable to expect that the applicant would have consulted the prison doctor again [first contact after 17 days of solitary confinement] had his problems been as grave as he alleges.[4]

---

[1] *Bonzi* (Switzerland) 7854/77 12 D.R. 85: see also 6032/73 (F.R.G.) 44D115.

[2] For methods to break a hunger-strike see 1753/63: *Recueil* (1964). *Ensslin, Baader, Raspe* (F.R.G.) 7572/76, 7567/76: 14 D.R. 64, 109. The Commission found on breach of Article 3 in the solitary confinement, as applied to these and to other members of the Baader-Meinhof group—the Rote Armee Fraktion: 6166173 2 D.R. 58.

[3] For a detailed account of the conditions of the solitary confinement of two detainees on remand see *Kröcher/Möller* (Switzerland) 8463/78 26 D.R. 24.

[4] 7630/76 (U.K.) 13 D.R. 113, 136; 8397/78 (Denmark) 27 D.R. 50.

Sterilization. The Commission has received a number of applications concerning acts of sterilization carried out under the Nazi regime, but had to declare them inadmissible *ratione temporis*, without considering the principle. The Commission, as already seen, observed that 'an operation of this nature might, in certain circumstances involve a breach of the Convention, in particular Articles 2 and 3'. The element of consent is critical. Is all sterilization without consent 'inhuman treatment' or is sterilization, as, for example, prescribed by law for certain sexual offenders,[1] acceptable? Again whose consent is required in the case of a married couple? While in the decision cited the Commission appears to have dispensed with the consent of the husband, it is to be observed that the medical indication was that the operation was necessary.[2]

Length of detention is not expressly mentioned in the Convention, which does not deal directly with the magnitude of penalties for criminal offences, or state that excessive terms of imprisonment could constitute a breach.[3] The U.K. Bill of Rights (1689) recognizes the principle, declaring that 'excessive bail might not be required or excessive fines imposed nor cruel and unusual punishment inflicted'.[4] Similarly a German court has held that the deprivation of certain civil rights in perpetuity will, if disproportionate to the offence, be 'inhuman treatment';[5] and this principle could certainly be applied to the deprivation of a person of citizenship or nationality.

A German Report on the Treatment of Long-Term Prisoners, prepared in the Council of Europe, held it to be 'inhuman to imprison a person for life without any hope of release' and 'that nobody should be deprived of the means of possible release'.[6] There followed a Council Resolution on the Treatment of Long-Term Prisoners,

---

[1] See references in debate in Consultative Assembly (September 1949): *T.P.* i. 208–9. Sterilization of a man at his own request has been held a crime in France: Court de Cassation, Sirey 1938.1.193.

[2] See *England: Bravery* v. *Bravery* [1954] 3 A.E.R. 59 for some difference of opinion on these issues in the Court of Appeal, and particularly the judgment of Lord Justice Denning.

[3] R14/56 (*de Becker*): Report § 263.

[4] Adopted as Eighth Amendment of the U.S. Constitution. The Fourteenth Amendment prohibits 'cruelty' in the execution of sentence.

[5] Oberlandesgericht, Köln (11.6.1963): N.J.W. (1963) 1748: (deprivation in perpetuity of capacity to take an oath, imposed for persons).

[6] European Committee on Crime Problems: XXV (1965) pp. 77.

calling for a review of long-term sentences at regular intervals 'after eight or fourteen years of detention' or before.[1] Again while the penalty of life imprisonment has been found to be not contrary to the Constitution in Italy or the Federal Republic of Germany, their constitutional courts have called for the allowance of conditional release from life imprisonment after a reasonable time as a matter of law, rather than an act of grace. The Commission, limited to the Convention, however, while it

recognises the desirability of such a requirement in the administration of criminal practice, it finds no provision of the Convention including Article 3 . . . which can be read as requiring that an individual serving a lawful sentence of life imprisonment must have that sentence reconsidered by a national authority, judicial or administrative, with a view to its remission or termination.[2]

But this refers to the length of sentence as such, and does not exclude the applicability of Article 3 to the conditions or effects of serving a prolonged sentence.[3]

Disciplinary measures or punishments are often complained of to the Commission as 'inhuman or degrading treatment'.[4] The compatibility of flogging as a penalty with Article 3 has not been determined, an application, in which the issue was raised, having been withdrawn and the statutory authorization for the penalty in the meantime repealed.[5]

Physical punishment of a prisoner, who is himself rebellious and violent, presents the particular difficulty of what use of force is necessary or proportionate; and so where it appeared from government reports that a violent prisoner, who was in fact a small man suffering from war injuries to the head, had been tied in a strait jacket by three warders, having been struck on the head with a rubber truncheon, and left for a number of hours in an isolation cell, the Commission made extensive inquiries in which the government authorities fully co-operated.[6]

---

[1] Resolution 76/2 (17.2.76).

[2] *Kotälla* (Netherlands) 7994/77: 14 D.R.

[3] *Bonnechaux* (Switzerland) 8224/78: 18 D.R. 100 (long detention remand of person of ill-health, given in fact adequate medical care—no documents found of Article 3); 9044/80 (Italy) 27 D.R. 200.

[4] The Standard Minimum Rules for the Treatment of Prisoners (Council of Europe: Resolution 73/5) are determined in 7408/76 (F.R.G.): 10 D.R. 221.

[5] 176/56: 2 *Yearbook* 174, 186.

[6] 2004/63: *Report of Commission*.

Prisoners have also complained of methods used to break a hunger strike on which they have embarked; these methods consisted of inducing thirst either by denial of water or by putting salt in milk or water given to the prisoner. The Commission has not found that they could not constitute 'inhuman treatment'.[1]

Confinement in isolation may, in the view of a German court, be contrary to Article 3, if it is harming the physical or mental health of the prisoner.[2]

Deportation and extradition. A similar question may arise in the converse way where a prisoner is to be deported or extradited to a country in which he expects ill-treatment. Is a complaint that deportation or extradition in such circumstances would be contrary to Article 3 compatible with the Convention at all? It might be said that, apart from the fact that the Convention does not impose on contracting States an obligation to grant a right of residence or asylum,[3] they are not responsible for the action of other States, and that, where the receiving country is not a party to the Convention, any action it may be expected to take is outside the competence of the Commission *ratione personae*. These formal objections have not, as will be seen, altogether commended themselves either to the Commission or to the national courts which have considered the issue.

The Commission has recognized in general that

L'expulsion d'un étranger peut, dans certaines conditions exceptionnelles, constituer un traitement inhumain ou dégradant au sens de l'Article 3 . . .[4]

and has given particular attention to the separation from wife and children, which expulsion may effect.[5] It has also said that

---

[1] 1753/63: *Recueil* (1964) i; 1760/63: *Recueil* 20. It appears from information given by the German authorities in 2007/63: *Receuil* (1965) i that the practice of adding salt to milk has been abandoned.

[2] Oberlandesgericht, Hamburg (13.6.1963): *N.J.W.* [1963] 1840. Isolation (Schwei-geabteilung) is authorized by S.P.O. § 116 (1). See 1392/62: *Recueil* (1965) i for an application, complaining of seven months' isolation, rejected for non-exhaustion of remedies. Compare Oberlandesgericht, Hamburg (16.10.1964): *N.J.W.* [1965] 357 (applying Prison Rules (Diest- und Vollzugsordnung) 967 (4) which provides that a medical certificate shall be required where any period of solitary confinement exceeds six months).

[3] See further under Article 5 (1) *f*.

[4] 984/61: *Recueil* 6 (the applicant stated that a surgical operation had rendered him 'intransportable'. The Commission found that, as the expulsion order had been deferred, no question of a breach of Article 3 arose in his case).

[5] 317/57: *Recueil* (1959). See further under Article 8.

the deportation of a foreigner to a particular country might in exceptional circumstances give rise to the question whether there has been 'inhuman treatment' within the meaning of Article 3. . . . [S]imilar considerations might apply to cases where a person is extradited to a particular country in which, due to the very nature of the régime of that country or to a particular situation in that country, basic human rights, such as are guaranteed by the Convention, might be either grossly violated or entirely suppressed . . .[1]

In considering applications protesting against expulsion to a country not a party to the Convention, the Commission has a task which, to compare small with great, has some analogy to that envisaged for the U.N. in Article 2 (6) of the Charter. In order to prevent, so far as it is competent to do so, a violation of the Convention rights by a country not a party to it, the Commission has to see whether contributory action by a contracting State may not be, however indirectly, a breach of the Convention. Here a distinction has to be made between the cases where the punishment, even for an offence of a political character, that can be expected, falls within the normal range of punishment for offences of the same kind, and those where, because the individual concerned served on what may be thought to be the wrong side[2] in campaigns of the Second World War or a civil war, his punishment may be greatly aggravated and vindictive. In any case, the expectation of a sentence of death is coming, as appears from the European Extradition Convention, Article 11, to be regarded as a bar to extradition or deportation at least in those countries which have to a great extent abolished it, though it plainly cannot as such be regarded as 'inhuman treatment' under the Convention, which expressly permits it. However, it might be so regarded as being wholly disproportionate to the offence and, in a decision which points up the principle, a German court has said:

Expulsion might be assimilated to [inhuman] treatment if the applicant had been sentenced to death in Czechoslovakia, or if he had been liable to the death penalty, or again if the sentence of imprisonment he was likely to incur had been out of proportion to that generally passed in Western countries . . . it is necessary to take into account the special circumstances of every case in order to judge whether expulsion constitutes inhuman treatment.[3]

[1] 1802/63: 6 *Yearbook* 480. See also 1465/62: 5 *Yearbook* 256 and 2143/64: *Recueil* 14, and for further discussion of this passage, read in the context of other Convention provisions, see under Article 5 (1) *f* below.

[2] See 2240/64 and 2396/65.

[3] Oberverwaltungsgericht, Berlin (27.9.1960): 3 *Yearbook* 640–2. The court found that the applicant had not been sentenced to death, and that the sentences imposed in

The question may also arise whether his delivery to another country may put his life in danger there, not through any positive action of the public authorities, but through their unwillingness or inability to protect him.[1]

degrading treatment/traitement dégradant

What is degrading belongs to the same order of ideas as respect for human dignity, which McDougal and Lasswell set among the basic human rights, distinguishing it from 'health, well-being and growth' and from 'security'.[2] Though certain applicants have complained of degrading treatment,[3] the Commission has not had occasion to express an opinion of its meaning.

What is degrading can again be a matter of subjective opinion: for example, an applicant had rejected a requirement that, in place of unemployment benefit, he work in municipal plantation services, secured normally for the disabled, on the ground that it was humiliating; but the Commission held that this was not degrading. But there would perhaps be broad agreement that the official non-recognition of change of sex could be degrading. So where an applicant had undergone an operation for change of sex from male to female, but the administrative authorities in the Federal Republic of Germany had refused to recognize a change of Christian name or to make any change in the birth register, a settlement of the application was reached.

Czechoslovakia for desertion and espionage, with which he was charged, fell within the usual limits set by Western countries. Contrast a finding of the Oberverwaltungsgericht, Münster (13.9.1955): *Die öffent. Verwaltung* [1956] 381 that the return of a foreign national or stateless person to a country 'behind the iron curtain' from which he had fled for political reasons was contrary to Article 3 of the Convention. But see now Bundesverfassungsgericht (30.6.1965): the abolition of the death penalty by Grundgesetz, Article 102, does not preclude the authorities of the Federal Republic from contributing indirectly, by extradition or deportation, to the imposition of the death penalty by another State: decision reported in *Journal of I.C.J.* (Summer 1966) 151.

[1] See, for example, *Zacharia* v. *Republic of Cyprus* [1962] 2 A.E.R. 438 discussed below under Article 5 (1) *f*; UN Declaration on Territorial Asylum 2312-XXII (14.12.1967); Interights (January 1985).

[2] See McDougal and Bebr, 'Human rights in the U.N.', 58 *A.J.I.L.* [1964] 605.

[3] e.g. 1352/62 (prisoner transported through town wearing prison uniform and handcuffed): 986/61: 5 *Yearbook* 98 (medical examination).

ARTICLE 4

(1) No one shall be held in slavery or servitude.

(2) No one shall be required to perform forced or compulsory labour.

(3) For the purpose of this Article the term 'forced or compulsory labour' shall not include:

  (a) any work required to be done in the ordinary course of detention imposed according to the provisions of Article 5 of this Convention or during conditional release from such detention;

  (b) any service of a military character or, in case of conscientious objectors in countries where they are recognised, service exacted instead of compulsory military service;

  (c) any service exacted in case of an emergency or calamity threatening the life or well-being of the community;

  (d) any work or service which forms part of normal civic obligations.

1. Nul ne peut être tenu en esclavage ni en servitude.

2. Nul ne peut être astreint à accomplir un travail forcé ou obligatoire.

3. N'est pas considéré comme 'travail forcé ou obligatoire' au sens du présent article:

  (a) tout travail requis normalement d'une personne soumise à la détention dans les conditions prévues par l'article 5 de la présente Convention, ou durant sa mise en liberté conditionnelle;

  (b) tout service de caractère militaire ou, dans le cas d'objecteurs de conscience dans les pays où l'objection de conscience est reconnue comme légitime, à un autre service à la place du service militaire obligatoire;

  (c) tout service requis dans le cas de crisis ou de calamités qui menacent la vie ou le bien-être de la communauté;

  (d) tout travail ou service formant partie des obligations civiques normales.

The Article is an expansion of Article 4 of the Universal Declaration[1] in that it introduces the idea of forced labour and enumerates certain forms of compulsory work which are not to be regarded as 'forced or compulsory labour' within the prohibition. Two versions were originally proposed, one identical with Article 4 of the Universal Declaration, and the other a compressed form of the final Article, only one exception being mentioned. A United Kingdom amendment of the second version[2] adapted the Article to almost its present form, the inclusion of work during conditional release in paragraph 3 (*a*) and rewording of the reference to conscientious objectors in paragraphs 3 (*b*) being effected later.[3] Minor changes in the French text of this paragraph also appear. No explanations of the amendments and additions are given, but it is possible that the rewording of paragraph 3 (*b*) was designed to avoid any inference that the Convention required contracting States to recognize conscientious objection to military service as a right as such. Article 4 has been adopted with certain changes as Article 8 of the First U.N. Covenant where the slave-trade is also prohibited and paragraph 3 (*a*) is slightly elaborated.

in slavery or servitude/en esclavage ou en servitude

No derogation is permitted from this first paragraph under Article 15.[4] While slavery, servitude, and forced labour have obvious elements in common, they are treated in Article 4, as in other declarations and conventions, as being distinct. Slavery and servitude both appear primarily to refer to the status of an individual or the condition of his life, while forced labour may characterize rather the kind of work or service, often incidental or temporary, which he performs. Slavery, on the other hand, is in essence the condition of being wholly in the legal ownership of another person, while servitude is, it seems, broader and in common with forced or compulsory labour can cover conditions of work or service, which the individual cannot change or from which he cannot escape.

---

[1] 'No one shall be held in slavery or servitude; slavery and the slave trade shall be prohibited in all their forms'; but see also Article 23 of the Declaration: '(1) Everyone has the right . . . to the free choice of employment, to just and favourable conditions of work . . . (3) Everyone who works has the right to just and favourable remuneration. . . .'

[2] Doc. CM/WPI (50) 2 (Committee of Experts: 6.3.1960): *T.P.* ii. 425.

[3] Apparently on 4.8.1950: *T.P.* iii. 730, and 14.6.1960: *T.P.* iii. 597 respectively.

[4] Compare I.M.T. Charter, Article 6 (*c*), declaring 'enslavement [of] any civilian population' a crime against humanity.

Slavery does not exist in any of the contracting States or of the overseas territories to which the Convention has been extended.

The forms of servitude, with which the U.N. Ad Hoc Committee on Slavery, reporting in April 1951, had concerned itself included debtbondage, being 'sold' into marriage, and the subjection of children to sham adoptions.

The supplementary slavery Convention (1956) elaborated these, and included a description of serfdom as:

The condition or status of a tenant who is by law, custom or agreement bound to live and labour on land belonging to another and to render some determinate service to such other person, whether for reward or not, and is not free to change his status. Article 1 (6)

The Commission applied this description to the notion of servitude in Article 4.

forced or compulsory labour/un travail forcé ou obligatoire

Some general comments are necessary on the expression itself.

It has become, at least in legal usage, a term of art; and historically it and the related ideas of corrective labour and recruited labour have been closely, and indeed primarily, associated with labour conditions in non-self-governing territories. It made perhaps its first international appearance in the League Mandates. The expression has been much discussed and its application generalized in a number of studies, recommendations, and conventions under the aegis of the League, the I.L.O., and the U.N. National legislation in many countries has also adopted it.

There is a question whether forced labour and compulsory labour are distinguishable, in the sense of direct and indirect compulsion respectively. In the preparation of the definition embodied in the Forced Labour Convention 1930, the Committee on Forced Labour rejected a Netherlands proposal to delete the words 'forced or', apparently on the ground that it was preferable to maintain the whole expression as used in the League B and C Mandates and the Slavery Convention 1926. In the Forced Labour Convention 1957 the words 'or compulsory' do not appear in the title, but were retained in the expression as used in the main body of the Convention; and it has been authoritatively said that, as a matter of experience, it is not always possible to distinguish between law and practice as regards forced labour in the strict sense and practice with regard to various forms of compulsion to labour.[1]

However, while it seems that in most cases a distinction between 'forced' or 'compulsory' labour is not, in practice at least, necessary, I.L.O. studies and recommendations suggest that the latter may be apt to describe certain forms of indirect compulsion to work.

The prohibition of Article 4 (2), qualified by paragraph 3, calls for understanding of the notion of 'forced or compulsory labour'.

A definition is to be found in the I.L.O. Convention No. 29, the Abolition of Forced Labour, in force in 1932.

For the purposes of this Convention the term 'forced or compulsory labour' shall mean all work or service which is exacted from any person under the menace of a penalty and for which the said person has not offered himself voluntarily.[2] Article 2 (1).

A supplementary convention, adopted in 1957 and in force in 1959, was I.L.O. Convention No. 105, which specified a number of prohibited purposes of the use of forced or compulsory labour. Article 1 requires contracting parties

... to suppress and not to make use of any form of forced or compulsory labour

(*a*) as a means of political coercion or education or as a punishment for holding or expressing political views or views ideologically opposed to the established political, social or economic system;

(*b*) as a method of mobilising and using labour for purposes of economic development;

(*c*) as a means of labour discipline;

(*d*) as a punishment for having participated in strikes;

(*e*) as a means of racial, social, national or religious, discrimination.

The phrase 'under the menace of a penalty' is ambiguous: it could mean that the work or service is required in execution of a penalty, or that a penalty may be imposed for a failure or refusal to perform the work or service. The latter is the more probable; but more important is the notion what is or is not voluntary. The voluntary element in the work or service being performed may affect in a number of ways the determination of whether it is forced or compulsory labour. First,

---

[1] *Report of the Committee of Experts on the Application of Conventions and Recommendations* (1962), para. 34: see also paras. 81, 82.

[2] e.g. *Cyprus* v. *Turkey* (6780/74: 6950/75) Report 10.7.1976.

while the provisions of Article 4 (3) (*a*) and (*b*) of the Convention are true exceptions to the prohibition of forced or compulsory labour, it is possible to read paragraphs (*c*) and (*d*) as belonging to a different order. What is accepted as a natural duty to the community may or should be so recognized by the individual, and work or service under paragraphs (*c*) and (*d*) may be done willingly as a duty. We have then here, not exceptions to the prohibition of forced or compulsory labour, but what is not forced or compulsory labour at all; it is excluded from Article 4 (2). Nevertheless, the extent of the duty of the individual to the community can be variable, not least under a regime of economic planning or development; and the margin between the planned use of labour and the direction of labour, between free and compulsory employment, can become almost indiscernibly narrow. While compulsory mobilization and use of labour for the purposes of economic development, which the Abolition of Forced Labour Convention forbids, may fall on the side of forced labour, the element of duty may place some compulsory social service, for example, for health or education on the other side. So the Constitution of India permits the imposition of 'compulsory service for public purposes', provided it is not discriminatory.[1] Other issues arise in the documents of professional employment.

The Commission had to consider Article 4 (2) in the *Iversen Case*.[2] The facts may be summarized as follows:

As a result of difficulties, which had arisen in the staffing of the public dental service in Norway, the Provisional Act for an obligatory public dental service for dentists was enacted[3] in June 1956 by the Norwegian Parliament, not without opposition there. Iversen had obtained a diploma in dentistry at Düsseldorf in 1958 and attended a

---

[1] Article 23 (2): this would include 'conscription ... for social service': *State of Himachal Pradesh* v. *Jorawar* [1953] A.I.R. 18, 19.

[2] 1468/62: 6 *Yearbook* 278–332.

[3] Its provisions material to the case were:

1. Persons who in 1955 or later have passed the examination in dentistry in this Kingdom, or have obtained approval of a foreign examination in dentistry giving it the same effect as the Norwegian examination in dentistry pursuant to Act of 8th July 1949, may, on the basis of a decision of the Ministry for Social Affairs, be required for a period of up to 2 years to take a position in public dental service which, though having been advertised, remains vacant.

4. Contravention of an assignment issued under the authority of this Act is punishable by fine, or by imprisonment up to 3 months.

S. 2 defined 'public dental service'; and s. 3 provided that travel allowances should be given and remuneration paid as stipulated for the post. The remuneration stipulated for Iversen was higher than that obtainable in a similar position in southern Norway.

supplementary course at the Norwegian Dental College, which was compulsory for all those with foreign diplomas seeking to qualify as dentists in Norway. Having qualified in September 1958 he performed his military service in northern Norway until December 1959 as an army dentist. On 4 December 1959 his application for a post in the public dental service in southern Norway was rejected and he was directed under the Act to take a position in the service in the Moskenes district in northern Norway; but, since he had performed his military service in the same region, with its severities of climate and terrain, his compulsory assignment to the dental service was limited to one year. After protest, he accepted the position and took it over on 11 January 1960. On 21 March he wrote to the Ministry of Social Affairs stating his intention to leave the post and on 20 May 1960 he did so. Proceedings were instituted against him in Sandefjord Town Court under s.4 of the Act, and on 20 February 1961 he was ordered to pay a fine of 2,000 kroner or go to prison for thirty days, for contravention of the Act.

He appealed to the Höyesterett (Supreme Court) submitting that the Act was contrary to the Constitution, that it was contrary to Article 4 of the Convention, and that in any case the Act was only applicable to those students who had given an undertaking, before commencing their studies in the Norwegian Dental College, to serve for a period in the public dental service after qualification.[1]

The Supreme Court dismissed his appeal. Of the five members three rejected all three objections, while two members upheld the third objection to the Act, and expressed no opinion on the others. With regard to Article 4 (2) Judge Hiorthöy, presiding, said:

> The position is much the same as regards the claim that the Law is invalid, as being contrary to Article 4 of the European Convention of 4th November 1950 for the Protection of Human Rights and Fundamental Freedoms. There is little doubt to my mind that the Convention's stipulation that no one shall be required to perform forced or compulsory labour cannot be reasonably interpreted as applying to the obligations of a public nature arising in the present case. The work in question is of short duration, well-paid, based on the professional qualifications of the person concerned and in immediate continuation of his completed studies. Even if, at the time, such service is, as

---

[1] This form of undertaking, which had been in use for a number of years before 1956 and a legal challenge to which in 1955 had in part led to the legislation of 1956, was not applicable to Iversen, since he had conducted his studies at his own expense abroad. The form of undertaking was abandoned on the entry into force of the Act.

may occur in many cases, contrary to the interests of the individual concerned, it is clear to me that it cannot be regarded as an infringement, let alone a violation, of Human Rights.

He added that, since he found no conflict between the Act and the Convention, there was no need to go into the question as to which must prevail.

The essence of the application of Iversen to the Commission was that his compulsory assignment to the public dental service in the Moskenes district was forced or compulsory labour contrary to Article 4 (2) of the Convention. He also claimed that Articles 8 and 11 had also been infringed. The Commission, finding unanimously that his complaints were manifestly ill founded under Articles 8 and 11 since the applicant had 'failed to produce any facts substantiating his allegations', was divided over the complaint under Article 4 (2). Six members considered the application manifestly ill founded; four members would have admitted it.[1]

Of the majority, four members considered that:

although Article 4, paragraph (3), of the Convention delimits the scope of Article 4, paragraph (2), by declaring that four categories of work or service do not constitute forced or compulsory labour for the purpose of the Convention, the expression 'forced or compulsory labour' is not defined in the Convention and no authoritative description of what it comprises is to be found elsewhere;

the concept of compulsory or forced labour cannot be understood solely in terms of the literal meaning of the words, and has in fact come to be regarded, in international law and practice as evidenced in part by the provisions and applications of ILO Convention and Resolutions on Forced Labour, as having certain elements, and that it is reasonable, in the interpretation of Article 4, paragraph (2), of the Convention, to have due regard to those elements;

these elements of forced or compulsory labour are first, that the work or service is performed by the worker against his will and, secondly, that the requirement that the work or service be performed is unjust or oppressive or the work or service itself involves avoidable hardship;

the attribution of these elements to 'forced and compulsory labour' in Article 4, paragraph (2), of the Convention is not inconsistent with the other provisions of that Article or of the Convention;

it is true that the Provisional Act of 1956 imposed obligatory service, but since such service was for a short period, provided favourable remuneration, did not

---

[1] As to this division of opinion on admissibility, see under Article 27 below.

involve any diversion from chosen professional work, was only applied in the case of posts not filled after being duly advertised, and did not involve any discriminatory, arbitrary or punitive application, the requirement to perform that service was not unjust or oppressive; the Law of 1951 was properly applied to Iversen when he was directed to take up the post at Moskenes; further, in the particular case of the Applicant, the hardship of the post was mitigated by the reduction in the required term of his services from 2 years to 1 year;

Two members of the majority considered that the service required of Iversen was covered by Article 4 (3) *c*, there being an emergency created by the threatened breakdown in the dental service for northern Norway:

the situation in 1956 and 1960 of the public dental service and school dental care in northern Norway was regarded by the Norwegian Government as an emergency threatening the well-being of the community in northern Norway;

in particular, in 1956, the Norwegian Government was confronted, in the exercise of its function, recognised in the Convention, of protecting public health, with a situation of the public dental service in northern Norway which had two elements; the inherent difficulties of administering the service caused by the scattered character of towns and settlements and the severe climate and intractable terrain; and a regional shortage of qualified dentists;

in the opinion of the Norwegian Government, there was the threat of a breakdown in the supply of volunteers from among whom the public dental service in northern Norway had hitherto been maintained;

the Law of 1956 was enacted by the Norwegian Parliament after a full and public debate;

the Commission has frequently held that, although a certain margin of appreciation should be given to a government in determining the existence of a public emergency within the meaning of Article 15 in its own country, the Commission has the competence and the duty to examine and pronounce upon the consistency with the Convention of a government's determination of this question [cf. *Lawless Report*, p. 85];

in the analogous circumstances of the present case, the Commission cannot question the judgment of the Norwegian Government and Parliament as to the existence of an emergency, as there is evidence before the Commission showing reasonable grounds for such judgment.

The minority was of the opinion that

the conditions under which the Applicant was required to perform his work in Moskenes as regards, for instance, salary, time-limit and professional facilities, do not as such exclude the applicability of Article 4 (2), . . . since the work in question was imposed upon the Applicant subject to penal sanctions;

. . . that the question of the applicability of Article 4 (3) *c* . . . requires further examination;

. . . having thus regard to the complexity of the legal problems raised by the Application and in view of the number of opinions which were, in the course of the deliberations, put forward in the Commission and even among the six members forming the majority, which voted in favour of the inadmissibility of this part of the Application, the members of the minority . . . are of the opinion that it should be declared admissible'.

The Provisional Act of 1956 was prolonged on its expiry in 1963, and the Supreme Court of Norway invoked the opinions of the majority in affirming that the legislation was not contrary to Article 4 (2).[1]

The provision of legal assistance *ex officio* by counsel, with less than usual or no remuneration, has been challenged more than once as 'forced and compulsory labour'. In a Belgian case the applicant was a pupil *avocat*, and was appointed to defend a Gambian national in Antwerp on a number of charges; and if he refused without good reason to conduct the defence, he could have been struck off the role of pupils by the Council of the *Ordre des Avocats*. The applicant conducted the defence of the accused up to appeal, his pupillage being terminated during the proceedings. When officially released from the case, he was told that, owing to lack of resources, no assessment of fees and disbursements could be made against the accused. The Commission and Court considered there was no breach of Article 4, but the Court differed in its reasoning from the Commission. Both had regard to I.L.O. Conventions Nos 29 and 105, and in particular to the I.L.O. Convention No. 29 deprivation of 'forced or compulsory labour' as

all work or service which is expected from any person under the menace of any penalty and for which the said person had not offered himself voluntarily.

The Court gave four reasons for finding no breach of Article 4:

The services to be rendered did not fall outside the ambit of the normal activities of an *avocat* . . . a compensatory factor was to be found in the advantages attaching to the profession, including the exclusive right of audience and of representation enjoyed by *avocats*. In addition, the service in question contributed to the applicant's professional training . . . the obigation

---

[1] 28.3.1966: *Norsk Retstidende* (1966) 474, 482–6.

[in securing for the accused the benefit of Article 6 (3) *c*] was founded on a conception of social solidarity, and cannot be regarded as unreasonable [being] of a similar order to the 'normal civic obligations' referred to in Article 4 (3) *d* ... Finally, the burden imposed on the applicant was not disproportionate ... there remained sufficient time for performance of his paid work ...[1]

The Commission has also held that the suspension of unemployment benefit, for refusal of the offer of a job in the municipal service, was not an imposition of compulsory labour.[2]

A limitation on voluntary action was expressed by the drafting of the Supplementary Convention on Slavery (1956) in the words:

It should not be possible for any person to contract himself into bondage.[3]

This principle has been expressed in municipal law. Thus

The law of England allows a man to contract for his or allows him to place himself in the service of a master, but it does not allow him to attach to his contract of service any servile incidents.[4]

Again the U.S. Supreme Court:

No State [of the Union] can make the quitting of work any component of a crime, or make criminal sanctions available for holding unwilling persons to labor.[5]

any work required to be done in the ordinary course of detention/tout travail requis normalement d'une personne soumise à la détention

Complaints to the Commission have been made of inadequate pay for prison work,[6] as already noted the Convention prescribes no material conditions, which the imposition of such labour must satisfy, Article 3 being the only control. Complaints[7] of detention in a labour institution (*Arbeitshaus* in Austria and Germany) by order of a court are excluded by Article 4 (3) *a* itself.

---

[1] *van der Mussele* (Belgium) Judgment No. 70 (23.11.1983). See also *Grussenbauer* (Austria) 4897/71: 42 C.D. 41; *Arrowsmith* (U.K.) 7050/76 19 D.R. 5.

[2] 7602/76 (Netherlands) 7 D.R. 161. For a general analysis see S. Trechsel, 'The Right to Liberty and Security of the Person', *Human Rights Journal* (1980) 1–88.

[3] U.N. Doc. A/2929 p. 33.

[4] *Davies* v. *Davies* [1887] 36 Ch. D. 359, 393 *per* Bowen L. J.

[5] *Pollock* v. *Williams* [1944] 322 U.S. 4,18.

[6] e.g. 833/60: 3 *Yearbook* 428.

[7] e.g. 982/61; 987/61; 1291/61: *Recueil* (19762) i.

any service of a military character/tout service de caractère militaire

This covers military service on *voluntary* engagement;[1] otherwise the clause is similar to Forced Labour Convention, Article 2 (2) *a*, which excepts

any work or service exacted in virtue of compulsory military service laws for work of a purely military character.

The qualification was there added in order to prevent the diversion of those doing compulsory military service to ordinary labour, which would then assume the character of forced labour.[2] However, in order to come within the exception, service is presumably not to be confined to participation in training, exercises, and active service, in the armed forces, but must cover at least some auxiliary services; for example, as already recorded, Iversen performed his compulsory military service as an army dentist, but the question whether this was service of a military character for the purpose of Article 4 (3) *a* was not put in issue in his application. On the assumption that it was, it might well be asked upon what principle it could be said that compulsory dental service to soldiers is not, but compulsory dental service to civilians in similar conditions is, forced labour and a violation of human rights.

conscientious objectors in countries where they are recognized/objecteurs de conscience dans les pays où l'objection de conscience est reconnue comme legitimé

No obligation is imposed by this paragraph on contracting States to make room for conscientious objectors; it merely recognizes that in some States conscientious objection to military service is permitted. This implies that such conscientious objection is an exercise of freedom of conscience under Article 9, but that a State may restrict it by allowing no exemption from military service, if it is necessary for the public safety in the sense of Article 9 (2). A Council of Europe Resolution[3] declares that:

---

[1] 3435–8/67 (U.K.) 28 C.D. 109.
[2] Similarly, unlawful refusal of exemption may constitute the service forced labour: 1758/63: *Recueil* (1964) i.
[3] Resolution 337 (1967).

1. Les personnes astreintes au service militaire qui, pour des motifs de conscience ou en raison d'une conviction profonde d'ordre religieux, éthique, moral, humanitaire, philosophique ou autre de même nature, refusent d'accomplir le service armé, doivent avoir un droit subjectif à être dispensées de ce service.

The Resolution invokes Article 9 of the Convention as its basis, enumerates certain procedural principles that should be followed in cases of conscientious objection to military service, and also the conditions that substitute service should satisfy:

C. Service de remplacement[1]

1. Le service de remplacement à accomplir au lieu du service militaire doit avoir au moins la même durée que le service militaire normal.[2]

2. Il faut assurer l'égalité, tant sur le plan du droit social que sur le plan financier, de l'objecteur de conscience reconnu et du soldat qui assure le service militaire normal.

3. Les gouvernements intéressés doivent veiller à ce que les objecteurs de conscience soient employés à des tâches utiles à la société ou à la collectivité — sans oublier les besoins multiples des pays en voie de développement.

Further discussion of issues arising on substitute service will be found in the *Grandrath Case* under Article 9.

emergency or calamity threatening the life or well-being of the community/le cas de crises ou de calamités qui menacent le vie ou le bien-être de la communaté

The reference to the well-being of the community appears to give a wider sense to emergency here than does Article 15, which speaks of 'a public emergency threatening the life of the nation'.

The expression 'emergency endangering the national safety' in the Hours of Work (Industry) Convention 1919, Article 14, was treated by the I.L.O. Conference as being equivalent to a 'threat to the existence of the life of the people' and to this notion it gave a rather strict interpretation, saying:

An economic or commercial crisis however, which concerns only special branches of industry, cannot be regarded as endangering the national safety

---

[1] See 5591/72 (Austria) 43 C.D. 61.
[2] See, for example, the law enacted in France in December 1963, requiring service *in lieu* of a duration double that of ordinary military service: *Le Monde* (13.12.1963).

within the meaning of Article 14, so that in this case the suspension of the Convention would not be justified.[1]

As already recorded, in the *Iversen Case* certain members of the Commission took the view that there were reasonable grounds[2] for the judgment of the Norwegian Government and Parliament that 'a breakdown in the supply of volunteers from among whom the public dental service in northern Norway had hitherto been maintained' was an emergency threatening the well-being of the community there.

normal civic obligations/obligations civiques normales

'Normal' here seems to describe, not obligations conceived in terms of some general principle, but those customarily accepted in a particular community though it is not of course the policy of the Forced Labour Conventions that all customs shall be immutable.

The Temporary Slavery Commission reporting in 1925[3] enumerated four kinds of work or service which might constitute forced or compulsory labour, but some of which were for public purposes:

occasional or periodical local services, usually unremunerated (*corvées*),[4] or levies according to regulations, usually remunerated work of general interest, ... such as the construction and upkeep of roads, resthouses, markets and telegraph lines ... which may necessitate the removal of labourers to a considerable distance from their homes for a longer or shorter period, and is generally remunerated

labour levies for 'exceptional tasks of public utility requiring a considerable amount of labour for a long period, such as the construction of railways, ports and canals'

---

[1] *International Labour Code* (1951) i. 210, n. 215. Contrast *Greece*: Council of State 1966 said that in the event of a strike or lock-out affecting a company in the field of public transport, the requisition of personal services and materials by legislation is not contrary to the constitutional provisions on freedom of labour and freedom of trade unions, and is not contrary to Article 4 of the Convention being covered by paragraph 3 (*c*).

[2] See further under Article 15 below.

[3] League Doc. A 19, 1925, vi.

[4] Derived from Law Latin *corvada*, a corruption of (*opera*) *corrogata*, i.e. any service or work, requisitioned in time of difficulty or stress, or in the feudal system required of a serf in lieu of rent or taxes. Compare villein tenure in England: 'Any considerable uncertainty as to the amount or kind of the agricultural services makes the tenure [of the villein] unfree. The tenure is unfree, not because the tenant holds at the will of the lord, in the sense of being removable at a moment's notice, but because his services, though in many respects minutely defined by custom, cannot be altogether defined without constant reference ot the lord's will' (Pollock and Maitland, *History of English Law*, i. 354).

the possibility of private enterprise availing itself of part of the native labour obtained by the application of the compulsory labour laws,

and the League Assembly, in approving the text of the Slavery Convention 1926:

While recognising that forced labour for public purposes is sometimes necessary: Is of opinion that, as a general rule, it should not be resorted to unless it is impossible to obtain voluntary labour and that it should receive adequate remuneration.

The concept of 'normal civic obligations' has been introduced in an attempt to make clearer what are essential public works or services, and has been decribed as:

work or service of a local character, required by law or recognised custom from the population or community as a whole, for the maintenance of communications, the preservation of food supplies, the provision of water supply, protection against fire, flood, avalanche or any similar calamity, and the maintenance or improvement of local utilities or amenties.

This appears to exclude work or service, which is either abnormal or involves the transfer of workers away from the locality or is directed towards some nation-wide objective.

Further, this description of 'normal civic obligations' is largely drawn from communities, which have generally simpler social and economic structures than the contracting States, and the expression will have differing connotations there.[1]

But 'normal civil obligations', whatever their precise extent in a particular community, cannot, it seems, be translated into a general subjection to direction of labour for economic purposes.[2] So I.L.O. Recommendation No. 35, associated with the Forced Labour Convention 1930, and, incidentally, cast in terms which might import a distinction between 'forced' and 'compulsory' labour and given a extended meaning to the latter, pointed to:

---

[1] The drafters of the First U.N. Covenant rejected a proposal to distinguish between 'normal civil obligations' in sovereign states, and 'minor communal services' in non-self-governing territories, an expression found in the Forced Labour Convention 1930: A/2929, p. 34, para. 25.

[2] See, for example, *Report of Ad Hoc Committee on Forced Labour* (1953), para. 258 on Polish Law of 7 March 1950, later repealed, providing for planned employment of graduates of vocational secondary schools and higher schools; and Abolition of Forced Labour Convention 1957.

The desirabilty of avoiding indirect means of artificially increasing the economic pressure upon populations to seek wage-earning employment, and particularly such means as

(*a*) imposing such taxation upon populations as would have the effect of compelling them to seek wage-earning employment with private under-takings;

(*b*) imposing such restrictions on the possession, occupation, or use of land as would have the effect of rendering difficult the gaining of a living by independent cultivation;

(*c*) extending abusively the generally accepted meaning of vagrancy;

(*d*) adopting such pass laws as would have the effect of placing workers in the service of others in a position of advantage as compared with other workers

and stressed

The desirability of avoiding any restrictions on the voluntary flow of labour from one form of employment to another or from one district to another which might have the indirect effect of compelling workers to take employment in particular industries or districts, except where such restrictions are considered necessary in the interest of the population or of the workers concerned.

Certain I.L.O. conventions contain related ideas. Thus in Convention No. 50 (Regulation of the Recruitment of Workers), 1939, 'recruiting' is stated to include

all operations undertaken with the object of obtaining or supplying the labour of persons, who do not spontaneously offer their services at the place of employment or at a public emigration or employment office or at an office conducted by employers' organisation and supervised by the competent authority.

ARTICLE 5

(1) Everyone has the right to liberty and security of person.

No one shall be deprived of his liberty save in the following cases and in accordance with a procedure prescribed by law:

1. Toute personne a droit à la liberté et à la sûreté. Nul ne peut être privé de sa liberté, sauf dans les cas suivants et selon les voies légales:

The subjection to the rule of all forms of arrest and detention is perhaps, after life itself, the most fundamental human right; and because in all countries it comes often into issue, the commentary on this Article must be of some length and elaboration. Further it is at a number of important points linked closely with other provisions of the Convention, and in particular with Article 6, so that it cannot be examined in isolation.

The First U.N. Covenant, Articles 9–13, goes far beyond Article 5 and establishes a code governing arrest and detention, the conditions of detention, and residence in and departure from a country, and the expulsion of aliens.

Everyone has the right/Toute personne a droit. ... No one shall be deprived/Nul ne peut être privé

These two clauses represent a combination of the drafts which formed part of the original Alternatives A and B of the Convention.[1]

A United Kingdom draft of Article 5 (1), as part of Alternative A, began with the second clause and contained substantially what became the provisions finally adopted,[2] while Alternative B contained two paragraphs, covering the whole of what is now Articles 2 and 5, and identical with Articles 3 and 9 of the Universal Declaration:

Article 2   1° (a) Everyone has the right to life, liberty and security of person
            3° (a) No one shall be subjected to arbitrary arrest, detention or
                    exile.[3]

There was dissatisfaction with the term 'arbitrary' which might be taken to mean illegal, or unjust, or both, and it was dropped in favour of a requirement that any deprivation of liberty follow a procedure prescribed by law,[4] and be limited to specified cases.

liberty and security of person/la liberté et la sûreté

The words 'of person' are essential in order to show that the personal liberty here described is, to borrow the words of Blackstone:[5]

the power of locomotion, of changing situation, or removing one's person to whatsoever place one's inclination may direct, without imprisonment or restraint, unless by due course of law.

---

[1] Alternative A was a draft Convention composed of detailed provisions under each Article, while Alternative B was cast rather in the form of statements of general principles: see A. H. Robertson, *Human Rights of Europe*, for an account of the evolution of these drafts.   [2] *T.P.* ii. 353.   [3] *T.P.* ii. 455.
[4] The First U.N. Covenant, Article 9 (1) retains both ideas.
[5] *Commentaries on the Laws of England* (1765) i. 134.

Liberty and security are the two sides of the same coin; if personal liberty spells actual freedom of movement of the person, security is the condition of being protected by law in that freedom. But some deprivations of liberty are permitted, security is 'guaranteed in absolute terms' in that an individual can be 'arrested and detained' only for the reasons and according to the procedure, prescribed by law,[1] where the deprivation of liberty is permitted. It appears that the right to liberty is not infringed by action, which is not aimed at arrest or detention; so where a ten-year-old girl was taken from school to police headquarters, for questioning about thefts in the school, was in an unlocked room for two hours and was taken home, the Commission found no deprivation of liberty.[2]

no one shall be deprived of his liberty/nul ne peut être privé de sa liberté

The forms of deprivation of liberty, which are permitted under Article 5 (1) further confirm the conclusion reached as to the sense in which 'liberty and security' are generally understood. But it is necessary to draw a distinction between three kinds of restraint, not all of which may constitute deprivation of liberty under Article 5 (1): control of movement, restriction of movement, and detention.

Control of movement. Typical controls, which may indirectly affect freedom of movement, are, in addition to the use of passports, systems of identity cards or papers, and the registration of aliens. Where identity cards are required, for presentation on demand or for movement between administrative divisions of a country, an unlawful refusal to issue one might be an interference with the security of the individual.[3] So the Swiss Federal Court has held that

Freedom of residence as guaranteed by Article 45 of the Federal Constitution also incudes the obligation of the canton of origin and the canton of previous residence not to impede or prevent a Swiss citizen from moving his place of residence by refusing to provide the necessary identification papers.[4]

Of aliens registration the Commission has said:

---

[1] *Arrowsmith* (U.K.) 7050/76 19 D.R. 5.
[2] 8819/79 (F.R.G.) 24 D.R. 158: for a general analysis see, S. Trechsel, 'The Right to Liberty and Security of the Person', *Human Rights Law Journal* (1980) 1, 88.
[3] As alleged in 2087/63, but the facts did not support the allegation.
[4] *Bundesgerichtsentscheid*, 53 [1927] i. 434, cited by R. Torovsky, op. cit.

... regulations requiring a foreigner to be in possession of a valid passport and to register with the local police, such as are frequently found in the national laws of the member States of the Council of Europe, are not in any way inconsistent with any of the rights and freedoms guaranteed in the Convention.[1]

The British Nationality Act (1981) has now created three categories of citizens: British citizen; citizens of British Dependent Territories; and British Overseas Citizens. The first two categories of citizens are those which belong, in the terms of the Act, respectively to the United Kingdom, including the Channel Islands, the Isle of Man, and to the Dependent Territories, to some of which the European Convention has been extended under Article 3.[2] The third category comprises those persons, who are U.K. citizens under the British Nationality Act (1948), but do not meet the conditions of citizenship of the other two categories. Only British Citizens have right of residence in the United Kingdom.

Restriction of movement. This may take the form of limitation of residence to a particular town or district, or prohibition of visits to or residence in certain places, or of journeys for certain purposes. It is primarily a denial of that freedom of movement within national territory, which is to be found expressed in a number of constitutions.[3]

Similarly the Fourth Protocol provides that, subject to the same permitted restrictions as have already been described on Article 3 (2):

Everyone lawfully (*régulièrement*) within the territory of a State shall, within that territory, have the right to liberty of movement (*le droit d'y circuler librement*) and freedom to choose his residence.

However, restrictions on this freedom are generally recognized as permissible in the interests of public order, health, or safety. So the Fourth Protocol provides that

No restrictions shall be placed on the exercise of these rights other than such as are in accordance with law and are necessary in a democratic society in the interests of national security or public safety, for the maintenance of *ordre public*, for the prevention of crime, for the protection of health and morals, or for the protection of the rights and freedoms of others. The rights ... may also be subject, in particular areas (*dans certaines zones déterminées*), to

[1] 830/60: *Recueil* (1961) ii.
[2] See under Article 63.
[3] *Federal Republic of Germany*: Grundgesetz, Article 11 (1), *India*, Constitution, Article 19 (1): 'All citizens shall have the right ... (*d*) to move freely throughout the territory of India; (*e*) to reside and settle in any part of the territory of India'.

restrictions imposed in accordance with law and justified by the public interest in a democratic society.[4]

These are wide-ranging exceptions, of a kind which will be considered below in the context of other provisions of the Convention. As far as Article 5 is concerned, vagrants may be detained under paragraph (*e*) and it would follow that they may, if necessary, be required to return to their own town or district, if they have one.[1]

Compulsory residence was seen as a deprivation of liberty, and a breach of Article 5,[2] where the applicant had been placed in residence at Cala Reale on the island of Asinara, off the north-west corner of Sardinia. Placed in detention on remand in February 1973, on a charge of conspiracy in the kidnapping of a business man, he was placed in the compulsory residence, when the time-limit of detention on remand expired, in January 1975, this being based on statutory authority.[3] He remained on Asinara until July 1976 when he was transferred by similar order to a district on the mainland.

The Commission and the Court both found a breach of the Convention in these circumstances. Particular significance was attached to the very small size of the area in which he was confined; the continuing supervision to which he was subject; the initial impossibility of making social contacts; and the length of his forced stay. The Court further noted that the Italian Ministry of the Interior decided in August 1979 to strike Asinara off the list of places for compulsory residence. The Court also rejected the claim of the Government that the applicant could be considered to be a vagrant.

But different issues may arise, where the restriction is imposed as a curb on political activities; there may be an infringement of other provisions of the Convention such as Articles 10 or 11, or even a deprivation of liberty not permitted under Article 5 (1).[4]

[1] Article 3 (3) and (4).
[2] So in Italy compulsory return (*rimpatrio con foglio di via obbligatorio*) of persons found outside the boundaries of their own town village, and giving no account of themselves, has been held to be consistent with Constitution, Article 13: 'No form of detention, inspection, or personal search, or any other restriction of personal liberty is permitted, except by a duly authorised act of the judicial authorities'. See 2208/64 and allied cases (vagrants in Belgium).
[3] *Guzzardi* (Italy) Judgment No. 39 (6.11.1980). See also 8918/80: 21 D.R. 250.
[4] Act of 1956 providing compulsory residence persons presenting a danger for security and public morality; and Act of 1965 directed against the mafia.
[5] The question was raised, but not decided, in habeas corpus proceedings in England, whether restriction orders requiring the petitioner to remain in a district of Northern Rhodesia, of about fifteen hundred square miles in extent, constituted

Detention. But 'detention' in Article 5 appears in general to be used in a narrower sense as being enforced confinement in a limited space, such as a house, a police-station or prison, a ship, or an aircraft. Similarly in a United Nations study it has been described as

... l'acte par lequel une personne est incarcérée dans un lieu déterminée, à la suite ou non d'une arrestation, et est soumise à des contraintes qui l'empêchent de vivre avec sa famille au d'exercer normalement son activité professionnelle.[1]

and the Commission has said:

the fact that the applicant has been in Germany since 1950 and unable to return to Switzerland cannot be regarded as constituting a detention under Article 5.[2]

Before passing to consider detention under Article 5, we may note the proposals by the Committee of Ministers[3] of the Council of Europe for the general sustitution, where practicable, of other forms of restriction or control for detention on remand, namely, surveillance in the home; injunction against leaving a particular place or district without the permission of the judge; order to appear periodically before certain authorities; surrender of passport or other identification papers; provision for security or bail. All these forms are represented in the practice of contracting States: thus all five are in use in Germany, Greece, Norway, and Sweden; the fourth is found in the Netherlands and Norway; and the fifth is commonly used in many countries.[4]

Several categories of detention, which are permissible as a deprivation of liberty under Article 5, can be distinguished, though as will be later seen there is some overlapping between them.

'detention': *ex pte Mwenya* [1960] 1 Q.B. 241. Conversely 'externment' of persons from a particular area of persons likely to cause disturbance there is permitted in India, subject to it being ordered for a limited time, and to the person affected being heard in opposition to the order: *Abdul Ratiman* v. *Emp* [1950] A.I.R. Bombay 374; *Tozammal* v. *West Bengal* [1951] A.I.R. Calcutta 322.

But a general and permanent prohibition of camping of nomads in a particular area was declared unlawful in *France*: Conseil d'État (20.1.65) cited in *Journal of I.C.J.* (Summer 1966) 142.

[1] U.N. Doc. E/CN 4/826, Rev. 1 (1964) 6.
[2] 830/60: *Recueil* (1961) i.
[3] Resolution (65) 11.
[4] But not in Sweden, and with severe restrictions in Denmark and Italy on the ground that admission to bail favours the rich.

First, *dentention under criminal law and procedure*: this covers detention under reasonable suspicion of a crime or to prevent further crime or escape (paragraph (1) *c*); serving of prison sentence after conviction, and preventive detention (paragraph (1) *a*); and remand in custody pending trial (paragraphs (1) *c* and (3)). The term 'preventive detention' has to be watched, as it is used in several different senses: as detention of recidivists,[1] or as detention to prevent an individual, who may or may not have been convicted of an offence, from engaging in activities regarded as politically dangerous;[2] or, very loosely, to indicate almost any form of detention other than the serving of a prison sentence. In what follows the term will be used only in the first sense.

Further, the classification of the intention under the domestic law may be such that a particular detention may be seen as a detention after conviction under Article 5 (1) *a*, or detention on remand under Article 5 (1) *c*, and one may follow the other.[3]

Second, *detention as a measure of social protection or control*: detention to compel compliance with a court order or other legal obligation (paragraph (1) *b*); detention of minors (paragraph (1) *d*); detention to control and help social misfits (paragraph (1) *c*). A penal element may be present in some of these cases of detention, but punishment is not its predominant purpose.

Third, what may be called *administrative detention*: detention to prevent the spread of disease (paragraph (1) *c*), and detention in connection with the admission or expulsion of persons to or from the country (paragraph (1) *f*).

save in the following cases/sauf dans les cas suivants

The stated categories of case, in which deprivation of liberty is permissible under the Convention, are, subject to the provisions of Article 15, exhaustive.

---

[1] In *England*: Criminal Justice Act 1948 as amended provides for corrective training and preventive detention: see ss. 20 and 21. Corrective training ranks as a form of imprisonment: *R.* v. *McCarthy* [1955] 2 A.E.R. 927; corrective training and preventive detention will follow any term of imprisonment already being served: *R.* v. *Cannell* [1953] 37 Cr. App.Rep. 158.

[2] e.g. in *South Africa* under the General Law Amendment 1962, s. 4, the Minister of Justice may 'at his discretion' order continued detention of any person who has completed a term of imprisonment for certain political offences. See further under Article 15 below.

[3] *Bonazzi* (Italy) 7975/77 24 d.R. 33.

in accordance with a procedure prescribed by law/selon les voies légales

The original draft used the expression 'legal procedure'. The present formula might appear even to place a shade more accent on procedure; but both drafts were represented in the French version by 'voies légales', so that no real shift of meaning can have been intended.

But the requirement that arrest or detention under Article 5 (1) must also be found in substantive law is marked by the use of the qualification 'lawful' in each of the six paragraphs, the omission of 'régulièrement' in the French text of Article 5 (1) c being apparently an oversight. This use of the qualification 'lawful' would, it seems, have been otiose, if it only looked back to and repeated the requirment of a procedure prescribed by law; further, a determination of the lawfulness of detention under Article 5 (4) could hardly be made exclusively in terms of the procedure followed. While 'lawfulness' is to be understood primarily in terms of the applicable domestic law, it may, where Article 5 is deemed to be incorporated in that law, import a reference back to the provisions of Article 5 itself,[1] particularly for the purpose of the exhaustion of domestic remedies.

As may be seen under paragraphs (1) c and f below, the procedure prescribed by law does not appear to be limited there to judicial process, but may in certain cases over administrative action. It does not, however, extend to the form of detention itself: for example, the material conditions of detention, or subject to paragraph (3), its duration.[2] So, saving the provisions of Article 3, the Convention ne contient aucune disposition relative au régime pénitentiaire auquel les personnes arretêes, condamnées ou internées pourraient avoir droit;[3]

nor is there any right guaranteed by the Convention to conditional release or release on pardon at any point during a term of imprisonment.[4]

---

[1] 858/60: 4 *Yearbook* 224, 236.
[2] 100/55: 1 *Yearbook* 162.   [3] 114/55.
[4] 1015/61: *Recueil* (1961) ii. Contrast First U.N. Covenant, Article 10 (2) and (3). See also 424/58: *Recueil* (1960) i ('le droit à l'octroi du régime du détain politique' is not a guaranteed right); 1403/62: *Recueil* (1963) ii ('. . . the Applicant objects to the manner in which his preventive detention is carried out; . . . in particular he complains that he is detained in the same building and subjected to the same conditions as persons serving criminal sentences of penal servitude', but the Convention does not require such separation of person serving a sentence of preventive detention).

Nevertheless, the gap in the Convention has been filled in the past by the work of the Committee of Ministers of the Council of Europe, in the adoption of the Standard Minimum Rules for the Treatment of Prisoners (1973),[1] of a number of supportive resolutions, and the appointment in 1980 of a Committee on Co-operation in Prison Matters: its task is to follow the development of the European prison systems, and to ensure the practical and effective application of the Standard Minimum Rules. The Rules do not rank as an international convention, but they have authority as formulated by government expertise and having wide acceptance; though the Commission has considered them to be not applicable in the armed services:

It is ... not established that the Minimum Rules should be considered as a yardstick to be followed by the member States of the Council of Europe for the treatment of persons imprisoned for a short period on disciplinary grounds.

It pointed up the gap in the Convention by further implying that conditions of detention, even if they failed to meet the Standard Minimum Rules, would not be contrary to the Convention unless they came within Article 3.[2]

It must also be pointed out that it is an inevitable consequence,[3] and in some cases in part the purpose, of the detention, permitted in its various forms under Article 5, that the detainee suffers restrictions upon the Convention rights that he could exercise if he were a free man. In other words, detention is itself a form of derogation from Convention rights and freedoms parallel to those forms expressly permitted, particularly in Articles 8–11, 15; as will be seen, for example, the restriction of correspondence of prisoners may in part be justifiable as much by the fact of detention as by recourse to provisions of Article 8 (2). It is for these reasons that the control of the Convention of arrest and detention are of prime importance.

(*a*) the lawful detention of a person after conviction by a competent court;

(*a*) s'il est détenu régulièrement après condamnation par un tribunal compétent;

---

[1] Resolution 73/5. See also C.E. Human Rights Files No. 5 (1981) D.D.H. 81/2.

[2] *Eggs* (Switzerland) 7341/76: 6 D.R. 176.

[3] So the Kammergericht, Berlin (9.12.1965), observed that freedom of expression in Article 10 is subject to certain natural limitations in case of lawful detention under Article 5: *N.J.W.* (1966) 1088.

after conviction/après condamnation

It might be thought that the word 'after' was an imprecise substitute for 'as a result of', but it is probable that the word was designedly chosen in order to express two separate ideas; sentence of imprisonment as a penalty for a particular offence, and preventive detention ordered for a recidivist after conviction on one of a series of offences. Such an order of preventive detention has been found by the Commission to be consistent with paragraph (1) a;[1] but it is an essential element that there should have been a conviction, though the order for preventive detention itself may be made in respect of the cumulation of earlier offences and convictions. Preventive detention, simply as a security measure, would not then be consistent with Article 5 (1).[2]

Where a court finds that action in fact of it is a contempt of court, punishable under its inherent jurisdiction by imprisonment, this would probably constitute a 'conviction' for the purpose of paragraph (1) a.

The position which may arise where the law, under which a detained person was convicted, is subsequently invalidated, will be examined under Article 7.

A further question, also connected with Article 7, is under what provision of Article 5 a person convicted under German law can be said to be detained. He is under German law still 'charged' (*Angeklagter*), and not yet 'convicted' (*Verurteilter*), until either the time-limit for appeal expires or the appeal is concluded. The following situation can arise,[3] the applicant was sentenced to fifteen months' imprisonment and his appeal was concluded after seven months. Since the appeal court affirmed the conviction, but did not deduct from sentence to be served the whole of the period spent in detention before the conviction became *res judicata*, on dismissal of the appeal the actual period spent in detention was longer than the sentence imposed.

If, on conviction by the trial court, the applicant commenced detention under Article 5 (1) a, the question arises whether the period of detention served is consistent with the spirit of the second sentence

[1] 99/55: 1 *Yearbook* 160 and 1185/61: *Recueil* (1962) ii (*Sicherheitsverwahrung* in Germany under StGB Articles 20*a*, 42*e*). Detention in Austria under Arbeitshausgesetz, Article 2, is similar: 606/59: 4 *Yearbook* 344.

[2] The original draft of paragraph (1) a included the words 'or as a security measure', but these were later struck out: *T.P.* ii. 351; iii. 724.

[3] 2479/65 (inadmissible for non-exhaustion of remedies).

of Article 7 (1); if on the other hand that detention is to be regarded as continuing detention under Article 5 (1) *c* and (3), 'trial' in paragraph (3) has to be understood as comprising proceedings on appeal, and the difficulties of this interpretation will be considered under that paragraph.

The continuance of detention can raise a further problem. An applicant had been ordered by the Lausanne Criminal Court to be sent to detention in 1965 for an indeterminate period as an habitual criminal. In August 1975 he was granted a conditional release for a probationary period of three years under supervision; but in October 1975 he was arrested on a charge of professional theft and in March 1976 the Lausanne Criminal Court sentenced him to seven months imprisonment, 168 days of detention on remand being deducted. Due for release in May 1976, his conditional release was revoked by the Head of Department of Justice of the Canton of Vaud, and his return to detention was ordered. The applicant claimed that this was an 'administrative detention', not covered by Article 5 (1) *b*. The Commission found that:

It cannot be questioned that the applicant's detention with effect from 9 May 1976 . . . constitutes in law the continuation of the detention ordered by the Lausanne Court in its judgment of 2 April 1965. This detention thus formally complies with the conditions laid down by Article 5 (1) *a*.

As to the question whether the administrative order for return to detention did not meet the requirements of Article 5 (4), that such detention should be the subject of separate court proceedings, the Commission found it unnecessary to answer it in general terms since the applicant had been able to make, and did make up to the Federal Court, an administrative law appeal; and this appeal related to both facts and law.[1]

competent court/tribunal compétent

The requirement that the detainee must have been convicted by a court implies a need for judicial process, involving an impartial finding of facts and application of the law of the land by an established tribunal. It excludes amongst other things detention by administrative order, a form of punishment. So, in accepting the Convention, Austria found it necessary to make a reservation that

---

[1] *Christinet* (Switzerland) 7648/76 Report 17 D.R. 35.

The provisions of Article 5 of the Convention shall be so applied that there shall be no interference with the measures for the deprivation of liberty prescribed in the laws on administrative procedure (BGBL. No. 172/1950)[1] (die in den Verwaltungsverfahrensgesetzen vorgesehenen Maßnahmen des Freiheitsentzüges) subject to review by the Administrative Court or the Constitutional Court as provided for in the Austrian Constitution.

Driving offences, punishable by detention at order of the Federal police under administrative regulations in force before Austria accepted the Convention, have been found by the Commission to be covered by the reservation.[2]

Paragraph 1 (*a*) does not, it seems, exclude courts of special jurisdiction, for example courts administering military law.

Foreign conviction. This question has arisen whether it is limited to courts within the jurisdiction of the contracting state where the person is detained: in other words, can a contracting State detain a person, consistently with paragraph 1(*a*), in respect of conviction by a court in another jurisdiction? The Commission has observed that the paragraph

ne renferme aucune distinction fondée sur l'emplacement du tribunal qui a statué; qu'il ne prohibe donc pas expressément l'exécution, par un État contractant déterminé, d'une condamnation à l'emprisonnement dont un individu a été frappé en dehors du territoire de cet État; que pareille prohibition ne ressort pas non plus implicitement du texte précité; qu'en effet, les progrès de la coopération internationale se manifestant de plus en plus dans le domaine judiciaire, les États se montrent mieux disposés que jadis à assurer l'exécution, dans leur ordre juridique interne, des décisions rendues à l'étranger, y compris les sentences pénales: que la Commission se refuse à croire que les États contractants aient voulu contrecarrer cette tendance lorsqu'ils ont élaboré et approuvé 'Article 5';[3]

The European Convention on Mutual Assistance in Criminal Matters[4] provides, amongst other things, for the exchange of information from criminal records,[5] but expressly excludes from the scope of

---

[1] Article 10 (1) in particular provides that the category and extent of the punishment for 'administrative offences' (*Verwaltungsübertretungen*) are to be determined by administrative regulations.
[2] 1047/61: 4 *Yearbook* 356; 1452/62: 6 *Yearbook* 268. See further under Article 64 below as to the character of the reservation.
[3] 1322/62: 6 *Yearbook* 494, 517.
[4] Entered into force, 12 June 1962.
[5] Article 22 and compare Article 13.

mutual assistance arrests and 'the enforcement of verdicts' (l'exécution des décisions d'arrestation et des condamnations).[1] However,
agreements exist between Scandinavian countries, under which fines
may be imposed and sentences of imprisonment served in the country
where the convicted person is found, and a similar agreement is
planned between the Benelux countries.[2]

The relation between the Federal Republic of Germany and the
D.D.R. creates special problems, and the Commission said that the
conclusion, cited above,

vaut a fortiori dans le cas où un État consent, comme on l'espère, à exécuter
des jugements qu'ils estime avoir été rendus non à l'etranger, mais sur une
portion du sol national que seules des circonstances historiques ont
soustraites à son pouvoir.[3]

However, the Federal Republic remains responsible for the observance of the Convention in the enforcement of judgments of courts in
the D.D.R., since

l'Article 5 de la Convention contient d'ailleurs des garantiers de nature à
empêcher que les États contractants n'exécutent à la légère des jugements ou
arrêts inconciliables avec les principes démocratiques ... la loi fédérale du
2 mai 1953[4] ... a précisément pour but d'établir un contrôle de la 'régularité'
de la détention et d'instaurer à cette fin une procédure particulière ... elle a
été respectée en l'espèce ...

and the Federal Constitutional Court has held that, while courts of the
D.D.R. are not, in terms of German law, foreign (im Ausland), their
judgments will not be enforced where they are contrary to the public
policy embodied in the Grundgesetz. So where a fugitive from the
D.D.R. had been convicted under legislation, the aim of which was to
seal off the economic order of the D.D.R. and restrict trade with the
Federal Republic, and which was also cast in imprecise terms and

---

[1] Article 1 (2).

[2] Compare also European Convention, Article 6 (2), which would it seems allow a
national of State A, who had been convicted in State B of an extraditable offence but
had escaped, to be dealt with by the competent authorities of State A, if it refused his
extradition on grounds of nationality.

[3] Ibid. 519.

[4] *Gesetz über innerdeutsche Rechts- und Amtshilfe in Strafsuche*, providing for enforcement
in the Federal Republic of D.D.R. court judgments, on fiat of the Public Prosecutor
(Generalstaatsanwalt).

capable of arbitrary construction, the penalty imposed was held not enforceable in the Federal Republic.[1]

Contempt of Parliament. Both House of the United Kingdom Parliament have a power to commit persons to prison for contempt, and this power is said to be derived from 'the medieval conception of Parliament as primarily a Court of Justice—"the High Court of Parliament" ',[2] having an inherent right to maintain its dignity and good order.[3] Up to the middle of the nineteenth century over a thousand instances of the exercise of the power of commitment by the House of Commons are said to be on record. While such a detention is plainly lawful, the question arises whether a House of Parliament is a 'competent court' in the sense of paragraph (1) *a*. Adjudication of a contempt is in effect a conviction, whether by a House of Parliament[4] or by the superior English courts exercising their inherent jurisdiction to prevent interference with the administration of justice,[5] and it appears then that a commitment to prison for contempt would be covered by paragraph (1) *a*.

(*b*) the lawful arrest or detention of a person for non-compliance with the lawful order of a court or in order to secure the fulfilment of any obligation prescribed by law;

(*b*) s'il a fait l'objet d'une arrestation ou d'une détention régulières pour insoumission à une ordonnance rendue, conformément à la loi, par un tribunal ou en vue de garantir l'exécution d'une obigation prescrite par la loi;

---

[1] Bundesverfassungsgericht (31.5.1960): *Juristenzeit*. [1960] 632, described with commentary by P. Abel, 10 *I.C.L.Q.* [1960] 346. The legislation in question was an Act for the Protection of Internal Trade (21.4.1950) and regulations concerning Punishment for Action against the Economic Order (23.9.1948).

[2] Erskine May, *The Law, Privileges, Proceedings and Usage of Parliament* (16th edn.), 90–3.

[3] In *Burdett* v. *Abbott* [1840] 14 East 1. Lord Chief Justice Ellenborough said at 150: 'Could it be expected that the Speaker with his mace should be under the necessity of going before a grand jury to prefer a bill of indictment for the power of self-vindication and self-protection in their [sc. the Commons] own hands? . . .' Cited ibid. 91.

[4] See *Brass Crosby's Case* [1771] 3 Wils. K.B. 188, per Lord de Grey C.J. For an instance of control by the courts of a parliamentary commitment for contempt, see in *India* a Presidential reference to the Supreme Court of a case of detention for contempt: *Legislative Assembly of Uttar Pradesh* v. *Allahabad High Court* [1964] Supreme Court, cited by *Journal of I.C.J.* (Summer 1965) 329.

[5] The Administration of Justice Act 1960 introduced the possibiity of appeal against conviction for contempt.

The terms of somewhat vague and general description, used in this paragraph, are it seems designed to cover both action by a court to secure the good administration of justice, and the fulfilment of certain civil obligations.

non-compliance with the lawful order of a court/ insoumission à une ordonnance rendue, conformément à la loi, par un tribunal

Typical orders would be injunctions, limiting or restraining particular actions by individuals, orders to compel the attendance of witnesses in the courts, and orders concerning the family, as for the custody of children or access to them. Examples are the refusal of a contentious litigant to submit to psychiatric examination;[1] and refusal to comply with a blood test ordered in a paternity suit;[2] and failure to pay a fine imposed for not securing the attendance of a child at school.[3] Disobedience to such orders or injunctions may also be treated as contempt of court.

any obligation prescribed by law/une obligation prescrite par la loi

It is difficult to give a precise meaning to this phrase, which cannot reasonably be extended to any obligation, which may arise or be recognized under the law. The Commission has said that it covers

. . . only cases where the law permits the detention of a person to compel him to fulfil a specific and concrete obligation, which he has until then failed to satisfy.[4]

The word 'prescribed' suggests specific obligations, imposed by law usually in statutory forms; but the meaning of 'concrete' remains unresolved, though the Fourth Protocol, Article 1, goes some way to limit the scope of the subparagraph by providing that:

No one shall be deprived of his liberty merely on the ground of inability to perform a contractual obligation.

It is necessary to distinguish the situation, in which the specific obligation can still be performed, from that in which is future

---

[1] 6659/74 (F.R.G.) 3 D.R. 92.
[2] 8278/78 (Austria) 18 D.R. 154.
[3] 6289/73 (Ireland) 8 D.R. 42.
[4] *Engel et al.* (Netherlands) 5100/71, 42 *Recueil* 61; Judgment No. 22 (8.6.1976).

fulfilment is to be secured. So where a Swiss national, performing military service in a training school of recruits, was placed under close arrest for five days for refusing to obey an order, the Commission held that:

... the purpose of the disciplinary arrest inflicted on the applicant was not to secure the fulfilment of any particular obligation. Whatever may the deterrent effect of close arrest, or for that matter of any penal or disciplinary sanction, it was ordered in this case as a punishment for past behaviour.[1]

But the refusal to make an affidavit, required by law in respect of personal possessions, was held to be a failure to perform a specific obligation, and deprivation of liberty as a means of compelling fulfilment of the obligation, was justified under Article 5 (1) *b*.[2]

The use of detention to secure the fulfilment of an immediate obligation, and indirectly as a warning against future breaches of obligation, is illustrated by the application of the Prevention of Terrorism (Temporary Provision) Act (1976) in the U.K. The Act provides that any person, arriving in or seeking to leave, the United Kingdom, may be examined to determine whether he had been involved in terrorism, or is subject to an exclusion order, or may be suspected of offences under the Act. Under the statutory order, the examining officer has authority to detain a person for up to seven days, without any warrant of arrest or detention. There are also statutory provisions authorizing search, fingerprinting and photography of persons so detained.

Three applicants, two U.K. Citizens and one an Irish citizen, arrived in Liverpool in February 1977 on a ferry from Dublin and were arrested, and detained for 45 hours in Bridewell Police Station in Liverpool. They were searched, fingerprinted, photographed, and interrogated, by the police; they were then released.

In a lengthy analysis of issues under Article 5, the Commission held that:

(*a*) the subparagraphs of Article 5 (1) are not mutually exclusive, but in the present case on examination of subparagraphs (*b*), (*c*) and (*f*) showed that only (*b*) was in issue;

(*b*) the requirement that the 'obligation' to 'specific and concrete' means that

---

[1] *Eggs* (Switzerland) 7341/76: 15 D.R. 35.
[2] 5025/71 (F.R.G.): 39 *Recueil* 95.

the person concerned must normally have had a prior opportunity to fulfil the 'specific and concrete' obligation incumbent on him and have failed, without proper excuse, to do so, before it can be said in good faith that his detention is 'in order to secure the fulfilment' of the obligation'.[1]

but this condition does not exclude: 'other limited circumstances of a pressing nature which could warrant detention in order to secure fulfilment of an obligation': § 175. Further, Article 5 (1) *b*

does not expressly require that there should have been such deliberate or negligent on the part of the detainee. It requires only that the purpose of the detention should be to secure the fulfilment of the obligation.

(*c*) the Statutory Order (1976) empowers an examining officer to examine persons, arriving or leaving the United Kingdom, for certain purposes and a person so examined may be 'required to submit to further examination'; this imposes a 'specific and concrete' obligation the fulfilment of which may be secured by detention, provided that fulfilment is:

a matter of immediate necessity and . . . the circumstances are such that no other means of securing fulfilment is reasonably practicable.

The Commission considered that this condition was met by the need to prevent terrorism in Northern Ireland.

(*c*) the lawful arrest or detention of a person effected for the purpose of bringing him before the competent legal authority on reasonable suspicion of having committed an offence or when it is reasonably considered necessary to prevent his committing an offence or fleeing after having do so;

(*c*) s'il a été et détenu en vue d'être conduit devant l'autorité judiciaire compétente, lorsqu'il y a des raisons plausibles de soupçonner qu'il a commis une infraction ou qu'il y a des motifs raisonnables de croire à la nécessité de l'empêcher de commettre une infraction ou de s'enfui après l'accomplissement de celle-ci;

Articles 5 (1) *c*, 5 (3), and 6 (1) are closely connected for they describe stages of a single process in the administration of criminal justice, the

---

[1] For example, 5025/71 (F.R.G.): 39 *Recueil* 95.

arrest, detention, and trial of an individual for a criminal offence. If we read them together, and leave out of account, for the moment, incidental matter, they appear to be saying something like this: An individual may be arrested and detained on the reasonable suspicion that he has committed an offence; he must then be brought promptly before a judicial officer, and must also be brought to trial for the offence within a reasonable time or released pending trial, it may be on bail or on some other condition to secure his appearance; and, once charged, he must be tried within a reasonable time.

Now, as will be seen, although this gives a rough picture of the content of these provisions, it could not, unless much elaborated, begin to serve as an interpretation: indeed the confused distribution of the ideas involved over two Articles, which deal generally with the distinct subjects of detention on the one hand and of trial on the other, the ambiguities of the language used to express these ideas, and certain divergences of established practice between contracting States, make these provisions among the most difficult in the Convention to construe and apply.

arrest or detention/arrêté ou détenu

The United Nations study cited earlier has described arrest as

... L'acte par lequel une personne est appréhendée par application de la loi ou par un autre moyen de coercition; elle comprend la période s'étendant entre le moment où l'intéressé est soumis à la contrainte et celui où il est amené devant l'autorité compétente pour ordonner le maintien de la détention ou la mise en liberté.[1]

It points up two aspects of arrest which must be considered: the manner in which it is effected, and the length of time for which a suspect may be held in custody solely on the basis of the arrest.

Lawful arrest takes various forms in the contracting states: arrest with a warrant issued by judicial authority; arrest without a warrant by an agent of public authority; and arrest by a private person. In all the contracting States[2] one or more of these forms are to be found in use according to particular circumstances, and, as might be expected, the

---

[1] E/CN 4/826, Rev. 1 (1964) 31.
[2] Arrest without warrant may be effected by police authority under inherent or statutory powers; further it may be limited to arrest *flagrante delicto*, as, for example, in Belgium, or extend to reasonable suspicion, as, for example, in the United Kingdom.

Commission has held that arrest without warrant is not inconsistent with Article 5,[1] in cases where it is permitted by the domestic law.[2]

Use of force. Force, in order to effect an arrest, is governed in the Convention only by Articles 2 and 3, already discussed. The Commission appears in one case to have adopted, as a criterion, the degree of force that is necessary and proportionate.[3]

The search of a person or his domicile, in connection with his arrest, belongs properly to Article 8, but the Commission has dealt with it under that Article as being part of the administration of criminal justice, saying[4]

Pour autant que le requérant se plaint de la perquisition effectuée à son domicile ... selon le paragraphe 2 dudit Article 8 il peut y avoir ingérence dans l'exercise du droit susmentionné [in paragraph 1 of the Article] pour autant que cette ingérence est prévue par la loi et constitue une mesure, qui dans une société démocratique, est nécessaire à la prévention des infractions pénales ...

Arrest outside the jurisdiction. This deserves special notice as difficult issues of law may be raised under paragraph (1) *c* where an individual is arrested outside the jurisdiction of the State, under the law of which he is charged, by officers of that State. The problem has to be looked at in two aspects: under the law of the place where the arrest is effected, and under the law governing the officers effecting it.

Such an arrest will not normally be lawful at the place where it is effected, but there may be an agreement in force between the two countries concerned permitting the arrest, either in the form of a treaty or administrative arrangement, or the local authorities may have in some other way assented to, or even assisted in, the arrest. The question will then arise whether that agreement or arrangement is valid,[5] or whether the consent or assistance were lawfully given under the local law.

---

[1] 176/56.

[2] See 89/55: 1 *Yearbook* 226 (warrant of arrest issued in error—release on discovery).

[3] 604/59: *Recueil* (1960) i.

[4] 530/59: *Recueil* (1960) i (house search and seizure of literature in connection with arrest). As to seizure of documents and other possessions for use in evidence, see further under Article 6 (3).

[5] The notion of validity here includes the competence of the parties to the agreement (police authorities; particular government departments) to make it: for *de facto* arrangements between government departments in cases of deportation, see under Article 5 (1) *f* below.

If the arrangement or consent is valid, the question will still arise whether the officers have effected the arrest within the scope of their authority, in particular, whether they were authorized to make the arrest under their own law, and whether the arrest fell within the limits of the arrangement or consent.

The Commission, in considering an arrest effected by Bavarian police officers, in executing a lawful warrant, in the precincts of the railway station at Salzburg, found that:

il y a lieu de noter qu'un accord a été passé entre la République d'Allemagne et l'Autriche en vertu duquel les autorités de police de la République Fédérale d'Allemagne peuvent valablement exercer leurs compétences dans l'enceinte de la gare de Salzburg; qu'il appert donc que la requête est manifestment mal fondée . . .[1]

Finally, it may be observed that the arrest of an individual outside the jurisdiction, found to be unlawful and therefore contrary to Article 5, will not of itself invalidate his continued *detention* within the jurisdiction in the sense of paragraph (1) *c*,[2] provided that detention is for the purpose prescribed in the paragraph.

for the purpose of bringing him before the competent legal authority/en vue d'être conduit devant l'autorité judiciaire compétente

The meaning and consequences of this claim are unclear. Is it saying that, to be justified under subparagraph 1 (*c*), the prime purpose of the detention must be to bring the person before the competent legal authority and meet the requirements of Article 5 (4); or is it saying that detention, justified on reasonable suspicion of an offence, to prevent the commission of an offence, or to prevent the escape of an offender, must also be 'effected' with a view of bringing the person before the competent legal authority.[3]

The objection to the first interpretation is that it makes the sub-paragraph a repetition of Article 5 (3); and the second interpretation is

---

[1] 990/61: *Recueil* (1961) ii.

[2] Unless it renders the dentention unlawful under the domestic law: see J. E. S. Fawcett, 'The Eichmann Case', 35 *B.Y.I.L.* (1962) 181.

[3] A passage in the Court judgment in the *Lawless* case could be so read: whereas it has been shown that the detention of G. R. Lawless from 13 July to 11 December 1957 was not 'effected for the purpose of bringing him before the competent legal authority . . .'.

supported by the French text—en vue d'être conduit—which characterizes the initial purpose not the process.

In the *Lawless* case, the Irish government argued that Article 5 (3) applied only to the first category of cases in subparagraph 1 (*c*)—the reasonable suspicion of an offence—but the Court rejected this saying that, Article 5 (3) and subparagraph 1 (*c*) must be read as a whole, and this

plainly entails the obligation to bring everyone arrested or detained in any of the circumstances contemplated by the provision of paragraph 1 (*c*) before a judge for the purpose of examining the question of deprivation of liberty or for the purpose of deciding on the merits.

The Court has not, however, resolved the need or purpose of subparagraph 1 (*c*). Its applicability to compulsory residence in the case of Guzzardi (Italy)[1] led to conflict of opinion: the majority considered that under the Italian statutes 'an order for compulsory residence as such, leaving aside the manner of its implementation, does not constitute deprivation of liberty'; but minority opinions expressed the view that the order was in fact covered by subparagraph 1 (*c*).

The use of a period of detention on remand for a given offence for police investigation of another offence may be inconsistent with Article 18;[2] further subparagraphs 1 (*b*) and (*c*) may in some degree overlap.[3]

What is at least clear is that subparagraph 1 (*c*), and Article 5 (3) in combination, need redrafting so that the aim and requirements of both provisions are clearly distinguished.

The meaning of the expression 'competent legal authority' is somewhat obscure. It appeared in the original draft of the paragraph, and remained unchanged, as did the French equivalent. It seems that the 'legal' means 'judicial', and that the whole expression is to be given the meaning, which appears in the expanded form in paragraph (3) of 'a judge or other officer authorised by law to exercise judicial power'.

---

[1] *Guzzardi*: Judgment No. 39 (6.11.1980).
[2] *Kamma* (Netherlands) 4771/71.
[3] 8073/77 (U.K.) 19 D.R. 223.

on reasonable suspicion of having committed an offence/ lorsqu'il y a des raisons plausibles de soupçonner qu'il a commis une infraction

The Commission may satisfy itself as to whether the suspicion is reasonable, or what is reasonably necessary under the paragraph, and will not always accept the finding of the authorities that it was reasonable.

But the Commission has not always stated the grounds of its finding of reasonableness, though it has said that

in determining what is a 'reasonable suspicion' . . . permitting the arrest or detention of a person under . . . paragraph (1) *c*, regard must be had to the circumstances of the case as they appeared at the time of arrest and detention . . .[1]

Further, the Commission has not found subsequent acquittal to be in itself an invalidation of the 'reasonable suspicion', on which arrest and detention was grounded,[2] where the applicant offered no evidence under paragraph (1) *c*.

to prevent his committing an offence or fleeing after having done so/de l'empêcher de commettre une infraction ou de s'enfuir après l'accomplissement de celle-ci

These expressions have an air of immediacy, as if they spoke of quick preventive moves by the police, and of 'hot pursuit'. But they come at the tail of a long sentence concerned with both arrest and detention, and while they plainly comprise immediate action in the form of arrest, they are also factors in detention, and are as such better considered under Article 5 (3).

(*d*) the detention of a minor by lawful order for the purpose of educational supervision or his lawful detention for the purpose of bringing him before the competent legal authority;

(*d*) s'il s'agit de la détention régulière d'un mineur, décidée pour son éducation surveilée ou de sa détention régulière, afin de la traduire devant l'autorité compétente;

---

[1] 343/57: 2 *Yearbook* 412; 1602/62: 7 *Yearbook* 165; 1932/62: 7 *Yearbook* 224; 8224/78; 15 D.R. 211.

[2] 1699/62: *Recueil* (1964) i (applicant had had thirty-five previous convictions).

No application has been made to the Commission under this paragraph, nor is it easy to imagine what circumstances are envisaged in the first clause.

It would be strange to equate attendance at school or other form of tuition with detention, as it is understood in the rest of Article 5, though we all know detention after school as a punishment; nor can detention here be equivalent to the normal custody of children.[1] It would be equally odd to treat the expression 'educational supervision' as containing a punitive element, some form of corrective training.

The preparatory work helps to explain the second clause. It is designed to enable public authorities to intervene for the protection of children, and the amendment adding the clause was explained in these words:

> Many children brought before the court have committed no offence at all, and the purpose of their detention is to secure their removal from harmful surroundings, so that they are not covered by Article 5 (1) c.[2]

This may explain why there is no mention of arrest in this paragraph.

(e) the lawful detention of persons for the prevention of the spreading of infectious diseases, of persons of unsound mind, alcoholics or drug addicts or vagrants;

(e) s'il s'agit de la détention régulière d'une personne susceptible de propager une maladie contagieuse, d'un aliéné, d'un alcoolique, d'un toxicomane ou d'un vagabond;

It would be a fair guess that this is one of the parts of the Convention that is already 'dated' and overtaken by practice, as Article 2 already has in great part. Further, the paragraph is inadequately drafted, bringing together, as it does, a number of quite distinct human situations under the single and simplicist notion of detention without any qualifications, including provisions for arrest.

Infectious diseases. The control of infectious diseases must be in general a matter of domestic law and administration, but all the contracting States operate, as part of that law, the International Sanitary

---

[1] See further under Article 8 below.
[2] *T.P.* iii. 724.

Regulations, adopted by the W.H.O. Assembly in May 1951.[1] Under these Regulations, as health authority

shall take all practicable means to prevent the departure of any infected person or suspect . . .[2]

while

On arrival of a ship, an aircraft, a train, or a road vehicle, an infected person on board may be removed and isolated.

However,

a person under surveillance shall not be isolated and shall be permitted to move about freely. The health authority may require him to report to it, if necessary, at specific intervals during the period of surveillance.

Unsound mind. The state of unsound mind creates a number of problems for the application of the Convention, concerning the authority to detain.

Normally detention will be ordered by a court, but detention by administrative order, for example by a local authority, is not unknown, and there may here be danger of a failure to assemble and appreciate properly the evidence indicating or contradicting a need for the order.[3] Paragraph (1) *e* is silent on the duration of such detention, but in some countries there is provision for periodicial review by the committing court of the continued need for detention.[4]

There are three situations, in which a person of unsound mind may be detained, that call for comment: detention for purposes of psychiatric examination control; or in direct consequence of having committed an offence; or after service of a term of imprisonment imposed on conviction.

A leading case is that of Fritz *Winterwerp*.[5] Originally committed to psychiatric hospital by the Amersfoort burgomaster, his term was extended by the Public Prosecutor; on application of his wife, and the Public Prosecutor, the District Court then ordered confinement of six months, and on further similar applications detention orders were

---

[1] *U.N.T.S.* i. 2302.

[2] Article 30 (2) *a*. An infected person is one suffering, or believed to be suffering, from a quarantinable disease, that is, plague, cholera, yellow fever, smallpox, typhus, and relapsing fever.

[3] See, for example, 1537/62: *Recueil* (1963) iii.

[4] e.g. *Denmark*—Penal Code, Article 70 (1) and 3; see 2518/65.

[5] (Netherlands) 6301/73; Report E.C.H.R.: Series B No. 31; Judgment E.C.H.R. No. 33 [24.10.1979].

made normally by the Regional Court. Four requests for discharge over a period of five years, were not sent by the Public Prosecutor to the Regional Court. In none of the earlier proceedings was he enabled to present his case in person or by a representative, or to challenge the medical evidence presented to the courts.

The Commission considered that, under Article 5 (1) *e*, a person must not be admitted to or kept in psychiatric detention without it being medically established and confirmed that his mental condition called for compulsory hospitalization; detention based only on statements of relatives or neighbours involved risk of abuse. In the present case, the Commission found that the mandatory provisions of Netherlands law regarding the procedure of hospitalization had been complied with; and that the absence or refusal of ensuing treatment could give rise to questions under Articles 3, 5 or 18, not in issue in this case.

However, the right of the person to present his own case and to challenge the medical and social evidence adduced in support of his detention was the absolute minimum for the judicial procedure envisaged by Article 5 (4); further, the refusal by the Public Prosecutor to refer requests for discharge to the courts, on the grounds that they would not be granted was a manifest denial of the right accorded by Article 5 (4).

The Court, to which the case was referred by both the Commission and the Netherlands Government, adopted similar reasoning and concluded that there had been compliance with the requirements of Article 5 (1) *e* but breaches of Article 5 (4).

Three minimum conditions, required by Article 5 (1) *e*, were adduced from the *Winterwerp* case, and applied in subsequent applications: an objective mental disorder must be established by a competent authority.

Transfer to a mental hospital for psychiatric examination is covered by the terms of paragraph (1) *b* itself,[1] but the question can arise whether a period of detention for this purpose is to count as part of the whole period of detention of a suspected person under Article 5 (3).

Where the law authorizes a court, on finding that the accused has committed the offence charged, to order his detention as being of unsound mind, the Commission has treated the detention as falling under paragraph (1) *a*.[2]

---

[1] See, for example, 680/60: *Recueil* (1960) ii; 973/61: *Recueil* (1962) i.

[2] 1293/61: *Recueil* (1926) ii (assault—detention for five years under Article 19 of

But the third situation, in which he is sentenced to a term of imprisonment to be followed by detention as of unsound mind, poses certain problems of the relation between responsibility, punishment, and social protection.

The notion of diminished responsibility (*verminderte Zurechnungsfähigkeit*)[1] introduces a new element, that a convicted person may be punished by a term of imprisonment, albeit reduced, under paragraph (1) *a*, and then ordered, as a measure of social protection, to be detained as of 'unsound mind' under paragraph (1) *c*. The Commission found no conflict here between these successive forms of detention, nor any basis of complaint under the Convention.

The Commission imposes no special procedural conditions on applications by persons known to be of unsound mind, and the substance of their applications are treated as any other.[2] The position of applicants who, though not detained, have been placed under guardianship for some or all purposes, or have been declared vexatious litigants in their countries, will be examined under Article 25.

Vagrancy. This takes many forms, and in dealing with it legislators have found it difficult to draw a clear line between alienation and social misconduct, or to decide whether it should be dealt with administratively or judicially. The provisions of law on vagrancy are often then confused and unsatisfactory, and we find them described as 'the most unconstitutional law yet lingering on the statute book',[3] or *un monstre juridique*. Where vagrancy is not itself an offence, but a vagrant may be detained for a long period by what is in effect an administrative decision, the question arises whether the requirement of Article 5 (4) is satisfied, that the lawfulness of his detention shall, if he demands, be determined by a court.[4]

Belgian 'Loi de défense sociale à l'égard des anormaux et des délinquants d'habitudes'). See also 2219/64: *Recueil* (1965) ii.

[1] *Germany*: StGB § 51 (2) provides that punishment may be mitgated ('kann die Strafe ... vermildet werden') if there is diminished responsibility by reason of loss of consciousness, or mental illness or weakness (wegen Bewußtsinnsstörung, wegen krankhafter Störung der Geistestätigkeit, oder wegen Geistesschwäche).

[2] See, for example, 1641/62: *Recueil* (1963) iii.

[3] Of the Vagrancy Act 1824 in England see Kenny, *Outlines of Criminal Law* (1952), ch. xxv.

[4] See 2208/64 concerning *Belgium*: Laws of 1.5.1849, Article 3, and 27.11.1891, Articles 6–8, 12–10 ('pour la répression du vagabondage et de la mendicité'), the issue being whether the *judge de paix*, when acting under these provisions, can be said to constitute a court.

A number of applications followed, the central complaint being that the magistrate (*juge de paix*), in ordering detention in the vagrancy centres[1] was acting really in an administrative capacity, there being no possibility of the lawfulness of the detention being determined. The Commission was of the opinion that the system was in breach of Article 5 (4), and that it then followed, that the work required of the detainees could not fall within the exception in Article 4 (3) *a*, and was therefore compulsory labour contrary to Article 4.[2] It was similarly held that the restriction of the correspondence of the detainees was contrary to Article 8.

The Court found for a breach of Article 5 (4), but not of Articles 4 or 8.[3] In August 1971 the 1891 Act was modified in Belgium, in light of the Court decision; and the new Act provided for appeals against the order of a magistrate for detention to the criminal courts, which were to decide within eight days.

In the case of psychiatric detention, the disorder must be of a kind and degree warranting compulsory confinement; and the continuance of confinement must depend on the persistence of the disorder.

So, where in the United Kingdom an applicant had been recalled into psychiatric detention, after a period of release for six years and no adequate explanation had been given to his solicitors by the authorities, there was a breach not only of Article 5 (2), but also of Article 5 (4), since the habeas corpus proceedings do not provide a sufficiently wide review of law and fact, and the Mental Health Review Tribunal does not render a decision; so the judicial requirements of Article 5 (4) are not met.[4]

In response to an application complaining of the conditions of detention in Broadmoor Hospital, the Commission sent a delegation of five members to visit the hospital. While finding the facilities and conditions of the hospital very unsatisfactory, the Commission decided by a majority vote, that they did not amount to treatment contrary to Article 3.[5] The extent to the term 'vagrant' was later raised but not determined in a later application; there the question was whether the applicant, placed in official guardianship in 1969, could

---

[1] 'Maisons de refuge'/'dépôts de mendicité', under 1891 Act.
[2] *de Wilde, Ooms and Versyp* (2832/66, 2835/66, 2897/66) (Belgium): E.C.H.R. Series B No. 10.
[3] Judgment No. 12 (18.6.1971).
[4] Judgment of the Court No. 46 (5.11.1981).
[5] 6870/75 (U.K.): 10 D.R. 37.

be regarded as a 'vagrant' under Article 5 (1) *e* when placed in a reformatory centre in 1975.[1]

(*f*) the lawful arrest or detention of a person to prevent his effecting an unauthorized entry into the country or of a person against whom action is being taken with a view to deportation or extradition.

(*f*) s'il s'agit de l'arrestation ou de la détention régulières d'une personne pour l'empêcher de pénétrer irrégulièrement dans le territoire, ou contre laquelle une procédure d'expulsion ou d'extradition est en cours.

unauthorized entry/de pénétrer irrégulièrement

That the Convention does not guarantee any right of entry or asylum has already been shown. Entry would be unauthorized if, among other circumstances, it was clandestine, or forbidden by administrative order, for example, the refusal by an immigration officer in the United Kingdom of leave to land.

action being taken with a view to deportation or extradition/une procédure d'expulsion ou d'extradition est en cours

Action must be taken to mean all steps necessary, including detention itself,[2] to effect extradition or deportation.

The process may, according to the differing practice among contracting States, involve judicial orders, ministerial action, or a combination of the two.[3] Further, we must distinguish the decision to extradite or deport an individual from the mode of execution of that decision.

Extradition and deportation are not measures governed as such by the Convention; and an application challenging an order either is then incompatible *ratione materiae*.[4] So:

---

[1] *Peyer* (Switzerland) 7397/76: application concluded by friendly settlement: 5 D.R. 105.

[2] Such detention must not be unduly prolonged, as where it can no longer lead to deportation in the reasonably near future. Amtsgericht, Köln (10.3.1965).

[3] Hence change of wording from 'proceedings' to 'action': *T.P.* iii. 351, 430, 449.

[4] 7256/75: 8 D.R. 163.

... the right of an alien to reside in a particular country is a matter governed by public law ... where the public authorities of a State decide to deport an alien on grounds of security, this constitutes an act of state falling within the public sphere ... Accordingly, even though the decision to deport the applicant may have consequences in relation to his civil rights, in particular his reputation, the State is not required in such cases to grant a hearing conforming to the requirements of Article 6 (1).[1]

Further, the deportation of an alien on grounds of State security does not rank as a penalty.

Nevertheless, the procedure of extradition or deportation must be conducted with reasonable diligence, and there must be recourse against an order being made; so the Commission did not consider that

... the right to make representations to the advisory panel (a body with no power to decide the matter) or to the Home Secretary (the authority responsible for the decision) can be seen as effective and sufficient remedies which the applicant is required to exhaust under Article 26 ...

Further, there must not only be a clear link between detention and deportation or extradition proceedings, in that the detention must be a necessary part of the proceedings, and limited to them,[2] but the length of detention must not be excessive or beyond what can be shown to be necessary.[3]

The European Convention on Extradition reserves to contracting states the right to refuse extradition of their 'nationals'. Further, the notion of deportation is necessarily limited to the expulsion of aliens; for it is

open as a matter of construction of the particular statute in which it is found ... [in this statute] the word 'deportation' is used in a general sense and an action applicable to all persons irrespective of 'nationality'.[4]

The great majority of applications to the Commision have been concerned with deportation rather than extradition; and the issues that have generally to be taken into account are the interference with family life, and the possible prospects for the person expelled in the recipient country.

---

[1] *Agee* (U.K.) 7729/76: 7 D.R. 164; 7902/77: 9 D.R. 224.
[2] *Caprino* (U.K.) 6871/75: 22 D.R. 5; 9058/80: 28 D.R. 160. Passage in aircraft on deportation is itself detention under Article 5 (1) *f*: 7376/76 (Sweden) 7 D.R. 123.
[3] *Lynas* (Switzerland) 9317/76: 6 D.R. 147.
[4] *Cooperative Committee on Japanese Canadians* v. *Attorney General for Canada* [1947] A.L. 87 P.C.

The impact of extradition or deportation on family life will vary with circumstances: for example, taking applications to the Commission, if a man is expelled, can his wife and children be reasonably expected to follow him; or does he have a parent or other relative without support; or can a couple living together be separated?

What order for expulsion is unreasonable in regard to family life will be a matter of fact, and it may, on investigation, sometimes be reversed.[1]

The prospect of ill-treatment in the recipient country of the person expelled has often been raised by applicants as an obstacle, usually to extradition. Before deciding that the prospect of ill-treatment is such as to bar extradition, the Commission has consistently called for evidence of possible treatment contrary to Article 3, and of how far it might be avoided. So, in the deportation from Denmark of 199 Vietnamese refugee children, including 152 Montagnards, the measures taken by the Danish authorities to secure, as far as practicable, the future safety of the children, were examined by the Commission at length;[2] the applicant was director of a body called Childrens' Protection and Security International, and was entrusted in effect with the care of the children on behalf of the parents, and consequently by a certain extension of Article 25, the Commission considered him 'as an indirect victim in that he has a valid personal interest in the welfare of the children'. It held that the expulsion was not collective, in the sense of the Fourth Protocol, because every individual case was investigated, and those aged 15 years or more were left free to stay in Denmark. Further, contact had been made with the U.N. High Commissariat for Refugees, and with the Red Cross, both Danish and South Vietnamese, to make practical arrangements for the re-establishment of the refugees. There are then 'no serious reasons to believe that the children would face treatment contrary to Article 3'.

The Commission has left open the question whether treatment to be feared under Article 3 is limited to action by public authorities or should be extended to cover possible action by autonomous groups.[3] Further, it has limited its approach to Article 3; here the then Consultative Assembly of the Council of Europe appeared to go further in a Recommendation (1961) which read:

---

[1] *Singh Uppal* (U.K.) 8244/78: 20 D.R. 29, ending in settlement.
[2] 7011/75 (Denmark): 4 D.R. 215.
[3] 7216/75: 5 D.R. 137; 8581/79: 29 D.R. 48.

3. Considering Article 3 of the Convention . . . which, by prohibiting inhuman treatment, binds contracting parties not to return refugees to a country where their life or freedom would be threatened.

This is close to saying that denial of asylum is inhuman treatment.

The European Convention on Extradition, which comes close to a codification of the practice,[1] deals with the problem of treatment in the recipient country in two ways. First:

If the offence for which extradition is requested is punishable by death under the law of the requesting Party, and in respect of such offence the death-penalty is not provided by the law of the requested party or is not normally carried out, extradition may be refused unless the requesting Party gives such assurance as the requested Party considers sufficient that the death-penalty will not be carried out. Article 11.

Secondly, extradition 'shall not be granted'

. . . if the requested Party has substantial grounds for believing that in request for extradition for an ordinary criminal offence has been made for the purpose of prosecuting or punishing a person on account of his race, religion, nationality, or political opinion, or that that person's position may be prejudiced for any of these reasons. Article 3 (2).

There are circumstances then in which a majority of the Convention countries may, or in fact must, refuse extradition on grounds under a potential breach of Article 3. But the Convention organs are precluded from invoking such grounds, as has been shown, *ratione materiae*. The question of the potential character of an offence, for which extradition is demanded, has surprisingly been rarely raised in applications to the Commission; but in one,[2] concerning the extradition of an I.R.A. activist from the United Kingdom to Ireland for an offence committed in Dublin, the difficulty of resolving the question, and the uncertainty of the provision of the European Convention on Extradition, were manifest. Article 3 (1) of that Convention states:

Extradition shall not be granted if the offence in respect of which it is requested is regarded by the requested Party as a political offence or as an offence connected with a political offence.

No definition of 'political offence' is offered, save that

---

[1] In force 18.4.1960. All councils of Europe members were parties at the end of 1984 except Belgium, France, Malta, Portugal, and the United Kingdom: two protocols, in force on 20.8.1979 and 5.6.1983 have six parties to them.

[2] 8299/78 (Ireland): 22 D.R. 51.

The taking or attempted taking of the life of a Head of State or a member of his family shall not be deemed to be a political offence for the purpose of this Convention. Article 3(3).

The question of the political character of an offence will arise further under Articles 9, 17, and 18.

(2) Everyone who is arrested shall be informed promptly, in a language which he understands, of the reasons for his arrest and of any charge against him.

2. Toute personne arrêté doit être informée, dans le plus court délai et dans une langue qu'elle comprend, des raisons de son arrestation et de toute accusation portée contre elle.

informed promptly/informée, dans le plus court délai

The Commission has held that there is no obligation under this paragraph to present the reasons for arrest or for the charge in writing:

> The applicant has repeatedly stated that he was never informed in writing of the reasons for his arrest and detention, but, on the other hand he has never expressly contested the statement of the Netherlands Government that he was duly informed; ... the said paragraph [2] does not require the information to be given in writing to the detained person ...[1]

The reasoning has a parallel in the third and fourth propositions, enunciated by Viscount Simon[2] as applicable to arrest without warrant:

> 3. The requirement that the person arrested should be informed of the reason why he is seized naturally does not exist if the circumstances are such that he must know the general nature of the alleged offence for which he is detained.
>
> 4. The requirement that he should be so informed does not mean that technical or precise language need be used. The matter is a matter of substance, and turns on the elementary proposition that in this country a person is prima facie entitled to his freedom and is only required to submit to restraint on his freedom if he knows in substance the reason why it is claimed that this restraint should be imposed.

It might be added here that 'informed' must require that the information be conveyed in language which the person understands, as

---

[1] 1211/61: *Recueil* (1962) ii.
[2] *Christie* v. *Leachinsky* [1947] A.C. 567 at 573.

well as in *a* language which he understands; and 'the reasons' must be the reasons.

It is clear that the information, to which a person is entitled under Article 5 (2), need be less specific and detailed than the charges made under Article 6; but the person should be:

> ... informed sufficiently about the facts and the evidence which are proposed to be the foundation of a decision to detain him. In particular, he should be enabled to state whether he admits or denies the alleged offence.[1]

In short, he must be enabled to make effective use of the proceedings envisaged in the first clause of Article 5 (3), or under Article 5 (4): but at the stage of arrest and detention envisaged in Article 5 (2), there is no need or right to have legal advice.[2]

Again, the reasons for arrest may be obvious: A convicted criminal was placed in compulsory residence in Italy by judicial order, and escaped to Costa Rica. Arrested by local authorities and given over to Italian police officers, he was brought back to Rome in an Italian Air Force aircraft, and the Italian warrant of arrest was read to him on his arrival. The Commission considered that, since the arrest in Costa Rica was outside the jurisdiction of the Convention, the communication of the warrant of arrest was as prompt as possible; in any case, he could be assumed to know what the purpose of his detention was.[3]

The application of the rule to arrest for the purpose of psychiatric detention must be obviously difficult.[4]

(3) Everyone arrested or detained in accordance with the provisions of paragraph 1 (*c*) of this Article shall be brought promptly before a judge or other officer authorized by law to exercise judicial power and shall be entitled to trial within a reasonable time or to release pending trial. Release may be conditioned by guarantees to appear for trial.

3. Toute personne arrêté ou détenue, dans les conditions prévues au paragraphe 1 (*c*) du présent article, doit être aussitôt traduite devant un juge ou un autre magistrat habilité par la loi à exercer des fonctions judiciaires et a le droit d'être

---

[1] 8098/77 (F.R.G.) 16 D.R. 111.
[2] *Gustaven* (Denmark) 8829/79.   [3] 8916/80 (Italy) 21 D.R. 250.
[4] 6998/75 (U.K.) 8 D.R. 106 (the applicant claimed the reasons given for his recall into psychiatric detention were 'brief and vague'; the application was settled).

jugée dans un délai raisonnable, ou libérée pendant la procédure. La mise en liberté peut être subordonnée à une
garantie assurant la comparution de l'intéressé à l'audience.

Some of the ground has already been cleared in the approach to this
difficult and important paragraph. We must now attack it directly.
The changes made during the drafting of the paragraph are not without interest. The draft preceding the final version[1] opened with the
words 'Anyone arrested or detained on the charge of having committed a crime, or to prevent his committing his crime, shall be
brought', and then continued as the text now stands. The differences
are that the notion of charge is used in place of reasonable suspicion,
and the possibility of flight is not covered. As so often in records of
preparatory work, no explanation appears for the changes, but two
results at least are clear: first, as already observed by the court in the
Lawless Case paragraph (1) *c* is in effect amalgamated with paragraph
(3); and secondly, the bringing of a charge against an individual for a
particular offence is not in the final version an essential factor in
paragraph (3), though it is in Article 6 (1).

brought promptly before a judge or other officer authorized by law to exercise judicial power/aussitôt traduite devant un juge ou un autre magistrat habilité par la loi à exercer des fonctions judiciaires

This clause then secures the purpose, which validates arrest or detention under paragraph (1) *c*, by making its fulfilment mandatory. There
are naturally variations of practice between the contracting States, but
in all a distinction is made between arrest or provisional arrest on the
one hand and detention on remand on the other,[2] and in all a limitation
is placed on the length of time for which a person may be held in custody
or arrest, prior to release on bail or detention on remand.

The authority for effecting an arrest varies: apart from possible
arrest in some systems by private persons, it may be effected by the

---

[1] *T.P.* ii. 426.
[2] The terminology can be confusing; for example, 'arrest' is in Austria *vorläufige
Verwahrungshaft*, not *Arrest*, which is detention; and *détention préventive* is in France and
Belgium the equivalent of detention on remand (*Untersuchungshaft* in Austria and
Germany). In the Netherlands four terms are to be found: *aanhouding en voorgeleiding*
(simple arrest) and *inverzekeringstelling* (*garde à vue*), and two forms of detention on
remand: *bewaring* and *gevangenhanding*, differing in their permissible duration.

police, or upon the prior or subsequent authorization of the public prosecutor, or by judicial order, which again may in some systems be issued by the investigating judge[1] or by the competent court itself. But detention on remand is invariably authorized by judicial order only.

The time limit within which a person held in custody on arrest must be brought before the competent judicial officer, in the sense of paragraph (3), varies but seldom exceeds forty-eight hours. Where periods of extension of custody on arrest are permitted, at the request of the police or public prosecutor, these periods are themselves limited, usually to the same length as the initial period.

The Court has examined at some length the role of an 'officer authorized by law to exercise judicial power'. It points out that Article 5 covers two forms of the exercise of judicial power: that by the recognized courts and judges, and that by specifically authorized officers of the administration of justice. Competent legal authority then in Article 5 (1) *c* is a synonym for 'judge or other officer authorised by law to exercise judicial power'; and, while 'officer' is not identical with 'judge', the former must have some of the attributes of the latter, if the protection of a person arrested is to be guaranteed:

The first of such conditions is independence of the executive and of the parties ... This does not mean that the 'officer' may not be to some extent subordinate to other judges or officers provided that they themselves enjoy similar independence. In addition, under Article 5 (3) ... the procedural requirement places the 'officer' under the obligation of hearing himself the individual brought before him ... the substantive requirement imposed on him the obligations of reviewing the circumstances militating for or against detention, of deciding, by reference to legal criteria, whether there are reasons to justify detention, and of ordering release if there are no such reasons.[2]

shall be entitled to trial within a reasonable time or to release pending trial/à le droit d'être jugée dans un délai raisonnable, ou libérée pendant la procédure.

The first question which arises is whether this clause expresses a right of the detainee or a duty of the competent authorities. What is at least

---

[1] This expression is perhaps to be preferred to 'examining magistrate' as the equivalent of *juge d'instruction* or *Untersuchungsrichter* or *Ermittlungsrichter*.

[2] *Schiesser* (Switzerland) Judgment (4.12.1979); 58 *I.L.R.* 684; *Meier* (Switzerland) 8485/79 22 D.R. 131. In the latter case the District Attorney performed only investigatory functions, and not prosecuting functions at the same time, so that Article 5 (1) *c* was met.

clear is that it poses alternatives: trial within a reasonable time or release pending trial. There are two reasons for thinking that, in the clause under discussion, the option is that of the authorities and not of the detainee; first, there is admittedly no *obligation* imposed by paragraph (3) to release pending trial a person, detained under paragraph (1) *c*, either with or without security, and therefore it could not be said that the detainee has a right to release under paragraph (3). It must logically follow that he cannot be said to have, under that paragraph, a *right* to trial within a reasonable time, given in any case by Article 6 (1). Secondly, it is in the main only the authorities who can judge of the time needed to prepare for trial. It will be seen that this reasoning would lead to the conclusions that paragraph (3) imposes upon the competent authorities a duty in the alternative either to provide for trial within a reasonable time after arrest or to release the detainee pending his trial; that the choice is theirs, not his; but that the choice is restricted in effect by the condition of reasonable time, so that, if the competent authorities find that trial is, for one cause or another, not practicable within a reasonable time, they must release him pending trial.

Meaning of 'trial'. But the uses of the word 'trial' in the clause are themselves ambiguous and there is some difference of the meaning between the English and French texts. In the English text 'entitled to trial' could mean entitled to be brought to trial, or to be tried in the sense of having the charge finally disposed of by the trial court. But the expression 'pending the trial' favours the first meaning, for, although 'pending' in English can, according to the dictionary, mean either 'during the continuance of' or 'up till', in such expressions as 'pending settlement' or 'pending trial' it has invariably the second sense. Further, to construe the words 'pending the trial' as being equivalent to 'during the continuance of the trial' would have the odd result that there would be no provision in the paragraph for release *before* trial. The natural meaning of the English text then appears to be that a detainee shall be either brought to trial within a reasonable time or released pending trial.

However, in the French text the word 'jugée' would normally mean judged or sentenced, the corresponding expression for a person brought to trial being 'mise en jugement'. Again *pendant la procédure* is somewhat wider than the English equivalent and could, it seems, cover any stage of the proceedings up to final judgment.[1] The meaning of the French text would then be that a detainee is entitled to judgment on the charge against him within a reasonable time or to release at the point, even during the trial, when the whole process has become unreasonably extended.

A further complication is introduced if it is argued that judgment is to be understood as meaning the decision which renders the case *res judicata* for all purposes under the domestic law; in case of conviction this may be, not the judgment and sentence of the trial court, but, as in some countries, the final decision on appeal.

Certain indications are to be found in the general context of paragraph (3). It must be remembered that in the process of detention and trial, different authorities are concerned: the preparation of the charge and of the case for the prosecution will in general be in the hands of the public prosecutor, and also in some systems the investigating judge, with the assistance of the police; but the appointment of the time and place of trial, and the conduct of the trial will be the responsibility of the competent court. Further, the first group will, subject to judicial control, be responsible for the continued detention of the accused, with which paragraph (3) is primarily concerned. If the English text is followed, so that the detainee must be brought to trial within a reasonable time or released, then the decision lies, subject to judicial control, with the first group, and is to be made solely in the framework of the current preparation of the case for trial. If the French text is followed, so that the detainee must be tried up to acquittal or conviction within a reasonable time or released, the competent authorities have to estimate in addition the data and duration of trial, before deciding whether or not the detainee must be released pending trial. This estimate is the harder to make where, as in the 'investigatory' system, the final determination of the charge or charges and delivery of the indictment (accusation; *Anklageschrift*) does not take place until a late stage in the process. On the other hand it might be argued that the French text gives greater protection to the detainee, for it must obviously be more difficult to justify refusal of release pending trial, if the probable duration of trial is to be added to the length of detention on remand before trial, for the purpose of determining what is a reasonable time under paragraph (3).

We may turn then to see how what is a reasonable time is to be

[1] It may also be noticed that in the German official translation 'trial' is represented by *Aburteilung* ('the act of passing final sentence on') and 'pending the trial' by *während des Verfahrens*.

determined, and whether this throws any light on the rest of the paragraph already discussed.

Periods involved. It is necessary first to make clear what periods of time are involved in Articles 5 and 6, and by what provisions of those Articles they are governed. They may be represented graphically (see Appendix 1).

It will be seen that in the period between charge and the beginning of the trial, Articles 5 (1) *c*, 5 (3), and 6 (1) are all operating together. This is an additional reason for thinking that Article 5 (3) does not give any substantive right to trial within a reasonable time. The extension of the operation of the various provisions over periods (*a*)–(*e*) will depend upon the conclusions reached as to the true meaning of these provisions.

The extension to periods (*a*) and (*c*) appears to be excluded, in the view of the Commission, by its finding that detention under paragraph (1) *c*, and therefore also under paragraph (3), is terminated by conviction of the accused:

la détention préventive [of the applicant] a cessé le . . . 1960, date à laquelle a statué le Landgericht . . . à partir de ce moment, elle s'est transformée, malgré pourvoi en cassation (Revision) de l'intéressé en une détention pénitentiaire entièrement compatible avec le paragraphe (1) a de l'Article 5 . . .[1]

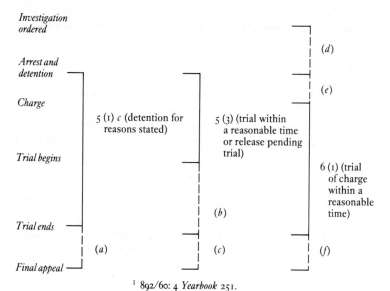

Extension of paragraph (3) over period (*b*) must depend on the conclusion reached as to the meaning of 'trial'. The elements of the problem have already been set out. The Commission has indicated that it takes the view represented in the French text. It has more than once expressly referred, in the context of paragraph (3), to the period between arrest and sentence on conviction by the court. In one application it considered the

reasonable or unreasonable nature of the delay between arrest and sentence (*entre l'arrestation et le jugement*)[1]

and in another it observed that the applicant had lodged several applications for release from detention (*Haftbeschwerden*)

entre son arrestation, et le jugement du 15 Janvier 1962 . . . qui ont inévitablement retardé le prononcé du verdict.

But the fact that the Commission has also cited two decisions together,[2] as representing its view, though one used one formulation and one the other, suggests that the difference of wording is not significant.

In one decision,[3] however, the Commission dealt with the period between arrest and the commencement of trial:

having regard to the very long period of time which elapsed before the applicant was brought to trial (*traduit en jugement*) in the present case and to the general circumstances of the case, the Commission does not consider that the applicant's complaint of an alleged violation of his right to trial within a reasonable time, under Article 5 (3) and Article 6 (1), can be said to be manifestly ill-founded . . .[4]

But in this case the applicant had made no complaint as to the length of the trial, nor did it appear necessary on the face of it[5] for the Commission to consider this *ex officio*. The language of the decision is here addressed to the actual complaint, of prolonged detention and

---

[1] Ibid. 253: see also 1103/61 for the same formulation. See Court book the same view in Wemhoff Judgment (27.6.1968) 1 E.H.R.R. 55.

[2] 1546/62, citing 892/60 and 920/60.

[3] 343/57: 2 *Yearbook* 452–4. Compare 1936/63 (Report of the Commission): three years' detention up to the date of commencement of trial found to be in all the circumstances unreasonable, no account needing to be taken of the subsequent period.

[4] However, this part of the application was rejected as inadmissible *ratione temporis* as regards that part of the period in question which antedated the entry into force of the Convention, and as regards the remainder for non-exhaustion of remedies. Compare 3168/67.

[5] The trial, of a case of some complexity, lasted from 16 June to 17 July 1954.

delay in coming to trial, and has therefore little bearing on the meaning of 'trial' in paragraph (3).

Extension to periods (*d*) and (*e*) depends in part upon the meaning of 'criminal charge (*accusation en matière pénale*)' in Article 6 (1), which will be examined under that paragraph. Here it is enough to point out that what is reasonable time there may be taken to run either from the formal charge or indictment (*Anklageschrift*) or, more broadly, from that moment when by some act, such as arrest on a warrant, the authorities, in the phrase of Lord Devlin, 'declare war' on the suspect.[1] But it does not appear that the extension of Article 6 (1) over periods (*d*) or (*e*), if adopted, would have any bearing on the application of Article 5 (3).

In the case of period (*f*), Article 6 (1), as it were, parts company at this point with Article 5 (1) *c* and (3); for, given that detention after judgment and sentence on conviction comes under Article 5 (1) *a*, the question may still arise whether appeal against that conviction is covered by the rule as to trial within a reasonable time, and is not settled by the exclusion of the period from Article 5 (1) *c* and (3). The extension will, however, depend then on whether the conviction is or is not *res judicata* in domestic law and whether, if so, proceedings on appeal can form part of 'trial' in Article 6 (1).

Reasonable time. From this survey of the various periods, into which the time between arrest and sentence may in practice be divided, it will be seen that there are two main Convention issues: first, what is a reasonable time in which to *detain* on remand a person suspected of or charged with committing an offence; and, second, what is a reasonable time in which to try him on that charge. Both issues will often raise their heads.

To determine then the proper scope and application of Article 5 (1) *c* and (3) on the one hand, and of Article 6 (1) on the other, is ensuring that detention and trial are not unreasonably prolonged, is a task intricate and difficult.

To consider now what is reasonable time under Article 5 (3), we must keep in mind not only that detention on remand is, like all detention, an exception, as it were, to the rule of liberty of the person, but also that there are large variations in the practice of the contracting States; and it is for this reason that it was not feasible to fix in the

---

[1] See under Article 6 (1) at p. 152.

Convention any absolute limit to the length of detention on remand. The Convention simply uses the criterion of what is reasonable.

The principle that detention on remand must be used with restraint, and subject to proper controls, has been expressed by the Committee of Ministers in a resolution,[1] already cited, which recommends that governments should act on the following lines:

(a) Remand in custody (*détention préventive*) should never be compulsory. The judicial authority should make its decision in the light of the facts and circumstances of the case.

(b) Remand in custody should be regarded as an exceptional measure.

(c) Remand in custody should be ordered or continued only when it is strictly necessary. In no event should it be applied for punitive ends.

(d) Any decision on remand in custody should state—as precisely as possible—subject-matter of the charge and the reasons underlying the detention. It must immediately be communicated to the person remanded in custody.

(e) Effective guarantees should be provided to prevent detention from extending beyond what is strictly necessary.

The following remedies (*garanties*) in particular should be taken into account (*envisagées*)

—limitation of the period of custody laid down by law or by the judicial authority;

—review *ex officio* at regular intervals;

—right of appeal to the judicial authority;

—right to be assisted by legal counsel.

(f) The person remanded in custody should be informed of his rights and the conditions on which they may be exercised.

In dealing with applications under Article 5 (3), and in particular the determination of what is a reasonable length of detention, the Commission has also proceeded 'in the light of the facts and circumstances of the case'. In the applications, referred to above, the Commission has said:

the reasonable or unreasonable nature of the delay between arrest and sentence must be considered not *in abstracto* but in the light of the circumstances such as the complexity of the case and the procedure followed by the applicant himself . . .[2]

---

[1] (65) 11.
[2] 892/60: 4 *Yearbook* 252.

and

the question whether a period of detention pending trial is reasonable or not is not a question to be decided in *abstracto* but to be considered in the light of the particular circumstances of each case . . .[1]

The particular circumstances, which the Commission has taken into account, may be grouped under three heads: the grounds of detention, the actual length of detention, and the character and requirements of the preparation for trial of the case against the detainee.

Grounds of detention. The possible grounds of detention under paragraph (1) *c* have already been examined,[2] and it was observed that, while they may initiate arrest and detention, they remain as factors in the continuance of detention. However, the prevention of other offences, or the prevention of escape, may over time diminish in importance, or disappear as grounds for continuing detention. As has already been observed, the Commission may satisfy itself as to the reasonableness or necessity of detention under paragraph (1) *c*, but it will, unless there is a strong indication to the contrary, treat a decision by a court, that the detention is necessary to prevent the commission of other offences or an attempt at flight, as a matter of 'fourth instance' and outside its review.

So it has remarked that

en l'état actuel du dossier, spécialement, la commission n'estime pas que le Landesgericht . . . et l'Oberlandesgericht . . . aient abusé de leur pouvoir d'appréciation en retenant l'existence d'un danger de faite . . .[3]

Length of detention. The actual length of time for which a person, suspected of or charged with an offence, may be detained on remand varies greatly in the practice of the contracting States. In some cases it may have been circumscribed by statute,[4] or by the common grant of release on bail, or by both; in others detention on remand may exceptionally continue for long periods, even for years, though it may be mitigated by periodical judicial review, by the detainee being not subject to a full prison regime, and by the subtraction of the period of

[1] 920/60: see also 1602/62 and 1936/63: 7 *Yearbook* 168, 224.
[2] Where a convicted person is placed in detention on remand, the detention is still governed by Article 5 (1) *a*: 8555/79 (Italy) 20 D.R. 139.
[3] 1599/62: *Recueil* (1963) iii.
[4] e.g. *England*: Habeas Corpus Act 1679, s. 4: Assizes Relief Act 1884; Administration of Justice Act 1960, s. 14; *Scotland*: Criminal Procedure (Scotland) Act 1887, s. 43, and *Wallace* v. *Lord Advocate* [1959] J.C. 71.

detention from the term of imprisonment actually served after conviction. Further, this extended use of detention on remand is often to be
seen in the institutional framework of the investigating judge (*juge
d'instruction*), unknown in the jurisdictions of the United Kingdom
and of Ireland. As to the assessment of the length of detention
imposed, there has been some difference of approach between the
Commission and the Court. The Commission devised seven criteria
to be applied according to the facts of a case. The Court, did not adopt
this method, saying:

... cases of alleged violation of Article 5 (3) must have been the subject of
domestic remedies, and therefore of reasoned decisions by national judicial
authorities. It is for them to mention circumstances which led them, in the
general interest, to consider it necessary to detain a person suspected of an
offence but not convicted. Likewise, such a person must, when exercising his
remedies, have invoked the reasons which tend to refute the conclusion drawn
by the authorities from the facts established by them as well as other circumstances which told in favour of his release.[1]

In a judgment given on the same day by a different chamber of the
Court, the seven criteria proposed by the Commission were analysed
at great length, but the judgment followed the different approach just
described.[2] In a subsequent judgment the Court said:

the persistence of suspicion does not suffice to justify, after a certain lapse of
time, the prolongation of the detention ... The Court is therefore led
necessarily, when examining the question whether Article 5 (3) has been
observed, to consider and assess the reasonableness of the grounds, which
persuaded the judicial authorities to decide [to continue detention][3]

Characteristic reasons given for continuing detention on remand
are the seriousness of the offence involved and the possibility of
further offences being committed by the detainee, if released;[4] the
dangers of suppression of evidence, or of absconding;[5] the requirements of the preliminary investigation; and excessive use of available
legal proceedings by the accused.[6]

---

[1] *Wemhoff* (F.R.G.) Judgment (27.6.1968): 1 E.H.R.R. 55.

[2] *Neumeister* (Austria) Judgment (27.6.1968): 1 E.H.R.R. 91.

[3] *Stögmüller* (Austria) Judgment (10.11.1969): 1 E.H.R.R. 155; see also *Matznetter*
(Austria) Judgment (10.11.1969): 1 E.H.R.R. 198.

[4] *Haase* 7412/76 (F.R.G.): 11 D.R. 78 three separate periods of detention extending
over two years found justified.

[5] 6738/79 (Switzerland): 21 D.R. 241 (in face of criminal proceedings following
extradition).

[6] *Bonnechaux* 8224/78 (Switzerland): 18 D.R. 100: 6541/74 (F.R.G.): 3 D.R. 86.

The Commission has been flexible in deciding what periods of detention it may take into account in finding whether the length is unreasonable. So a period lying outside its competence *ratione temporis*, for example before its ratification of the Convention or acceptance of Article 25, may still be added to a period of detention within the competence, in order that the detention may be assessed as a whole in terms of its length.[1]

Again, although Article 5 (1) *c* does not extend to detention for the purpose of extradition, Article (1) *f* is to be understood as requiring it to be lawful, that the detention process be conducted, not only without abuse of authority, but with reasonable diligence and regard to time.[2]

The applicability of Article 5 (3) to detention in military service raises the organic question what element of criminal law, pointing to Article 6 (1), is to be found in the dealing with offences against military discipline; and also, in applications concerning detention following refusal to perform military service in the Netherlands, the functions of the Auditeur-Militair and Officer-Commissaris had to be considered as 'competent legal authorities' under Article 5 (3).[3]

As regards the principle of fair proportion between the duration of detention on remand and the penalty to be expected German courts have pointed to what is really at stake, even where the detainee is under a milder regime than convicted prisoners.[4]

The Bundesgerichtshof has considered[5] these problems in terms which must be set out at length:

It must then always be put to proof whether it is really necessary for effective criminal prosecution (*zur Sicherung der Strafverfolgung*) that an individual, who is still only suspect and whose guilt has not yet been judicially established should be deprived of his freedom. The starting point for this necessary appreciation must then be the doer and his act; from this it at once follows that duration of detention on remand must not be out of proportion to

---

[1] *Ventura* 7438/76 (Italy): 23 D.R. 5: see also 6701/74 Austria: 5 D.R. 69.

[2] *Lynas* 7317/75 (Switzerland): 6 D.R. 141.

[3] *de Jong, Baljet* (Netherlands) 8605/79, 8806/79: 24 D.R. 144; *van der Sluis et al.* (Netherlands) 3362/81: 28 D.R. 212.

[4] Landgericht, Köln (9.6.1964): *N.J.W.* [1964] 1816; Amtsgericht, Köln (10.3.1965): 8 *Yearbook* 558. There may of course be special circumstances aggravating the effects of detention on remand, such as bad health, or detriment to business depending on personal attention of detainee: see 790/60, and 1936/63. For its effect on the family of the detainee see 2294/64: 7 *Yearbook* 352.

[5] Judgment (10.1.1966): *N.J.W.* [1966] 924. The Bundesverfassungsgericht (15.12.1965) has also said that neither the gravity of the offence nor the degree of culpability can in themselves justify arrest or detention: *N.J.W.* (1966) 243.

the seriousness of the offence (*Bedeutung der Tat*) and to the punishment that may be expected. . . . Account must be taken then—independently of the grounds for detention established by law (suspicion, and danger of flight of repetition of offences, or of concealment of evidence)—of the punishment to be expected as well as of the seriousness of the offence; and all these appreciations depend upon the information available at the time (*auf den jeweiligen Stand der Ermittlungen*). Here it must not be forgotten that the weight and significance of particular circumstances can rapidly change in the course of the proceedings. Further it is always to be kept in mind that, as a ground for detention on remand, it is sufficient that there be suspicion that an offence has been committed, and this suspicion must in German law be strong (*dringender*) and under the Convention, in the absence of provisions of domestic law requiring a higher test, it must be reasonable (*hinreichender*); but in the trial itself (*Hauptverhandlung*) the guilt of the accused must be fully demonstrated, so that he will be entitled to acquittal, if the suspicion is not transformed, on the basis of the evidence produced at the trial, into a firm conviction of the court that he is guilty. It follows that, if the question as to what punishment is to be expected has to be answered before the trial, it must be answered in terms of what punishment would have to be expected, if the trial court were to be convicted of the guilt of the accused and pass judgment on him on the basis of the evidence established up to the point where it created suspicion strong enough to order detention on remand. That is the meaning of 'punishment to be expected' in light of the information available at the time.

Therefore just as strong suspicion is—aside from other possible grounds of detention—sufficient to justify a detention order, so when we come to the question of the permissible length of detention on remand in light of the punishment to be expected, it will be enough if, on the information available at the time, suspicion is so strong that punishment may be expected which is not out of relation to the period of detention already served. The German code of criminal procedure employs here a negative formulation, namely, that the length of detention must 'not stand out of proportion' to the magnitude of the offence and the punishment to be expected. In the literature and in various court decisions,[1] we often find a positive conception, that the length of detention 'should in no circumstances exceed the punishment to be expected for the offence. . . . The court is of the opinion that there are no differences here in respect of the requirements determining the length of detention, so that in effect detention on remand must 'stand in a commensurate relation' (*in angemessenen Verhältnis*) with the seriousness of the offence and the punishment to be expected. As in the contexts already described, so here strong suspicion may serve as a basis for the calculation of punishment (*genügt . . . für Strafzumessungstatsachen*).

---

[1] The court here cited the decisions referred to above, p. 000, n. 1.

The court is seeking to draw a line between reasonable suspicion and a presumption of guilt.[1] Conscious of the danger that detention on remand may come to the point where it becomes punitive, that is, justifiable only on the hypothesis that the detainee is guilty and will almost certainly receive a like or longer term of imprisonment, the court introduces the notional element of a term of imprisonment that might be imposed for what the detainee is reasonably or strongly suspected as having done.[2] The length of this notional term becomes an indicator of what is reasonable time in Article 5 (3).

Preparation for trial. We now turn to the character and requirements of the preparation for trial of the case against the detainee. The essence of the problem has been expressed in a decision of the Belgian Court of Cassation:[3]

> Que le 'délai raisonnable' n'est pas écoulé lorsque des actes d'instruction, nécessaires à la manifestation de la vérité, sont encore en cours et que ces actes sont accomplis sans retard injustifié . . .
> Qu'il s'ensuit qu'en décidant que l'intérêt public et notamment les nécessités urgentes de l'instruction, exigeaient le maintien de la détention préventive du demandeur, l'arrêt [against which appeal was brought] n'a violé . . . l'article 5 de la Convention . . .

In other words, the proper investigation of the case and its preparation for trial may be, for various reasons, prolonged, but it may also appear necessary to detain the accused while it is going forward.

The conflict between the public interest and the liberty of the individual has to be resolved by the principle of limiting detention to a reasonable time. In considering what is reasonable time in paragraph (3) in such cases, the Commission has taken account both of the complexity and difficulty of the case, and of the conduct of the applicant while under detention.

The complexity or difficulty of a case under investigation is not itself a ground of detention of a suspect, recognized by paragraph (1) *c*, but it is a factor which, in combination with others, may prolong detention.

Where the offences charged dated from nearly twenty years before and

---

[1] For a further development of the idea see BVerfG. (15.12.1965): *N.J.W.* [1966] 243.
[2] The court expressly rejected, as the measure, the term of imprisonment demanded by the prosecution at the trial.
[3] 16.3.1964: *Pasicrisie Belge* (1964), no. 7/8, 762.

it was required to prepare under unusual circumstances . . . a trial on a large scale in order properly to determine not ony the question of the applicant's guilt, but also the extent to which the guilt of others might be taken into account in estimating the degree of the applicant's responsibility.

detention on remand for nineteen months was found not unreasonable.[1]

Again,

whereas, in the present case, allowance must be made in particular for the large number of offences imputed to the Applicant, which could not fail to affect the time required to conduct a preliminary investigation of his case; whereas it is also to be taken into account that the investigations involved other persons who were accused together with the Applicant; whereas, in particular, the medical observation and examination of the co-defendant Z as to his criminal responsibility[2] delayed the proceedings against the Applicant; whereas, furthermore, in the main hearing in 1963, the Applicant's counsel applied for an adjournment with the result that the proceedings against the Applicant and Z were detached from the main proceedings and the Applicant was tried at a later date; whereas, finally, between September 1963 and his conviction and sentence in January 1964, the Applicant made various appeals which, whilst they left the reasons for his continued detention on remand under the constant control of the German judicial authorities, inevitably delayed further the delivery of a verdict; whereas, in conclusion, an examination of the case does not reveal that the detention of the Applicant was unduly prolonged; whereas, consequently, it does not disclose any appearance of a violation of Article 5, paragraph (3).[3]

The decision last cited concerns also the conduct of the applicant. On the one hand, the Commission has attached importance to detention on remand being under periodic judicial control:

whereas the documents in the case show that the reasons for the detention were under constant review by the courts.[4]

But this control may itself lead not only to delay in the preparation of the case for trial but to prolongation of detention:

. . . the said detention cannot be regarded as having been unduly prolonged, in view of the complex nature of the applicant's case and in view of the fact that

---

[1] 920/60; *Recueil* (1961) ii (charges of crimes against humanity during the Second World War).

[2] For psychiatric examination of detainee, see also 1546/62.

[3] 2077/63: 7 *Yearbook* 268.

[4] 530/59: 3 *Yearbook* 184, 192.

the grounds of his detention were under continual consideration, control by the German courts as a result of the many applications submitted by the applicant and speedier proceedings . . . were thereby prevented . . .[1]

and may be subject to abuse by the applicant:

whereas the applicant filed numerous complaints against his arrest and against the seizure of his letters, which prevented the authorities pressing forward the enquiry, as the file of the case was constantly being sent from one department to another . . .[2]

or carried to the length of challenges to the impartiality both of the investigating judge and the judges of the competent court.[3]

The test of abuse here is perhaps whether the applicant has manifested an intention to delay or obstruct the proceedings. If, as in some systems, a detainee on remand is entitled to make periodic applications to the court for provisional release, it can hardly be held against him if he exercises the right; indeed, it could under the Convention be a failure to exhaust remedies if he did not do so.

This points up the fact that, when the Commission has surveyed the 'particular circumstances' of the detention complained of, it has still to decide what weight must be given to each before it can come to an opinion as to whether or not there has been a breach of Article 5 (3). As we have seen, the actual length of detention, the term of imprisonment that may be expected on conviction, the complexities and difficulties of investigating the case and preparing it for trial, the system of investigation and the way it is applied,[4] the material and moral effects of the detention, the conduct of the detainee, have all to be brought into a common focus. The actual length of detention may be so short that the complaint if manifestly ill founded, for no criminal procedure would be workable without the possibility of detention on remand; but it may be so long that the other 'particular circumstances' fall away without weight in the conclusion that the length of detention is unreasonable.

What is overriding is that detention on remand must be strictly

---

[1] 297/57: 2 *Yearbook* 204, 210, 212. Compare Indian Constitution, Article 22 (2), and *Punjab* v. *Ajaib Singh* [1953] A.I.R.: S.C. 10.

[2] Whether documents should be copied to avoid such delays, *quaere*.

[3] 2516/65.

[4] Compare *Koch Case* [1928] U.S.-Mexico Claims Commission: 4 *R.I.A.A.* 408, 410 (detention pending trial for nearly eight months held unjustifiable, the case being not complicated and there being no evidence of any investigation being carried on during the period).

justified, both as to its grounds and its length, and must not decline into a mere administrative convenience for the prosecution.[1]

Release may be conditioned by guarantees to appear from trial/La mise en liberté peut être subordonées à une garantie assurant la comparution de l'intéressé à l'audience

Bail is not specifically mentioned, perhaps because in some contracting states it is frowned on as unduly favouring persons of means, and seldom used.[2]

Since, if it appears that the trial of a detainee cannot be had in a reasonable time, he must be released pending trial, it must follow that release must not be, in effect, denied by being hedged round with too onerous guarantees. But the amount of bail would be outside the purview of the Commission, unless there appeared an element of abuse.[3]

(4) Everyone who is deprived of his liberty by arrest or detention shall be entitled to take proceedings by which the lawfulness of his detention shall be decided speedily by a court and his release ordered if the detention is now lawful.

4. Toute personne privée de sa liberté par arrestation ou détention a le droit d'introduire un recours devant un tribunal, afin qu'il statue à bref délai sur la légalité de sa détention et ordonne sa libération si la détention est illégale.

entitled to take proceedings/a le droit d'introduire un recours devant un tribunal

The principle of judicial control of every arrest or detention, whatever its form or purpose, is laid down in this paragraph, and is applied in the practice of all the contracting States. The practice of course varies

---

[1] Compare General Law Amendment Act 1962 in *South Africa*, s. 17, of which permits the detention for ninety days of persons, arrested on suspicion of committing certain political offences, for purposes of interrogation. The detainee must be visited weekly by a magistrate, but other visitors must have police permission. Detention may be ordered for a further period of ninety days 'unless he has replied satisfactorily to all questions'. No court is competent to release the detainee.

[2] In England indigent prisoners may obtain the assistance of the Official Solicitor in applying for release on bail: see Rules of the Supreme Court, O. 79, Rule 9.

[3] For a complaint of excessive bail see 1936/63: 7 *Yearbook* 236, 238, 242. For bail practice generally in *England* see M. Zander, *Criminal Law Review* (1967), 25, 100, 128.

and may take a generalized form, such as the application for a writ of habeas corpus in England; or more often the form of special proceedings, usually statutory, by way of application to the competent court or judge with an opportunity of appeal, and designed to cover the particular kind of arrest or detention of which the applicant complains.

The character and scope of this judicial control have a number of features illustrated in applications to the Commission, for the procedural guarantees, which Article 5 (4) calls for, necessarily vary. So the Court has said:

The judicial proceedings referred to in Article 5 (4) need not, it is true, always be attended by the same guarantees as those required under Article 6 (1) for civil or criminal litigation. . . .[1] None the less, it is essential that the person concerned should have access to a court and the opportunity to be heard either in person or where necessary, through some form of representation, failing which he will not have been afforded the 'fundamental guarantees of procedure applied in matters of deprivation of liberty'.[2]

First, there is the relation between Article 5 (4) and the provisions of 5 (1). A sentence of detention following conviction under 5 (1) *a* is final, even if it is for life imprisonment, in that its continuance cannot be challenged by recourse under 5 (4).[3] Again there can be no review under 5 (4) of the correctness of the conviction, on which the detention is based; however, if the continuing detention rests on unsoundness of mind of the detainee under 5 (1) *e*, this is a matter of fact that can be investigated under 5 (4).[4]

A second issue that arises is the range of the judicial process envisaged by 5 (4). Given that military discipline does not fall outside the scope of Article 5 (1), was solitary confinement in the military detention centre of Basel prison covered by 5 (1) *a*.[5] This provision

applied to any 'conviction' occasioning deprivation of liberty pronounced by a 'court', whether the conviction be classified as criminal or disciplinary in the internal law of the state in question.[6]

The chief military prosecutor, who directs the administration of military justice, had rejected the appeal of the applicant against the

---

[1] See the *de Wilde, Ooms and Versyp Judgment* (18.6.1971) § 78.
[2] Judgment in note above at § 76.
[3] 9089/80 (U.K.): 24 D.R. 227; following *Engel* Judgment No. 22 (8.6.1976).
[4] *Caprino* 6871/75 (U.K.): 22 D.R. 5; *van Droogenbroeck* Judgment No. 50 (28.11.1981).
[5] *Eggs* 7341/76 (Switzerland): 15 D.R. 35.
[6] *Engel* Judgment No. 22 (8.6.1976) para. 68.

measure. The Commission, after examining the organization of the military service, found:

a merging of powers, in the office of the chief military prosecutor, which is hardly compatible with the requirements of a judicial authority and guarantor of individual freedom.

In contrast, the Social Defence Committee in Belgium, which has the competence to order internments, was found to be independent in its composition both from the executive and the parties, and to provide adequate guarantees in its procedure—legal assistance, hearing of the applicant in person, and capacity of the applicant to present counter evidence.[1]

The Commission originally left open the question has for the principles of Article 6 (1) are applicable to the proceedings envisaged in 5 (4) in particular the principles of fair hearing and determination. But a move forward has been made by the Commission and the Court.[2]

The applicant, convicted of housebreaking, was sentenced to two years' imprisonment by the Bruges Court of Summary Jurisdiction; and, as he was a recidivist, the Court ordered that he be placed at the disposal of the Minister of Justice for ten years on the expiry of the sentence. At this time, however, he was not kept in detention, but given conditional liberty to ensure rehabilitation. Failure to comply with one of the conditions of release led to reimprisonment and release several times.

As regards the detention 'after conviction', confirmed by the Ghent Court of Appeal, the Court considered that there was a sufficient link between them within Article 5 (1) *a*, since the discretion granted to the Minister of Justice was to be exercised within the framework of the Law on Public Protection (Loi de défense sociale), under which the order, placing the detainee at the disposal of the Minister, was made, and of the sentence itself. The Recidivists Board has only an advisory function to supply the Minister with an opinion 'on the advisability of releasing recidivists and habitual offenders . . . and on the conditions' that should be attached to their release.

The Court concluded that, while Article 5 (4) does not empower the Convention organs to substitute their own discretion for that of the decision-making authority,

---

[1] 6858/74 (Belgium): 3 D.R. 139.
[2] *van Droogenbroek* Judgment No. 50 (24.6.1982) (Belgium).

... the review should however be wide enough to bear on those conditions which, under the Convention, are essential for the 'lawful' detention of a person,

and the detention

would no longer be in conformity with the Convention if it ceased to be based on reasons that are plausible and consistent with the objectives of the Social Protection Act.

Some final remarks may be made on Article 5 (4) in its applicability to extradition and deportation, and to psychiatric detention.

Extradition and deportation. Paragraph (1) *f* differs from almost all the other paragraphs of Article 5 (1), and in particular paragraph (1) *c*, in that the purpose of arrest and detention, permitted under it, is a matter of incontrovertible fact, namely, the decision of the competent authority to extradite or deport. So, while, for example, reasonable suspicion or likelihood of escape or being of unsound mind or a vagrant, are matters of the appreciation of evidence, the decision to extradite or deport is a brute fact. If we leave aside the cases, in which such a decision or order is made by a court and in which therefore an issue could hardly arise under Article 5 (4), we find this fact reflected in the practice of contracting States, in which the decision to extradite or deport is normally a ministerial or administrative act, and must, in the majority of cases, involve arrest and detention however brief. What then is the extent of the protection given by the Convention, and in particular Article 5 (4)?

We must recall here the distinction made above between the decision and order to extradite or deport, the lawfulness of that order, and the lawfulness of the detention necessary to carry it out.[1] The Commission has said that

en autorisant l'arrestation ou la détention régulières, d'une personne contre laquelle une procédure d'expulsion ou d'extradition est en cours, l'article 5 (1) *f* de la Convention confirme du reste que le domaine de l'extradition, comme celui de l'expulsion ... ne compte pas, par lui-même, au nombre des matières que régit la Convention;[2]

---

[1] A similar distinction is made in German law between the grounds and lawfulness of extradition or deportation (*materialrechtliche Würdigung des Sachverhaltes*) and the lawfulness of detention (*formellrechtlichen Haftvoraussetzungen*).

[2] 1405/62: *Recueil* (1963) ii. See also 1211/61: *Recueil* (1962) ii.

and so while there may be a question whether the extradition or deportation order is consistent with other provisions of the Convention, such as Articles 3 or 8, the lawfulness of the order under domestic law, the questions whether, for example, the case falls within the terms of the applicable extradition agreement, or whether a political offence is involved, or whether the order is in excess of authority or is a *détournement de pouvoir*, fall as such outside the competence of the Commission under Article 5 (4). The European Extradition Convention makes no reference to the Human Rights Convention, and indicates in Article 22 that rules of domestic law are to be followed in response to requests for extradition.

Article 5 (4) is directed to the lawfulness of the detention, and not to the merits of the decision to extradite or deport, or to the lawfulness of the order executing that decision.[1] It follows that Article 5 (4) is satisfied where there is a determination by a court of the authority in law for detention with a view to extradition or deportation. It may of course be that under the domestic law the court is competent to pass upon the lawfulness of the order for extradition or deportation, as well as on the lawfulness of the detention, and it may be that in some cases the second will entail the first. But a contracting State is not, it seems, obliged by Article 5 (4) so to extend the competence of the court.

Psychiatric detention. The position of those of unsound mind presents problems of access to justice, required by Article 5 (4), and also of the determination of the lawfulness of their detention. So the Court has said:

... it is essential that the person concerned should have access to a court and the opportunity to be heard either in person or, where necessary, through some form of representation ... Mental illness may entail restricting or modifying the manner of exercise of such a right, ... but it cannot justify impairing the very essence of the right. Indeed, special procedural safeguards may prove called for in order to protect the interests of persons, who on account of their mental disabilities, are not fully capable of acting for themselves.

In a later case[2] the Court derived from the deficiencies it found in the *habeas corpus* proceedings, available to a detainee in the Divisional Court in England, the principles upon which the decision as to the

[1] 858/60: 4 *Yearbook* 224. Compare Cour d'Appel, Bruxelles (31.8.1962): *Journal des Trib.* (1962) 498; *Caprino* 6871 (75) (U.K.): 12 D.R. 14.
[2] *X. v. United Kingdom: Judgment* No. 46 (5.11.1981) pp. 56–8.

lawfulness of detention should be based under Article 5 (4). The Judgment needs quotation at length:

In *habeas corpus* proceedings, in examining an administrative decision to detain, the court's task is to inquire whether the detention is in compliance with the requirements stated in the relevant legislation and with the applicable principles of the common law. According to these principles, such a decision—even though technically legal on its face—may be upset inter alia, if the detaining authority misused its powers by acting in bad faith or capriciously or for a wrongful purpose,[1] or if the decision is supported by no sufficient evidence or is one which no reasonable person could have reached in the circumstances.[2] Subject to the foregoing, the court will not be able to review the grounds or merits of a decision taken by an administrative authority to the extent that under the legislation in question these are exclusively a matter for determination by that authority.

The Court recognized that *habeas corpus* proceedings can be an effective check on arbitrariness, where emergency measures for detention of persons of unsound mind are taken, and are of short duration:

on the other hand, in the Court's opinion, a judicial review as limited as that available in the *habeas corpus* procedure in the present case is not sufficient for a continuing confinement. . . . The review should, however, be wide enough to bear on those conditions which, according to the Convention, are essential for the 'lawful' detention of a person on the ground of unsoundness of mind, especially as the reasons capable of initially justifying such detention may cease to exist . . . This means that in the instant case, Article 5 (4) required an appropriate procedure allowing a court to examine whether the patient's disorder still persisted and whether the Home Secretary was entitled to think that a continuation of the compulsory confinement was in the interests of public safety.[3]

Under the Mental Health Act (1959) s.66, the Home Secretary has discretion[4] to hold, release, or recall, a person of unsound mind in detention. The Court found the system inconsistent within Article 5 (4).[5]

---

[1] See *R.* v. *Governor of Brixton Prison. ex pte Sarno* [1916] 2 K.B. 42: *R.* v. *Governor of Brixton Prison, ex pte Soblen* [1962] 3 A.E.R. 641.

[2] *Shahid Igbal* [1978] 3 W.L.R. 884; *Zamir* v. *Secretary of State* [1980] 2 A.E.R. 768.

[3] For the application of *habeas corpus* proceedings, being found adequate, to detention under the U.K. Prevention of Terrorism Act (1976) see *McVeigh et al.* (U.K.) 8022/77: 25 D.R. 15.

[4] The Home Secretary is under no obligation to submit medical or other evidence, justifying detention, to the Divisional Court.

[5] A claim for release on licence from service of sentence after conviction, even for life

speedily/en bref delai

What is the length of time that may be acceptable for the procedures of Articles 5 and 6 will vary, despite the similarity of the language. 'Promptly/aussitôt' in Article 5 (3) implies immediate transfer of the detainee to a judicial authority; 'speedily/en bref delai' implies that detention must be terminated without delay, if its lawfulness is challenged in a court, and is by due process found wanting; while 'reasonable time/delai raisonnable' in Article 6 (1) applies to extended civil litigation or criminal process, in which appeals may come into account. In general, the length of time taken by these various procedures will depend on their purpose and structure, and the actual conduct of them by the authorities and by the individual concerned.

The Court has drawn attention to the distinctions that must be drawn, in the application of 'speedily' in Article 5 (4), on the one hand, between detention ordered by an administrative body or by a court at the close of judicial proceedings; and on the other hand, between normal imprisonment and psychiatric detention, which calls in any case for review at reasonable intervals.[1]

and his release ordered if the detention is not lawful/et ordonne sa libération si la détention est illégale

It would be natural perhaps to assume that, where detention is found to be unlawful or no longer justifiable, release of the detainee would follow as of course. But an application against the Netherlands raised the question whether the courts were competent to order release, after passing on the lawfulness of detention with a view to extradition or deportation. In the words of a Netherlands court:[2]

the issue of admitting and expelling foreigners is a matter involving the exercise of governmental authority and is therefore not subject to judicial examination, unless in a particular case there is a question of détournement du pouvoir or a wholly arbitrary act on the part of the State.

In an earlier application[3] the Commission had said:

imprisonment, is not a challenge to the lawfulness of the detention under Article 5 (4), as a claim for release from psychiatric detention may be: 9089/90 (U.K.) 34 D.R. 227.

[1] *Luberti* Judgment No. 75 (Italy) (23.2.1984).
[2] Arrondissementzrechtbank, Rotterdam (6.6.1963).
[3] 1211/61: *Recueil* (1962) ii.

it is true that Dutch law does not provide for any specific procedure by which he might have challenged the deportation order as such; whereas, however, the Applicant had, according to the general principles of Dutch law, the possibility of taking action before the courts on the grounds that his detention and subsequent deportation from the Netherlands constituted an abuse of power on the part of the authorities which were responsible for the measures taken against him; whereas the Applicant has not availed himself of this possibility and therefore has not exhausted the remedies available to him under Dutch law;

The procedure described is governed by Civil Code, s. 1401. According to practice under this section, the court may, if it finds, for example, that a detention order is unlawful as being a *détournement de pouvoir* or *abus de pouvoir*, give a declaratory judgment to that effect, or direct payment of compensation, or order *restitutio in integrum*, or order discontinuance of the wrong with a fine in addition of each day of non-compliance. Since the court had a discretion as to which of these courses it might adopt, an applicant maintained that, in the case of detention found to be unlawful under the section, release was not mandatory, and that, while the procedure satisfied the main part of Article 5 (4), the final clause was not met. But, even if the conformity of the procedure with Article 5 (4) was not apparent on the face of s. 1401 and the practice, no breach of the paragraph could be established unless it could be shown that the court had, in a given case of unlawful detention, failed to order release. This the applicant failed to show either in his own case or any other.[1] The position has now been placed beyond doubt by new legislation[2] which makes an order for release from detention mandatory in the circumstances described.

Detention that is unduly prolonged may also lose the character of being detention with a view to extradition or deportation. Administrative difficulties or delays may arise in the way of sending the detainee out of the country. Where they are of his own making and in his own interest, the continued detention could hardly be improper. So where detention was prolonged, first to enable the detainee to come to an arrangement with the authorities of his country of nationality as to his treatment after deportation, and later to challenge the order for deportation in the courts, the Commission found no reason for complaint.[3] But where, after a deportation order had been made, it

[1] 1983/63: *Recueil* 20. See also 2621/65.
[2] Vreemdelingenwet (Aliens Act) 13.1.1965: *Staatsblad* 40.
[3] 1983/63.

was reported that there was no possibility in the foreseeable future of deporting the detainee either to Yugoslavia, of which he was a national but whose authorities showed no readiness to grant a passport, or to any other country, a German court refused to renew the detention order and released the detainee, saying:

... Further, a longer period of detention would offend against the Convention of Human Rights, and in particular the principles laid down in Article 5; for it would be out of proportion to the intended objective, and would, by becoming in effect of indefinite duration, lose its character of a provisional measure (*verliert wegen ihrer im Ergebnis unbestimmten Dauer den Charakter einer vorläufigen Massnahme*).[1]

(5) Everyone who has been the victim of arrest or detention in contravention of the provisions of this Article shall have an enforceable right to compensation.

5. Toute personne victime d'une arrestation ou d'une détention dans des conditions contraires aux dispositions de cet article a droit à réparation.

This paragraph, which appeared in the first United Kingdom draft, was struck out by the Committee of Experts on the grounds that 'it might be held to impose on States Parties to the Convention an obligation to ensure the payment of damages, for example, by persons ordered to pay them as a result of a civil action',[2] but it was reinstated by the Conference of Senior Officials, which reported that the paragraph created

the right to compensation to repair the harm ... suffered as a result of arrest and illegal detention. The action should be taken against the person or persons responsible.[3]

The second sentence, as will be seen, is not very happily worded.

---

[1] Amtsgericht, Köln (10.3.1965). Compare Fugitive Offenders Act 1881, c. 7, in U.K. which provides that a fugitive offender committed to prison may, if not conveyed out of the country within one month, be discharged out of custody 'unless sufficient cause is shown to the contrary': *in re Shuter* (No. 2 [1959] 3 A.E.R. 481 (committal had been on 15 July and flight arranged was postponed to 17 August: held that, given serious character of the offences, a delay of a day or two was not unreasonable). A similar provision is to be found in Extradition Act 1870, s. 12.

[2] Doc. CM/WP 1 (50) 15 (16.3.1950).

[3] Doc. CM/WP 4 (50) 19 (19.6.1950).

victim/victime

The use of this emotive word is not, as will be seen under Article 25 where it appears again, altogether easy to understand. If it simply describes a person who has been subjected to arrest or detention it seems otiose; or the paragraph might be read as not giving a right to compensation for technical errors, which might have caused no real injury or even inconvenience, as requiring proof of some special damage. A third possibility is that the word is not used to express the extent of injury at all, but rather to exclude claims for compensation by 'strangers': in other words, only the individual, who has himself been arrested or detained, has a right to compensation under the paragraph.

An early decision[1] of the Commission gives some support to the second construction without, however, excluding the third. It appears that by an error a warrant of arrest had been issued by the competent judge and the applicant had been arrested at 7.15 in the morning; he was, however, released, on discovery of the error, the same morning. The Commission held his complaint of deprivation of liberty to be manifestly ill founded, but did not elaborate.[2]

shall have an enforceable right to compensation/a droit à réparation

The English and French texts are a little out of step. The word 'enforceable' is not represented in the French text and appears to add nothing to the sense of the clause. Further 'réparation' has a slightly wider connotation than 'compensation', which would normally mean payment of money or money's worth, and for which 'dédommagement' or even 'dommages-intérêts' might have been expected as the equivalent.

It is plain that the right to compensation is conditioned on a breach of one of the provisions of Article 5:

> The right of an individual to claim compensation under the Article for a wrongful detention is conditional upon a finding of a breach by a Respondent Government of at least one of the specific provisions of Article 5.[3]

[1] 89/55: 1 *Yearbook* 226.

[2] His request for legal aid had been rejected by the competent courts, on the ground that there was no causal link between the arrest complained of and the loss of employment and a bicycle, and ill health, alleged by him, and therefore his action for damages against the issuer of the warrant had no chance of success.

[3] 760/60, 791/60: *Recueil* (1961) i; confirmed by the conclusion of the court in the *Lawless Case*: 4 *Yearbook* 486.

But how is the breach to be found? If the provisions of Article 5 are held to form part of the domestic law of a particular contracting State, upon a holding by its courts that an arrest or detention was unlawful as being contrary to one of those provisions, the right to compensation under paragraph (5) would be directly enforceable under the domestic law. Denial of the right would then be a new breach of the Convention that could, subject to the exhaustion of domestic remedies,[1] be a matter of application to the Commission.

It is necessary to distinguish here the following elements:

(*a*) the lawfulness of a measure of detention under the domestic law;
(*b*) the consistency of a measure of detention with paragraphs 5 (1) or (4);
(*c*) right to compensation where measure is inconsistent with paragraphs 5 (1) or (4).

The Commission does not have to investigate (*a*), but only to determine (*b*) and then, if necessary, make a recommendation on (*c*).

(*a*) is then a question of fact. The unlawfulness of the measure of detention will be established formally or subtantially by a domestic court, evidence of which will be presented to the Commission.[2] It will be then for the Commission to determine whether this unlawful detention is a measure inconsistent with one of paragraphs 5 (1)–(4): (*c*). If a breach of the Convention is then found, (*b*) will be then applied.

ARTICLE 6

(1) In the determination of his civil rights and obligations or of any criminal charge against him, everyone is entitled to a fair and public hearing within a reasonable time by an independent and impartial tribunal established by law. Judgment shall be pronounced publicly but the press and public may be excluded from all or part of the trial in the interests of morals, public order, or national security in a democratic society, where the

---

[1] See in *Germany*: Bundesgerichtshof (10.1.1966): *N.J.W.* (1966) 726. Article 5 (5) accords a directly enforceable remedy to the injured party (*unmittelbare Schadenersatzansprüche*). The court observed that in the adoption of the Convention it had not been considered necessary to pass an executory law (*besonderes Ausführungsgesetz*) in addition to the law adopting it (*Zustimmungsgesetz*).

[2] *Huber* 6821/74 (Austria): 6 D.R. 65; and 7950/77 (Austria): 19 D.R. 21.

interests of juveniles or the protection of the private life of the parties so require, or to the extent strictly necessary in the opinion of the court in special circumstances where publicity would prejudice the interests of justice.

1. Toute personne a droit à ce que sa cause soit entendue équitablement, publiquement et dans un délai raisonnable, par un tribunal indépendant et impartial, établi par la loi, qui décidera, soit des contestations sur ses droits et obligations de caractère civil, sout du bien-fondé de toute accusation en matière pénale dirigée contre elle. Le jugement doit être rendu publiquement, mais l'accès de la salle d'audience peut être interdit à la presse et au public pendant la totalité ou une partie du procès dans l'intérêt de la moralité, de l'ordre public ou de la sécurité nationale dans une société démocratique, lorsque les intérêts des mineurs ou la protection de la vie privée des parties au procès l'exigent, ou dans la mesure jugée strictement nécessaire par le tribunal, lorsque dans des circonstances spéciales la publicité serait de nature à porter atteinte aux intérêts de la justice.

This paragraph establishes the principle of fair hearing in certain judicial proceedings, and rules concerning publicity of those proceedings.

The first sentence retained in great part its original form throughout the drafting process,[1] but one not insignificant change was made towards the end. It had read: 'In the determination of any criminal charge against him or of his *rights and obligations in a suit at law*'.... The French text, which has a different syntactical structure and has remained unchanged throughout, has, for the words italicized, 'ses droits et obligations de caractère civil'.

Both texts were so worded in the draft of the Convention forwarded by the Consultative Assembly to the Committee of Ministers for their session in Rome on 3–4 November 1950. It appears that on 3 November, the day before the Convention was signed, a committee of legal experts was still working on 'minor points of drafting'.[2] This

---

[1] It is now substantially the same as the second and third sentences of the First U.N. Covenant, Article 14 (1).

[2] *T.P.* iv. 1007–1119.

paragraph is not mentioned in their report, but in the final text the
expression 'civil rights and obligations' appears in subtitution for the
words italicized. The purpose of this change is not clear but, given the
constant form of the French text, it can hardly have been other than
simply to bring the English expression more closely into linguistic line
with the French.

The earlier history of these expressions[1] does not reveal any
decisive factor. Article 10 of the Universal Declaration speaks of the
'determination of his rights and obligations and of any criminal charge
against him'. An earlier French version of the text had contained the
qualification 'en matière civile', but this had been voted out by the
General Assembly Third Committee.[2] Article 13, now Article 14, of
the C.P.R. Covenant reverted to the earlier language, 'droits et
obligations de caractère civil', which was represented in English by
'rights and obligations in a suit at law', and there is some evidence that
the intention of the drafters was to confine the terms to litigation
between individuals, and to exclude, in particular, from Article 6 (1),
administrative proceedings or decisions.[3]

Yet the U.N. Commission of Human Rights at its sixth session
appears to have been of the opinion that the expression did or should
apply to any contentious proceedings; and it stressed the importance
of Article 14

since, in the last analysis, the implementation of all the rights in the Covenant
depended upon the proper administration of justice.

Whatever its precise meaning the language of Article 13, later
Article 14, of the C.P.R. Covenant was, as already indicated, taken
without change into the first draft of Article 6 (1) of the Convention.

A right to access to justice, to the courts which may administer it, is
necessarily entailed by Article 7;[4] but there is not any formulation of it
in the Convention, or recognition in Article 6 of the ways in which it is
obstructed in common practice.

A series of applications from individuals in prison in the United
Kingdom complained of prevention of correspondence or communication with a solicitor, where legal advice was being sought for

---

[1] See J. Velu, 'Le problème de l'application aux juridictions adminsitratives des
règles de la Convention européenne des Droits de l'Homme relative à la publicité des
audiences et des jugements', *Revue D.I. et D. Comp. Belge* (1961) 129.

[2] Op. cit. 142–6.   [3] Op. cit. 151–6.

[4] *Golder* Judgment No. 13 (U.K. (21.2.1975) § 35.

possible action over alleged ill-treatment in prison. The practice was to require any such complaint to be handled wholly by internal procedure, and any correspondence relating to it would be stopped. One application was settled on particular facts in 1972,[1] but in November 1981 a change of practice was made relating to the settlement of the application. Without admitting any admission of a breach of the Convention, the Government stated that:

Prisoners will continue to be required to raise complaints about prison treatment through the appropriate internal channel so that the prison authorities may know about the complaint, investigate it, and take any action that may be necessary. However, the prisoner will not have to await the outcome of the investigation before being able to raise the complaint internally.[2]

The costs of legal proceedings are obviously a limitation on the right of access to the courts, particularly where there is no possibility of free proceedings or repayment of costs;[3] and the requirement of payment of security for costs can in some circumstances amount to a denial of access.[4]

The place of immunity from jurisdiction of the courts demands more explanation than it has been given; for it is at least an exception to the rule of Article 6, to which the Convention text itself is not adjusted. The Commission has observed that:

The principle of immunity in respect of such statements [in Parliament] is generally recognised as a consequence of an 'effective political democracy' within the meaning of the Preamble to the Convention ... This affords absolute protection to persons making such statements ... The applicant does not have any right in United Kingdom law to protection of his reputation in so far as it may be affected by the statements complained of.[5]

Again, an applicant, injured while on duty in the voluntary armed forces of the United Kingdom, was granted a pension in lieu of any right of action against the State. Under the Crown Proceedings Act

---

[1] 4115/63: 36 *Recueil* 43.

[2] *Reed* (U.K.) 7360/76: 25 D.R. 9. See also *Hilton* (U.K.) 5613/72: 4 D.R. 177 and C.M. Decision 24.4.79; *Kiss* (U.K.) 6224/1973: 7 D.R. 55 and C.M. Decision 19.4.1978. The effect of the 'internal ventilation' requirement still came into consideration in Campbell (7819/77) 14 D.R. 186, and *Fell* (7878/77) 23 D.R. 102.

[3] 6202/79 (Netherlands): 1 D.R. 66, and 2158/78 (U.K.): 21 D.R. 95 (refusal of legal aid).

[4] 7973/77 (Sweden): 17 D.R. see 1307/61 (F.R.G.) (imposition of security for costs). Related in effect is constraint to pay a fine by way of settlement of criminal proceedings: *de Weer Judgment* (Belgium) No. 35 (27.2.1980).

[5] *Agee* (U.K.) 7729/76: 7 D.R. 165, 175.

(1947) 9, 10, no member of the armed forces, who has suffered injury while on duty, shall subject the Crown, or any other person considered liable in tort to an action, if the Minister of Social Services certifies a right of that member to a pension. The Commission, leaving aside the question whether any 'civil rights' of the applicant could be involved in the case, considered that s. 10 operated as a *defence* in the event of any action being brought, and that 'the mere existence of this defence [did not mean] that the applicant was denied access to the courts'.[1] There are two lines of reasoning apparent in these decisions. On the one hand it is said that, given the immunity of Parliament, the individual has no civil right in law in respect of statements made in Parliament,[2] and Article 6 (1) does not therefore come in to account. On the other hand, it is suggested that immunity is a *defence* to any action brought, and is absolute. The first line is perhaps logically to be preferred, though its consistency with Article 17 of the Civil and Political Rights Covenant can be questioned; of the second line it may be asked in what sense is the defence *absolute*, and whether, for example, Parliament can withdraw the immunity of a member in respect of a statement made.

determination/. . . décidera

The words relate primarily to the decision on the merits of the case, and to its finality; but such determination may be part of the judicial or the administrative process. It is necessary then to distinguish judicial and administrative decisions; and this can be further illustrated in the relation of Article 6 (1) to proceedings under Article 5.

The distinction is shown in two cases described below. In one there was the involvement of an administrative authority indirectly in the dismissal of an individual from employment; in the other there was restrictive regulation of an insurance company, in the exercise of statutory powers.

In the contract of employment the functions of the employer and of the related administrative authority were seen to be separable. The employee was an interior decorator working under contract with a limited liability company in the Hague. The company, acting under the terms of the special decree on Labour Relations, requested the

---

[1] 7443/36 (U.K.): 8 D.R. 216. See also U.K. State Immunity Act (1978).
[2] The right to respect for reputation has been recognized as a civil right by the Commission: 8366/78 (Luxembourg): 16 D.R. 196.

Director of the Regional Office to authorize the termination of the contract and dismissal of the employee, such authorization being required by the statue. On the claim by the employee that Article 6 had not been complied with—no hearing before the Director of the Regional Labour officer—the Commission found that:

... the procedure of which the applicant complains concerns relations between the relevant administrative authority ... and the employer. It is incontestable that the decision on dismissal rests ultimately with the employer himself. The Commission considers therefore that, even if it is admitted that the procedure in question may have affected the rights and obligations deriving from the relations between the applicant and his employer, it cannot be considered in any way to have decisively determined civil rights and obligations within the meaning of Article 6 (1) ...[1]

The question whether proceedings under Article 5 (3) or (4) could involve the determination of 'civil rights and obligations' and so attract Article 6 (1) was earlier left open by the Commission.[2] But it has later said that the classification of a prisoner in Category A (high security) did not involve 'civil rights and obligations',[3] and that an order for deportation is not a 'determination' of them, though it may of course effect them, for the right of an alien to enter and reside is separate[4] being derived from public law.

In general, hearings or enquiries preliminary or auxiliary to trial, and interlocating proceedings, are excluded from the full applications of Article 6 (1). The conclusion was reached by the Court in the Neumeister case,[5] in which it interpreted Article 5 (4) in terms of its language in comparison with Article 6 (1):

[Article 5 (4)] while requiring that such proceedings [against detention on remand] shall be allowed, stipulates that they should be taken before a 'court'. This term implies that the authority called upon to decide thereon must possess a judicial character, that is to say, be independent both of the executive and of the parties to the case; it in no way relates to the procedure to be followed. In addition, the provision in question also lays down that such remedies must be determined *speedily*, (the French text uses the somewhat less expressive term 'bref délai'). This clearly indicates what the main concern must be in this matter. Full written proceedings or an oral of the parties in the

---

[1] 8974/80 (Netherlands): 24 D.R. 187. The second case: *Kaplan* (U.K.) 7598/76 is described below.   [2] 1599/62.
[3] 8575/79 (U.K.): 20 D.R. 202.   [4] 7901/77 (U.K.): 9 D.R. 224.
[5] Judgment (27.6.1968) §§ 22–5; see also 6541/74 (F.R.G.): 1 D.R. 82.

examination of such remedies would be a source of delay, which it is important to avoid in this field.

Post-trial proceedings. Proceedings subsequent to trial may take the
form of appeal, against conviction or sentence in criminal matters;
revision, or retrial.[1] Unlike the C.P.R. Covenant, which in Article
15 (5) confers a right of 'review by a higher tribunal' in criminal
matters, neither Article 6 nor any other provision of the Convention
requires any of the proceedings by way of appeal, revision, or retrial,
to be made available as of right. It follows that Article 6 does not
govern applications for leave to appeal, or for revision, or for retrial.
Further, where under the domestic law there is provision for any of
these proceedings the modalities are solely determined[2] by that law.

Nevertheless, the proceedings by way of appeal, revision, or retrial
must be conducted so as to assure justice according to law. So where
Article 349 (2) of the German Code of Criminal Procedure provides
that an appeal may be rejected by the Supreme Court (Bundesgerichtshof) without an oral and public hearing of the parties, the
Commission found that Article 6 (1) was applicable, but that there was
no inconsistency with it, given that

the Public Prosecutor and Applicant, notwithstanding the fact that they were
not present at the hearing, had the possibility of presenting their arguments to
the court in writing[3]

so that equality was preserved.

Again, whether the possibility of further appeal is open,

it should be considered whether the notion of a fair trial within the meaning of
Article 6 (1) ... might not signify that a court must state in detail the reasons
for its decision in order that, on appeal from that decision, the defence might
be properly safeguarded ...[4]

Constitutional appeals although, as will be seen, they are ex-
haustible remedies for the purpose of Article 26, are no exception to
the principle just stated. The Commission has observed that the

---

[1] See p. 146 below for an explanation of these terms.
[2] But subject probably to the principle of non-discrimination embodied in Article 14:
see, for example, a decision of the Bavarian Constitutional Court (16.1.1961): 42–vi–59
(the categories of persons entitled to appeal to the Constitutional Court must be defined
objectively and must not discriminate against aliens).
[3] 599/59: *Recueil* (1961)i.
[4] 1035/61: *Recueil* (1963) i. See further below under 'fair hearing'.

appeal committee (Dreiausschuss) of the Federal Constitutional Court in Germany

n'avait pas pour fonction de juger l'affaire elle-même, mais uniquement de décider si les conditions régissant la saisine de la Cour avaient bien été remplies; ... que cette décision ne constitue pas une décision relative soit à une contestation ... soit au bien-fondé [in sense of Article 6 (1)] ... qu'il en résulte que ... le Comité de Trois Juges n'était pas un Tribunal auquel sont applicables les dispositions de l'Article 6 ...[1]

and this remains true even if the applications committee

en rejetant le recours constitutionnel aurait pu, dans une certaine mesure, se prononcer également sur le bien-fondé de la requête.[2]

However, the position might be different if an appellate court were, in the interest of justice, to treat an application for leave to appeal as, in effect, the appeal itself and to proceed to determine it.

A distinction must also be made, for purposes of Article 6 (1), between appeal against conviction and appeal against sentence, only the former ranking as a continuing determination of a criminal charge. Thus the provisions of Article 6

relate to the establishment of the guilt of the accused and do not concern the determination of the actual penalty to be inflicted upon the convicted person within the range of penalties authorized by the relevant penal law.[3]

The position under the Convention of applications for revision or retrial and of proceedings, where they are allowed, will be considered further below.

civil rights and obligations/droits et obligations de caractère civil

Two approaches are possible to this expression: to construe it in terms of the domestic law of the contracting State in which it comes in issue, or to assign a general meaning to it. On the first approach, civil rights would be found to have a wider connotation in some countries than

---

[1] 436/58: 2 *Yearbook* 386, 390.

[2] 441/58: 2 *Yearbook* 391, 396, having regard to Article 91*a* of the Statute of The Constitutional Court: see also 673/59: *Recueil* (1961) i; 4 *Yearbook* 594, and 742/60: ibid. 290; and 1552/62: *Recueil* (1963) iii.

[3] 343/57: 4 *Yearbook* 588. Compare *Germany*: Bayerischer Verfassungsgericht (19.6.1959) (Article 6 contains *procedural* guarantees).

others, and it would not be a correct approach to the interpretation of
a treaty. The Commission has rejected it saying:

la Commission tient à constater qu'il n'y a pas lieu de rechercher si le droit
revendiqué constitue un 'droit civil' aux termes du droit autrichien; qu'en
effet, la notion de 'droits et contestations de caractère civil', employée à
l'article 6 § 1 de la Convention, ne saurait être interprétée comme simple
renvoi au droit interne de la Haute Partie Contractante mise en cause, mais
ou'il s'agit bien au contraire, d'une notion autonome qu'il faut interpréter
indépendamment des droits internes des Hautes Parties Contractantes même
si les principes généraux du droit interne des Hautes Parties Contractantes
doivent nécessaire être pris en considération lors d'une telle interprétation;[1]

But in treating it as a 'notion autonome' we are still faced with alternative constructions. Here the abrupt alteration of the text, already
described, in the preparatory work serves only to obscure the issue.
The expression 'civil rights' has in English a political rather than a
legal flavour, being close to the rotunder 'civil liberties'. These rights
and liberties attach to the individual as πολιτικὸν ξῷον, to be maintained not so much against other individuals as against the community
as a whole, and particularly against the State as the focus of its power.

Where the expression has been given statutory form it has been
broadly interpreted. So the Judicial Committee of the Privy Council
held that an Act of the Parliament of Canada was *ultra vires* since

its provisions were concerned directly with the civil rights of both employers
and employed in the Province . . . for it set up a Board of Inquiry which could
summon them before it, administer to them oaths, call for their papers, and
enter their premises . . . It interfered further with civil rights when, by section
56, it suspended liberty to lock-out or strike during a reference to the Board,[2]

---

[1] 1931/63. Compare 808/60: '. . . the question whether a right or obligation is of a civil
nature within Article 6 (1) . . . does not depend on the particular procedure prescribed
by domestic law for its determination but solely on an appreciation of the claim itself': 5
Yearbook 122 (action for defamation classified in Austrian law as a criminal proceeding).
For a full review of the decisions of the Commission in 423/58; 808/61; and 1931/63 and
an analysis of 'civil rights' in Article 6 (1) see *Austria*: Verfassungsgerichtshof
(14.10.1965): *Österr. Juristen-Zeitung* [1966] 409. Compare also in *Germany*: Bundesgerichtshof (20.7.1964): decision of a disciplinary tribunal on the professional conduct of
an advocate not covered by Article 6 and in particular Article 6 (2): *N.J.W.* (1964). 2119.
[2] *Toronto Electric Commissioners* v. *Attorneys General for Canada and Ontario* [1925] A.C.
396, 403, construing British North America Act 1867, s. 92 (13) reserving 'property and
civil rights' in a Province to the Provincial legislature.

and again that Federal Legislation, which prohibited 'the manufacture importation, sale or possession' of any substitute for butter, made in whole or part from any fat other than of milk or cream, affected 'civil rights' in the Province and was *ultra vires*.[1] These constructions appear to be saying that among the civil rights involved in these cases were broad rights to freedom of industrial action, to privacy, and to engage in trade.

A broad construction of 'civil rights and obligations' in Article 6 (1) would then cover all rights or obligations enforceable at law, regardless of whether the parties were individuals, corporations, or public authorities, or the State itself. It has some support in the fact that the expressions 'civil rights' or 'civil and political rights' have been adopted to describe the contents of the C.P.R. Covenant, which corresponds of course at many points to Section I of the European Convention; for if Section I is therefore to be regarded as embodying 'civil rights', that is rights and freedoms of the individual as member of a political community, it would seem natural to construe the expression as it appears in Article 6 (1) in the same way.

The alternative construction is narrower. Borrowing the municipal law distinction between private law and public law, it would limit civil rights and obligations to those arising or perhaps capable of arising, in the co-ordinate legal relations between individuals. 'Civil' would then be understood as denoting rights and obligations under civil as distinct from administrative law, criminal law, constitutional law, and so on. This construction conforms better with the French text, which, it will be recalled, remained unchanged throughout the preparatory work.

The Commission, without attempting a comprehensive definition for purposes of Article 6 of 'civil rights and obligation', has inclined towards the narrower construction.

It will be convenient to illustrate, first, areas of public policy and administration, where, in the view of the Commission, the contacts and relations between individuals and public authority do not involve and cannot give rise to civil rights and obligations. So the Commission has said that:

---

[1] Dairy Industries Act [R.S.C. 1927, c. 45], s. 5a: *Canadian Federation of Agriculture* v. *Attorney General for Quebec* [1951] A.C. 179. Compare also *in re Storgoff* [1945] S.C.R. 526, 578: 'criminal proceedings abound with civil rights'.

... by building regulations, promulgated in the public interest by the State as the supreme authority, especially standards concerning building heights and provisions for the implementation thereof, do not give rise to legal relations between owners and the State which could be termed civil rights and obligations within meaning of Article 6 (1) ...[1]

An applicant, in an earlier case, complained of a decision of the City of Hamburg to widen the street, in which his house was situated; he had refused to sell to the competent authority a small portion of his front garden to assist the widening. He challenged the decision in the administrative courts, and appealed to the Federal Administrative Court, without success. He made a number of complaints of the court proceedings to the effect that requirements of Article 6 has not been observed. The Commission held that:

... the proceedings that the applicant had instituted before the administrative courts did not concern the determination of any of his private rights in relation to his property. The purpose of his complaint was to obtain a judgment from the courts setting aside an administrative act, which the authorities had taken in the execution of their aim to provide for safe roads. Accordingly, the relevant proceedings concerned the exercise of the duties and powers of the competent authority in the implementation of the above aim, as well as the rights of the individual arising out of this bilateral relationship, which clearly falls in the domain of public law.[2]

Pensions, which are granted from State funds and are non-contributory, again are outside the reach of civil rights.[3]

Entry to and residence in a country is not a civil right; and a

---

[1] 9607/81 (Switzerland): 28 D.R. 248. But fixing compensation for the taking of property in the public interest is a determination of civil rights, given the tortious element: *Andorfer Tonwerke* (Austria) 7987/77: Report; compensation for victims of Nazi persecution is, in contrast, solely a matter of public law: 7014/75 (F.R.G.) 5 D.R. 134.

[2] 5428/72 (F.R.G.): 44 *Recueil* 49: Article 6 (1) does not therefore extend to an *actio popularis*. The reasoning is similar in *Gonriet* v. *Union of Post Office Workers* [1977] 3 A.E.R. 70 (House of Lords). A similar distinction is made between a property right and the procedure for its acquisition: so ownership of a patent involves civil rights and obligations, but the formalities to be complied with to acquire a valid patent do not attract Article 6 (1): 7830/77 (Austria) 14 D.R. 200, 8000/77 (Switzerland) 13 D.R. 81.

[3] 5715/72 (F.R.G.): 44 *Recueil* 77 (claim by family for war-pension relying exclusively on public law and outside Article 6 (1)); as also 8149/78 (Austria) (grant of non-contributory pension to those injured in a mountain rescue operation); and unilateral payments of insurance in military service (no contract): 8341/78 (Switzerland): 20 D.R. 161 and 3959/69 (Austria) 35 *Recueil* 109.

decision to deport an alien does not constitute a determination of civil rights;[1] it is in fact 'a discretionary act by a public authority'.[2]

Appointments and dismissals in the public service do not involve civil rights and obligations, and even where, as often in Convention countries, there are disciplinary boards or administrative courts competent to handle disputes or complaints, the requirements of Article 6 are not applicable to the proceedings. So where an assistant judge (*Hilfsrichter*) was dismissed by an administrative decision of the president of the Land Court of Appeal (Oberlandesgericht), and the decision was affirmed by the administrative court of appeal (Oberverwaltungsgericht), the Commission said:

... the case of the Applicant concerns the question of his admission to a permanent post as a public servant with the German administration; and, ... it is clear that the determination of the Applicant's right to be admitted to a permanent post does not fall within the meaning of Article 6 because this question is not one of a determination of the Applicant's civil rights or obligations ...[3]

Taxation, though plainly a matter of public law, may give rise to questions under Article 6. Article 1 of the First Protocol recognizes the right of the State 'to secure the payment of taxes', but it does not prescribe how this may be done: in particular it does not require that the assessment or exaction of tax shall of necessity be subjected at some point to judicial review: in other words, the imposition and collection of taxes can, consistently with Article 1 of the Protocol, be left exclusively in the hands of the executive without reference to the courts, provided the law established so prescribes. So a formal inquiry in which a tax officer is only gathering information and has no power to impose any tax liability is not bound by the principle *audi alteram partem*.[4] But suppose the fiscal legislation establishes agencies to review tax assessments, made by executive authority but challenged by

---

[1] 7902/77 (U.K.): 9 D.R. 224, repeating 3325/67 (U.K.): 25 *Recueil* 117.

[2] 8244/78 (U.K.): 17 D.R. 149.

[3] 423/58; 9937/69: 32 *Recueil* 61. Similar reasoning was applied to exclude from civil rights and obligations issues of religious practice of a minister in the state church system in Denmark. The applicant had made it a condition of baptism that the parents of child should attend five periods of religious instruction: his refusal to abandon the practice was referred to an advisory Court. The Commission held that no civil rights were involved and that Article 6 (1) was not applicable to any action taken by the Church Ministry: 7374/76: 5 D.R. 157. But see *obiter dicta* on civil rights of Social Insurance Office employee: *Preikhzas* 8504/74 (F.R.G.) 16 D.R. 5.

[4] *Guay* v. *Lafleur* [1965] 47 D.L.R. 2ᵈ 226 (no infringement of Canadian Bill of Rights, 1960 5.2(*e*)).

the taxpayer, and requires agencies in effect to act quasi-judicially, and suppose further that decisions of the agencies are themselves subject to appeal to the higher courts. Must the agencies conduct themselves as tribunals governed by the provisions of Article 6 (1), and must the higher courts, when considering their decisions on appeal, be held to be governed by those provisions? We return to this below.

Public authority and public law prevail in the administration of justice. So proceedings on a request for legal aid, provided from public funds are not covered by Article 6 (1);[1] and the classification of a prisoner in Category A in United Kingdom prisons, as being a danger to security, does not involve any civil right.[2] Nor is the more privileged classification of membership of the House of Lords a civil right.[3]

But professional employment and services, whether public or private, raise difficult issues under Article 6, that arise from their forms of organization: in particular, what is the range of civil rights and obligations in these professional services, and how far can private and public criteria be maintained, and does the establishment of institutions of control—tribunals, diciplinary boards, commissions, and so on—require that such institutions comply with the principles of Article 6 (1)?

In a leading application,[4] a medical specialist was owner and director of a clinic, and the authorization of its management was withdrawn by the Provincial Government (Wiesbaden) in November 1967, and his licence to practise as a doctor was withdrawn. Appeals to the administrative courts, and to the Federal Constitutional Court were unsuccessful; and the proceedings in the administrative courts and their decisions were delayed over a number of years. He complained in his application of the length of the administrative court proceedings, and of the termination of his licence to practise as a doctor, the grounds of which were the subject of those proceedings.

The Commission had first to consider whether Article 6 (1) was applicable to these proceedings, whether in fact civil rights and obligations were involved. Two views were expressed; five members considered that the professional practice of medicine implied a number of rights and obligations, which were civil in that they were part of

---

[1] 3825/69 (F.R.G.): 32 *Recueil* 56.
[2] 8575/79 (U.K.): 20 D.R. 202.
[3] 8208/78 (U.K.): 16 D.R. 162.
[4] *König* 6232/73 (F.R.G.): Report 1. 1977: Judgment No. 26 (26.4.1978).

the relationship of doctor and patient, and that therefore the revocation of the licence to practise or run a clinic was an administrative act
reflecting these civil rights and obligations; five other members considered that the practice of a profession was an exercise of the right to
work, which is a 'fundamental right', and a civil right under the Convention in so far as it is not an exercise of public power or the administration of public services. Six members found Article 6 (1) to be not
applicable to the proceedings in issue as they related to action by the
State in exercise of specific powers *jure imperii*, and not *jure gestionis*.
Nine members, one abstaining, constituted a majority in finding that,
Article 6 (1) being applicable, the proceedings in question had
exceeded a reasonable time. The Court considered that the rights
asserted by the applicant—to run his clinic and to continue to exercise
the practise of medicine—were rights of a 'private character', which
was not altered by the supervision imposed in the interests of the
public health, or by the exercise by the medical profession of its
responsibilities towards society at large; and therefore that the proceedings, being decisive for such private rights and obligations, were
governed by Article 6 (1). The Court also found that the proceedings
had exceeded a reasonable time.[1]

Parallel applications were brought by three Belgian doctors, who
had been suspended from practice by Provincial Councils of the *Ordre
des Médecins* (Medical Association).[2] Le Compte[3] had been suspended
for three months for contesting, through the press, decisions taken
against him for criticisms he had made of the organs of the *Ordre*. van
Leuven and de Meyer had been suspended from practice for one
month for systematically limiting their fees to amounts that could be
reimbursed by Social Security, and taking part in publicity in the
magazine, which was found offensive by their colleagues.

The ten Provincial Councils of the *Ordre* were each composed of
medical practitioners, and two assessors, being judges of first instance
courts. The Provincial Councils are competent to terminate a licence
to practise medicine, or to subject its exercise to contain restrictions,
and this is described among the functions of the Councils as:

---

[1] Judgment §§ 91, 93.
[2] Established by an Act (25.7.1938), and reorganized by Royal Decree No. 79
(10.11.1967). All physicians, surgeons, and obstetricians must, in order to practice, be
registered in the *Ordre*.
[3] *Le Compte* (6874/74), *van Leuven and de Meyer* (7238/75) (Belgium): Report (4.12.79)
Judgment (23.6.1981).

to ensure observance of the rule of professional conduct for medical practitioners and the upholding of the reputation, standards of discretion, probity and dignity of the members of the *Ordre*. They shall to this end be responsible for disciplining misconduct committed by their registered members or in connection with the practice of the profession and serious misconduct committed outside the realm of professional activity, whenever such misconduct is liable to damage the reputation or dignity of the profession.[1]

Appeals against decisions of Provincial Council may be made to one of the two Appeal Councils;[2] and further to the Court of Cassation, which may pronounce on the legality of the decisions and the observance of the formal requirements.

The Commission considered that Article 6 (1) was applicable to the proceedings; that the Appeal Council, though prescribed by law and independent, could not be regarded as impartial in its composition; and that appeal to the Cour de Cassation could not remedy this, given the limits on its jurisdiction.

The Court elaborated its reasoning on the applicability of Article 6 (1):

The Court considers that a tenuous connection or remote consequences do not suffice for Article 6 (1), in either of its official versions (contestation sur/ determination of), civil rights and obligations must be the object—or one of the objects—of the *contestation* (dispute); the result of the proceedings must be directly decisive for such a right ... That right was directly in issue before the Appeals Council and the Court of Cassation ... it is by means of private relationships with their clients or patients that medical practitioners in private practice, such as the applicants, avail themselves of the right to continue to practise; in Belgian law, these relationships are usually contractual or quasi-contractual and, in any event, are directly established between individuals on a personal basis and without any intervention of an essential or determining nature by a public authority. Accordingly, it is a private right that is at issue, notwithstanding the specific character of the medical profession—a profession which is exercised in the general interest—and the special duties incumbent on its members.

The Commission and the Court both found the system inconsistent with Article 6 (1). But it might be asked whether the notion of private relationship, as described by the Court, is not too narrow; and whether, for example, negligence by a doctor towards a patient in a

---

[1] Royal Decree No. 79 Article 6 (2).
[2] Composed of five medical practitioners and five Court of Appeal Judges, each group having appointed substitutes, and a judge having a casting vote.

national health service does not create civil obligations under Article 6 (1).

Again while the regulation of the professions is largely internal, covering in particular the conditions of admission to the profession, and of conduct within it,[1] Article 6 (1) might be seen to apply indirectly in some circumstances. So where:

le requérent se plaint de ce qu'il a été déchu, dans un procès non conforme a l'article 6 (1) de la Convention de Sauvegarde des Droits de l'Homme et des Libertés fondamentales, du droit d'être enregistré comme avocat stagiaire (Rechtsanwaltsanwärter) et de pratiquer en tant que tel bien que ce droit soit garanti par l'article 18 de la Constitution autrichienne (relatif a la liberté de choisir une profession) et constitue un 'droit civil' aux termes du droit autrichien;

... suivant l'interpretation que la Commission a donné a cette notion autonome [cf. parmi d'autres, la décision de la Commission sur la recevabilité de la requete No. 423/58], la contestation sur le droit d'être admis a une fonction publique *n'est pas une contestation portant sur les 'droits et obligations de caractère civil'* au sens de l'article 6 § 1 de la Convention; que la contestation sur la decheance du droit d'exercer et d'accéder à la fonction d'avocat ne peut, non plus, être considerée comme une contestation sur un droit de caractère civil vu notamment les caractères propres à la profession d'avocat; que l'article 6 § 1 de la Convention ne s'applique pas en l'espèce.[2]

It is to be observed here that the conditions of admission to, and exclusion from, the professional status of Rechtsanwaltsanwärter, were prescribed by Austrian law. The decision whether these conditions were satisfied in a particular case is determined on appeal by an administrative body (*Oberste Berufungs-und-Disziplinar-Kommission*). This body has, nevertheless, in its composition and its procedure, most of the characteristics of a judicial tribunal: it has a legally qualified bench; it hears witnesses and receives written evidence; the State, the legal profession, and the appellant, are all represented before it by counsel; and its decision, taken by a majority, is final. Must it then act as an independent and impartial tribunal and give the appellant a fair hearing, in conformity with Article 6 (1)?

The effects on civil rights and obligations by action of administrative authority were surveyed at length by the Commission in an

[1] Subjection to the rules of the medical profession of professional contracts concluded by its members, even if it takes the form of a decision of a Provincial Council, does not involve Article (1): 8782/79 (Belgium): 25 D.R. 243.

[2] 1931/63. The statutory regulation of the accountancy profession, hitherto unregulated, in the Netherlands was raised in *van Marle et al.* 8543/79: 21 D.R. 180.

application resting on the following facts.[1] The applicant had acquired control of an insurance company in the United Kingdom. In November 1975 the Secretary of State for Trade served notices on the applicant and the company that he was considering exercising his powers under the Insurance Companies Act (1974) s. 79 to impose restrictions on the company's business, on grounds of certain conduct of the applicant as controller of the company. After written and oral representations made on behalf of the applicant, the Secretary of State served notice on the company in February 1976, imposing restrictions under s. 29 on its ability to enter into insurance contracts. The Commission held that the conduct of an insurance business was a commercial activity in the private sector, and was an exercise of a civil right for the purposes of Article 6 (1), even though it could be subject to administrative authorization and supervision in the public interest. Then

In the Commission's view the essential role of Article 6 (1) in this sphere is to lay down guarantees concerning the mode in which claims or disputes concerning legal rights and obligations (of a 'civil' character) are to be resolved. A distinction must be drawn between the acts of a body which is engaged in the resolution of such a claim or dispute and the acts of an administrative or other body purporting merely to exercise or apply a legal power vested in it and not to resolve a legal claim or dispute. Article 6 (1) would not, in the Commission's opinion, apply to the acts of the latter even if they do affect 'civil rights' . . . Its function would not be to decide ('décidera') on a claim, dispute or 'contestation'.[2]

It is not easy to determine at what point the act of administrative authority decisively affects a civil right. So in a town-planning scheme in Stockholm a zonal expropriation permit was granted by the Government to the City Council under the Building Act (1947); and under the Expropriation Act (1917) a time-limit of five years was set by the Government, within which expropriation might be affected. Further, prohibitions on construction of buildings on specified parcels of land were also imposed, subject also to time-limits. Two applications were brought complaining of the effects on properties of these measures.[3] Sporrong claimed that the expropriation permit,

---

[1] *Kaplan* (U.K.) 7598/76: Report 21 D.R. 5. The *Ringeisen Judgment* No. 13 (16.7.71), often quoted, is not precise in saying that Article 6 (1) 'covers all proceedings the result of which is decisive for private rights and obligations'.

[2] Report § 154. See also 8974/80 (Netherlands): 24 D.R. 187. For similar reasoning on determination of a criminal charge see 343/57: 4 *Yearbook* 582.

[3] *Sporrong/Lönnroth* (7151.7152/75): Report (5.3.1979): Judgment No. 52 (24.9.1981).

ultimately cancelled, and the prohibition on construction, covering a parcel of land owned by him, had been in force for total periods of twenty-three and twenty-five years respectively. Mrs Lönnroth had property in Stockholm, occupied by two buildings, was subject to an expropriation permit and prohibition on construction for eight and twelve years respectively. The Sporrong Estate did not attempt to sell the property affected at any time; Mrs Lönnroth made seven attempts to sell her property, but prospective buyers withdrew after consultation with the city authorities.

The Commission and the Court disagreed on the applicability of Article 6 (1) to the expropriation permits. The Commission held, no doubt on the reasoning expressed in the Kaplan Report, that the issue of such permits was not itself a taking of property or resolution of any claim to property,[1] or a determination of civil rights, it not being contested that property rights are civil rights. The Court was unable to share this view. It said that:

It is of little consequence that the contestation (dispute) concerned an administrative measure taken by the competent body in the exercise of public authority . . .

and further that, given the question whether the long time-limits granted in the applicants' case were inconsistent with Swedish law—disputed by the Government, the applicants were entitled to have this question of domestic law determined by a tribunal: in short, it was not the administrative character of the permits that was decisive, it was rather their effect upon the value of the properties that demanded a determination under Article 6 (1).

It is tempting to argue that, where the domestic law of a Convention country prescribes a judicial or quasi-judicial process for determining certain rights and obligations, even when these are not civil rights or obligations in the narrower sense so far described, the provisions of Article 6 (1) should nevertheless be applicable to the process.

Two other questions concern the determination of civil rights and criminal charges under Article 6: do the provisions of the Article regulate procedure only, or do they give substantive rights? Can the individual waive under domestic law rights guaranteed by Article 6?

As to the first, it might be said that Article 6 simply contains rules to be observed by the courts, if and when they are seised of the deter-

---

[1] 8428/72 (F.R.G.): 44 *Recueil* 49, quoted above.

mination of civil rights or criminal charges. But the French text 'Toute personne a droit ...' certainly, and the English word 'entitled' probably, are to be read as meaning that every person, who has or believes he has a civil right or obligation, or has been charged with a crime, has the right to have the issue brought before the courts and determined. The narrower view would permit the State to bring a criminal charge and refuse either to withdraw or prosecute it, an inadmissible conclusion.

The second question was considered by the Commission in the following application.[1] The applicant entered into a contract with a German school in Spain, a corporate body under Spanish law. The contract was concluded in Bonn, was countersigned by an official of the Foreign Ministry (*Auswärtiges Amt*) and included a clause providing that any dispute arising should be arbitrated by an authorized agent (*zuständiger Vertreter*) of the Federal Republic. The applicant was later dismissed by the school management, and its decision was confirmed by a German Consul in the district. As regards the effect of the arbitration clause, the Commission said:

> ... the inclusion of an arbitration clause in an agreement between individuals amounts legally to partial renunciation of the exercise of those rights defined by Article 6 (1); ... nothing in the text of that Article nor of any other Article of the Convention explicitly prohibits such renunciation; ... the Commission is not entitled to assume that the Contracting States, in accepting the obligations arising under Article 6 (1), intended to prevent persons coming under their jurisdiction from entrusting the settlement of certain matters to arbitration; ... the disputed arbitration clause might have been regarded as contrary to the Convention if [the Applicant] has signed it under constraint, which was not the case; ... it may however be queried whether the original validity of the consent, from which the arbitration clause assumes its legal force, might not subsequently be affected if the arbitrator, in carrying out the functions conferred on him by that clause, conducted himself in a manner incompatible with the spirit of the Convention and particularly Article 6; this question does not however arise in the present case.

It would appear from these observations, of the nature of *obiter dicta*, that submission to arbitration, entailing the renunciation of judicial recourse in the sense of Article 6, may be vitiated either by constraint or by the subsequent misconduct of the arbitrator: and, in the latter circumstances, the misconduct of the arbitrator would not be in itself a

[1] 1197/61: 5 *Yearbook* 88.

breach of Article 6, but would be a bar to any denial of the right of the applicant to judicial recourse in accordance with that Article.

criminal charge/accusation matière pénale

Since a criminal charge must be determined, in the conditions prescribed in Article 6, within a reasonable time, two related questions arise: in what circumstances can an individual be properly said to be facing a criminal charge, and at what point does the period of 'reasonable time' begin to run? The second question will be considered in its place below.

The Commission has drawn three distinctions, between charge and other forms of process, between charge and conviction, and between criminal and disciplinary charges.

It has said that proceedings to decide whether, for example, sentence is to be suspended or remitted,[1] or its conditions of service changed, do not fall under Article 6 (1) since there is no determination of a charge:

So

... under Article 411 [of the Austrian Code of Criminal Procedure] the function of the Landesgericht was not to determine the 'civil rights or obligations' of, or a 'criminal charge' against the Applicant within the meaning of Article 6, but solely to decide, subsequently to the conviction of the Applicant, whether a pardon or a commutation of the sentence should be recommended to the President of the Republic . . .[2]

Similarly proceedings, in which an order revoking release on probation was subject of appeal, or in which the court had to decide 'only the question whether or not the Applicant should be extradited . . . and, if so, to which of the countries which had requested his extradition',[3] or in which the execution is requested in the Federal Republic of Germany of a sentence imposed by an East German Court,[4] do not involve the determination of a 'criminal charge' under Article 6 (1).

Again Article 410 of the Austrian Code of Criminal Procedure provides that, where a conviction has become *res judicata*, and the trial

[1] 606/59: 4 *Yearbook* 144.

[2] 864/60: 3 *Yearbook* 340.

[3] 1918/63: 6 *Yearbook* 184. Similar proceedings of preliminary judicial investigation are not covered by Article 6 (1): 8541/74 (F.R.G.): 1 D.R. 8L.

[4] 1322/62: Collection 1–30 p. 161. The process of settlement under Article 28b is not a determination of a charge or guilt: *Neubecker* (F.R.G.) 6281/73: 3 D.R. 30.

court is satisifed of the existence of mitigating circumstances, that did not exist or were unknown at the time of conviction, it may seise the Oberlandsgericht of an application for reduction of sentence.

The Commission has held that the hearing and determination of the application does not fall under Article 6 (1), since neither civil rights nor a criminal charge are in issue.[1]

The point at which a person ceases to be charged or accused under Article 6 (1) and becomes a convicted person under Article 5 (1) *a*,[2] or to put it another way, the point at which the charge becomes *res judicata*, is important for determining the extent of his rights under Article 6 (1). Where there is a form of appeal, the point will normally be either the determination of final appeal, or the expiry of the time-limit of appeal. So, not only does Article 6 or any other provision of the Convention give no right to retrial, or revision of conviction or sentence,[3] but where there is under domestic law provision for retrial under certain conditions, the proceedings on application for a new trial are not governed by the provisions of Article 6. Thus the Special Court of Revision in Denmark

does not form part of the ordinary hierarchy of judicial instances and can neither confirm nor invalidate the decisions of the ordinary courts. It can only decide whether a case, which has been finally decided by an ordinary court shall be reopened and a new trial ordered . . .[4]

Again, where an application to the Commission had sought a retrial under Article 353 of the Austrian Code of Criminal Procedure, the Commission said

Whereas at the time of seeking this redress the Applicant was no longer an accused person within the meaning of Article 6 of the Convention, but was a convicted person, who was faced with a judgment amounting to *res judicata* which he was attempting to have quashed by invoking facts and evidence which he claimed were new; whereas the task of the Regional Court and the Court of Appeal of Vienna was merely to determine the admissibility of the

---

[1] 1038/61: Collection 1–30 p. 112. But the rights assured by the *partie civile* in criminal proceedings are 'civil rights' for the purposes of Article 6 (1): 142/62: 6 *Yearbook* 355.

[2] For a distinction between a convicted and an accused fugitive criminal see Extradition Act 1870, ss. 10, 26, and *in re Caborn-Waterfield* [1960] 2 W.L.R. 792, discussed by Paul O'Higgins, 9 *I.C.L.Q.* (1960) 498 and 10 (1961) 339, and between appeal against conviction and against length of sentence: 6501/74 (F.R.G.) 1 D.R. 80.

[3] 1098/61: *Recueil* (1961) ii, following 704/60.

[4] 343/57: 4 *Yearbook* 582.

said requests; whereas these two courts were not seised of any criminal charges against the Applicant, whether it be the initial charge or that which the Public Prosecutor might have newly formulated or repeated if the requests had been declared admissible.

However it is to be noticed that the Commission excepted the case where the court hearing the application for retrial is confronted with a new formulation of the charges or, it seems, additional charges.

In an unusual case the penalty provisions of the German Traffic Code (Strassenverkehrszulassungsordnung) were found by the Federal Constitutional Court to be unconstitutional on the technical ground that they had been embodied in an ordinance and not in a statute. The applicant, who had been convicted of a traffic offence under another undisturbed provision of the Traffic Code, claimed that the principles of Article 6 (1) applied to proceedings for the revision of his sentence. The Commission rejected his application on the ground that since his conviction remained *res judicata*, revision of his sentence did not involve the determination of a criminal charge.[1]

shall be entitled/a droit

This expression may be construed in two ways. First, it may be read as meaning that it is only when civil proceedings or criminal proceedings have been initiated by or against an individual that the provisions of Article 6 (1) operate; alternatively, it may mean that, whenever the individual believes that his civil rights or obligations are in issue, or when a charge is made against him, he is entitled to have that issue or charge determined in accordance with the provisions of Article 6. From the first construction it would follow that, for example, a criminal charge could be brought against an individual but that he could not claim any entitlement under Article 6 to have the charge proceeded with or withdrawn. The Commission has rejected this construction.[2]

fair hearing/entendue équitablement

The assurance of fair hearing in the determination of civil rights and obligations and criminal charges is not less vital than the control of detention. In the words of a Chief Justice of Canada

---

[1] 2136/64.
[2] 2257/64.

The principle that no one should be condemned or deprived of his rights without being heard, and above all without having received notice that his rights would be put at stake, is of a universal equity . . . [N]othing less would be necessary than an express declaration of the legislature to put aside this requirement, which applies to all courts and to all the bodies called upon to render a decision that might have the effect of annulling a right possessed by an individual.[1]

It is right that it should not be circumscribed in the Convention by attempts or exhaustive definition. The Commission has said that it

cannot be determined *in abstracto* but must be considered in the light of the special circumstances of each case.[2]

Further there are two other principles which, in the view of the Commission, govern the determination of what is a fair hearing under Article 6: the rights specified in Article 6 (2) and (3) are not exhaustive of the content of fair hearing in Article 6 (1); and for this determination the trial in question must be taken as a whole. So in the *Nielsen case*[3] the Commission said

Article 6 of the Convention does not define the notion of 'fair trial' in a criminal case. Paragraph 3 of the Article enumerates certain specific rights which constitute essential elements of that general notion, and paragraph 2 may be considered to add another element. The words 'minimum right', however, clearly indicate that the six rights specifically enumerated in paragraph 3 are not exhaustive, and that a trial may not conform to the general standard of a 'fair trial', even if the minimum rights guaranteed by paragraph 3—and also the right set forth in paragraph 2—have been respected. The relationship between the general provision of paragraph 1 and the specific provisions of paragraph 3, seem to be as follows:

In a case where no violation of paragraph 3 is found to have taken place, the question whether the trial conforms to the standard laid down by paragraph 1 must be decided on the basis of a consideration of the trial as a whole, and not on the basis of an isolated consideration of one particular aspect of the trial or one particular incident. Admittedly, one particular incident or one particular aspect even if not falling within the provisions of paragraph 2 or 3, may have been so prominent or may have been of such importance as to be decisive for the general evaluation of the trial as a whole. Nevertheless, even in this con-

---

[1] *L'Alliance des Professeurs Catholiques de Montreal* v. *Labour Relations Board of Quebec* [1953] 4 D.L.R. 161, 174 *per* Rinfret C.J.

[2] 1013/61: 5 *Yearbook* 164.

[3] 343/57: Report of the Commission: 4 *Yearbook* 518 at 548–50.

tingency, it is on the basis of an evaluation of the trial in its entirety that the answer must be given to the question whether or not there has been a fair trial.

It follows from this relationship between Article 6 (1) and the remainder of the Article that, while the specific rights in Article 6 (2) and (3) are expressed to be limited to persons charged with criminal offences, the principles embodied in them may be also applicable in civil proceedings.

The distinction between criminal and disciplinary charges is to be found in the law and practice governing the armed services, the civil service, and the professions. The Supreme Court of India has held that the competent authority has a discretion, in a proceeding against a civil servant for misconduct, to conduct it by departmental inquiry or by criminal prosecution, and that such discretion was not inconsistent with the equal protection of the law, required by Article 14 of the Constitution.[1] The Convention, however, does not contemplate such discretion. If the charge is, in effect, criminal, Article 6 (1) with its procedural conditions becomes applicable. But what is a 'criminal charge'. While in the interpretation of the principle, set down in Article 6 (1), by the Commission and the Court, criteria were evolved for determining what is a criminal charge, the Court came finally to the conclusion that this issue could be avoided. The development appears in applications concerning disciplinary proceedings in the armed services and in the professions.

In the *Engel judgment* of the Court, five soldiers serving in the Netherlands Army[2] had brought applications, asserting breaches of a number of provisions of the Convention, including Articles 5 and 6, arising from various penalties passed on them by their respective commanding officers for offences against military discipline. Dona and Schul were editors of the periodical of the Conscript Serviceman's Association, and one issue was considered to tend to undermine military discipline. The other three had been absent or late from duty. The penalties imposed,[3] being forms of detention were not inscribed in the applicants' universal needs, nor were the offences covered by the ordinary criminal law. The applicants had appealed to the complaints officer and finally to the Supreme Military Court, which confirmed the decisions in issue but in one of the cases reduced the penalty imposed.

---

[1] *Partap Singh* v. *State of Punjab* [1964] A.I.R. 72, 100.
[2] Engel, van der Wiel, de Wit, Dona, Schul.
[3] Committed to a disciplinary wait for three months (de Wit, Dona, Schul).

The disciplinary law, applicable to the Netherlands Army was set out at the time of the measures complained of in the Military Discipline Act (27.4.1903), the Regulations on Military Discipline (31.7.1922), the Military Penal Code (27.4.1903) and the Army and Air Force Code of Procedure (9.1.1964). A military criminal law was also in force, proceedings under it being held at first instance before a court martial. The measures complained of in these applications were confined to the disciplinary law, described above. The Court remarked that charges against Dona and Schul came within the Military Penal Code 5.147.[1]

The Court in considering whether criminal charges were involved in the sense of Article 6 (1), began by saying that, while states may maintain or establish a distinction between criminal law and disciplinary law, and may designate particular acts or omissions as criminal offences under the ordinary law, or as disciplinary offences, or as both, there must be limits to designation of offences as disciplinary instead of criminal,[2] for otherwise the principles of Article 6 (1) could be evaded:

Hence, the Court must specify limiting itself to the sphere of military service, how it will determine whether a given 'charge' vested by the State in question . . . with a disciplinary character none the less counts as a 'criminal' within the meaning of Article 6 . . . The very nature of the offence is a factor of great import. When a serviceman finds himself accused of an act or omission allegedly contravening a legal rule governing the operation of the armed forces, the State may in principle employ against him disciplinary law rather than criminal law.

If then an offence is no more than a contravention of a rule 'governing the operation of the armed forces', and has no other particular accountability, it may be fairly treated as a disciplinary offence.

However, supervision by the Court does not stop there. Such supervision would generally prove to be illusory if it did not also take into consideration the degree of severity of the penalty that the person risks in incurring. In a society subscribing to the rule of law there belong to the 'criminal' sphere deprivations of liberty liable to be imposed as a punishment, except those

---

[1] Covering 'endeavours to undermine discipline in the armed forces', and imposing a term of imprisonment not exceeding three years.

[2] The Rehabilitation of Offenders Act (1974) (U.K.) s. 2(1) covers offences that have been subject to 'service disciplinary proceedings', or to any 'court or person authorised [under the statue of service] to award a punishment'.

which by their nature duration or manner of execution cannot be appreciably detrimental.

As the Court said, it was confining its judgment to penalties in the armed services, essentially forms of detention. Other penalties, such as fines or dismissal from employment, were not then considered; and the judgment then can offer severity of penalty as no more than a broad indication of the criminality of an offence.

The Commission has adopted the three criteria indicated by the Court—classification of the offence under domestic law, the nature of the offence, and the degree of severity of the penalty imposed—in finding whether a criminal charge under Article 6 (1) is involved in disciplinary measures in the armed services.[1] Its findings have tended to treat penalties other than deprivation of liberty, or those 'belonging to the criminal sphere', as outside the notion of criminal charge, even though the impact on the individual may have been serious: for example, dismissal from service of a police officer for 'appropriating one gallon of petrol for his personal use' and for other breaches of duty, about which he had been warned;[2] and transfer of a major in the Portuguese army to the reserve list for political activities.[3]

The Commission had earlier consistently held that the proceedings of disciplinary boards or tribunals in the professions fell outside the scope of Article 6 (1) in a number of applications; for example, action of the disciplinary committee of the Bar Association in Austria against a member found to be overcharging in practice, was held to be incompatible with Article 6 (1);[4] and so was the complaint of a Belgian architect, struck off its register by the Order of Architects, a statutory professional body, for breach of its rules, in respect particularly of use of publicity and of fees charged.[5] Here the Commission observed that

la poursuite disciplinaire . . . ne peut pas être considérée comme faisant partie du droit pénal,

and so no 'criminal charge' under Article 6 (1) was involved. But the decision does not make clear whether 'droit penal' here means Belgian law or is to be understood autonomously. In a recent judgment of the Court[6] the interpretation of Article 6 in this area has become markedly

---

[1] *Eggs* (7341/76) (Switzerland): Report 15 D.R. 35, 64: 8778/79 (Switzerland): 20 D.R. 240.   [2] 8496/69 (U.K.): 21 D.R. 168.
[3] 9208/80 (Portugal): 26 D.R. 262.   [4] 2793/66 (Austria): 23 *Recueil* 125.
[5] 4040/69 (Belgium): 37 *Recueil* 25.
[6] *Albert/Le Compte* (Belgium) No. 58 (28.5.1982).

more complicated. In the case of Albert, the Brabant Provincial Council of the *Ordre des Médecins* had, after written exchange and hearing, suspended his right to practise medicine for two years in connection with various certificates of unfitness to work issued by him to patients, and two earlier suspensions from practice following criminal convictions. The Commission considered that, while 'civil rights and obligations' were in issue in the disciplinary measure taken against him, he had not been subject to a 'criminal charge'.

The Court said:

For its part, the Court does not believe that the two aspects, civil and criminal of Article 6 (1) are necessarily mutually exclusive ...[1] None the less, the Court does not consider it necessary to decide whether in the specific circumstances, there was a 'criminal charge'. In point of fact paragraph 1 of Article 6, violation of which was alleged by the two applicants, applies in civil matters as well as in the criminal sphere ... Dr. Albert relied in addition on paragraph 2 and on sub-paragraphs 2 (*a*), (*b*) and (*d*) of paragraph 3, but, in the opinion of the Court the principles enshrined therein are, for the present purposes, already contained in the notion of a fair trial as embodied in paragraph 1; the Court will therefore take these principles into account in the context of paragraph 1.[2]

In short, the principles of Article 6 (2) and (3) are 'applicable mutatis mutandis, to disciplinary proceedings subject to paragraph 1 in the same way as in the case of a person charged with a criminal offence'.[3]

It appears to follow from this interpretation that

(*a*) to subject the member of a profession to disciplinary measure for professional misconduct is a form of accusation;

(*b*) Article 6 (1) is applicable to any such disciplinary measures that involve or affect any civil rights and obligations of the accused;

(*c*) the right to a fair hearing granted by Article 6 (1) in respect of such measures necessarily includes the standard requirements, expressed in Article 6 (2) and (3) (*a*), (*b*) and (*d*);

(*d*) any disciplinary board or tribunal, taking such measures must grant the accused a fair hearing, as described, it being irrelevant

---

[1] It cited the judgments in the cases of *Engel*, *König*, and *le Compte et al.*

[2] The Court considered Articles 6 (2) and (3) (*a*), (*b*) and (*d*) in detail, but found no violation.

[3] Paragraph 39. The principle was expressed by the Commission in 852/60: 4 *Yearbook* 354.

whether the accusation is a 'criminal' charge in the sense of Article 6 (1).[1]

The disciplinary punishment of prisoners serving sentence can raise the applicability of Article 6 (1). The Commission has so far used the criteria proposed in the *Engel Judgment*. So where an applicant serving a prison sentence had been, as he said, assaulted by a prison officer, and had then had imposed on him by the Board of Visitors the loss of 80 days remission of sentence the Commission applied these criteria: in particular, 'loss of remission does not constitute deprivation of liberty'.

The Commission concluded unanimously that there had been no contravention of Article 6 in these cases.[2] In short, what was decisive was that the judge rapporteur drafted the decision of the court on the basis of written pleadings, and that the Generalprokurator, without being represented at the non-public session of the court or purporting to influence its decision, indicated his agreement by the single word 'einverstanden'. Further, since the appeal against sentence had been brought by the accused, and not by the Public Prosecutor, the court had under Austrian law no power to increase the sentence and so bring about a *reformatio in peius*: the sentence of Hopfinger was unchanged and that of Ofner in fact reduced.

Again where the Generalprokurator was himself in the non-public session of the court, the appellant being neither present nor represented, but limited his intervention to the statement that in his opinion the appeal against sentence was ill founded, and withdrew before the deliberation of the court, the Commission found no breach of Article 6.

A strong case the other way was one in which the Public Prosecutor appealed for an increase in the sentence of the trial court, the Generalprokurator addressed the Supreme Court in the absence of the accused or his representative, and the sentence was in fact increased. Here the application was declared admissible, and the applicant was thereby enabled to take advantage of the Austrian legislation described below, and on a rehearing his sentence of imprisonment was reduced.[3]

---

[1] This proposition is expressed in the U.K. Prison Rules (196475.49(2)) '. . . at any inquiry into a charge against a prisoner, he shall be given a full opportunity of hearing what is alleged against him and of presenting his own case.'

[2] So decided by the Committee of Ministers: 6 *Yearbook* 710–12.

[3] 1446/62: 6 *Yearbook* 252.

However, where again the Public Prosecutor had successfully appealed for an increase of sentence, but the Generalprokurator had not, in the opinion of the Commission, played a more active role in the Supreme Court than in the *Ofner—Hopfinger Cases*, there was no breach of Article 6 found.

Prominent among the issues that arise in the assessment of 'fair hearing' are the admissibility of evidence; the equality of arms; the personal participation of a party in the proceedings, and the motivation of any judgment or order. The Commission has constantly stressed that these are all governed by domestic law, the question then being whether that law or its application can be shown to be inconsistent with Article 6 or other provisions of the Convention, and that for the determination of these issues the proceedings in question must be investigated and assessed as a whole.[1]

The *admissibility of evidence* has formed the basis of numerous applications to the Commission, the great majority being manifestly ill-founded either because the domestic rules governing evidence are reasonable, or because the admission or exclusion of evidence by the court cannot be shown to have been a denial of justice. In its own words, it is with the 'proper presentation of the case', and not with an evaluation of the evidence, that the Commission is concerned.[2]

Article 6 (3) *d* does not grant the accused an unlimited right to demand the hearing of witnesses in court; and it may admit confidential information from prisoners, who have a legitimate interest in remaining anonymous, but counter-evidence must be allowed.[3] Again press statements attributing a 'dangerous character' to the accused may be admitted, if the evidence on which the statements are based is uncontested.[4]

The principle of the *equality of arms* (*l'égalité des armes*; *Waffengleichheit*) is an expression of the rule *audi alteram partem*, and implies that each party to the proceedings before a tribunal must be given a full opportunity to present his case, both on facts and in law, and to comment on the case presented by his opponent. This opportunity must be equal between the parties and limited only by the duty of the

---

[1] e.g. 7945/77 (Norway): 1 D.R. 228 following *Nielsen case*: 343/57. 4 *Yearbook* 518.

[2] 6172/73 (U.K.): 3 D.R. 77.

[3] 8417/76 (Belgium): 16 D.R. 200.

[4] *Baader et al.* 7572/76 (F.R.G.): 14 D.R. 64. In this case the conduct of the accused, in failing to appear at certain stages of the proceedings, was held to justify continuance *in absentia*.

tribunal to prevent in any form an undue prolongation or delay of the proceedings.

The Commission strives to observe the principle of the equality of arms in its own proceedings, and has had to consider a number of applications[1] claiming that it has not been observed in certain Austrian criminal proceedings.

The criminal proceedings in issue were applications to have a conviction quashed (*Nichtigkeitsbeschwerde*), and appeal against sentence (*Berufung*), these being the only means of recourse against trial court decisions. *Nichtigkeitsbeschwerde* lay only to the Supreme Court (Oberster Gerichtshof), while *Berufung* lay to the court of second instance (Oberlandesgericht), but might be combined with a *Nichtigkeitsbeschwerde*. Both forms of proceedings had two characteristic features: first, that both courts heard and determined a *Berufung* in non-public session, and second, that it was determined 'after hearing' (*nach Anhörung*) the Attorney-General (Generalprokuratur) in the case of the Oberster Gerichtshof or the Public Prosecutor (Oberstaatsanwalt) in the case of the Oberlandesgericht, but without 'hearing' the accused.

The first feature was protected by a reservation made by Austria under Article 64 of the Convention.

The second feature, however, demanded closer inspection. If we take first proceedings in the Supreme Court, we shall see that, in the leading cases of Ofner and Hopfinger, the Commission considered three elements to be material to the question whether the equality of arms was observed: the role of the Generalprokuratur as securing respect for the law (*Wahrung des Gesetzes*) rather than the conviction of the accused; the precise circumstances in which the 'hearing' of the Generalprokuratur took place; and the effective result of the proceedings for the accused, and in particular whether there was for him a *reformatio in peius*.[2]

The same principles governing the equality of arms are applicable to proceedings before the court of second instance (Oberlandesgericht) as

[1] See for example, *Chorzow Factory Case (Merits)* [1928] P.C.I.J.: Ser. A, 17 at 7. The court 'in the case allows the parties, in accordance with established precedent, to amend their original submissions ... subject only to the condition that the other party must always have an opportunity of commenting on the amended submissions'. See also, for example, *Inland Revenue Commissioners* v. *Hunter* [1914] 3 K.B. 423 at 428: 'No communication shall be made by one party to a judicial tribunal without the knowledge of the other party.'

[2] *Ofner* 524/59 (Austria), *Hopfinger* 617/59 (Austria): 6 *Yearbook* 680, 780.

appear from another group of applications, of which the leading cases were those of *Pataki* and *Dunshirn*.[1] In both cases the Public Prosecutor appealed against the sentences imposed upon the applicants. Written pleadings were filed, and the case-files were submitted to the chief Public Prosecutor (Oberstaatsanwalt) 'for information and opinion'. In both cases the case-files were returned to the Oberlandesgericht with an endorsement to the effect that the appeal should be allowed on the grounds already set out in the written pleadings. The Oberlandesgericht heard the appeals in non-public sessions, the decision in each case being endorsed to the effect that the Oberstaatsanwalt had been present and had 'addressed the court'. In neither case were the applicants present or represented. The sentences were increased in the case of Pataki from three to six years' imprisonment,[2] and in the case of Dunshirn from, in effect, fourteen months' to fifty-four months' imprisonment, the court likewise finding no extenuating circumstances. The Commission, observing that although the *Pataki—Dunshirn Cases* differed on the facts from the *Ofner—Hopfinger Cases*, not least in the different roles of the Oberstaatsanwalt and Generalprokurator, the principles applicable were the same, said:[3]

In the present cases, the problem is whether the presence of the Public Prosecutor, without the presence of the accused or his counsel, at the session of the Court of Appeal when the case was heard and decided in conformity with Section 294, paragraph (3), of the Code of Criminal Procedure, constituted an inequality in the representation of the parties, which is incompatible with the provisions of the Convention.

It is not possible to establish with certainty whether the Public Prosecutor has taken an active part on the deliberations of the Court. No records of the deliberations were kept. Even on the assumption, however, that the Public Prosecutor did not play an active role at this stage of the proceedings, the very fact that he was present and thereby had an opportunity of influencing the members of the Court, without the accused or his counsel having any similar opportunity or any possibility of contesting any statements made by the Prosecutor, constitutes an inequality which, in the opinion of the Commission, is incompatible with the notion of a fair trial.

The Commission therefore reaches the conclusion that the proceedings conducted in the present cases on the basis of section 294, paragraph (3), of the

---

[1] *Pataki* 596/59 (Austria); *Dunshirn* 789/60 (Austria): 6 *Yearbook* 714.

[2] The court found no extenuating circumstances, contrary to the view of the trial court, and increased the sentence so as to bring it within the range of five to ten years' imprisonment, prescribed by statute for the offences committed.

[3] 6 *Yearbook* 730.

Code of Criminal Procedure, as it was then worded, were not in conformity with the Convention.

It is to be noted that in these cases the third element, the presence of *reformatio in peius*, weighed also against the fairness of the hearing.

The equality of arms may also be infringed by some communication between the prosecution and the judge, not disclosed to the defence. Such a problem was posed by the *croquis* system in Austria, now abolished. The *croquis* was a sketch or outline of the position and argument, which the Generalprokuratur proposed to adopt at the oral hearing on *Nichtigkeitsbeschwerde* or *Berufung*; the *croquis* was sent to the Supreme Court in advance of the hearing, but was not communicated to the applicant; however, the practice was changed following certain applications to the Commission, and the *croquis* was made available to the defence before the hearing.[1] However, in a later case, the *croquis* contained material, in the form of a so-called *pro domo* note, not disclosed to the defence; in a settlement of the application, the Austrian Government stated that

By his ordinance of 24 January 1980 concerning the enactment of new regulations on the official communications between the Supreme Court and the Attorney General (Generalprokuratur). The President of the Supreme Court has amended the Supreme Court's Rules of Procedure in such a way as to leave no room for any *pro domo* notes.[2]

An inequality of arms can be established by the burden of costs of proceedings, and the denial or inadequacy of legal aid. So Article 6 (3) *c* provides for legal aid in criminal proceedings; and

despite the absence of a similar clause for civil litigation, Article 6 (1) may sometimes compel the State to provide for the assistance of a lawyer when such assistance proves indispensable for an effective access to count either because legal representation is rendered compulsory, as is done by the domestic law of certain Contracting States for various types of litigation, or by reason of the complexity of the procedure or of the case.[3]

Analogous problems of the 'equality of arms' have arisen on applications on German criminal proceedings. So an applicant, charged with a form of manslaughter (*fahrlässige Tötung*) after a traffic

---

[1] Described at length in 1418/62 (Austria) 6 *Yearbook* 222.
[2] *Peschke* 8289/78 (Austria): Report (13.10.1981) 25 D.R. 182. For a similar *croquis* system in Belgium, not found to be contrary to Article 6 (1): See *Jespers* 8463/78 (Belgium): Report (14.12.1981).
[3] *Airey* (Ireland): Judgment No. 32 (9.10.1979) § 26.

accident, was acquitted by the trial court (Schöffengericht) but convicted and fined by the Landgericht on appeal by the Public Prosecutor. On his appeal against conviction (Revision), the written pleadings of both sides were submitted to the Oberlandesgericht with a handwritten note by the Generalstaatsanwalt that, in his opinion, the appeal might be dismissed as being manifestly ill founded.[1] The Commission considered that

this intervention did not add to the [written pleadings] any legal arguments which might have called for further pleadings from the defence

and that the principle of equality of arms was not infringed.[2]

In the course of the examination by the Commission of the Pataki–Dunshirn and related applications, Austrian legislation was enacted in two stages, which modified the sections of the Code of Criminal Procedure that had been in issue so that their procedural application would be in future consistent with Article 6, and also provided for the re-examination under the new procedure of the cases of individuals whose applications had been declared admissible by the Commission. Consequently the Commission in its Report to the Committee of Ministers on the *Pataki—Dunshirn Cases* went on

to propose that the Committee of Ministers take note of this Report, express its appreciation of the legislative measures adopted in Austria with a view to giving full effect to the Convention of Human Rights, and decide that no further action should be taken in the present cases.[3]

The Committee of Ministers adopted this proposal.[4]

Personal appearance. The right to be present in person in civil proceedings is not expressly guaranteed by Article 6. However, the Commission has pointed out that

the question arises whether in certain classes of case or in certain sets of circumstances the right to a fair hearing guaranteed by Article 6, paragraph 1, implies a right to be present in person at the hearing of the case, and whereas

---

[1] Under German Code of Criminal Procedure, Article 349 (2).

[2] 1035/61: 6 *Yearbook* 180, 190. See also 1169/61: 6 *Yearbook* 520, 574–8.

[3] 6 *Yearbook* 734. For the text of the Austrian Federal Act (Strafprozessnovelle 1962: 18.7.1962) amending and supplementing the Code of Criminal Procedure, particularly Articles 294 and 296, see 5 *Yearbook* 344–50; for the text and explanatory memorandum of Austrian Federal Act 18/63: 26.3.1963, on the reopening of appeal proceedings in certain criminal cases, see 6 *Yearbook* 804–16.

[4] Resolution (63) DH 2: 6 *Yearbook* 736–8. For this procedure see under Article 31 below.

one class of cases in which this question appears to arise with particular force is a case where the personal character and manner of life of the party concerned is directly relevant to the formation of the Court's opinion on the point which it is called upon to decide; and whereas, furthermore, a case in which a parent, following upon a divorce, makes an application to the Court for a right of access to a child of the marriage is without doubt a case of this kind;

WHEREAS, also, the right to a fair hearing guaranteed by Article 6, paragraph 1, of the Convention appears to contemplate that everyone who is a party to civil proceedings shall have a reasonable opportunity of presenting his case to the Court under conditions which do not place him under a substantial disadvantage vis-à-vis his opponent.[1]

So in proceedings in cassation in a criminal matter, where the court

did not have to decide the material facts, nor the degree of culpability or criminal liability of the party concerned [so that] his 'personal character and manner of life' would not have been directly relevant to the formation of the court's opinion

a wholly written procedure met the requirements of fair hearing.[2] Where then, in order that justice may be done, it is necessary for the court to see, hear, and form a view of, the individual himself, there will be at least prima facie a breach of Article 6 if proceedings are conducted in his absence, because he has been expelled from the country or his admission is refused.[3]

The position of an individual, seeking to appear as a witness on his own behalf or to plead his own case, is different and will be considered under Article 6 (3) below.

Motivation of decision. The requirement that the decision of a court be motivated rests upon the principles that justice must be seen to be done, and the hearing seen to be fair, and that procedural obstacles must not be put in the way of appeal or revision by a defective statement of the facts or law on which the decision is based.

It is an element in that openness, which is essential in any tribunal.[4]

---

[1] 434/58: 2 *Yearbook* 354, 370. See also 696/60.

[2] 1169/61: 6 *Yearbook* 520, 572. 7211/75 (Switzerland) 7 D.R. 104.

[3] See 172/56: 1 *Yearbook* 211; and 434/58: 2 *Yearbook* 354, but in both cases there had been in effect a failure to exhaust domestic remedies. Contrast proceedings limited to plea of nullity on points of law, where personal appearance is not necessary: 8251/78 (Austria) 17 D.R. 166. As to failure of accused to appear see *Colozza* 9024/80 (Italy) 23 D.R. 138.

[4] *Report of the Commission on Administrative Tribunals and Enquiries 1957* (Cmnd. 218), § 41: 'We have already expressed our belief . . . that Parliament in deciding that certain

As regards the presentation and appreciation of evidence in criminal proceedings, the Commission said in the *Nielsen Case*:[1]

> It is of course impossible to know what has motivated the jury to give the answers they did on the question of Schouw Nielsen's guilt. But this does not immediately concern the Commission under the Convention. Whether the jury and the Court have appreciated the evidence correctly or not, is a question on which the Commission is not called upon to pronounce. The task under the Convention is to decide whether evidence for and against the accused has been presented in a manner, and the proceedings in general have been conducted in such a way, that he has had a fair trial.

While the Commission cannot control the appreciation of a court of the evidence before it, the question may arise whether the decision complained of is properly based on that evidence, in the sense that the court has not taken account of the facts or evidence not presented or commented on by the parties or otherwise known to them.

The Commission, in answer to an applicant who complained that, in not accepting the statements made by him on oath, the courts had in effect denied him a fair hearing, said

> the right to a fair hearing does not require a court automatically to base its decision on the statements of one or other party made on oath but to appreciate impartially all the matters of fact and of law submitted to it by both parties with reference to the particular issues which it is called upon to decide.[2]

Narrowly construed this could be read as stating that a court does not deny a fair hearing to one of the parties before it merely because it rejects, wholly or in part, his evidence, though given on oath. But this obvious answer could have been sufficiently made by the first clause, and, on a wider construction, the latter part of the statement might be read[3] as saying that fair hearing requires that a court base its conclusions and order on the evidence submitted to it by, or at least known to,[4] the parties.

The possibility of appeal or revision has also been considered by the

decisions should be reached only after a special procedure must have intended that they should manifest three basic characteristics: openness, fairness and impartiality. The choice of a tribunal rather than a Minister as the deciding authority is itself a considerable step towards the realisation of these objectives, particularly the third.'

[1] 343/57: 4 *Yearbook* 568.　　　　　　　　　[2] 911/60: 4 *Yearbook* 222.

[3] Compare a similar trend seen by H. W. R. Wade, *Annual Survey of Commonwealth Law* (1965) 123, commenting on *R.* v. *Deputy Industrial Injuries Commissioner, ex pte Moore* [1965] 2 W.L.R. 89.

[4] This would include facts or matters of which the court could take judicial notice.

Commission as requiring at least in criminal proceedings, motivation of a court decision. Where in Germany the Landgericht had, giving reasons, denied a motion by the applicant for a visit of inspection by the court to the scene of a traffic accident, and the oberlandesgericht had dismissed his appeal without reasons stated, as being manifestly ill founded, the Commission said that the Court of Appeal might be assumed to have adopted the reasoning of the court below, but that

a second consideration must be taken into account, namely whether or not a further appeal was open to the Applicant; . . . in cases where such possibility is open to a convicted person, it should be considered whether the notion of a 'fair trial' with the meaning of Article 6, paragraph (1) . . . might not signify that a court must state in detail the reasons for its decision in order that, on appeal from that decision, the defence might be properly safeguarded.[1]

There appears to be no reason why this principle should not be extended beyond the particular circumstances envisaged by the Commission in that passage.[2]

public hearing/entendue publiquement

Another element in the openness, necessary in a tribunal, is public hearing. The members of the public have an interest in overseeing the administration of justice carried on in their name. Proceedings conducted in the presence of any members of the public, including representatives of the press, who choose to attend, appear to satisfy this test. But the permitted exceptions in Article 6 (1) are so extensive that it is doubtful whether the requirement of public hearing under the Convention is likely in practice to yield much protection. They go far beyond the exceptions allowed by the Lord Shaw of Dunfermline in a thunderous judgment[3] in which he said:

The three exceptions which are acknowledged to the application of the rule prescribing the publicity of Courts of Justice are, first, in suits affecting wards;

---

[1] 1035/61: 6 *Yearbook* 192. In that case the decision of the Court of Apeal was final.
[2] See in *United Kingdom*: Tribunals and Inquiries Act 1958, s. 12, requiring statement of reasons for decisions by a large number of listed adminsitrative tribunals, or by Ministers, if such statement is requested and subject to certain limitations for national security and the interests of persons primarily concerned.
[3] *Scott* v. *Scott* [1913] A.C. 417. The Registrar had ordered a petition for nullity of marriage to be heard *in camera*. The respondent applied to have the petitioner and her solicitor attached for contempt of court for publishing an account of the proceedings. The court granted the application, and the Court of Appeal held that it had no jurisdiction to intervene. The House of Lords asserted jurisdiction and found no contempt as the Registrar was incompetent to order a hearing *in camera*.

secondly, in lunacy proceedings; and thirdly, in those cases where secrecy, as for instance the secrecy of a process of manufacture or discovery or invention—trade secrets—is of the essence of the cause.

These exceptions are perhaps too narrowly drawn—for example, the needs of national security may, as Article 6 (1) recognizes, sometimes require the exclusion of the public—but certain other exceptions in Article 6 (1) are so large and loosely expressed as to cover almost any denial of public hearing. In the first plae, the decision to exclude the public is placed wholly in the discretion of the court, of which Lord Shaw observed:

> To remit the maintenance of constitutional right to the region of judicial discretion is to shift the foundations of freedom from rock to sand.

In particular, it is difficult to imagine in what 'special circumstances' not already covered by other wide exceptions, a court might be of opinion that it was 'strictly necessary' to prevent publicity from prejudicing 'the interests of justice'.[1] But it is not difficult to imagine what Bentham or Lord Shaw would have said of so large a breach in the protection of rights.

Secondly, the expression 'public order', 'l'ordre public' in the French text, suffers here from its usual ambiguity. Does it mean simply order in the court and its precincts, or is it some vaster concept of public policy? Again what is the extent of the protection that may be given to 'the private life of the parties'? Is it to be confined to the ground on which Lord Shaw based his first two exceptions, that they are concerned with 'transactions truly *intra familiam*',[2] or does it cover the exclusion from publicity of revelations that may be perhaps uncomfortable, politically inconvenient, or commercially damaging?[3]

The question has arisen before the Commission whether the

---

[1] A Belgian court invoked this exception in ordering that both preliminary investigation and trial be conducted *in camera* of certain narcotics offences, on the ground that publicity given to the names of the drugs involved would 'jeopardise the interests of justice' by suggesting the use of habit-forming drugs: Tribunal Correctional, Brussels (27.1.1965) 645/Soc./63. It is not easy to see why the exception in the interests of justice was preferred. See also BGH (16.6.1964): *N.J.W.* [1964] 1485. See 1913/63: (sexual offences involving young boys).

[2] A Belgian court has suggested that the test is whether 'the repercussions of a public hearing would be so grave and far-reaching as to endanger the emotional ties or family situation of the individual concerned or his near relations': Tribunal Correctional, Brussels (17.3.1966) 8668/B/65.

[3] As to trade secrets, see K. J. Partsch, *Die Rechte und Freiheiten*, etc., p. 158, n. 508.

requirement of fair and public hearing implies a right to an oral hearing; and is closely related to personal appearance of parties to proceedings. The Commission has not attributed a literal meaning to the word 'hearing',[1] but has given pre-eminence to the need for adequate presentation of testimony and argument, either orally or in writing. So in a case of extradition it said:

it appears from the transcripts of those hearings that the Applicant had full opportunity to state his case and to expound the grounds upon which he not only claimed that his extradition had been demanded for reasons other than those mentioned in the extradition request, and consequently should be refused by the Respondent Government, but also invoked the right to political asylum; ... furthermore, from the outset of the proceedings, the Applicant was represented by competent legal counsel who in writing submitted to the courts in question relevant arguments on behalf of the Applicant ... the Commission finds that the Applicant was given full opportunity of stating his case, be it in person before the investigating judge (Ermittlungsrichter) or through submission of written pleadings ...[2]

Where the procedure prescribed is limited to written pleadings, it would be reasonable for the judgment of the court to be communicated to the parties in writing. Yet Article 6 (1) states explicitly that judgment is to be delivered publicly,[3] and indeed proceedings conducted on the basis of written pleadings are not likely to be easily comprehended and overseen by members of the public in attendance. The dilemma is perhaps resolved by treating 'fair and public hearing' as essentially a single process: it mut be fair and it must be seen to be fair, but the second requirement may within limits give way to the first.

Austria has made the requirement of public hearing a subject of reservation under Article 64.[4] Under *SPO*, Articles 285 *d* and 294, as

---

[1] However, a German court has so intepreted 'public hearing' in Article 6 (1) though excluding from its scope all administrative proceedings: Oberlandesgericht, Bavaria (21.9.1960): *N.J.W.* [1960] 270. Contrast *Gopalan* v. *State of Madras* [1950] India, Supreme Court: S.C.R. 88: 'I am not prepared to accept the contention that a right to be heard orally is an essential right of procedure even according to the rules of natural justice.'

[2] 1802/63: 6 *Yearbook* 462, 482. See also 599/59, where the applicant 'had the possibility of presenting arguments in writing in support of his appeal' so that the proceedings were not, despite the absence of an oral hearing, inconsistent with Article 6.

[2] The ruling of the German Federal Supreme Court that a judgment, given upon wholly written pleadings, may itself be communicated in writing to the parties consistently with Article 6 (1), may then, on a strict reading of the Article, be questioned: Bundesgerichtshof (27.6.1957): *N.J.W.* [1957] 1480.

[4] *Collected Texts*, 5th ed., Section 5; and see 2243/64: *Recueil* 17.

authorized by Bundesverfassungsgesetz, Article 90, provide that under certain conditions an appeal (*Berufung*) or plea of nullity (*Nichtigkeitsbeschwerde*) may be dismissed at a non-public hearing (*nichtöffentliche Beratung*). The reservation states that Article 6 of the Convention shall not prejudice the principles laid down in Article 90.

The Court, after considering the French and English texts of Article 6 (1), and finding that in terms they might be seen as stricter than Article 14 (1) of the Covenant—judgment 'shall be made public/sera public', did not feel 'bound to adopt a liberal interpretation' since:

... many member States of the Council of Europe have a long-standing tradition of recourse to other means, besides reading out aloud, for making public the decisions of all or some of their courts, and especially of their courts of cassation for example, deposit in a registry accessible to the public . . . It considers that in each case the form of publicity to the given to the 'judgment' under the domestic law of the respondent State must be assessed in the light of the special features of the proceedings in question and by reference to the object and purpose of Article 6 (1).[1] *Within a reasonable time/dans un delai raisonnable*

Two questions arise on this requirement: between what points of time does the period run; and what facts must be taken into account to determine what is reasonable?

For *civil* proceedings the Court has set certain criteria for determining what is reasonable since:

The reasonableness of the length of proceedings coming with the scope of Article 6 (1) must be assessed in each case according to the particular circumstances . . . The Court has regard, *inter alia*, to the complexity of the factual and legal issues raised by the case, to the conduct of the applicants and the competent authorities and to what was at stake for the former; in addition, only delays attributable to the State may justify a finding of a failure to comply with the 'reasonable time' requirement . . .[2]

The conduct of the litigants in raising the issues in the proceedings that require new evidence or argument,[3] or in themselves apply for deferment or interruption of the proceedings.[4] The delays attributable to the administration of justice as a system may be in length unaccept-

---

[1] *Pretto* (Italy): Judgment No. 71 (25.10.1983) § 26; see also Axen (F.R.G.): Judgment No. 72; *Sutter* (Switzerland): Judgment No. 74 (22.2.84).
[2] *Zimmermann/Steiner* (Switzerland): Judgment No. 66 (13.7.1983) § 24.
[3] *Buchholz* (F.R.G.) Judgment No. 42 (6.5.1981).
[4] *Zand* 7360/75 (Austria), Report 15 D.R. 70, 84.

able,[1] but may often be due to the workload of the courts;[2] the court observed the significant increase in the volume of litigation in the Federal Republic of Germany, resulting from 'deterioration in the general economic situation'.[3] The use of test case procedure may deal with a multiple list of action.[4]

It has been said, in a number of applications,[5] that the point in time from which the period of Article 6 begins, in *criminal* proceedings is that at which the action of the authorities, by way particularly of arrest or charge, causes 'serious repercussions' on the position of the individual.

In stating that the period of reasonable time runs between charge and sentence, the Commission has not indicated whether the later point is the end of trial at first instance or the moment at which the sentence becomes *res judicata*, which could in some systems be the conclusion of an appeal. Since the Convention does not guarantee any right of appeal for a convicted person, it could be said that the period of reasonable time ends properly at the end of trial. However, it may be necessary to distinguish between forms of appeal: thus, for example, appeal may in some systems be brought against sentence by the public prosecutor or against the conviction itself by the Attorney General, or his equivalent, 'for the protection of the law'. Where either sentence or conviction is not *res judicata* until conclusion of the appeal, and these proceedings are unduly protracted, the time in which the charge has been determined may cease to be reasonable in the sense of Article 6.

The Commission and the Court have been agreed that the criteria for the determination of what is 'reasonable time' in Article 6 are the complexity of the facts and law in issue, the conduct of the authorities interim the system of criminal justice, and the conduct in the proceedings of the accused.[6]

These are matters in great part of circumstantial evidence: for example, the length of time taken for the proceedings may be in itself

---

[1] *Karrer et al.* 7464/76 (Austria) Report 16 D.R. 42; *König Judgment* (F.R.G.), No. 27 (28.6.1978) §§ 110, 111.

[2] 8737/79: 23 D.R. 220.

[3] *Buchholz* in n. 11 above.

[4] 8954/80 (F.R.G). 26 D.R. 194 (proceedings against zone planning permission for the construction of a new airport near Munich).

[5] Exemplified in *Hätti* 6181/73 (F.R.G.) 6 D.R. 22; *Bocchieri* 6323/73 (Italy) 8 D.R. 59.

[6] Applied in 1936/63 and later formulated in the *Neumeister Judgment* No. 8 (27.6.1968); *Ringeisen Judgment* No. 13 (16.7.1971).

questionable;[1] the complexity of the proceedings may be even increased by the system in use;[2] the effect of flight abroad may be material,[3] as may the consquent reduction of sentence of a convicted person as reparation.[4] It is not then possible to provide a general interpretation of what constitutes 'reasonable time' in Article 6.

The Belgian Court de Cassation had dismissed the appeal of the applicant on points of law because the documents before it did not, in its view, show any intervention in the case by the judge, when working in the public prosecutors department. But the Court did not find this conclusive, saying:

In order that the courts may inspire in the public the confidence which is indispensable, account must also be taken of questions of internal organisation. If an individual, after holding in the public prosecutor's department an office whose nature is such that he may have dealt with a given matter in the course of his duties, subsequently sits in the same case as a judge, the public are entitled to fear that he does not offer sufficient guarantees of impartiality.

This expresses the counter-presumption, but the critical words 'may have dealt' show the reasoning confused, for the Court held, in disagreement with the Cour de Cassation, that the trial judge 'did in fact play a part in the proceedings' in the public prosecutor's department.[5]

In a detailed examination of a summing-up to the jury, and other observations in court in absence of jury, the Commission found no evidence of partiality in the judge.[6] But the counter-presumption principle was hardly observed in the following Austrian case.[7] The applicant was charged of assault with intent to rob in the office of a travel agency; the foreman of the jury was employed by a tourist organization, which owned the travel agency, and the jury, composed of three judges and eight other individuals, returned a unanimous verdict of guilty. The Commission found the application inadmissible.

---

[1] *Haase* 7412/76 (F.R.G.) 11 D.R. 78 (seven years can be justified only by 'special circumstances') and *Eckle* 8130/78 (F.R.G.) 16 D.R. 120.

[2] See *Neumeister* in n. 18 (23 persons involved in 22 offences, comprising 32,000 pages of evidence, but on 12 charges, initially investigated, the applicant was convicted on one only).

[3] *Kofler* 8261/78 (Italy) 25 D.R. 157.

[4] 8182/78 (F.R.G.) 25 D.R. 142.

[5] Judgment No. 31.

[6] 5574/72 (U.K.) 3 D.R. 10.

[7] 7428/76 (Austria) 13 D.R. 36.

within a reasonable time/dans un délai raisonnable

Two questions arise on this requirement: between what points does the period run, and what facts must be taken into account in the determination of what is reasonable?

The Commission has affirmed that the words in criminal proceedings

refer to the period that elapses between the charge and the sentence, and not that between the offence and the charge, as is quite clear from the English text as well as the French[1]

We have to ask then at what point a person is charged for the purposes of Article 6. At least four possible phases can be discerned in the period between the commission of an offence and the beginning of the trial of a person charged with it. He may have passed from being simply a witness of the act to being suspected of having committed it. The suspicion may be hardened to the point where the is charged with a specific offence in respect of the act; and finally a formal indictment may be delivered on the basis of which trial can commence.

In the various legal systems of the contracting states not all these phases are clearly distinguished nor is the position of the individual necessarily the same in each phase.[2] For example, the point at which the individual becomes bound to answer questions under interrogation or ceases to be so bound not only vary with the forms of criminal investigation and procedure but are by no means easy to determine in a given case.[3] Again, the individual may, particularly under the inquisitorial procedure in use in France and to a large extent in Germany and Austria, be arrested and detained, or his personal effects and papers seized, a considerable time before a formal charge of a specific offence against him.

Construction of the word 'charge' in Article 6 in terms of any particular system of law or procedure would therefore lead only to uneven

---

[1] 1545/62: 5 *Yearbook* 270, 276 (the applicant complained in effect of the delay between the alleged offence and the presentation of the charge).

[2] The last two are exemplified by the distinction in German criminal procedure between *Angeschuldigter*, a person against whom a public charge (*öffentliche Klage*) has been brought, and *Angeklagter*, the person after the indictment (*Anklageschrift*) has been delivered and the main proceedings opened (*Eröffnung des Hauptverfahrens*).

[3] See, for example, *The Accused—A Comparative Study*: ed. J. A. Coutts (1966), pp. 3–8, and under particular countries.

and artificial results. A criterion of when an individual is charged must be sought, which can be generally applied without reference to technical differences of procedure, and which depends not upon what is in the minds of the police or investigating authority, but upon their overt acts.[1] A certierion is suggested by a vivid expression used by Lord Devlin. Writing of English pre-trial procedure he said:[2]

> The caution, charge or arrest is the 'declaration of war' at which the interrogee ceases to be the good citizen helping the police as 'neutral inquirer', and becomes the accused, no longer bound to assist or to reply to questions.

The Commission has adopted a criterion of this order,[3] which might in some cases cover period (*d*) in the diagram considered under Article 5 (3) above.

An unusual form of the problem appears where, in German criminal procedure, a new trial is ordered of a convicted person; from the time of the reopening of the procedure (*Wiederaufnahme des Verfahrens*), he resumes his status of an accused and he is transferred from imprisonment as a convict to a place of detention pending trial (*Untersuchungsanstalt*). It is arguable thus that, in terms of the Convention, he ceases to be detained under Article 5 (1) *a*, but becomes once more a person detained under Article 5 (1) *c*, to whom the provisions of Article 5 (3) apply.[4]

In stating that the period of reasonable time runs between charge and sentence, the Commission has not indicated whether the later point is the end of trial at first instance or the moment at which the sentence becomes *res judicata*, which could in some systems be the conclusion of an appeal. Since the Convention does not guarantee any right of appeal for a convicted person, it could be said that the period of reasonable time ends properly at the end of trial. However, it may be necessary to distinguish between forms of appeal: thus, for example, appeal may in some systems be brought against sentence by the public prosecutor or against the conviction itself by the Attorney General, or his equivalent, 'for the protection of the law'. Where either sentence or conviction is not *res judicata* until conclusion of the appeal,

---

[1] As to the subjective elements in the process by which the individual passes from being a witness, to a suspect and to a person charged, see Lord Kilbranden in *The Accused—A Comparative Study*, pp. 60, 61, discussing Scottish pre-trial procedure.

[2] *The Criminal Prosecution in England* (1962), ch. 2.

[3] 1936/63: Report of the Commission (27.5.1966) at 84.

[4] 1873/63.

and these proceedings are unduly protracted, the time in which the charge has been determined may cease to be reasonable in the sense of Article 6.

As to reasonableness, it seems that the period between charge and sentence must neither be so short as to impair the rights guaranteed under Article 6 (3) and in particular subparagraph (*b*), nor longer than necessary to prepare and conduct a fair trial of the charge: and in particular it must not be so long as to render the trial unfair through destruction or deficiency of evidence. Here the complexity of the case, already considered in connection with Article 5 (3),[1] the system and conduct of its investigation and of its trial, and the contributions, if any, to delay by the individual concerned, must all be taken into account.[2]

The requirement of determination within a reasonable time is less energetic and exacting than that of the NATO Status of Forces Agreement 1953, Article VII-9, which provides that

> Whenever a member of a force or civilian component or a dependant is prosecuted under the jurisdiction of the receiving State he shall be entitled:
> *a*. to a prompt and speedy trial;[3]

This language, unlike that of Article 6 (1), distinguishes between the interval between charge and commencement of trial and the length of trial itself, but there is still little authority[4]—and perhaps given the great variety of material circumstances that have to be considered, there cannot be—on what constitutes prompt and speedy trial. So in the *El Oro Mining and Railway Company Case*[5] the Great Britain–Mexico Claims Commission said that it would

> not attempt to lay down with precision just within what period a tribunal may be expected to render judgment. This will depend upon several circumstances, foremost among them upon the volume of work involved by a thorough examination of the case:

---

[1] See p. 107 above.

[2] 1936/63 (Report of Commission). See also 2120/64, 2516/65: and 2654/65: Schertenreb 8339/78 (Switzerland) 23 D.R. 137.

[3] The remaining provisions of the section are parallel to Article 6 (3) of the Convention.

[4] See R. B. Ellert, *NATO Fair Trial Safeguards*, 20, 25–7.

[5] [1937] 5 *R.I.A.A.* 191, 198.

But 'wrongful delays in giving judgment' will constitute a denial of justice;[1] and in criminal proceedings protracted hearings without apparent need to get further evidence,[2] or repeated adjournments,[3] will constitute undue delay. Further, lengthy proceedings leading to a conviction, which is ultimately quashed, are a denial of justice.[4]

by an independent and impartial tribunal/par un tribunal indépendant et impartial

A question arises whether rights and obligations covered by Article 6 (1) must be referred directly to a court, or whether the provision is met, if there is initially an administrative decision with subsequent control by the courts. The Austrian Constitutional Court has, in a full examination of the whole provision, in two cases,[5] decided that it is so met. The court observed that it might be argued that subsequent judicial control (*Nachprüfung*) did not satisfy the requirements of Article 6 (1) for three reasons: first, that in Austria the function of the Constitutional Court and the Administrative Court is to supervise rather than to determine; second, that they rule only on appeals, for the confirmation or setting aside of decisions; and third, that they are not competent to investigate the facts fully. The court rejected this reasoning. First, Article 6 (1) did not in terms require that a matter be referred directly (*unmittelbar*) to a tribunal. Secondly, a decision of either court in cassation obliges the administrative instances concerned to give effect in the case before it of the legal consequences of that decision. Thirdly, neither the Constitutional Court nor the Administrative Court were, even before the advent of the Convention, precluded from examining the facts of a case; in particular, the Administrative Court was expresssly authorized to quash an administrative decision, if the statement of facts was inadequate or if there was a substantial divergence between the decision and the facts stated.[6] But the introduction of Article 6 (1) as a *constitutional* provision in Austrian law[7] means that the competence of both courts is, as far as

---

[1] *Fabiani Case* [1892] Moore I.A. 4878, 4895.

[2] *Chattin Case* [1927] U.S.–Mexico Claims Commission: 4 *R.I.A.A.* 282, 292 (nearly four months spent in determining an application for release pending trial).

[3] *Salem Case* [1934] 2 *R.I.A.A.* 1161, Nielsen diss. See also R. B. Ellert, op. cit., at 27.

[4] *Dyches Case* [1929] U.S.–Mexico Claims Commission: 4 *R.I.A.A.* 458, 461.

[5] Verfassungsgerichtshof (14.10.1965): *Österr. Juristen-Zeitung* [1966] 248, 409.

[6] Verwaltungsgerichtsgesetz, ss. 41 and 42.

[7] Verfassungsgesetz (4.3.1964) Abs. ii: *B.G.B.I.* No. 59.

may be necessary, enlarged in order that a fair hearing of the matter in issue may be secured.

The often fine distinction between independence and impartiality turns mainly, it seems, on that between the status of the tribunal determinable largely by objective tests and the subjective attitudes of its members, lay or legal. Independence is primarily freedom from control by, or subordination to, the executive power in the State; impartiality is rather absence in the members of the tribunal of personal interest in the issues to be determined by it, or of some form of prejudice.[1]

The independence of a tribunal is secured under Article 6 by its members being not answerable at any stage to anyone in the hierarchy of government,[2] and being irremovable during the exercise by the tribunal of its functions.[3] Further, the transfer of cases from a plenary court to divisions or chambers does not put their independence in question.[4]

The role of law officers in the courts has called for a distinction between the tasks of prosecution and advice: so the position and functions of the Generalprokuratur in Austria in military proceedings in the Supreme Court were described as follows:

His task is in a more objective way to ensure respect of the law in criminal proceedings and he does not, like a prosecutor, have the additional task to see that reasonably suspected persons are convicted and adequately punished.[5]

So, where a plea of nullity is made, if the Generalprokuratur is not a party to the proceedings, but makes observations on the draft decision of the Judge-Rapporteur, and, if he expresses disagreement, the Supreme Court conducts an oral hearing: otherwise it considers the draft decision in private. The Commission remarked that

This circumstance is certainly not of itself even prima facie that the court sitting in private was subject to any discretion [by the Generalprokuratur], and was not an independent and impartial tribunal . . .[6]

---

[1] K. J. Partsch, *Die Rechte und Freiheiten der europäischen Menschenrechtskonvention* (1966), p. 155, makes an analogous distinction between *Staatsunabhängigkeit*, *Parteienunabhängigkeit*, and *Gesellschaftsundabhängigkeit*.

[2] *Zand* 7360/76 (Austria) Report 15 D.R. 70.

[3] *Sutter* 8209/76 (Switzerland) 16 D.R. 166.

[4] *Pretto* 7984/77 (Italy) 16 D.R. 92: *Axen* 8209/78 (F.R.G.): Judgment No. 72 (8.12.1983).

[5] *Ofner* and *Hopfinger* 524/59 and 617/59.

[6] *Huber* 5523/72 (Austria) 46 *Recueil* 99.

The impartiality of a tribunal and its members may be sometimes more difficult to determine than its independence. There is on the other hand a generally accepted presumption that the established courts and tribunals are impartial in the conduct of cases before them, and consequently the burden of proof of partiality lies upon those who claim it in a given case; on the other hand, the administration of justice necessarily requires that a claim of partiality must be considered in a given case on the facts taken as a whole, and here the evidence may demonstrate some partiality in the conduct of the judicial proceedings, or it may be sufficient to create a counter-presumption of partiality. So where a trial judge had been previously head of section in the Brussels public prosecutor's department and had taken some part in the preparation of the case against the accused,[1] the Court said:

It would be going too far to the opposite extreme to maintain that former judicial officers in the public prosecutor's department were unable to sit on the bench in every case that had been initially examined by that department, even, though they had never had to deal with the case themselves ...

Similarly, in considering the effect of press reports of trial proceedings,[2] hostile to the accused, the Commission said:

... it is clear that in certain cases, and in particular in cases where laymen participate as jurors in the proceedings, this guarantee may be seriously impaired by a virulent press campaign against the accused, which so influenced public opinion and thereby the jurors, that the hearing can no longer be considered to be a 'fair hearing' within the meaning of Article 6. ... In the present case the Applicant has not submitted any evidence, for example any passage in the text of the relevant decisions, which could lend the Commission to conclude that the articles appearing in the ... newspaper ... did so influence the jurors ...[3]

Where there is local prejudice against the accused, intensified by press articles, he must, before claiming a breach of the Convention, have sought, if it is possible, a change of venue. In the *Pfunders Case*[4]

---

[1] *Piersack Judgment* (Belgium) No. 53 (1.10.1982) § 30.

[2] Issues of contempt of court may arise, and generally a distinction must be made between the periods before and during trial, after trial, and before the conclusion of appeal: *R. v. Duffy, ex pte Nash* [1960] 2 Q.B. 188 in *England*; and after conclusion of appeal: *Attorney General v. Butterworth* [1963] 1 Q.B. 696. Scottish practice is stricter: see *Stirling v. Associated Newspapers* [1960] J.C. 5; and *McAlister v. Associated Newspapers* [1954] S.L.T. 14. For the possibility that communications by the police or authorities before trial may prejudice a fair hearing, see 2343/64: *Recueil* 22.

[3] 1476/62.

[4] 788/60: 4 *Yearbook* 166: the accused were seven German-speaking inhabitants of the Italian Tyrol charged with murder of an Italian *Guardia di Finanze*.

the Austrian Government claimed that there was a breach of Article 6 (1) of the Convention, since

four out of six jurors were of 'Italian ethnic origin' and were 'particularly liable to be swayed by the Italian press campaign, the political tension, the vehement argument of the Public Prosecutor' . . .,

but the Commission held that, since

the Italian Government have shown that according to Article 55 (2) of the Code of Criminal Procedure an accused may in any event apply for a change of venue on the grounds of *suspicion légitime* and that the persons concerned in this case did not do so either at first instance or on appeal,

there had been a failure to exhaust local remedies.

The suggestion that the principle *stare decisis* may impair the independence or impartiality of a tribunal has been rejected by the Commission. An applicant had been convicted of collaboration with the enemy in Norway, and alleged a breach of Article 6 (1) in that the Oslo District Court (Lagmannsrett) and the appeal committee of the Supreme Court (Höyesterrett) had refused a retrial, in face of new submissions, on the ground that they were bound by previous decisions on whether there was a state of war in Norway after June 1940. The Commission pointed out that the District Court and the appeal committee

found that the submission by the Applicant of new evidence and argument did not justify a departure from jurisprudence which had been established by the Norwegian courts over a long period; and that it is evident that the reliance by a tribunal on established and appropriate jurisprudence has no relation to the notion of a tribunal acting in a manner which is not independent and impartial.

Where a tribunal repudiates, on other than legal grounds, a line of defence put forward by the accused, and in effect compels its abandonment, there is a lack of impartiality and so no fair hearing.[1]

Contempt of court. The term is used here because it described certain rules, which are designed to prevent the impairment of the

---

[1] 1727/62: 6 *Yearbook* 370 (the President of the Court of Appeal, acting as *juge-rapporteur*, described the defence at the trial as 'invraisemblable, scandaleux, mensonger, ignoble et répugnant' and indicated that the court would have to consider whether the sentence imposed 'était suffisante, en égard au système de défense adopté'): *Report of Sub-Commission* (friendly settlement) 17.2.1965: *Recueil* 15 (compensation paid).

administration of justice, and so save to maintain fair hearing. Under the Convention it can be said that the court process must not be subjected to outside interference, particularly by statements or publications, which could influence the court, or at least make it questionable whether justice is being really done.

The Commission has more than once had to observe the impact of articles or statements in the press on court proceedings. So the start of the trial of members of the Baader-Meinhof group (Red Army Fraction Rote Armee Fraktion) was proceeded by a 'press campaign tolerated—if not organized—by the public authorities', in which the applicants[1] were described as 'bandits' and 'gangs of murderers'. They had died in fact in course of the trial. Their applications being maintained, the Commission observed that:[2]

... the press, and even the authorities responsible for crime policy, cannot be expected to refrain from all statements not about the guilt of the accused persons but about their dangerous character where uncontested information is available to them (prisoners convictions, use of firearms on arrest, liberation of Baader by force etc.). The exceptional measures surrounding the trial were admitted by such as to foster the public conviction that the applicants were criminals. The measures and the statements made by the authorities were however a response to the acts and declarations of the applicants and other members of the Red Army Fraction, and were not designed to create artificially a climate of opinion unfavourable to the accused, who were moreover tried by professional judges and not by a jury, which is by its nature more easily influenced.[3]

The Commission found no denial of fair hearing on these grounds.

In a leading case under the Convention,[4] the Court had to consider an injunction, granted in the English courts, restraining the publication of an article describing the production and sale of the drug thalidomide, which was subject to proceedings in the courts. It is necessary to summarize the facts.

Between 1959 and 1962 a numbr of babies had been born deformed, allegedly because their mothers had taken thalidomide as a tranquilizer or sleeping pill during their pregnancy. Civil actions for damages were brought against Distillers (Biochemicals) Ltd., the

---

[1] *Ensslin, Baader, Raspe* 7572/6 (F.R.G.): 14 D.R. 64.
[2] Ibid. p. 112.
[3] 1476/62: 11 Cok. Dec. 31 (press campaign found not to have influenced a jury).
[4] *Sunday Times Case* (U.K.) Judgment No. 30 (26.4.1979).

manufacturers and sellers of the drug, and had reached the stage of settlement negotiations in 1972. In September 1972 the *Sunday Times* published an article entitled: 'Our Thalidomide Children—A Cause for National Shame', and declared its intention to publish a long article tracing the history of the manufacture, history, and sale of the drug in 1961. In October 1972, Distillers (Biochemicals) Ltd. approached the Attorney-General, claiming that the published article was a contempt of court, given the litigation still outstanding, and he in turn sought and was granted an injunction[1] to restrain the publication of the proposed second article. The House of Lords directed the High Court to order that:

... Times Newspapers Ltd ... be restrained from publishing or causing or authorising or procuring to be published or printed, any article or matter, which prejudges the issues of negligence, breach of contract, or breach of duty, or deals with the evidence relating to any of the said issues, arising in any actions pending or imminent against Distillers ... in respect of the development, distribution or use of the drug 'thalidomide'.

The Commission having by a majority found that the injunction was contrary to Article 10 of the Convention, referred the case to the Court. The Court, in its judgment, recognized two forms of interference of the administration of justice by the press: pressure and prejudgment. The notion of pressure had been described in *Vine Products Ltd.* v. *Green*,[2] in which it was stated that:

It is a contempt of this court for any newspaper to comment on pending legal proceedings in any way which is likely to prejudice the fair trial of the action. That may arise in various ways. It may be that the comment is one which is likely in some way or other to bring pressure to bear upon one or other of the parties to the action, so as to prevent that party from prosecuting or from defending the action, or encourage that party to submit to terms of compromise which he might otherwise not have been prepared to entertain, or influence him in some other way in his conduct in the action ...

The language is ambiguous as to whether both criminal and civil proceedings are covered by the rule, though it can be assumed that they are.

The House of Lords in its reasoning indicated another kind of

---

[1] The High Court granted an injunction but this was reversed by the Court of Appeal; but on further appeal the House of Lords restored the injunction: *Attorney General* v. *Times Newspapers Ltd* [1973] 3 A.E.R. 54.

[2] [1966].

pressure, as an element in contempt of court, pressure on the public at large that could invite prejudicial discussion of issues and so inhibit recourse to the courts.[1]

The 'prejudgment principle' was largely taken for granted by the court, which referred to various authorities quoted by the House of Lords, and said:

Even if the court does have certain doubts concerning the precision with which the principle [prejudgment] was formulated at the relevant time, it considers that the applicants were able to foresee, to a degree that was reasonable in the circumstances, a risk that publication of the draft article might fall foul of the principle.

The court concluded then that, given that the injunction was a registration of freedom of expression under Article 10 (1), it was nevertheless legitimate under Article 10 (2) 'prescribed by law', and had the purpose of 'maintaining the authority and impartiality of the judiciary'. But a final question remained under Article 10 (2). Was the injunction 'necessary in a democratic society' for the purpose indicated. The Court and the Commission both found that, in all the circumstances in particular the undisputed public concern, need for the public to have information to 'serve as a brake on speculative and unenlightened discussion, and the fact that the proceedings in the court against Distillers Ltd. had reached a stage of settlement negotiations, making it doubtful whether the issue of negligence would fall to be detrimental by the courts, the inspiration was not "necessary" under Article 10 (2); and this finding the court found strengthened by the fact that the injunction was discharged by reference only to the "pressure principle" and not the "prejudgment principle" '.

It would not be easy to draw from the reasoning of the court, and of the national courts, in this case, any precise rules for the protection of fair hearing in the courts from interference from the press,[2] but the Contempt of Court Act (1981) makes an advance; s. 5 provides that:

A publication made as or as part of a discussion in good faith of public affairs or other matters of general public interest is not to be treated as a contempt of court under the strict liability rule, if the risk of impediment or prejudice to particular legal proceedings is merely incidental to the discussion.

---

[1] So Lord Justice Phillimore in the Court of Appeal said that 'an attempt to stir up public feeling against a party is a serious contempt'.

[2] A helpful study is P. J. Duffy, 'The Sunday Times case: Freedom of Expression Contempt of Court and the ECHR' 5 *Human Rights Review* (1980) 17.

The proceedings must be 'active . . . at the time of publication' and must be 'seriously impeded or prejudiced' for the Act to apply: s. 2. The 'strict liability rule' is described as 'the rule of law whereby conduct may be treated as a contempt of court as tending to interfere with the course of justice in particular legal proceedings, regardless of intent to do so': s. 1.

The relationship between 'good faith' and 'regardless of intent', and the determination of what is 'merely incidental', do not make the application of the structure easy. The obligations of a non-judicial body[1] to act fairly in conducting an investigation was considered by the Court of Appeal in a case involving the United Kingdom Race Relations Board. Lord Scarman said:

The Board was created so that in the sensitive field of race relations compliance with the law and the resolution of differences could first be sought without recourse to the courts with their necessarily open and formalised judicial process. . . . The procedures are not adversatorial but conciliatory; settlement, not litigation, is the business of the Board, and it is left to the Board to decide how best to perform the functions which the Act requires it to perform, namely, investigation, the formation of opinion, conciliation, and if all else fails, the taking of legal proceedings in the county court.

The Court of Appeal was satisfied with the practice of the Board in delegating to its staff the task of containing needed information by investigation or inquiry. Lord Denning, Master of the Rolls, said:

Every member of a judicial body must have access to all the evidence and papers in the case, he must have heard all the arguments, and must come to his own conclusions. The maxim *delegatus non potest delegare* applies strictly to judicial functions. But it is different with a body exercising administrative functions or which is making an investigation or conducting preliminary inquiries especially when it is a numerous body. The Race Relations Board has twelve members. The employment committee has seven members. It is impossible to suppose that all of them need to sit to determine a matter. Nor that all of those who sit should have read all the papers or heard all the evidence . . . a quorum must have done so.

The independence of tribunals is in great part a matter of their structure, function and relationship to executive power. Impartiality is

---

[1] The Contempt of Court Act (1981) s. 19 states that a court 'includes any tribunal or body exercising the judicial power of the State'; but what is such a tribunal or body has not been more closely defined.

to be assessed in light of the special circumstances of a case, and it may not always be obvious.[1]

established by law/établi par la loi

While this requirement plainly prohibits the establishment of extraordinary courts by mere executive order,[2] it does not necessarily mean that a tribunal, established by law, but not composed *according to law*, is necessarily inconsistent with Article 6. So, in the view of the Commission, administrative errors in the composition of the tribunal must have led to a denial of justice, before they can be impugned under Article 6:

the composition of the jury is an administrative matter which does not as such concern the 'establishment' of the court; . . . any administrative error is to be taken into account only insofar as the error caused such prejudice to the Applicant as to amount to a denial of justice . . .[3]

The Austrian Supreme Court had also found that 'such mistakes of administration', as had occurred in the case, could not be made a ground for quashing the conviction for faulty composition of the court.[4]

Judgment shall be pronounced publicly, but the press and public may be excluded from all or part of the trial/ Le jugement doit être rendu publiquement, mais l'accès de la salle d'audience peut être interdit à la presse et au public

Certain aspects of the permitted exceptions to publicity have already been discussed.

[1] In 5574/72 (U.K.): 3 D.R. 10 (the foreman of the jury was an employee of the organization, which owned the travel agency, burgled by the accused).

[2] But not the conferment of specialized jurisdiction on a normal court: 1216/61: *Recueil* (1963) i (Third Criminal Chamber of Landgericht, Coblenz, competent to try offences committed in the exercise of public office; bribery and breaches of security by private persons; and false declarations by persons and under oath: found by the Commission not to be an 'extraordinary court').

[3] 1476/62: *Recueil* (1963) ii (certain jurors had been admitted as 'principal jurors' though not included in the official list; the court was established under Article 14*a*, and functioned under Chapter 19 of the Austrian SPO).

[4] SPO § 345 (1) '. . . if the Court or jury was not set for hearing, if all the judges or jurors did not assist at the entire trial or if a disqualified judge or juror took part in the trial'.

Must the pronouncement of judgment always be public, or is it part of the trial so as also to fall under the permitted exceptions to publicity? Two considerations support the first construction; First, the term 'trial' does not necessarily include every stage of the whole proceedings from charge or commencement of action up to judgment; in particular, interlocutory proceedings in civil cases and preliminary investigations in criminal matters are frequently conducted without press or public having effective access, though the principle of publicity is observed both in the presence of the parties or their representatives and in the subsequent disclosure in court of the results of those proceedings or investigations. The reference in the French text to 'la salle d'audience' possibly also suggests that 'trial' is to be understood as the main hearing.[1] Secondly, since it is the judgment which is of decisive importance for the accused or the parties and is the expression by the court of the will of the community, it should be always public.

Some miscellaneous points must be mentioned in connection with Article 6 (1). First, as is perhaps obvious from its wording, it confers no right on a private individual to bring, or cause to be brought, criminal proceedings against another.[2] Secondly, in most countries there is a procedure for controlling vexatious litigants, in which the 'querulant' will be prevented from litigating in all matters or in prescribed matters save with the leave of a court or through an appointed guardian *ad litem*. The Commission has held that such a limitation is not a denial 'du droit à une bonne administration de la justice', and is not therefore contrary to Article 6 (1).[3]

Everyone charged with a criminal offence shall be presumed innocent until proven guilty according to law/ Toute personne accusée d'une infraction est présumé innocente judqu'à ce que sa culpabilité ait été légalement établié

The Commission has said[4] that these words

---

[1] In the German translation it is rendered as *Verhandlung*, rather than *Verfahren*, which also perhaps indicates a distinction between the hearing and the pronouncement of judgment. K. J. Partsch, *die Rechte und Freiheiten*, p. 157, however, regards the translation as misleading.

[2] 809/60.   [3] 412/58.

[4] 343/57: 2 *Yearbook* 446. For the relation between presumption of innocence and reasonable suspicion see 176/56 (Report of the Commission) pp. 462–71. The principle

cannot be understood as guaranteeing to an accused person that he will have no prejudicial opinions concerning his guilt or innocence expressed by a witness at his trial.

From this it would follow that it is only some act or omission by the court itself, which can operate as a failure of presumption of innocence. Here it may be remarked that the presumption of innocence does not imply where lies the main burden of proof at the trial of the charge, that is to say, upon the prosecution to prove the guilt of the accused beyond a reasonable doubt. The presumption of innocence does not necessarily have this function; for example, in Germany there is no such distribution of the burden of proof, since it is the duty of the court to do all that is necessary to discover the truth[1] and it is the presiding judge who conducts the trial, examines the accused, and admits all necessary evidence; nevertheless the principle *in dubio pro reo* prevails in German criminal procedure.[2]

Ther term 'charged' is not to be understood as limiting the rule to criminal proceedings. It does not mean that

... the authorities may not inform the public about criminal investigations. They do not violate Article 6 (2) if they state that a suspicion exists, that people have been arrested, that they have confessed etc. ... However, the Commission stresses that in its view, public authorities, in particular those involved in criminal investigations and proceedings, should be careful when making statements in public, if at all, about matters under investigation and on the persons concerned thereby, in order to avoid as much as possible that those statements could be misinterpreted by the public and possibly lead to the applicant's innocence being called in question even before tried.[3]

This repeats in substance an earlier decision,[4] which also said:

It is a fundamental principle embodied in this Article which protects everybody against being treated by public officials as being guilty of an offence before this is established according to law by a competent court.

It would be better to stay with this brief principle than to qualify it, as is done in the decisions quoted. It is difficult to see how aspects of

also covers necessary preliminary inquiries, e.g. medical or psychiatric examination. 986/61–5: *Yearbook* 198, and see *Germany* Bundesverwaltungsgericht (25.10.1960): *N.J.W.* [1961] 571.

[1] S.P.O. § 244 (2).
[2] See K. Neumann in *Manual of German Law*, ii. 149 (H.M.S.O., 1952).
[3] 8361/78 (Netherlands) 27 D.R. 37, 43.
[4] *Krause* 7986/77 (Switzerland) 13 D.R. 73.

suspicion and arrests, and even more of confessions, do not call innocence in question. Perhaps the reservation 'if at all', points to the right course.

Two aspects of the presumption of innocence have come before the Commission in the admissibility of evidence of past convictions and in the imposition of costs in cases of *non liquet*, acquittal, or discontinuance of proceedings.

Previous convictions. The admissibility, during the hearing and before sentence, of evidence of previous convictions of the accused varies among the contracting states. The variation may be explained in part by differences in the composition and functions of the court, and the trial procedure. The court may or may not have lay members and where there are jurors their function may or may not be limited to determinations of fact and guilt; again the proceedings may be divided into two stages, the determination of guilt and the imposition of sentence on conviction, or there may be no such division. The question whether the admission during the hearing of evidence of previous convictions impairs the presumption of innocence has to be answered in terms of these differences and the reasons for them. Where an applicant had been charged in Denmark with two acts of rape in 1963, and evidence of a conviction for rape in 1956 and of other convictions for sexual offences was given to the jury during the hearing, the Commission said:[1]

... when interpreting such fundamental concepts as 'fair hearing' ... and 'presumption of innocence', ... the Commission finds it necessary to take into consideration the practice in different countries which are members of the Council of Europe; ... it is clear that in a number of these countries[2] information as to previous convictions is regularly given during the trial before the court has reached a decision as to the guilt of the accused; ... the Commission is not prepared to consider such a procedure as violating any provision of Article 6 of the Convention, not even in cases where a jury is to decide on the guilt of an accused.

---

[1] 2518//65: 8 *Yearbook* 370; 2742/66: 9 *Yearbook* 550.

[2] *Austria*: S.P.O. § 252 (2); *Germany*: S.P.O. § 249; *Denmark*: Retsplejeloven Article, 877 (2); *Italy*: Cod. di Proc. Pen. Article 464; all allow production of evidence of previous convictions during the hearing; *Norway*: Straffeprosessloven, Article 337, imposes more restrictions on admissibility. In *England* there is no absolute prohibition, the test of admissibility being the relevance of evidence of previous convictions to the charge being tried.

In *Germany* Oberlandesgericht, Stuttgard (2.3.1964) held that a court may not, consistently with Article 6 (2), revoke an order for release on probation because the prisoner is subject to new *charges* not yet brought to trial: *N.J.W.* [1964] 1585.

On the first it is necessary to distinguish recidivism, where the evidence of previous convictions is not directed to the determination of a charge, but to the implementation of social policy. So, in considering preventive detention in institutions for recidivists, the Commission said

... the committal to such institutions is not as such primarily based on a finding of guilt, but rather on the general assumption that persons with a serious criminal record may also in future constitute a danger to society. The passing of a judgment concerning a person's dangerousness does not in itself violate the presumption of innocence.[1]

It has been asked what benefit or burden there may be for the accused where there has been some form of acquittal, or a discontinuance of the proceedings:

One cannot deduce from Article 6 (2) a general duty of the State to compensate any accused, who was not finally convicted by a competent court, for the period spent in detention on remand.[2]

This would run against the provisions of Article 5 (5).

The imposition of costs following the discontinuance of proceedings was challenged by the accused in two applications, which both led to friendly settlements.[3] Neubecker was left to pay his own costs. He accepted in settlement a declaration that the discontinuance of the proceedings rendered the judgment against the applicant 'devoid of any effect' and 'no opinion concerning the applicant's guilt can be inferred from the judgment or the [discontinuance] decision . . .'.

In a third application, which was also settled, a prosecution had been brought for the publication of two poems by the applicant, on Christmas and on the imagined return of Christ to Earth. The charge was the infringement of freedom of worship and belief under Article 261 of the Swiss Criminal Code. The applicant was acquitted, but ordered to pay all the costs of the proceedings. The Federal Court dismissed his appeal against the order, saying that, while no suspicion remained after the acquittal, 'the provocative tone of the poems and the absence of suitable commentaries' gave sufficient grounds for the

[1] 9167/80 (Austria) 26 D.R. 248.
[2] 7950/77 (Austria) 19 D.R. 213 (the holding by the Court of Appeal that the Act on compensation for Criminal Detention did not apply, where the criminal proceedings were quashed by a Presidential grant of pardon; was not, in the view of the commission, inconsistent with Article 6 (2).
[3] *Neubecker* 6281/73 (F.R.G.) 8 D.R. 5; *Liebig* 6650/74 (F.R.G.) 17 D.R. 5.

imposition of costs, which the community should not have to bear. It is not easy to see how the contents of the poems, which had been the subject of the prosecution and the acquittal, could be relied on to justify the imposition of costs. In the settlement the Swiss Government, without any admission of any breach of the Convention, undertook to assume the payment of all the costs, including those of the fees to the applicant's lawyers.[1]

Further, there is no right derivable from Article 6 (2) for an accused not finally convicted, to have compensation for detention on remand,[2] or for loss of assets, including payment of lawyers fees.[3]

3. Everyone charged with a criminal offence has the following minimum rights:

   (a) to be informed promptly, in a language which he understands and in detail, of the nature and cause of the accusation against him;

   (b) to have adequate time and facilities for the preparation of his defence;

   (c) to defend himself in person or through legal assistance of his own choosing or, if he had not sufficient means to pay for legal assistance, to be given it free when the interests of justice so require;

   (d) to examine or have examined witnesses against him and to obtain the attendance and examination of witnesses on his behalf under the same conditions as witnesses against him;

   (e) to have the free assistance of an interpreter if he cannot understand or speak the language used in court.

3. Toute accusé a droit notamment:

   (a) être informé, dans le plus court délai, dans une langue qu'il comprend et d'une manière détaillée, de la nature et de la cause de l'accusation portée contre lui;

   (b) disposer du temps et des facilités nécessaires à la préparation de sa défense;

   (c) se défendre lui-même ou avoir l'assistance d'un

---

[1] *Geerk* 7640/76 (Switzerland) 16 D.R. 56.
[2] 7950/77 (Austria) 19 D.R. 213; *Eckle* 8130/78 (F.R.G.) 24 D.R. 232.
[3] 9037/80 (Switzerland) 24 D.R. 221.

défenseur de son choix et, s'il n'a pas les moyens de
rémunérer un défenseur, pouvoir être assisté gratuitement par un avocat d'office, lorsque les intérêts de la
justice l'exigent;

(*d*) interroger ou faire interroger les tèmoins à charge et
obtenir la convocation et l'interrogation des témoins à
décharge dans les mêmes conditions que les tèmoins à
charge;

(*e*) se faire assister gratuitement d'un interprète, s'il ne
comprend pas ou ne parle pas la langue employée à
l'audience.

Paragraph 3 is subtantially that contained in a draft amendement to
Article 6 introduced by the United Kingdom in the Committee of
Experts in March 1950.

charged with a criminal offence/accusé

It is not entirely clear at what point the minimum rights set out may be
said to begin. It is possible that the point of time at which a person
becomes charged for these purposes may not be the same as that from
which the period of reasonable time after charge runs in Article 6 (1).
Thus paragraphs (*d*) and (*e*) present no difficulty, for they are related
essentially to the trial itself, when the formal charge or indictment
must of necessity have been presented. Further, paragraph (*a*) must
relate to the contents of the formal charge or indictment itself, rather
than to the position at some prior stage, such as arrest; otherwise there
would be an overlap with Article 5 (2).

A question may, however, arise, at least in the inquisitorial system of
criminal procedure, as to whether paragraphs (*b*) and (*c*), operate as
do the remaining paragraphs, at or from the delivery of the formal
charge or indictment, or whether from an earlier point of time when
the person may be said to be charged in the sense of Article 6 (1).

has the following minimum rights/a droit notamment

The English and French expressions do not essentially differ and it is
clear that the rights set out in Article 6 (3) are not necessarily
exhaustive of the requirements of fair hearing under Article 6 (1).[1]

---

[1] Se 343/57 (Report of the Commission, pp. 79–80); 788/60 (Report of the Com-

The Commission has said that Article 6 (3) does not give any protection against self-incrimination, holding that

the Convention only guarantees the rights set forth in Article 6 (3) to persons 'charged with a criminal offence' and . . . the provisions of that paragraph do not extend those rights to persons who are heard as witnesses but who are not accused persons, even if the statements made by such persons might result in subsequent criminal proceedings against them.[1]

It would seem to follow *a fortiori* that an accused person is not protected by Article 6 (3) from being compelled to give evidence tending to incriminate him on either the offence charged or other offences. It would be a matter of controversy whether nevertheless the accused is protected by the principle of fair hearing under Article 6 (1) from being compelled to give such evidence at his trial.[2]

Also missing, perhaps surprisingly, from the rights guaranteed by the Convention is the principle of double jeopardy. An Austrian citizen had been convicted of robbery and sentenced in Germany to twenty-five months' imprisonment, of which he served seventeen; he was then deported to Austria where he was put on trial on the same charge and sentenced to five years' imprisonment,[3] the German sentence served being taken into account. On his application alleging that it is contrary to the Convention to punish a person twice for the same crime, the Commission

does not find that Article 6 or any other Article of the Convention guarantees either expressly or by implication the principle of *non bis in idem*.[4]

A failure to observe one or more of the prescribed rules in Article 6 (3) can in general be rectified by an acquittal;[5] and the accused cannot, after acquittal, complain of bias or other disadvantages in the proceedings.[6]

mission, pp. 224–5), quoted above at p. ooo. Compare *Austria*: Verwaltungsgerichtshof (27.6.1960): 3 *Yearbook* 622.

[1] 1083/61: *Recueil* (1962) i.
[2] As to pre-trial procedure see J. A. Coutts (ed.), *The Accused* (1965) 5. For a strong challenge to the rule against self-incrimination see Lord Kilbranden, ibid. at 66. 'It is hard to see how an innocent man can incriminate himself, and if a guilty man does so, so much the better.'
[3] Austrian Penal Code, Article 36: an Austrian citizen, who has committed a crime abroad, shall on his return to Austria be dealt with under the Penal Code without regard to the *lex criminis*, though sentence imposed abroad is to be taken into account.
[4] 1519/62: 6 *Yearbook* 348; 7680/76 (F.R.G.) 9 D.R. 190.
[5] 5575/72 (Austria) 1 D.R. 44.
[6] 8083/77 (U.K.) 19 D.R. 223.

(a) **to be informed promptly/être informé dans le plus court délai.**

The notion of promptness seems to be out of place in this context, and to have strayed in from Article 5 (2). It is particularly inappropriate in the inquisitorial system of procedure, where the charge may be formulated at a relatively late stage of the pre-trial process. At the trial itself, on the other hand, the notion could have little meaning.

in a language which he understands/dans une langue qu'il comprend

It is to be observed that the Convention does not given an accused person a right to be charged or tried in the language of his choice. Articles 6 (3) *a* and *c*, and 14, seek only to ensure that differences of language shall not prevent a fair hearing, or be used as a basis of discrimination, in the administration of justice. In countries where more than one language are in common use, either generally or in particular areas, it may often be hard to determine whether the accused has or has not an adequate understanding of the language in which he is charged or tried.[1] The difficulty is increased where the accused has political motives for objecting to the use of a particular language for these purposes.

in detail, of the nature and cause of the accusation/d'une manière détaillée, de la nature et de la cause de l'accusation.

The principal elements in the charge or accusation, which appears to call for precision, are the acts or omissions alleged against the accused, their legal classification, and the formulation of the offence as so classified.

Of the degree of precision in general necessary under Article 6 (1) and (3) *a* the Commission has said that

the information to which a person is entitled concerning the charges made against him is more specific and more detailed in connection with his right to fair trial . . . than in connection with his right to liberty and security of person.[2]

---

[1] Compare *Erumeru* v. *Erumeru* [1965] Nigeria M.L.R. 411.

[2] 343/57: 2 *Yearbook* 462. The conclusion of the Commission that Nielsen 'was informed of the nature and cause of the accusation against him in sufficient detail and

As to the first two elements, calling for precision,

... dans le cadre du droit à un procès équitable garanti par l'ensemble des prescriptions de l'Article 6, l'accusé a droit à être informé non seulement de la *cause* de l'accusation, c'est à dire, des faits matériels qui sont mis à sa charge et qui sont à l'origine de son inculpation, mais aussi de la nature de l'accusation, c'est à dire la qualification juridique des faits matériels; ... cette information sur la nature et la cause de l'accusation paraît d'autant plus nécessaire qu'aux termes du § *b* de l'Article 6; ... il existe en effet[1] un lien logique entre les paragraphes 3*a* et 3*b* ...

so that a change in the classification of the offence must be made known to the accused.

The formulation of the offence, particularly where it is not a statutory offence, may be too indefinite. An application was directed against the provisions of an Austrian statute prohibiting neo-Nazi activities.[2] Proscribed activities were set out in detail in Section 3 *a–f* of the Statute, while Section 3 *g*, under which the applicant was convicted, prescribed several penalties for particularly dangerous activities of a National Socialist nature carried on in ways other than those set out in Section 3 *a–f* ('auf andere als die in denn §§ 3 *a* bis 3 *f* bezeichnete Weise'). The applicant maintained that the provision was essentially vague and failed to specify the actions, other than those already covered by Section 3 *a–f*, that could constitute an offence under it. The Austrian Government said in answer that

Convinced of the danger of the revival of National Socialism, the legislator deemed it essential, in addition to specifying a number of offences, to insert a general clause providing for the punishment of any 'activity' of a National Socialist nature,

and such activities were to be understood only in the sense of 'a pattern of behaviour (*komplexes Handeln*)', manifesting 'typical National Socialist ideas'. The Commission found that

the terms of the charge drafted against him under Section 3 *g* ... created a justiciable offence consistent with the Convention;

that in this respect there was no violation on the part of the Respondent Government of Article 6 (3) *a*' was confirmed by the Committee of Ministers acting under Article 32 (1): 4 *Yearbook* 592.

[1] 524/59 (Report of the Commission) 31–2.
[2] 1747/62: 6 *Yearbook* 424. The statute was the *Verfassungsgesetz über das Verbot der NSDAP*.

in particular, the direction of the presiding judge to the jury that a
necessary element under Section 3 g was 'an intention to undermine
the democratic government in Austria in order to revive National
Socialism'; and the findings of the jury

indicate the nature of the acts in question, the circumstances in which they
were committed and the period during which the acts were perpetrated.

The Commission found no appearance of a violation of either Article
6 (3) a or 6 (1) of the Convention.

(b) to have adequate time and facilities for the preparation of his defence/disposer du temps et des facilités nécessaires à la préparation de sa défense

The substantive provisions of subparagraphs (b) and (c) are closely
linked with subparagraphs (a) and Article 6 (1) itself. Whether the
provisions extend to the preliminary investigation of offence,
involving the accused, has been left open by the Commission.[1]

The Commission summarized the provisions of Article 6 (3) in an
early decision, stressing the need, in any given case involving their
application, to survey the underlying facts and the proceedings as a
whole—'il faut tenir compte de l'ensemble de la situation faite à la
défense et ne pas l'apprecier seulement en la personne de la
l'accusé'.[2]

Areas of defence which have come into account under Article 6 (3)
are access to legal advice; the availability of court files; and access to
documentary evidence in the hands of the prosecution.

The accused must be free to consult the lawyer of his choice,
subject to reasonable conditions.[3] So the Commission has said that
correspondence from prison, and other communication, with a lawyer
for purpose of defence, must be allowed, but the lawyer cannot claim
for himself the facilities recognized in paragraph 3 (b).[4] The Standard
Minimum Rules for the Treatment of Prisoners, adopted by the

---

[1] 8463/78 (Switzerland) 26 D.R. 24.
[2] *Ofner* 524/59 (Austria) 3 *Yearbook* 322.
[3] 1850/63; 7854/77 (Switzerland) 12 D.R. 185; *Schertenleib* 8337/78 (Switzerland) 17
D.R. 181. See also International Commission of Jurists—Arrested Persons and their
Communications, a report submitted to the U.N.: E/C.N.4/N.B.110 (1964).
[4] 7909/74 (Austria) 15 D.R. 160.

Committee of Ministers of the Council of Europe,[1] do not cover legal advice in regard to complaints, or other proceedings. Rule 36 provides:

2. It shall be possible to make requests or complaints to an inspector of prisons during his inspection. The prisoner shall have the opportunity to talk to the inspector, or to any other duly constituted authority entitled to visit the prison, without the director or other members of the staff being present.

3. Every prisoner shall be allowed to make a request or complaint, under confidential cover, to the central prison administration, the judicial authority or other proper authorities.

Rule 38 (1) provides that

Prisoners who are foreign nationals shall be allowed reasonable facilities to communicate with the diplomatic and consular representatives of the State to which they belong.

As regards this Rule, the Commission has held that the rights of communication, implied in Article 6 (3) *b*, do not include access to the embassy of the nationality of the Prisoner.[2]

Access to the court files must be given to the defence when it is needed; and it may also be an adequate substitute for attendance of the accused or his legal representative at particular hearings.[3]

Access to documentary or other evidence in the hands of the prosecution may also be required, though this may raise administrative difficulties, or more seriously the rule of privilege of certain official documents from disclosure: the latter, as part of the general problem of access to governmental information and files, will be considered under Article 10 (2) below.

In conclusion on Article 6 (3) *b* it must be noted that the Commission has suggested that the rights of defence must prevail:

In short, Article 6 (3) *b* recognises the right of the accused to have at his disposal, for the purpose of exonerating himself or of obtaining a reduction in his sentence, all relevant elements that have been or could be collected by the competent authorities. The Commission considers that if the element in question is a document, access to that document is a necessary 'facility/facilité

---

[1] Resolution 73/5.
[2] 1184/61.
[3] E.g. the hearing by an investigating judge of witnesses abroad: 6566/77 (F.R.G.) 1 D.R. 84.

necessaire' if, as in the present case, it concerns an act of which the defendant is accused, the credibility of testimony etc.[1]

There is some uncertainty as to whether Article 6 (3) *b* is applicable to proceedings for reduction of sentence, since it is arguable that no determination of a criminal charge is involved; and the Commission has found that deportation, while appeal against sentence was in progress, conviction having become final, was an interference with rights under Article 6 (3) *b*.[2] But it may be that Article 6 (3), as its language suggests covers everyone 'charged with a criminal offence/ tout accusé' regardless of the form or purpose of the proceedings.

(c) to defend himself in person or through legal assistance of his own choosing or . . ./se défendre lui-même ou avoir l'assistance d'un défenseur de son choix et . . .

It appears from this clause that the accused may at his trial either defend himself or obtain legal assistance, the choice being his; and that legal assistance is to be understood as comprising advice or representation or both. Where he is represented by a lawyer, the accused cannot claim under Article 6 a right to attend the hearing in person at any stage.

The right to choose a lawyer for the defence depends upon the accused having sufficient means to pay his fees,[3] and this was the subject of criticism in the Conference of Senior Officials in June 1950,[4] but the text remained.

The choice is not only limited to the trial stage, but also by the regulations that may be made governing the appearance of lawyers before the courts. So a requirement that appeal against conviction, or appeal to a constitutional court, may be made and conducted only by a legal representative, is not inconsistent with paragraph 3 (c).[5]

The administration of criminal justice in Italy, in the provision of free legal aid, and in the appointment of counsel of the accused by the

---

[1] *Jespers* 8403/78 (Belgium) Report 27 D.R. 61, 88.

[2] 6501/74 (F.R.G.) 1 D.R. 80.

[3] 646/59: 3 *Yearbook* 272.

[4] The French and Italian representatives thought that the rule discriminated against those without sufficient means, since they could receive legal assistance only when it was considered that justice required it: *T.P.* iii. 652.

[5] 727/60: 5 *Yearbook* 308 (since Article 6 (1) does not oblige contracted States to provide unrestricted access to appellate courts, the conditions of access may include a requirement of legal representation).

competent authority, came up in three applications which went finally
to the Court. The careful judgments of the Court do not in effect offer
new or comprehensive interpretations of Article 6 (3) *c*, given that it
was the circumstance of each of the cases, which were complex and
decisive. It is then sufficient to record the judgments.[1] Nevertheless,
the Commission has made a number of interpretations of Article 6
(3) *c*. In the first place, it is limited to criminal proceedings, and no
claims can be made under it in civil or administrative litigation.[2]
Further, where the applicant withdrew his counsel and made no
personal appearance in the proceedings, no invocation of the Convention could be made by him.[3] The choice between personal participation and legal representation depends upon the domestic law, in
statute or rules of court;[4] and it is open to the body responsible for
professional conduct to hold that it would be improper for a lawyer to
act in a particular case, given personal interest or involvement.[5]

Further, the Commission has said that the right in question

is not an absolute right, but limited by the right concerned to make regulations
concerning the appearance of lawyers before the Courts; . . . the State has full
discretion to exclude lawyers appearing before the Courts,[6]

But this discretion must, it is believed, be exercised in good faith, and
not so as to deny a fair hearing under Article 6 (1).

**or, if he has not sufficient means to pay for legal assist-
ance, to be given it free when the interests of justice so
require/et, s'il n'a pas les moyens de rémunérer un
défenseur, pouvoir être assisté gratuitement par un
avocat d'office, lorsque les intérêts de la justice l'exigent**

This clause generalizes the rule underlying the practice to be found in
one form or another, in all the contracting States.[7] The criteria for the

---

[1] *Artico Judgment* No. 37 (13.5.1980); *Pakelli Judgment* No. 64 (25.4.1983); *Goddi Judgment* No. 76 (7.4.1984).

[2] 3944/69 (F.R.G.) 33 *Recueil* 5.

[3] 8386/78 (U.K.) 21 D.R. 126. A change of rules, enabling personal appearances for a litigant and eliminating *pro domo* notes, was made in Austria in part the settlement of application 8289/78 (*Peschke*) 25 D.R. 182.

[4] 8923/72 (Norway) 3 D.R. 43; 7592/76 14 D.R. 64.

[5] 8295/78 (U.K.) 15 D.R. 242.

[6] 722/60: 5 *Yearbook* 104.

[7] For a penetrating comparative study of legal aid see N. S. Marsh, 'Legal Aid and the Rule of Law—A comparative outline', *Journal of I.C.J.* ii (1960) 95–115. See also

grant of legal aid are that the means of the applicant are insufficient to meet the costs involved and that it is in the interest of justice, because of the factual complexity or legal difficulty of the case, or because an issue of public importance is involved, that the defence be conducted by a lawyer. So

le droit à l'assistance gratuite d'un avocat d'office n'est donc reconnu qu'en faveur de tout 'accusé', c'est-à-dire d'une personne accusée d'une infraction pénale, à condition que l'accusé n'ait pas les moyens de rémunérer un défenseur de son choix et dans la mesure oú les intérêts de la justice exigent l'assistance d'un défenseur.[1]

While the Convention then

ne contient aucune clause similaire en faveur de ceux qui comme le requérant, sont ou entendent devenir parties à une instance de caractère purement civil[2]

the requirement of fair hearing under Article 6 (1) may nevertheless make representation by a lawyer necessary, though the contracting States are not required to provide for it in civil matters.[3] A criterion of the requirement is legal difficulty, so

lorsqu'une affaire ne suscite pas de litige grave d'ordre juridique, mais exige simplement l'établissement correct des faits le refus d'accorder aux parties le droit d'être représentées ou assistées, dans la procédure par des avocats ne peut être considéré comme constituant un refus d'entendre la cause équitablement.[4]

The principle that only an accused is entitled to free legal aid under Article 6 (3) *c* excludes any such entitlement in order to maintain a private prosecution[5] or an action as *partie civile* in a criminal matter.[6] The Commission has excluded extradition proceedings from the

R. Ginsburg and A. Bruzelius, 'Professional Legal Assistance in Sweden', 11 *I.C.L.Q.* (1962) 997. See also *England*: Report of the Departmental Committee on Legal Aid in Criminal Proceedings, 1966 (Cmnd. 2934), and M. Zander, *Modern Law Review* (1966).

[1] 919/60: *Recueil* (1961) ii. Insufficiency of means can be only a 'temporary exemption from 1055' 9365/81 (F.R.G.) 28 D.R. 229.

[2] 739/60: *Recueil* (1961) i; see also 89/55, 134/55, 180/56: 1 *Yearbook* 226, 232, and 236; 727/60: 3 *Yearbook* 302.

[3] 2308/64.

[4] 1013/61: 5 *Yearbook* 165 (lawyers only admitted before Arbeitsgericht in Germany if sum in dispute exceeds 300 DM, or it is necessary to safeguard the rights of the parties—sum involved in the Applicant's case was under 100 DM); 2545/65.

[5] 808/60: 5 *Yearbook* 108.

[6] 1341/62, and 1359/62: *Recueil* (1963) i.

reach of the provision, presumably on the ground that the criminal charge or charges, which are the ground of the requisition, are not within the jurisdiction of the respondent State. So.

in accordance with Article 59 of the [Austrian] Code of Criminal Procedure the courts were called upon to decide only the question whether or not the Applicant should be extradited; ... accordingly, during the proceedings before the Austrian courts, the applicant was not 'charged with a criminal offence' within the meaning of [paragraph (3) c].[1]

However, proceedings on appeal, at least where the applicant is respondent, have been held by the Commission to be covered by paragraph 6 (3) c, on the ground that if the applicant has no professional legal assistance the proceedings cannot be regarded as fully 'contradictory':

the denial to an accused person of legal assistance on appeal or the exclusion of his lawyer from the hearing of that appeal raises the ... issue of 'equality of arms'.[2]

But an application for a retrial is not a proceeding covered by paragraph 6 (3) c, since the accused has become a convicted person.[3]

The difference of language between the English and French texts, where 'legal assistance' is rendered by 'défenseur' and 'avocat d'office', has been passed on by the Commission which refused to give a technical meaning to the term 'avocat':

the preparatory work on Article 6 (3) c confirms that the word 'avocat' ... is not to be understood in the technical sense of the term but in the sense of legal assistance ... in the case in question, although it is clear that *Gerichtsreferendar* G. is not an 'avocat' he is nevertheless a competent 'défenseur', when instructed to provide the accused with 'legal assistance'.[4]

As has already been observed, the choice of an *avocat d'office* rests with the State under paragraph 3 (c),[5] and the Commission has held that the State is free to regulate the conditions of legal aid to exclude particular practitioners, and that it is not in general responsible for the

---

[1] 1918/63: *Recueil* (1963) iii.
[2] 834/60: 6 *Yearbook* 150: 1135/61: 6 *Yearbook* 194; 1446/62: 6 *Yearbook* 260; 1567/62: *Recueil* (1963) iii. It may be noted too that, in Germany and Austria at least, the accused remains 'charged' in the sense of Article 6 (1) and (3) until the conclusion of any appeal.
[3] 623/59: *Recueil* (1961) i.
[4] 509/59: 3 *Yearbook* 182.
[5] 1242/61: *Recueil* (1962) ii.

conduct of the case by the *avocat d'office* appointed.[1] But the regulation of the grant of free legal aid is still controlled by the interest of justice under paragraph 3(*c*) itself and by the requirements of Article 6 (1) and 3 (*b*). So, while the *avocat d'office* need not be known to the accused,[2] the principle that he must be one in whom the accused may, in all the circumstances of the case, have confidence[3] seems to be implied in Article 6. Further, frequent changes of *avocat d'office* in the course of a single case may obstruct the defence,[4] though on the other hand courts pressed with work cannot be expected to grant constant adjournments in order to enable a new *avocat d'office* to acquaint himself with the case.

(*d*) to examine or have examined witnesses against him and to obtain the attendance and examination of witnesses on his behalf under the same conditions as witnesses against him/interroger ou faire interroger les témoins à charge et obtenir la convocation et l'interrogation des témoins à décharge dans les mêmes conditions que les témoins à charge

The question arises whether paragraph 3 (*d*) confers a right on the accused to be confronted with witnesses,[5] and is closely linked with the requirement that the examination of all witnesses shall be under the same conditions.

In the *Fundres/Pfunders Case*,[6] the Trent Court of Appeal had ordered an inspection on the spot (*descente en lieu*) of the place where the body was found of the Guardia di Finanze whose death the accused were charged with having caused. The inspection was carried

---

[1] 300/57; 722/60: 5 *Yearbook* 106. In 1251/61: *Recueil* (1963) i the Commission impliedly recognized that there may exceptionally be grounds for State responsibility.

[2] 1807/63: *Recueil* (1963) iii. For a case of frequent changes of *avocat d'office* in the course of the proceedings, see 1850/63 (Report of the Commission).

[3] Germany: Bundesverfassungsgericht (181.12.1958): *Entsch. des BVerfG*. ix, p. 36.

[4] 1850/63.

[5] Compare NATO Status of Forces Agreement, Article VIII. 9: 'Whenever a member of a force or civilian component or a dependant is prosecuted under the jurisdiction of a receiving State he shall be entitled . . . (*c*) to be confronted with the witnesses against him.'

[6] 788/60: Report of the Commission, 120–43. Compare *Karamat* v. *The Queen* [1956] A.C. 256 P.C.: absence of the appellant from *descente en lieu* by the court did not invalidate it, there being no suggestion that evidence had been produced outside the scope of the 'view' as ordered.

out by the Court in the presence of two Guardie di Finanze, witnesses for the prosecution, one of whom had found the body, and of two lawyers for the defence. The Austrian Government maintained that the failure of the Court to order the presence of the accused at the inspection was contrary to Article 6 (3) *d*. The Commission, two members dissenting, concluded:

> Now, it should be noted that the main purpose of the Court of Trento in deciding to visit Fundres/Pfunders and in summoning Calvia and Lombardo [the other Guardie], appears to have been to ascertain the original position of the body in the stream bed. Calvia and Lombardo were likely to be able to supply information on this point. The accused on the contrary, according to their statements during the trial, had not seen how Falqui's body had come to be in the [River] Roaner and remained lying there. In these circumstances, the interests of the defence during the examination of Lombardo and Calvia could be safeguarded by counsel just as well as by the accused themselves and, as is known, Mr. Dander and Mr. Sand [defence lawyers] were actually present at the inspection. The Commission infers from this that the order in dispute of 10th March 1958 did not infringe Article 6 (3) *d* in this respect.
>
> Once at the scene of the crime, the Court of Appeal agreed to extend the scope of the inquiry: at Mr. Dander's request, it allowed the accused Luigi/ Alois Bergmeister, who was present, to be questioned on the circumstances of the brawl which had preceded Falqui's death. Bergmeister's statements related, among other things, to the exact spot where Falqui had been struck and had fallen before running off towards the bridge; they contained, with regard to the place, certain particulars on which it would have been easier for Bergmeister's co-accused to express an opinion than for their counsel. It would therefore have been better if Bergmeister had not been heard in the absence of the seven prisoners.
>
> The Commission notes, however, that the hearing took place at Mr. Dander's express request, made on the spot, and that neither the latter nor his colleague, Mr. Sand, asked for an adjournment of the hearing to enable the other accused to be present.

The inference that may be drawn from this appears to be that there may be circumstances in which the confrontation of the accused and witnesses against him is necessary in order to satisfy the requirements of Article 6, but that the right may be regarded as waived if the defence does not request confrontation in a particular case.[1]

---

[1] See *Report*, p. 149, for a dissenting opinion that: 'Every accused has a personal right whether the accused so requests or not. It is of the same nature as the right of an accused person to be treated according to the law. ... It follows that the judge is bound to guarantee accused persons this right automatically.'

Connected is the problem of the admissibility of hearsay evidence, on which practice in the contracting States is variable. In Germany an objection to the admissibility of statements to the police by unnamed persons (*anonyme Gewährsleute*) was rejected on the ground that it was the police, and not the unnamed persons, who were before the court as witnesses; and therfore, in the view of the court, there was no inconsistency with Article 6 (3) *d*.[1]

witnesses/témoins

Who may be a witness is, as will appear below, to be determined by the court. Paragraph 3 (*d*) has been held by the court to cover experts, whether summoned by the parties[2] or the court.[3]

A right of the accused to be heard as a witness in his own behalf has been recognized by the Commission as falling primarily under Article 6 (1) rather than paragraph 3 (*d*):[4]

insofar as the Applicant alleges violation of Article 6, paragraph (3) in that he was not heard as a witness by the above Court, it is first to be pointed out, as appears from the text of the decision by the District Court of Vienna, that the Applicant was heard as a party to the case and was given a full opportunity of submitting to the Court his version of the facts of the case and his legal arguments; whereas, secondly, it is to be observed that paragraph (3) does not deal specifically with the question in what capacity parties in a case should be heard by the Court; whereas this question falls rather for consideration under the principle of according an accused person a fair hearing within the meaning of Article 6, paragraph (1); whereas the Commission held in a previous decision (No. 434/58–S. against Sweden) that

'the right to a fair hearing guaranteed by Article 6, paragraph (1) of the Convention appears to contemplate that everyone who is a party to civil proceedings shall have a reasonable opportunity of presenting his case to the Court under conditions which do not place him at a substantial disadvantage vis-à-vis his opponent.'

Whereas in the present case the District Court of Vienna, although it heard the Applicant as a party and the plaintiff as a witness, nevertheless permitted

---

[1] Bundesgerichtshof (1.8.1962): *N.J.W.* (1962) 1876.

[2] 1290/61: *Recueil* (1963) i.

[3] 1167/60: 6 *Yearbook* 218. The appointment by the court of an expert to prepare a *rapport d'expertise* does not engage the responsibility of the State under the Convention; 1045/61: *Recueil* (1962) i.

[4] 768/60: *Recueil* (1962) i. See also 1092/61: 5 *Yearbook* 212 (no Convention right to be heard as a witness in one's own case).

the Applicant to represent his case as fully as did the plaintiff; whereas the procedure adopted by the District Court in the present case did not place the Applicant at such a substantial disadvantage as to violate the principle of 'fair hearing' within the meaning of Article 6 (1).

The Commission does not consider that Article 6, as it stands, protects any witness from self-incrimination. So where

the Applicant's second complaint concerns an alleged right for a person not to be compelled to give evidence in circumstances where such evidence would, or would tend to, incriminate him; at the hearing of the case against X. on 11th August 1959 the Applicant was apparently faced with the alternative either of stating the truth and thus exposing himself to subsequent prosecution on charges of using threats against X. or of commiting perjury which would expose him to the risk of criminal proceedings;[1]

but the provisions of paragraph 3

do not extend those rights to persons who are heard as witnesses but who are not accused persons, even if the statements made by such persons might result in subsequent criminal proceedings against them; whereas it follows that the right claimed is not as such included among the rights and freedoms guaranteed by the Convention.[2]

under the same conditions/dans les mêmes conditions

The Commission has, in describing the purpose of paragraph 3 (d), emphasized this qualification as showing that an accused it not entitled to call witnesses without limit:

the text in question is intended to place the indicted, prosecuted or accused person on an equal footing with the prosecution as regards the hearing of witnesses, but not to give him a right to call witnesses without restriction.[3] . . . The competent judicial authorities of the contracting States accordingly remain free, on condition that the Convention and in particular the above-mentioned principle of equality is complied with, to establish whether the hearing of a witness for the defence is likely to be of assistance in discovering the truth, and if not to decide against calling such witness . . .[4]

---

[1] But the First U.N. Convenant, Article 15 (3) g, protects against self-incrimination.
[2] 1083/61: *Recueil* (1962) i.
[3] The Commission referred for confirmation to the *travaux préparatoires*: *T.P.* iii. 653 [Report of Senior Officials (19.6.1950) 15–16].
[4] 1134/61: 4 *Yearbook* 382. See also 788/60: *Report of the Commission*, p. 116. See also 753/60; 3 *Yearbook* 320; 1913/63: *Recueil* (1965) i.

So in Belgium it has been held that paragraph 3 (*d*) does not deprive the court of its discretionary power to determine whether the testimony of a witness has probative value.[1]

While the appreciation of the probative value will be normally outside the competence of the Commission, as being a matter of 'fourth instance', it must if necessary satisfy itself that the refusal to hear a witness has not offended against the principle of equality in paragraph 3 (*d*).[2]

(*e*) **to have the free assistance of an interpreter if he cannot understand or speak the language used in court/ se faire assister gratuitement d'un interprète, s'il ne comprend pas ou ne parle pas la langue employée à l'audience**

A German court has liberally extended this provision to cover the free[3] assistance of an interpreter during the preliminary investigation (*Untersuchung*).[4]

A difficulty in the paragraph as drafted is that it does not show how the understanding or lack of understanding of the language by the accused is to be proved.[5] The NATO Status of Forces Agreement, Article VII 9, says simply that 'if he considers it necessary' he shall be entitled to have the services of a competent interpreter, though this does not indicate at whose charge.

The Commission has said that paragraph 3 (*e*) does not in any case confer a general *liberté linguistique*, in which the accused can insist on

---

[1] *Ministère Public* v. *Belaid* [1962] Cour de Cassation: *Pasicrisie Belge* 1283–40. Compare *Redmond* v. *Tapson* [1882] 22 Ch. D. 430 *per* Jessel M.R.: 'The Court has still power to say, when the witness attends, that the witness shall not be examined, or that he shall be examined in open court. It can always restrain the abuse of the power to summon witnesses.'

[2] 1706/62: *Recueil* 21 at 42 (failure to invoke refusal before the Supreme Court, on a plea of nullity, a non-exhaustion of remedies). See also 1097/61: *Recueil* (1963) i.

[3] Compare *Denmark*: Copenhagen City Court (25.4.1966) (fees of an interpreter are costs of the court. In *Belgium*, a Decree of 28.12.1950 makes a convicted person liable for costs of interpretation from languages not in common use (French, Dutch, and German). But the courts do not appear to apply the rule strictly: Tribunal Correctionel, Bruxelles, 11.5.1965: 19.5.1965: (no costs ordered to be paid for Spanish interpretation); similarly in *Germany*: Amtsgericht, Bremerhaven, 18.10.1962, citing Article 6 (3) *e* of the Convention: 5 *Yearbook* 362.

[4] Amtsgericht, Bremerhaven (18.10.1962): *N.J.W.* (1963) 827: 5 *Yearbook* 362.

[5] See, for example, 2686/65.

being tried in a particular language.[1] But it may not always be easy to determine whether the applicant has been *mute of malice* at his trial and concealed his understanding of the language of the court in order to obtain trial in the language of his choice.

It would not, it is believed, be a sufficient compliance with paragraph 3 (*e*) that counsel for the accused could understand the language used but that the accused could not.[2]

The Court, making an extensive analysis of Article 6 (3) *e*,[3] said in particular that the terms 'free/gratuitement':

denote neither a conditional remission, nor a temporary exemption, nor a suspension, but once for all exemption or exoneration ... To read Article 6 (3) *e* as allowing the domestic courts to make a convicted person bear these costs would amount to limiting in time the benefit of the Article and in practice to denying that benefit to any accused person who is eventually convicted.

Further, even if an interpreter is appointed by the court,

making such an appointment admittedly eliminates in principle the serious drawbacks that would arise were an accused to defend himself in person in a language he did not master or fully master rather than incurring additional costs. Nevertheless ... the risk remains that in some borderline cases the appointment or not of an interpreter might depend on the attitude taken by the accused, which might in turn be influenced by the fear of financial consequences.

The imposition of costs on the accused after acquittal has also been considered by the Commission.[4]

ARTICLE 7

(1) No one shall be held guilty of any criminal offence on account of any act or omission which did not constitute a criminal offence under national or international law at the time when it was committed. Nor shall a heavier penalty be imposed than the one that was applicable at the time the criminal offence was committed.

---

[1] 2332/64: *Recueil* 21. Compare 808/60: 5 *Yearbook* 124, on which see further under Article 14 below.

[2] See, for example, *Hemapala* v. *The Queen* [1963] A.C. 859 P.C.

[3] *Lüdicke, Belkacem and Koc* (F.R.G.), Judgment No. 23 (28.11.1978) §§ 40–2 repeated in effect in *Öztürk Judgment* (F.R.G.) No. 73 (21.2.1983).

[4] *Temeltasch* 3116/80 (Switzerland): Report (5.5.1982).

(2) This Article shall not prejudice the trial and punishment of any person for any act or omission which, at the time when it was committed, was criminal according to the general principles of law recognized by civilized nations.

1. Nul ne peut être condamné pour une action ou une omission qui, au moment où elle a été commise, ne constituait pas une infraction d'après le droit national ou international. De même il n'est infligé aucune peine plus forte que celle qui était applicable au moment où l'infraction a été commise.

2. Le présent article ne portera pas atteinte au jugement et à la punition d'une personne coupable d'une action ou d'une omission qui, au moment où elle a été commise, était criminelle d'après les principes généraux de droit reconnus par les nations civilisées.

This Article has its origins in Article 11 (2) of the Universal Declaration of Human Rights, and in fact paragraph (1) reproduces that paragraph exactly except for the substitution of the word 'criminal' for 'penal'. This significant change was made in the early stages of the drafting of a United Nations Convenant. The reason was that the majority seven members of the U.N. Human Rights Commission, considered[1] that the concept of a penal offence (*la responsabilité pénale*; *Strafbarigkeit*) was too narrow, in that Article 11 (2) could be read as meaning that the principle of non-retroactivity would cover any offence, which was not defined as a crime with a penalty prescribed; and that, in particular, the validity of the judgment in the Nuremberg trial of major war criminals might be cast in doubt. The expression 'criminal offence' was considered to be wider, as embracing not only penal offences in the strict sense, but any evil act worthy of punishment, and so to be particularly apt in a context which covered both national law and international law, the prescription of penalties being hardly developed under the latter. The minority, six members, opposed this change as an abandonment of the principle *nulla poena sine lege*; but, although Article 7 of the Convention and the First U.N. Convenant, Article 15, in effect stress also the principle *nullum crimen*

---

[1] For an account of the discussions and references see K. J. Partsch, *Die Rechte und Freiheiten der Europäischen* MRK 171–3.

sine lege, they do not substitute it; and the second sentence of Article 7 (1) is an extension of the first principle, which would not be in place if it had been abandoned.

In the drafting of the European Convention the expression 'penal offence' was retained for some time, the French equivalent being 'un acte délictueux'. The use of the latter expression emphasizes the breadth of concept intended. The substitution of the word 'criminal' for 'penal' appears to have been the work of the Conference of Senior Officials;[1] though no explanation is given, the change is in line with the earlier discussions of this Article, and of its fellow in the First U.N. Covenant. The French equivalent was later changed to 'une infraction', perhaps to be more directly in keeping with criminal law concepts than 'un acte délictueux'.

The second paragraph of Article 7, which is repeated substantially in the C.P.R. Covenant, Article 15 (2), was intended to confirm that, in the words of the Committee of Experts,[2] the text of the first paragraph

did not affect laws which, under the very exceptional circumstances at the end of the second World War, were passed in order to suppress war-crimes, treason and collaboration with the enemy, and did not aim at any legal or moral condemnation of these laws.

Article 7 as it stands does not embody the principle *non bis in idem*. The Commission so found[3] where the applicant, an Austrian citizen, had been sentenced to twenty-five months' imprisonment in Germany for robbery there and to deportation to Austria. After serving two-thirds of the sentence he was deported to Austria, where he was tried and convicted of the same offence, and sentenced to five years' imprisonment.[4] The Commission, having examined the issue *ex officio* since the applicant invoked no Article of the Convention, could not find that

Article 6 or any other Article of the Convention guarantees either expressly or by implication the principle of *non bis in idem*.

The Commission, through its President, drew attention of the Committee of Ministers to this apparent gap in the Convention, and

---

[1] CM/WP 4 (50) 19, 16 rev. (19.6.1950): *T.P.* iii. 667.

[2] Report: CM/WP 1 (50) 15 (16.3.1950): *T.P.* iii. 485.

[3] 1519/62: 6 *Yearbook* 346. The First U.N. Covenant, Article 15 (7), adopts the principle of *non bis in idem*.

[4] Under Strafgesetz, Article 36, which provides that an Austrian citizen, who commits a crime abroad, shall on return to Austria be tried for the crime, without regard to the *lex loci criminis*, though any punishment imposed abroad shall be taken into account in imposing sentence.

pointed out that the European Convention on Extradition, 1960, had adopted the principle.[1] The European Committee on Crime Problems, to which the matter was referred for its opinion, suggested that the application of the principle on the international plane should be confined

to acquittals, and to those convictions where the penalty or measure imposed has been served, or where the fact that the penalty has not been served is due to a decision to that effect by the country imposing the sentence, or where, following ascertainments of guilt, no sanction has been imposed.

The Committee advised that rules to cover such application would be better placed in the Convention on the International validity of Criminal Judgments than in a protocol to the Human Rights Convention.

The Commission has observed that Article 7 (1)

... does not merely prohibit—except as provided in paragraph (2)—retroactive application of the criminal law to the detriment of the accused, it also confirms in a more general way, the principle of the statutory nature of offences and punishment (*nullum crimen*, *nulla poena sine lege*) and prohibits in particular, extension of, the application of the criminal law *in malam partem* by analogy.[2]

The necessary reference to the internal law of a contracting state can raise a question of 'fourth instance', which will be discussed under Article 19 below. The Commission has said,[3] in regard to Article 7 (1), that:

... la violation éventuelle du droit interne [application of the law as no longer in force] entraine la reonnaissance de la Convention, de sorte que la Commission peut et doit la constater sans s'eriger pour autant en une court de 'quatrième instance'.

held guilty/condamné

This expression is to be understood as meaning conviction for an offence by a competent court, and is not of course applicable in the determination of civil rights. Further, the detention on remand, or

[1] Article 9: 'Extradition shall not be granted if final judgment has been passed by the competent authorities of the requested Party upon the person claimed in respect of the offence or offences for which extradition is requested ...'

[2] 1852/63 (F.R.G.): 8 *Yearbook* 198; see also 1169/61 (F.R.G.): 6 *Yearbook* 588.

[3] 1169/61.

release from prison on probation, of a person charged, cannot be taken as holding him guilty so as to attract Article 7.

In an application of great legal complexity[1] involving rent control in West Berlin, the main issues were whether or not an order prohibiting price increases (*Preisstoppverordnung*) of the 1936 was still in force after the war, and whether the legislation, which according to the applicant had superseded it, did not preclude the penal sanction imposed on him for increasing the rent of a flat in a building owned by him. The applicant invoked Article 7. In rejecting the application, the Commission made some general observations on the sense of the Article and particularly on the task of the Commission in applying it: since it necessarily involves for the Commission a *renvoi* to domestic law, the Commission can, without functioning as a 'fourth instance',[2] and indeed must consider whether the form and application of the municipal law in question is consistent with Article 7.[3]

The Commission said:

. . . ce paragraphe ne se borne pas à prohiber—sous réserve du paragraphe 2— l'application rétroactive de la loi pénale '*in peius*'; . . . il consacre, plus généralement, le principe de la légalité des délits et des peines ('*nullum crimen, nulla poena sine lege*'); il interdit, en particulier, l'application extensive de la loi pénale '*in malam partem*' par voie d'analogie, ainsi que le Gouvernement de la République Fédérale d'Allemagne l'a rappelé dans ses observations écrites sur la recevabilité de la présente requête; . . . la Commission se réfère, sur ces différents points, à sa jurisprudence constante [cf. les décisions sur la recevabilité des requêtes N°. 217/56 (*Annuaire* i, p. 239), 223/56, 268/57 (*Annuaire* i, p. 240), 272/57, 309/57, 780/60, 1028/61 (*Annuaire* iv, p. 335), 1063/ 61, 1103/61 (*Recueil* viii, p. 126), 1162/61, 1445/62 (*Recueil* xii, p. 113), 1446/62 et 1599/62 (*Recueil* x, p. 11)];

. . . du principe de la légalité des délits et des peines découles également, de l'avis de la Commission, l'impossibilité de condamner une personne en vertu d'une loi pénale abrogée, lorsque les faits incriminés sont postérieurs à cette abrogation qu'en effet, pareille condamnation aurait trait à 'une action ou une omission qui, au moment où elle a été commise, ne constituait pas une infraction d'après le droit national', l'article 7 § 1 ne distinguant pas entre l'action ou omission qui 'ne constituait plus' une infraction et celle qui n'en constituait 'pas encore' une;

---

[1] 1169/61: 6 *Yearbook* 520, 588.

[2] For this notion see under Article 19 below.

[3] For an instance, see 780/60: *Recueil* (1961) i and 1063/61: 5 *Yearbook* 190. See also 1732/62: *Recueil*(1964) i: sentence imposed not inconsistent with provisions of Austrian S.P.O., but longer than was apparently intended by the court—Generalprokurator admitted an error of calculation (*Gedankenfehler*).

... la Commission, chargée de veiller au respect de la Convention par les États contractants (article 19), a compétence pour s'assurer, au besoin d'office, que les juridictions nationales ne continuent pas d'appliquer une loi pénale qui n'est pas en vigueur; ... si, d'ordinaire, il ne lui appartient pas de contrôler la bonne observation du droit interne par ces juridictions (cf. p. ex. *Annuaire* iii, p. 233, requête N°. 458/59, et *Recueil* viii, p. 57, requête N°. 1140/ 61), il en va autrement dans les matières où la Convention renvoie au droit interne, ce qui est précisément le cas de l'article 7; qu'en ces matières, la violation éventuelle du droit interne entraîne la méconnaissance de la Convention, de sorte que la Commission peut et doit la constater sans s'ériger pour autant en une Court de 'quatrième instance';

... il importe peu, d'autre part, que l'abrogation d'une loi pénale soit expresse ou implicite, pourvu que le droit interne de l'État intéressé n'ignore pas cette dernière forme d'abrogation;

The issue of 'fourth instance' in a similar context arose before the Permanent Court in its advisory opinion on the constitutionality of certain amendments to the Danzig Criminal Code. Judge Anzilotti considered the Court incompetent to give an opinion since the consistency of the amendments with the Constitution of the Free City was wholly a question of 'municipal law, with which the Court is not reputed to be acquainted and of which it is certainly not an organ',[1] and the courts of Danzig were competent to determine the constitutionality of enacted laws. This reasoning does not meet the point that the treaty of Versailles, Article 103, in establishing the League as guarantor of the Danzig Constitution required it to pass on the constitutionality of decrees, and that the Senate minority parties, in having the issue brought to the League Council through the High Commissioner, were not limited under League procedure by any rule of exhaustion of remedies in the Danzig courts. The court said:

It is clear that, though the interpretation of the Danzig Constitution is primarily an internal question of the Free City, it may involve the guarantee of the League of Nations as interpreted by the Council and by the Court. It is also clear that, when the constitutionality of decrees issued by the Senate is challenged, this may raise questions the solution of which depends upon the interpretation of the Constitution. ... [I]n order to give the opinion for which it asked, the Court will have to examine municipal legislation of the Free City, including the Danzig Constitution.[2]

---

[1] *Certain Danzig Legislative Decrees Case* [1935] P.C.I.J.: A/B 65 at 64.
[2] Ibid. at 50.

The task of the Commission, in dealing with applications under Article 7, is in a way analogous, though the distinct functions of the League Council and the Permanent Court in the Danzig case are in a way combined in it.

constitute a criminal offence under national or international law/ne constituait pas une infraction d'après le droit national ou international

The rule of *nullum crimen sine lege* requires that the offence de defined[1] and commonly known as such.[2] The Permanent Court analysed this principle in considering an amended provision of the Danzig Criminal Code, which read:

> Any person who commits an act which the law declares to be punishable or which is deserving of penalty according to the fundamental conceptions of a penal law and sound popular feeling shall be punished.[3] If there is no penal law directly covering an act, it shall be punished under the law of which the fundamental conception applies most nearly to the said act.

The Permanent Court observed of this provision:[4]

> It is not a question of applying the text of the law itself. . . . It is a question of applying what the judge (or the Public Prosecutor) believes to be in accordance with the fundamental idea of the law, and what the Judge (or the Public Prosecutor) believes to be condemned by sound popular feeling. . . . [U]nder the new decrees a man may find himself placed on trial and punished for an act which the law did not enable him to know was an offence, because its criminality depends entirely upon the appreciation of the situation by the Public Prosecutor and by the Judge. Accordingly, a system in which the criminal character of an act and the penalty attached to it will be known to the Judge alone replaces a system in which this knowledge was equally open to both the Judge and the accused. Nor should it be overlooked that an individual opinion as to what was the intention which underlay a law, or an individual opinion as to what is condemned by sound popular feeling, will

---

[1] 1747/62: 6 *Yearbook* 442, and see under Article 6 (3) *a*.

[2] Compare *Entick* v. *Carrington* [1765] 19 St. Tr. 1030 *per* Lord Camden C.J.: Justification for trespass must be 'maintained by the text of the statute law, or by the principles of the common law' and 'the silence of the books is an authority' against such justification.

[3] Article 2: 'Bestraft wird, wer eine Tat begeht, die das Gesetz für strafbar erklärt oder die nach dem Grundgedanken eines Strafgesetzes und nach gesundem Volksempfinden Bestrafung verdient. . . .'

[4] *Certain Danzig Legislative Decrees Case* [1935] P.C.I.J.: A/B 65 at 52, 53, 56.

vary from man to man. ... It is true that a criminal law does not always
regulate all details. By employing a system of general definition, it sometimes
leaves the Judge not only to interpret it, but also to determine how to apply it.
The question as to the point beyond which this method comes into conflict
with the principle that fundamental rights may not be restricted except by law
may not be easy to solve. But there are some cases in which the discretionary
power left to the Judge is too wide to allow of any doubt but that it exceeds
these limits. It is such a case which confronts the Court in the present
proceedings.[1]

The Commission has interpreted the expression 'national law' to
mean law found applicable to the offence under conflict rules and as
therefore not limited to the law of a contracting State. So where an
applicant complained that the inscription in his police record
(*Strafregister*) of convictions in Eastern Germany for offences
committed there was inconsistent with Article 7, on the ground that
they did not constitute criminal offences under the law of the Federal
Republic of Germany, the Commission said, rejecting the application:

> ... the inscription on the Applicant's *Strafregister* of his previous conviction
> cannot legitimately be considered as meaning that he was put on trial by the
> authority inscribing the conviction in his *Strafregister* and 'held guilty of a
> criminal offence' within the meaning of Article 7.... [T]he Applicant has not
> disputed that the conviction ... was in regard to acts which did constitute a
> criminal offence under the law applicable at the place where, and the time
> when, he was convicted.[2]

at the time when it was committed/au moment où elle a été commise

The principle of non-retroactivity is essential to Article 7,[3] but it does
not it seems cover provisions which are to the *advantage* of the
accused. So where the applicant was charged under a statute,
amended between the time of the commission of the offence and the
prosecution, the Commission considered the form of charge milder
than under the earlier statute and said that the application of a new
penal provision *in mitius* was fully consistent with Article 7.[4]

---

[1] It may be asked whether these limits were not also exceeded in *Shaw* v. *Director of
Public Prosecutions* [1962] A.C. 220, 267: see Lord Shawcross, *Revue Belge de droit international* [1965] 297, 204: and *Canadian Bar Review* [1964] 561.

[2] 448/59: 3 *Yearbook* 270.

[3] 327/57. *Rooney* v. *North Dakota* [1906] 196 U.S. 319 is to the same effect.

[4] For retroactive penal law see *South Africa*: General Law Amendment Act 1962, s. 4,
empowering the President to declare by Proclamation that organizations are unlawful

Has there been a change in the law between that presumed to be in force when the offence was committed and that applied in the trial and conviction?

An amendment of the law may be to the advantage or the disadvantage of the accused. In an early decision, the Commission, finding in a statute amended after the offence had been committed, that the form of charge was milder than in the earlier statute, held that the subsequent charge and conviction did not contravene Article 7. But it later held that Article 7 does not guarantee, where there is such an amendment of the law, that the accused has any right to the application of the more favourable provisions.[1] The reason for this appears to be that there is no provision in Article 7, which, as the Covenant, Article 15 (1), expressly states:

If, subsequent to the commission of the offence, provision is made by law for the imposition of the lighter penalty, the offender shall benefit thereby.

As far as interpretation of the law goes, reference to and reliance in precedent is not a retroactive application of the criminal law,[2] but the new interpretation of the law may be disputable under Article 7. So the publisher and editor of a magazine, designed for homosexuals, and published in the United Kingdom were prosecuted for the common law offence of blasphemous libel when an issue of the magazine contained a poem, which attributed to Jesus Christ promiscuous homosexual practices with the Apostles and others. The substance of the applications by the publisher and editor will be seen below under Article 10; while here the issue under Article 7 was whether the courts had not in fact introduced new law, in saying that, given the manifest intention of the publisher and the editor to publish the issue containing the article, it was not necessary to establish an intention to blaspheme at least on the part of the editor; in short, the publication involved a strict liability. The Commission concluded:

Despite the admission of the Court of Appeal and the majority of the House of Lords that a point of principle was involved in the determination of this question, which required clarification, it is equally clear that the application of a test of strict liability and the exclusion of evidence as to the publisher's and editor's intention to blaspheme did not amount to the creation of a new law in

as from 8 April 1960, no court having competence to pronounce on the validity of such a Proclamation.

[1] 7900/77 (F.R.G.): 13 D.R. 70.   [2] 6689/74 (U.K.): 3 D.R. 95.

the sense that earlier case law clearly denying such strict liability, and admitting evidence as to the blasphemous intentions, was overruled.[1]

The time element also came into account under Article 7 in the age of the offender chosen for fixing of sentence.[2] Under the Penal Code an order for committal to prison of a recidivist could not be made unless conviction was pronounced after his twenty-fourth birthday. The applicant was so convicted, and an order made, but in respect of crimes commited before the date. The Commission found no breach of Article 7, since:

The law was thus both in force and appliable to the applicant's behaviour, and only its actual enforcement depended on the applicant's age at the time of conviction.

nor shall a heavier penalty be imposed than the one that was applicable at the time the criminal offence was committed/De même il n'est infligé aucune peine plus forte que celle qui était applicable au moment où l'infraction a été commise

The rule of *nulla poena sine lege* rests upon the same principles as the rule of *nullum crimen sine lege*, so that neither the conditions, that may be imposed on release on probation, nor preventive detention or *emprisonnement subsidiaire* for recidivism[3] rank as additional penalties in the sense of Article 7. But conviction and sentence that have become *res judicata* cannot be varied.[4]

The penalty 'applicable' may be the penalty prescribed, or, where the law prescribes penalties within a range or leaves the imposition of sentence to the discretion of the court, the penalty that might reasonably be expected.

What an 'applicable' penalty is for the purpose of Article 7 is open then to debate. Where the law prescribes for the particular offence penalties within a range, it might be said to be the maximum penalty;

---

[1] The law-making function of the House of Lords on appeal was described in *Knuller v. Director of Public Prosecutions* [1973] *A.C.* 435.

[2] 9167/80 (Austria): 26 D.R. 248.

[3] See 1445/62: *Recueil* (1963) ii.,

[4] See *Bulletin of I.C.J.*, No. 16 (July 1963), 5–15, for substitution of death penalties for imprisonment in Burundi after its independence for offences committed while the territory was still in a Trusteeship.

but either in this case or where the law prescribes no particular penalty, leaving the imposition of sentence to the discretion of the court, it might be said to be the penalty customarily imposed or reasonably to be expected. So the Bill of Rights 1689 in England that 'excessive fines [ought not to be imposed] nor cruel and unusual punishments inflicted'.

In so far as the Commission has suggested that Article 7 incorporates a principle of restrictive interpretation of provisions of the criminal law,[1] it is possible that, for example, an unusual term of imprisonment might be found to be inconsistent with Article 7.

... criminal according to the general principles of law recognized by civilized nations/criminelle d'après les principes généraux de droit reconnu par les nations civilisées

The purpose of paragraph (2) has already been explained, and was described by the Commission as

de préciser que cet Article n'affecte pas les lois qui, dans les circonstances tout à fait exceptionnelles qui se sont produites à l'issue de la deuxième guerre mondiale, ont été passées pour réprimer les crimes de guerre et les faits de trahison et collaboration avec l'ennemi, et ne vise à aucune condamnation juridique ou morale de ces lois.[2]

The Federal Republic of Germany, in accepting the Convention, made a reservation that

it will only apply the provisions of Article 7 paragraph 2 . . . within the limits of Article 103 (2) of the Basic Law of the German Federal Republic. This provides that 'any act is only punishable if it was so by law before the offence was committed'.[3]

The Commission has suggested that

en formulant cette réserve, la République Fédérale . . . semble avoir accepté, en ce qui la concerne, une extension des obligations découlant normalement de l'article 7,

---

[1] 1162/61: *Recueil* (1963) i.

[2] 268/57: 1 *Yearbook* 241. Compare 77/55; 931/60: *Recueil* (1961) ii and 1038/61: 4 *Yearbook* 324, 336. Compare 214/56 (*de Becker Case*): 2 *Yearbook* 226.

[3] 'Eine Tat kann nur bestraft werden, wenn die Strafbarkeit gesetzlich bestimmt war, bevor die Tat begangen wurde.' For the distinction between *Strafwürdig* and *Strafbar* here see K. J. Partsch, *Die Rechte und Freiheiten*, p. 178.

but did not find it necessary, on the particular facts of the application, to consider this further.

It appears that the general principles of law, invoked in paragraph (2), are to be distinguished from international law in paragraph (1) in particular here by the fact that paragraph (2) contemplates rules of municipal law, which are common to many countries, but which may or may not be recognized as rules of international law. It may be observed that the C.P.R. Covenant, Article 15 (2), which is in substance the same as Article 7 (2) of the Convention, uses the expression recognized by the 'community of nations' in place of 'civilized nations', but it is doubtful whether there is any intention to alter the sense of the provision.

ARTICLE 8

(1) Everyone has the right to respect for his private and family life, his home and his correspondence.

(2) There shall be no interference by a public authority with the exercise of this right except such as is in accordance with the law and is necessary in a democratic society in the interests of national security, public safety or the economic well-being of the country, for the prevention of disorder or crime, for the protection of health or morals, or for the protection of the rights and freedoms of others.

1. Toute personne a droit au respect de sa vie privée et familiale, de son domicile et de sa correspondance.

2. Il ne peut y avoir ingérence d'une autorité publique dans l'exercice de ce droit que pour autant que cette ingérence est prévue par la loi et qu'elle constitue une mesure qui, dans une société démocratique, est nécessaire à la sécurité nationale, à la sûreté publique, au bien-être économique du pays, à la défense de l'ordre et à la prévention des infractions pénales, à la protection de la santé ou de la morale, ou à la protection des droits et libertés d'autrui.

The first paragraph is derived from the Universal Declaration, Article 12,[1] but it is cast, paradoxically perhaps, in a vaguer and less comprehensive form; for not only is the prohibition against attacks upon honour and reputation omitted, but the concept of respect belongs to the world of manners rather than the law. What began in the Teitgen proposals as 'inviolability', and became 'immunity from arbitrary interference',[2] then protection from governmental interference (*immixtions gouvernementales*),[3] ended tamely as 'respect'.[4] These changes may in part reflect various opinions, expressed in the Consultative Assembly but overruled, that 'in these cases [under Article 8] no rights regarded as essential for the function of the democratic institutions were at stake'.[5]

The C.P.R. Covenant has substantially restored Article 12 of the Universal Declaration, and reads:

1. No one shall be subjected to arbitrary or unlawful interference with his privacy, family, home or correspondence, nor to unlawful attacks on his honour and reputation.
2. Everyone has the right to the protection of the law against such interference or attacks.

The preparatory work also reveals hesitations between the expressions 'privacy' and 'private life', and 'family' and 'family life', the inclusion of 'life' in both cases prevailing.

The association of family, home, and correspondence in the first paragraph suggests that it is designed, primarily at least, to protect the physical framework of personal life: the family from separation, the home from intrusion, and correspondence from being searched or stopped. But that it goes to inner life as well applications to the Commission have shown.

private and family life/vie privée et familiale

These words are doubtless to be read disjunctively, but they are closely linked. Among the relatively few applications involving private

---

[1] 'No one shall be subjected to arbitrary interference with his privacy, family, home, or correspondence, nor to attacks upon his honour and reputation. Everyone has the right to the protection of the law against such interference or attacks.'

[2] *T.P.* i. 69 and 72; ii. 456: Report of Committee of Experts: Alternative B (16.3.1950).

[3] United Kingdom draft: *T.P.* iii. 612.

[4] Report of Conference of Senior Officials (17.6.1950): *T.P.* iii. 625.

[5] *T.P.* i. 199.

life in itself it is possible to distinguish, those in which the situation presented is hardly recognizable as one of private life; those involving aspects of criminal proceedings; and those that present major problems: the rights of pregnancy, the status and regulation of homosexuality, and the interference with communications.

Examples of the first group may be quickly disposed of, for they could not be more manifestly ill-founded: so keeping a dog is not part of private life under Article 8 (1);[1] nor are the compulsory wearing of seat-belts an interference with it.[2] Since the decision about dogs—perhaps even they have 'rights'—may be challenged, the reasoning of the Commission may be quoted:

> The Commission cannot however accept that the protection afforded by Article 8 of the Convention extends to relationships of the individual with his entire immediate surroundings, in so far as they do not involve human relationships and notwithstanding the desire of the individual to keep such relationships within the private sphere. No doubt the dog has had close ties with man since time immemorial. However, given the above considerations this document alone is not sufficient to bring the keeping of a dog into the sphere of the private life of the owner.

It might be said that the qualified protection given to private life by 'respect', excludes the criminal law process with its social purpose, from Article 8 (1); and that justification for some of its measures does not have to be sought in Article 8 (2). So statements made by an accused in the Magistrates Court, which were communicated to the Chief Constable and all the city police, were part of public proceedings, and their communication was not an interference with the private life of the accused;[3] and the control of the correspondence of prisoners, however private, is to be regarded as an inherent condition of detention.[4] However, a compulsory blood test carried out as part of paternity proceedings is an interference with private life, necessary for the protection of the rights and freedoms of others under Article 8 (2).[5]

The computerized recording of personal data is a new and hardly controlled development.[6]

---

[1] 6825/74 (Iceland) 5 D.R. 86.
[2] 8707/79 (Belgium) 18 D.R. 255.
[3] 3868/68 (U.K.) 34 *Recueil* 10.
[4] 4144/69 (Luxembourg) 33 *Recueil* 27.
[5] 8278/78 (Austria) 18 D.R. 154.
[6] The Convention on Data Protection (28.1.1981) had 13 signatories but only one ratification (Sweden) by 10.1983.

The control of *pregnancy* by law, enacted in most countries, is
illustrated by developments in the Federal Republic of Germany from
1974, when the Fifth Criminal Law Reform Act was adopted. Under
Article 218 of the Criminal Code (1871), as amended and applied in
other legislation and court decisions, any abortion, except one
indicated on medical grounds to save the life or health of the mother,
was punishable. The Reform Act (21.6.1974) enlarged and liberalized
the law, setting out the circumstances, in which the termination of
pregnancy would be permissible, and in which it would remain
unlawful. A critical provision was Article 218 (*a*), which read:

An abortion performed by a doctor with the pregnant woman's consent shall
not be punishable under Article 218 if no more than twelve weeks have
elapsed after conception.

After the promulgation of the Act, its entry into force was
suspended by the Federal Constitutional Court by a provisional ruling
at the request of the Land Government of Baden-Württemberg; and
proceedings were instituted in the Court for a review of the Act under
the Basic Law (Grundgesetz) (1940), by 193 members of the Bundestag
and five Länder. The Court ruled that Article 218 (*a*) of the Reform
Act was incompatible with Article 2 (1), first sentence, of the Basic
Law read in conjunction with Article 1.[1] Following this judgment the
Fifteenth Criminal Law Act (21.6.1976) revised the Act of 1974,
maintaining the principle that abortion is wrongful, but providing that
termination of pregnancy shall not be punishable, if performed by a
doctor, it being advisable in order to avert from the pregnant woman
the danger of a distress so serious that she cannot be called to continue
the pregnancy, and there being no way or means of averting the
distress that she could be expected to bear.

In particular, abortion is permitted if continuance of the pregnancy
would endanger her life or health, or if it is feared that the child might
suffer from incurable injury to health, or if the pregnancy was the
result of a sexual offence. Further, the Act provides that the pregnant
woman is exempt from any charge, if the abortion is performed by a

---

[1] Article 2 (2): 'Jeder hat das Recht auf Leben und körperliche Unversehrtheit'
(Everyone has the right to life and freedom from bodily injury); Article 1: 'Die Würde
des Menschen ist untastbar' (The dignity of man shall be inviolable). It is not clear how
these propositions are related to the Bürgerliches Gesetzbuch (Civil Code). Article 1:
'Die Rechtsfähigkeit des Menschen beginnt mit der Vollendung der Geburt' (Man's
capacity for rights begins at actual birth).

doctor within the first 22 weeks of pregnancy, and she has made use of medical and social counselling.

For the Constitutional Court it appears, in its reliance on the quoted provisions of the Basic Law, that it is the right of life of the unborn child that is decisive. The Commission does not expressly follow this, saying:[1]

60 The Commission does not find it necessary to decide, in this context whether the unborn child is to be considered as 'life' in the sense of Article 2 of the Convention, or whether it could be regarded as an entity which under Article 8 (2) could justify an interference 'for the protection of others'. There can be no doubt that certain interests relating to pregnancy are legally protected e.g. shown by a survey of the legal order in thirteen High Contracting Parties . . .

61 The Commission therefore finds that not every regulation of the termination of unwanted pregnancies constitutes an interference with the *right to respect* for the private life of the mother. Article 8 (1) cannot be interpreted as meaning that pregnancy and its termination are, as a principle, solely a matter of the private life of the mother. In this respect the Commission notes that there is not one member State of the Convention which does not in one way or another, set up legal rules in this matter . . .

and after reviewing the legislation in issue:

63 In view of this situation the Commission does not find that the legal rules complained about by the applicants interfere with their right to respect for their private life,

The reasoning is difficult to follow, not least because no explanation is offered of what elements of pregnancy are not part of private life, or of what regulation of the termination of unwanted pregnancies would constitute an interference with the right to respect for private life.

The Commission has held at least that the private life of the mother of an unborn child excludes any claim by her husband, and father of the child, to object to a termination of pregnancy:

. . . any interpretation of the husband's and potential father's right under Article 8 of the Convention, to respect for his private and family life, as regards an abortion which his wife intends to have performed on her, must first of all take account the right of the pregnant woman, being the person primarily concerned in the pregnancy and its continuation or termination to respect for her private life.

[1] *Brüggemann and Scheuten* 6959/75 (F.R.G.): Report 10 D.R. 100.

The claim of the husband was declared then to be incompatible with Article 8.[1]

On the place of *homosexual relations* under the Convention, important questions remain unanswered. The Commission has held that homosexual relations are part of private life, but may be justifiably restricted under conditions set out in Article 8 (2).[2] In an application against the continuance of the law in Northern Ireland,[3] criminalizing male homosexual acts and enacted by statutes of 1861 and 1885, the Commission considered that the prohibition of consensual homosexual acts between males over 21 years of age was not justified. The case was sent to the Court, which came to the same conclusion by fifteen votes to four. The court pointed out that there is a better understanding of homosexuality, in that in the great majority of Convention countries, including the United Kingdom,[4] it was no longer found necessary or appropriate to penalize male homosexual acts; and that in Northern Ireland the authorities have in recent years refrained from enforcing the law against consenting males over the age of 21; and that there was on the other hand public opposition in Northern Ireland to proposed change in the old law. The Court concluded that there could not in all the circumstances, be 'pressing social need' to maintain the old law, criminalizing private homosexual acts between adult males capable of valid consent.[5] Neither the Commission nor the Court entered into Article 14, although the applicant had maintained before the Commission that, in restrictions on homosexual conduct, there was still no basis in terms of Article 8 (2) for distinguishing between male and female conduct; homosexual acts between consenting adult women were not then contrary to the law of Northern Ireland or of the United Kingdom. Further, the Court did not, as the Commission had, consider whether restrictions on homosexual relations might be based on the prosecution of morals under Article 8 (2);[6] though recognizing

[1] 8416/79: 19 D.R. 244.

[2] 7215/75 (U.K.): *Yearbook* (1978) 36.

[3] *Dudgeon* 7525/76 (U.K.): 11 D.R. 117.

[4] Homosexual acts in private between two consenting males over 21 ceased to be offences in England and Wales under the Sexual Offences Act (1967) and in Scotland, under the Criminal Justice (Scotland) Act (1980).

[5] Judgment no. 45 (22.10.1981): *Yearbook* (1981) 444. The Commission has observed that the age above which the criminal law shall no longer apply 'may be fixed within a reasonable margin and vary depending on the attitude of society': 5935/72 (F.R.G.): 3 D.R. 46.

[6] The seizure by public authority of issues of a homosexual magazine was held, given its contents, to be justified for 'the protection of morals' under Article 8 (2): 7308/75

that 'the moral climate of Northern Ireland', evidenced by the opposition to legislative change, had to be taken into account, it expressly left this issue to 'the national authorities'. It follows that on this approach, as in corporal punishment in the Isle of Man, it is in the end public opinion and not the Convention, that prevails.

The life and status of a transsexual were in issue in complaints against the inadequacy of Belgian law, in that the birth certificate remained conclusive of status for all legal and administrative purposes. The applicant, born a female child, had changed to male sex at the age of 28 after thirteen operations carried out over three years. The Commission considered that in the law and practice there was failure to respect his private life, and also a denial of right to marry under Article 12. The Court, to which the case was referred, held that there had been a failure to exhaust domestic remedies, and did not therefore proceed with the case.[1]

We come now to family life,[2] linked as it is with private life.

The identification of family relationships is a task of public authority and particularly immigration officials, and it must not be exercised 'perversely, arbitrarily, or otherwise, in denial of the right ... to respect for family life'.[3] The 'family' includes, in addition to a married couple and their children, the children of the first and second marriage,[4] and a grandparent in cohabitation;[5] and the determination of paternity, by means of a compulsory blood-test, is not intervention in private and possibly family life justifiable under Article 8 (2) for the protection of the rights of others. An adopted child and parent constitute a 'family', in the view of the Commission, so that the State 'cannot separate two persons united by an adoption contract', but has no positive obligation to grant a particular status—of adoption' to them.[6] The statement, and its qualification, are not easy to reconcile.

(U.K.) 16 D.R. 82. In an early decision on homosexuality the Commission invoked the protection of 'public morals', without making clear the *public* factor: 530/59: 3 *Yearbook* 188.

[1] 7654/76: 11 D.R. 194 (Report 1.3.1979).
[2] It is a matter of fact: 7224/75 (U.K.) 12 d.R. 32. A broad view of what constitutes home and family life is in the judgment of Lord Reid in *Race Relations Board* v. *A.G.* [1975] AC 259.
[3] *Kamel* 8378/78 (U.K.) 30 D.R. 168. The use of a patronymic name for a family is objective and reasonable: 8042/77 (Switzerland) 12 D.R. 202.
[4] 8604/79 (F.R.G.): 20 D.R. 206.   [5] 8924/80 (Switzerland): 24 D.R. 183.
[6] 6482/74 (Netherlands): 7 D.R. 75. The relationship of foster mother and child for whom she has cared and to whom she is deeply attached involves her 'private life', but whether it constitutes 'family life' was not pursued: 8257/78 (Switzerland): 13 D.R. 248.

The Commission has long recognized extramarital relationships as constituting 'family life' where the couple is in established cohabitation—a 'common household'.[1]

The place of the child of an unmarried mother was raised in an application from Belgium.[2] Under Belgian law no legal bond between an unmarried mother and her child resulted from birth by her voluntary and received recognition, or by affiliation by a formal deed, both being challengeable by third parties. The legal bond created was limited to that between child and mother, and the inheritance and property rights of the child were severely restricted. Paula Marckx, an unmarried mother, brought applications on behalf of herself and of her daughter Alexandra, whom she had 'recognized' soon after her birth and adopted a year later. The Commission held that the principle and procedure of recognition, acquired under Belgian law, was contrary to Article 8 and also to Article 14, and that 'simple' adoption did not remedy this.

The Court reached the same conclusion:

36 ... The necessity to have recourse to such an expedient [recognition] derived from a refusal to acknowledge fully Paula Marckx's maternity from the moment of the birth. Moreover, in Belgium an unmarried mother is faced with an alternative; if she recognises her child (assuming she wishes to do so), she will at the same time prejudice him since her capacity to give or bequeath her property to him will be restricted;[3] if she desires to retain the possibility of making such dispositions as she chooses in the child's favour, she will be able to renounce establishing a family tie with him in law ... the dilemma is not consonant with 'respect' for family life; if it thwarts and impedes the normal development of such life.

37 As regards Alexandra, only one method of establishing her maternal affiliation was available to her under Belgium, namely to take legal proceedings (recherche de paternité: Civil Code Articles 341a–c) ... Quite apart from the conditions of proof that have to be satisfied, the legal representative of an infant needs the consent of the family council before he can bring ... an action for the declaration as to status; it is only after attaining majority that the child can bring such an action himself ...

---

[1] 7289/75 (Switzerland) 9 D.R. 57.

[2] *Marckx* 6833/74: Report (10.12.1977): Judgment No. 31 (13.6.1979).

[3] Civil Code, Article 908 provides that recognized 'illegitimate' children 'only receive by disposition *inter vivos* or by will no more than their entitlement under the title 'Inheritance on Intestacy' which is a maximum of three-quarters of what a 'legitimate' child inherits, if the mother has other heirs.

As regards the fact that an illegitimate child, whether recognized or adopted remains a stranger to his parents' families, the Court said:

45 In fact the legislation makes provision for some exceptions—and recent case-law is tending to add more—but it denies a child borne out of wedlock any rights over the estates of his father's or mother relatives (Civil Code, Article 756) it does not expressly create any maintenance obligations between him and those relatives and it empowers his guardian rather than those relatives to give consent where appropriate to his marriage ...

The Court, in finding breaches of Article 8 in these circumstances, also by demonstrable reasoning found breaches of Article 14 in relation to Article 8. Some of these issues will be reviewed further in the care of children.

Another important implication of the reasoning of both the Commission and the Court was, as stated by the Court, that:

Article 75 of the Convention entitles individuals to contend that a law violates their rights by itself in the absence of an individual measure of implementation if they run the risk of being directly affected by it.

This says, in effect, that legislation can be restrictive by its existence as well as its enforcement.

Care of children. Another question of the extent of family life under Article 8 is whether it is confined, as between parents and children, to legitimate children or legitimated children. The question falls into two parts: Does family life for purposes of Article 8 embrace the illegitimate child at all? If so, is the recognition of a status of illegitimacy itself consistent with respect for 'family life' in Article 8?

The Commission has given an affirmative answer to the first part of the question, in respect of the relationship of the child to his or her mother,[1] or to the natural father,[2] or to both. This answer is in line with the practice of the Commission that it will not in general construe a word or phrase in the Convention in terms of the domestic law of the country concerned in an application; for here the Convention rights of natural parents would vary with the rights accorded to them under domestic law.

The second part of the question is more difficult, but the Commission appears to have indirectly answered it in the negative. A

---

[1] 514/59: 3 *Yearbook* 204; 2707/66.
[2] 1475/62: *Recueil* (1963) ii.

German citizen had unsuccessfully sought custody of his six-year-old natural daughter, who had been taken by order of the District Court (*Amtsgericht*) from the custody of her mother, for neglect of her parental duties, and placed in the care of the competent local authority (*Stadtjugendamt*). In German law illegitimate children are given certain protection under the constitution,[1] but the natural father, though he has a legal duty to support his natural child, has not legal right of custody or access; however, he may apply for a declaration of legitimacy (*Ehelichkeitserklärung*).[2]

The Commission said:

... the Applicant, although unable to invoke the Convention ... before the Federal Constitutional Court ... could have lodged a constitutional complaint ... alleging that the decision of the District Court violated Article 6 of the Basic Law.[3]

If a declaration of legitimacy were to be regarded as a remedy, which must be exhausted, then the status of illegitimacy, which is indeed recognized by Article 6 (5) of the Basic Law, could not in itself be regarded as inconsistent with Article 8 of the Convention; for the recourse has not the effect of removing the status but only of correcting its effects in particular cases.

How far may the State intervene in the parental care of children? In 1979 the Swedish Parliament adopted an amendment to the Code of Parenthood which read:

A custodian shall exercise the necessary supervision over the child with due regard to the child's age and other circumstances. The child shall not be subjected to corporal punishment or any other form of humiliating treatment.

The provisions of the Code of Parenthood form no part of the Penal Code, and no sanction attaches to their breach. However, the applicants, three couples and a divorcee, members of a Protestant Free church congregation in Stockholm, complained of such restrictions of the corporal punishment of their children, which they analysed at some length; in particular, they relied on religious

---

[1] Grundgesetz, Article 6 (5): Legislation (*die Gesetzgebung*) shall provide the same conditions for the bodily and spiritual development (*Stellung in der Gesellschaft*), of illegitimate children, as for legitimate children.

[2] Viz. *legitimatio per rescriptum principis* under BGB s. 1723, for which there is no equivalent in English law. The declaration lies within the discretion of the court.

[3] 1475/62: *Recueil* (1963) ii.

doctrine invoking Biblical texts[1] and Luther's Large Catechism. They pointed out that the Central Social Board of Stockholm, to which the new amendment to the Code of Parenthood had been submitted for consideration, maintained that:

special efforts of information [should be innovated in respect of] extreme religious groups which have argued for so-called loving chastisement as a systematic part of the upbringing of children.

It appears that the applicants considered such chastisement as including 'blows, beatings, boxing the ears'.

There was naturally extended argument between the Government and the applicants on the application. However, the Commission said:

The exact practical effects of the provision about which the applicants complained remain obscure. The applicants have not been directly subjected to any enforcement or other procedure arising from their disagreement with the Code, which might constitute an interference with their rights. They have further contended that the provisions of the Code may be relied upon in deciding questions as to the custody of children, but again they have not illustrated this submission . . . Furthermore, the information provided by the Swedish Government tends to confirm that this incomplete law is without any direct practical effect beyond that of attempting to encourage a reapparaisal of the treatment of children.

The Commission concuded that the amendment of the Code of Parenthood did not constitute an interference amounting to lack of respect for the family lives of the applicants.[2]

Custody. The care of children involves three distinct notions: guardianship, custody, and access. Where the parents of a child are divorced or separated, either may claim and be given custody of the child, the other having a right of access; or in some systems the guardianship of the child may be assigned to a local welfare authority and custody given to an individual. Under Article 8 neither parent, in case of separation or divorce, has a prior right of custody as against the other. So the Commission has said that

it is plain that the right of one particular parent to the custody of an infant as against the other parent is not, as such, included among the rights and

---

[1] Including Hebrews 12:6.
[2] 8811/79 (Sweden): 29 D.R. 104, 113. *G. Hendriks* 8429/78 (Netherlands): 18 D.R. 225; C.M. Resolution 82/4 (10.12.1982).

freedoms set forth in the Convention, and that the appreciation of the question which parent should be given the custody of an infant is, in principle, governed by the law of the domestic courts . . .[1]

This does not mean of course that where the domestic law assigns a priority of guardianship to one parent in general or in prescribed circumstances, there is an inconsistency with the Convention.

The Commission has also on several applications asserted that interference with family life, by separation of the child from its parents for purpose of custody, may be justified in the interests of the child,[2] and it has also invoked the 'protection of health and morals' clause in Article 8 (2).[3]

The close link between the two paragraphs of Article 8 on the care and upbringing of children is illustrated in an eloquent passage in a separate opinion of Judge Sir Hersch Lauterpacht,[4] in which he warns against too sharp a distinction between individual and social interests:

For it is clear that the distinction between the protection of the child and the protection of society is articifical. Both the laws relating to guardianship and those relating to protective upbringing are laws intended primarily for the protection of children and their interests. At the same time, the protection of children—through guardianship or protective upbringing—is pre-eminently in the interests of society. They are part of it—the most vulnerable and the most in need of protection. All social laws are, in the last resort, laws for the protection of individuals; all laws for the protection of individuals are, in a true sense, social laws.[5]

Access. Of children whose parents are divorced or are living apart under judicial separation the Commission has said that while their custody must in general be assigned to one of the parents, there being under the Convention no priority of claim, but that

the parent who is deprived of the custody of an infant may not be prevented, under Article 8 (1), from access to that infant unless special circumstances, as defined in paragraph 2 of that Article, so demand . . .[6]

[1] 172/56: 1 *Yearbook* 216; also 785/60: *Recueil* (1961) i; 1488/62: *Recueil* (1963) ii.

[2] 900/60: *Recueil* (1962) i; 845/60: ibid.

[3] 514/59: 3 *Yearbook* 204. But see 2805/67, where the care of the child prevails over the claims of the parents, as being part of 'the rights and freedoms of others'.

[4] *Guardianship of Infants Convention (1902) Case* [1958] I.C.J. Rep. 55 at 85.

[5] Compare U.N. General Assembly Resolution 1386–xiv (20.1.1959): Declaration of the Rights of the Child.

[6] 172/56: 1 *Yearbook* 217. The same applicant made two subsequent applications to the Commission: 434/58: 2 *Yearbook* 354 and 911/60: 4 *Yearbook* 198.

the circumstances primarily envisaged being 'the protection of the health and morals' of the child.[1] The terms of paragraph 2 in the view of the Commission leave

a considerable measure of discretion to the domestic courts in taking into account, when deciding on questions of access of the children, factors in the case which might appear to them to be critical for the protection of the health and morals of the child.

Nevertheless, it was still for the Commission to consider whether the measures taken were or were not justified under Article 8 (2).[2]

Separation of spouses. Many forms and consequences of separation have been brought to the Commission, which has taken, and perhaps had to take, less generous views than the German Constitutional Court.

Since the communication of a detainee with his wife or family is part of private life and correspondence under Article 8 (1), the denial of communication must be shown to be necessary under Article 8 (2). So where the applicants had been arrested on arrival at Liverpool from Ireland and detained for 45 hours for 'purpose of examination',[3] and denied any opportunity to contact their wives, the Commission quoted the Shackleton Report:

147 The affect on the family of the detained person must not be overlooked. Unless there are specific reasons relating to the danger that accomplices will be alerted the police should fulfil any request from the person detained that his family be notified of his arrest and should be prepared to answer any reasonable request for information about him from his close relatives throughout the period.

---

[1] 1329/62: 5 *Yearbook* 208. The transfer of a child into the custody of a parent living under a régime where the principles and standards of the Convention are not observed, raises questions analogous to those in extradition cases: see 2707/66, and for the concept see in *Germany*: Bundesverwaltungsgericht (15.12.1955): *Entsch. des BVerwG* 3. 58 (expulsion of husband to Italy—obligation of wife to follow not contrary to Article 3 of the Convention since there is a rule of law in Italy as in Germany).

[2] 312/57: 2 *Yearbook* 353; 1449/62: 6 *Yearbook* 266; same reasoning applied in 2306/64: *Recueil* 21 (father in preventive detention—visits of twelve-year-old child and correspondence with him forbidden, child being in guardianship of the competent local authority—measures considered by the Commission to be *assez rigoureuses* but within the margin of appreciation). See also 911/60: 4 *Yearbook* 222.

[3] Under the Prevention of Terrorism (Temporary Provisions) Act (1976) and Order made under it.

It found that there was no evidence before it to show specific reasons why in the present case the wives of the applicants could not be notified of their whereabouts; it found them in breach of Article 8.[1]

Expulsion[2] of one spouse where it appears possible that the other can follow is not, in the view of the Commission, interference with family life under Article 8 (1). It appears that the burden is on the applicant or spouse to show that, if one is deported, the other can follow and so they continue living together.[3] But it is not clear what kind of evidence is needed to do this. A couple, a U.S. citizen and a Brazilian national, were living together in the United Kingdom, in what constituted 'family life' under Article 8 (1). He had been formerly employed as an agent of the C.I.A., and she had been imprisoned for two years in Brazil, with allegations of ill-treatment, for his political activities. The grounds of deportation order against him which he denied, were that he had contacts, and was engaging in activities, harmful to the security of the United Kingdom. It was asserted that, given her active hostility to the Government of Brazil, she might not be granted an entry visa to the United States. The Commission said:

The applicant and his common law wife, who have apparently been living together in England since 1973, are both aliens and are of different nationality. They have been resident in the United Kingdom on a temporary basis and it has not been shown that they will be unable to make reasonable arrangements to live together outside the United Kingdom, even if they would prefer to remain.

The conclusion is neither reasoned nor responsive to the undisputed facts, revealing practical difficulties for the couple to live together outside the United Kingdom.[4]

A German national had obtained a residence and work permit in 1961 in Switzerland, married a Swiss national in 1965, and he lost his job in 1968 and was finally deported in 1972. The applicant made short visits to his wife and in the course of one of these visits was arrested, and sentenced to a term of imprisonment for disobeying the order of expulsion. The Commission observed that:

---

[1] *McVeigh et al.* 8022/77 (U.K.): Report 25 D.R. 15; 6564/74 (U.K.) 2 D.R. 105.

[2] The Commission has held, since 214/56, that the Convention guarantees no right of entry to or residence in a particular country.

[3] e.g. 5269/71 (U.K.) 39 *Recueil* 104 (expulsion to Cyprus): 5301/71 (U.K.) 43 *Recueil* 82 (expulsion to India).

[4] 7729/76 (U.K.) 7 D.R. 164.

... the applicant has in no way proved that the fact of having to leave Switzerland amounted to interference with his private life and an obstacle to his married life. In particular, he has not explained for what reason his wife was prevented from joining him in the Federal Republic of Germany in order to render married life possible.[1]

Nor were the Swiss authorities required to explain why they and the Federal Court could not accept at least short visits to his wife.

In Commission findings in applications on the effects of expulsion on family life, two alternative approaches appear: to determine the links of the family with the countries concerned, or to give priority under Article 8 (2) to the requirements of immigration control. For example:

In deciding whether an interference has arisen [in cases of expulsion] the Commission considered the practicability and reasonableness of the close members of family concerned accompanying or following the applicant. A further factor to be considered is the links which the deportee and the other members of the family have with the destination country and in particular whether there are further members of the family or relatives there ...

The reference to the immigration control was subsidiary only for:

Even assuming that her circle of acquaintances established during her stay in Germany to constitute relationships recognised as private life within the meaning of Article 8 (1) ... the Commission concludes that her deportation cannot be regarded as an interference with her right to respect for such relationships since the applicant knew and acknowledged at all material times that her presence ... was temporary and subject to revocation.[2]

The alternative and tougher approach was taken in later cases where, for example:[3]

... the Commission notes that the applicant was deported for having defied immigration controls [overstaying] and this his marriage was contracted at a time when the applicant was aware that he was at risk with his irregular immigration status. There do not appear to be any insurmountable obstacles

---

[1] 3031/75 (Switzerland): 6 D.R. 124. The situation is different where the wife of a deported husband makes the choice, for her own reasons, to remain: 5269/71 (U.K.) 39 *Recueil* 104; and, where a Syrian citizen was to be deported; 'It may be possible for his wife and children to follow him to Syria, but in the circumstances they may have a valid reason for not doing so'. 6537/73 (F.R.G.): 1 D.R. 77.

[2] 9478/81 (F.R.G.): 27 D.R. 243 (the applicant was an Indonesian citizen).

[3] 9082/80 (U.K.): 28 D.R. 160.

to the applicant's wife and child following him to Pakistan. The applicant's wife is not a United Kingdom citizen, only acquiring a right to abode in the United Kingdom in 1975. The applicant's child, although having United Kingdom citizenship by birth in the United Kingdom, is of an adoptable age.[1]

However, even though holding that the deportation constituted an interference with the right of the applicant to respect for his family life, the Commission attached 'significant weight' to the reasons for the deportation:

It finds with regard to the second paragraph of Article 8 that there are no elements concerning respect for family life which might outweigh valid consideration relating to the proper enforcement of immigrating controls. In this respect the Commission would emphasise the close connections between the policy of immigration control and consideration pertaining to public order.

The deportation order was then justified as being necessary for the 'prevention of disorder'.

The Commission generalized this criterion, saying:

It finds with regard to the second paragraph of Article 8 that there are no elements concerning respect for family life which might outweigh valid considerations relating to the proper enforcement of immigration controls.

The need of separation of spouses, of a wife from an alcoholic and violent husband may require State action, by legislation or otherwise, to secure it. So

... although the object of Article 8 is essentially that of protecting the individual against arbitrary interference by the public authorities, it does not merely compel the State to abstain from such interference: in addition to this primarily negative undertaking there may be positive obligations inherent in an effective respect for family life.[2] In Ireland, many aspects of private and family life are regulated by law. As regards marriage, husband and wife are in principle under a duty to cohabit but are entitled in certain cases to petition for a decree of judicial separation . . . Effective respect for private or family life obliges Ireland to make this means of protection effectively accessible.

However, in the actual circumstances the applicant was not in a position, in which she could apply to the High Court, largely owing to

---

[1] It appears that, in regard to family life under Article 8, it is the condition of a child, and not his or her parental status that is decisive: see 8245/78 (U.K.) 24 D.R. 98.

[2] 9285/81 (U.K.): 29 D.R. 205 repeating the reasoning in 8245/78 (U.K.): 24 D.R. 98.

costs, to obtain recognition in law of her *de facto* separation from her husband; she was then a victim of a violation of Article 8.[1]

The denial of entry to members of the family, who seek to join other members—spouses, parents, children, and so on—can be in breach of Article 8.

In 1970 applications were brought by 31 East African Asians,[2] largely from Uganda, complaining of the refusal of the United Kingdom to admit them to Great Britain or to allow them to stay there permanently. The Commission found a violation of Article 3 in 25 of the applications; and of Article 2 and 14 taken together in three cases. The Committee of Ministers, not having the requisite majority, made no decision on these findings. However, the United Kingdom government adopted measures to facilitate the entry of United Kingdom passport holders, and all 31 applicants came to be settled in the United Kingdom.

home/domicile

The protection of the home from entry or search, by the police, or other public authority, which appears to be given in paragraph 1, is largely nullified by the permitted derogations in paragraph 2. In particular, the expression 'in accordance with the law', though somewhat stronger in the French 'prévue par la loi', would accommodate a general power of police search, without warrant or specific statutory authority. Further, the interests of national security, the prevention of disorder or crime, or the protection of morals, are so broad that they could be used to justify a variety of entries and searches.

Where an applicant to the Commission had been arrested on charges under the law proscribing homosexual offences, his home was searched by the police, and books, pamphlets, letters, and his address book taken, which led to searches of the homes of others.[3] The Commission described the search of the home and seizure of papers as an interference 'necessary for the prevention of disorder or crime and for the protection of public morals, which was the position in this case'. The authority in law for the action of the police does not appear from the report of the decision.[4]

---

[1] *Airey* (Ireland): Judgment No. 31 (3.10.1979).

[2] 4403/70–4419/70 and others: (10.2.1970 to 3.6.1970).

[3] Compare the opinion expressed by Horridge J. in *Elias* v. *Pasmore* [1934] 2 K.B.

[4] 530/59: 3 *Yearbook* 188, 190. See also 604/59: 3 *Yearbook* 238 (search of home justified by authorities on ground that the applicant had not obeyed the directions of the police

The widescale eviction of Greek Cypriots from their homes by the Turkish invading forces in 1974 led to over 170,000 homeless people in northern Cyprus; and its violation of the convention was manifest.[1]

The expropriation of land or buildings has provoked far fewer applications than might have been expected. A case, declared inadmissible, may be described not least for its complexities. In April 1977 the Hull City Council, in the United Kingdom, declared sixteen clearance areas, in one of which the applicant's house was situated and made a single Compulsory Purchase Order for those areas, under the Housing Act (1957). Proceedings by the applicant to have the order quashed, ending in rejection by the Court of Appeal, exhausted remedies.

The Commission found that the court proceedings had established that the Clearance Order and the consequential compulsory purchase of the applicant's house were lawful in English law, and that, given the conditions of housing in the area,

... in the light of the general risk to health which the area in question posed and the pressing need to rehouse those living in these conditions, that the interference in question was justified under the terms of Article 8 (2) ... as in accordance with the law necessary in a democratic society for the protection of health and the rights of others.[2]

The Commission also found Article 13 and Article 1 of the First Protocol inapplicable.

The scope of the term 'home' was considered in an application arising from legislation in the island of Guernsey, which in 1970 made the occupation of all dwelling houses subject to licence; individuals satisfying certain residential qualifications did not require a licence. In a house listed as a controlled dwelling, for which a licence was required, the applicant and his wife, who was exempt from the licence requirement, lived together until 1973 when they separated. The applicant continued to live in the house, to which he had the legal title, but a licence was refused him. The Commission considered that, given that the applicant had legal title to the house, and lived in it with his wife, it was his 'home' and that it

and was suspected of carrying arms—no complaint made by the applicant as to the search).

[1] 6780/74 and 6950/75 (*Cyrpus* v. *Turkey*): 4 E.H.R.R.—Report of Commission §§ 208–10.

[2] 9261/81 (U.K.) 28 D.R. 177.

... remained the applicant's home also after his separation from his wife. Her leaving their common household gave no rise to changes in that respect. ...

The Commission held that:

... the refusal of the Housing Authority to grant the applicant a licence and their order that he should vacate his premises interfered with his right to respect for this home ...

but that the order was justified under Article 8 (2).[1]

correspondence/correspondance

The term, both in English and French, means communication in writing, and this is emphasized by the equivalent in the German official text (*Briefverkehr*). The German courts have been inclined to treat conversation, either direct or by telephone, as being part of private life, rather than of correspondence, in Article 8 (1). So it has been held that tape recording of a conversation, without the speaker's consent, is a breach of Article 8 (1),[2] unless the speaker is pursuing an unlawful purpose.[3]

Wire-tapping is an old practice, but electronic devices and the computer have made it sophisticated in its extent, and its data recordable. It has been the subject of two important applications, culminating in judgment of the Court; the comparison of the practice in the Federal Republic of Germany[4] and the United Kingdom is here interesting, and legislation is in progress in the United Kingdom following the judgment of the Court.[5]

In the Federal Republic of Germany, two statutes were enacted in 1968, one amending Basic Law, Article 10, and the other (G10) giving effect to the amendment. By the amendment to the Basic Law, Article 10 reads:

(1) Secrecy of the mail, post and telecommunications shall be inviolable.

(2) Restrictions may be ordered only pursuant to a statute where such restrictions are intended to protect free democratic constitutional order or the existence or the security of the Federation or of a *Land*, the statute may

---

[1] *Wiggins* (U.K.) 7456/76 13 D.R. 40.
[2] Bundesgerichtshof (20.5.1958) 27. 284.
[3] OLG, Celle (13.5.1965): *N.J.W.* [1965] 1677.
[4] *Klass et al.* (F.R.G.): Judgment No. 23 (6.9.1974): *I.L.R.* vol. 58 p. 423. See P. J. Duffy: 'The Case of Klass and others', *Human Rights Review* (Spring 1979) 20.
[5] *Malone* (U.K.): Judgment No. 82 (2.8.1984).

provide that the person concerned shall not be notified of the restriction and that legal remedy through the courts shall be replaced by a system of scrutiny by agencies and auxiliary agencies appointed by the people's elected representatives.

G10, implementing Article 10 (2),[1] is an elaborate statute, and only its provision relevant to our present theme need be described.

Under Article 1 the competent authorities may open and inspect mail and post, read telegraphic messages, listen to and record[2] telephone conversation, where there are factual indications for suspecting a person of planning, committing, or having committed offences, punishable under the Criminal Code, against the peace or security of the State, the democratic order, external security, and the security of the allied armed forces. These surveillance measures are permissible only if investigation of facts by another method is without prospect of success or is considerably more difficult; and an application to use them may be made by the head of one of the Agencies for the Protection of the Constitution of the Federation of *Länder*,[3] the Army security office, or the Federal Intelligence Service (Bundesnachrichtendienst), to the supreme *Land* authority, the Minister of Defence, or the Minister of the Interior, according to the jurisdiction in which the case fails.

Measures ordered by one of these authorities must be discontinued once the required conditions of their use cease to exist, and in any case after three months unless there is a fresh application. Under Article 1 (5) § 5 the person subject to the surveillance is not to be notified of the measures affecting him; however, the Constitutional Court quashed this provision as being incompatible with Article 10 (2) of the Basic Law, and ruled that the competent authority must inform the person concerned, as soon as notification can be made without jeopardizing the purpose of the restriction.

This surveillance system is subject to extensive administrative and

---

[1] Bundesamt für Verfassungsschutz; verfassungsschutzhehorden.
[2] Gesetz zur Beschränkung des Brief-Post-und Fernmeldegeheimnisses (Law on Restriction on the Secrecy of the Mail, Post, and Telecommunications) referred to as G10.
[3] As regards the recording of information obtained by surveillance or computer see the Lindup Committee Report on Data Protection (U.K.) (December 1978) Cmnd 7341, and the European Convention on Data Protection, adopted by the C.E. Committee of Ministers in 9. 1980, reviewed by A. Evans, 'Computers and privacy' (1980) 130 N.L.J. 1067.

judicial control. In the first place, the measures ordered are supervised by an official 'qualified for judicial office', who examines the
information obtained in order to decide whether its use would be
compatible with the G10, and whether it is relevant to the object of the
measure: he transmits to the competent authority only the information
satisfying these conditions, and destroys the remainder.

The competent Minister[1] must provide monthly an account of the
measures, which he has ordered, to the G10 Commission,[2] and report
at least once every six months to a Board composed of five members of
Parliament. The G10 Commission has the task of deciding whether a
person subject to surveillance is to be notified; the Minister concerned considers *ex offico* whether, on discontinuance of the surveillance, or at regular intervals thereafter, the person is to be notified,
submits his decision to the G10 Commission for its approval. The G10
Commission may also decide *ex officio*, or on the application of a
person believing himself to be subject to surveillance, on the legality
or necessity or measures, and if the decision is negative the Minister
must terminate them immediately.

Finally, while according to Article 9 § 5 of G10, 'there shall be no
remedy before the courts in respect of the ordering and implementation of restrictive measures', a person believing himself under surveillance may challenge it before the Constitutional Court, if he can
advance evidence to substantiate his complaint. The Court noted in
particular:

... G10 contains various provisions designed to reduce the effect of surveillance measures to an unavoidable minimum and to ensure that the surveillance is carried out in strict accordance with the law. In the absence of any
evidence or indication that the actual practice is otherwise, the Court must
assume that ... the relevant authorities are properly applying the legislation in
issue.

and that that legislation was justifiably enacted as being necessary in
the interests of national security, and for the prevention of the disorder or crime, under Article 8 (1). The conclusion had this form
because the five applicants (a judge, a government legal officer, and

---

[1] In Federal matters. The *Länder* Parliaments have set up similar supervisory
systems.

[2] Appointed to supervise the application of G10. It is composed of a chairman,
qualified to hold judicial office, and two assessors. The Commission is independent of
the administration.

three lawyers) had not been themselves subject to surveillance, but were challenging the content and impact of the statute.

Malone was a British citizen arrested in 1977 and charged with offences concerning the dishonest handling of stolen goods. Two trials, in each of which the jury failed to agree, led to acquittals in May 1979. In his application to the Commission, he complained of police surveillance, claiming that since 1971 his correspondence had been intercepted and his telephone lines taped; during the first trial it was admitted by the prosecution that one telephone conversation, to which he was a party, had been interrupted. After this first trial, the applicant instituted proceedings against the Metropolitan Police Commissioner; he sought declarations that the interception, monitoring, or recording conversations on his telephone lines were unlawful, even if done pursuant to a warrant issued by the Home Secretary. His action was dismissed by the Vice-Chancellor, Sir Robert Megarry on 28.2.1979. He held that:

(a) since the tapping was effected from wires outside the subscribers premises, no issue of trespass on the premises arose;
(b) there was no general right of privacy in English Law and no particular right to hold a telephone conversation in the privacy of one's home without molestation;
(c) while there was no specific power in law to tap telephones, there was no rule of law making it unlawful.[1]

Sir Robert Megarry suggested that tapping 'cries out for legislation'.[2] In its Report the Commission considered that the interception measures, authorized by recognized rules of common law going back at least to 1710, which did not lay down with reasonable certainty the principle conditions and procedures for the issue of warrants. The issue of back warrants authorizing interruptions by the police was regulated solely by administrative justice; and such interceptions were therefore not carried out 'in accordance with the law' under Article 8 (2).

The Commission has been principally concerned with the special problem of the rights of prisoners in the matter of their

---

[1] The practice is set out in *The Interception of Communications in Great Britain* Cmnd. 7873 (April 1980), summarized in the Commission decision on admissibility in the Malone case: 26 D.R. 105. Interception may be authorized by the Secretary of State.
[2] A bill has been laid before Parliament (June 1985).

correspondence. Here is it necessary to separate correspondence of
prisoners with the Commission. The Commission has held that freedom to correspond with the Commission is not a right guaranteed in
Section I, and in particular Article 8, of the Convention, but is
protected by Article 25, under which we shall consider it.

The correspondence of prisoners may be subject to control or
restrictions in a number of ways: the number of letters a prisoner may
be permitted to write may be limited, or there may be restrictions as to
the addresses or subject-matter of his letters; again his letters will
usually be scrutinized by prison officials, he may be required to alter
or delete certain passages, or a letter may be simply stopped. In
Germany, for example, the courts have a part in the control of the
correspondence of prisoners.

A preliminary question arises under the Convention as to whether
the freedom of correspondence of a prisoner is inherently limited to
his detention under Article 5, or whether this is not so, the only
restriction that can be imposed being those permitted by Article 8 (2).
In support of the first view, it might be said that it is of the very nature
of detention under Article 5 (1) $a-c$ that the continuity of normal life
is broken, not least in family separation, and that the prisoner therefore loses any right to conduct correspondence. But it could be
objected that Article 8 (1) speaks of every person, without qualification, having a right to respect for his correspondence; and that in any
case so extreme a conclusion goes beyond the practice of the contracting States.

But the second approach is not without difficulties. On what provision of Article 8 (2), for example, would it be possible to base a
prison regulation that only one letter a week may be written? It could
hardly be for the prevention of disorder or crime, since that is secured
by scrutiny of the letters written by prisoners before they are
dispatched. A possible approach might be made on the lines that,
while detention consistent with Article 5 (1) does not entail loss of all
right to carry on correspondence, 'respect' for correspondence in
Article 8 (1) does not, quite apart from Article 8 (2), involve an
unlimited freedom in the matter; that prison regulations, placing a
reasonable limitation on the number of letters a prisoner may write, or
on the addresses to whom they may be sent, are part of the regime of
detention permitted under Article 5; and the control of correspondence by scrutiny and, if necessary, stopping of letters falls under
Article 8 (2).

... [I]n the view of the Commission the measure commonly adopted in the law of democratic societies of permitting prison authorities to examine the correspondence of prisoners under their charge clearly falls within the exceptions permitted in this paragraph of Article 8 ...[1]

Such examination requires that letters be written in a language which can be handled by the examiners without undue difficulties. So where the applicant[2]

semble bien ne pas avoir offert aux autorités pénitentiaires de joindre à ses lettres rédigées en polonais une traduction en langue française établie ou supervisée par un traducteur assermenté, sans le concours duquel les dites autorités ne pourraient guère contrôler sa correspondance dans le cadre des lois et règlements en vigueur

and had not addressed himself to the 'service des cas individuels', his complaint under Article 8 was held to be manifestly ill founded.

As far as addresses are concerned, correspondence with lawyers has been already considered under Article 6, and the Commission has found that restrictions on letters by prisoners to the press are consistent with Article 8:

... in the present case, the letter withheld by the prison authorities was addressed to a newspaper editor and not, as originally indicated by the Applicant, to a person who could be considered to have an official capacity connected with the Applicant's right of defence; ... communications by prisoners to the press cannot in any way be considered matters of such importance as not to fall under the exception in paragraph (2) [prevention of disorder or crime] if the authorities should have objections to such correspondence.[3]

But there is the danger that letters may be stopped, not because it is *necessary* for the prevention of disorder or crime, but because it is administratively inconvenient to have complaints, which they may contain of prison conditions, brought to outside notice. The danger is slight, where there is adequate machinery for dealing with complaints. It is not easy for the Commission to determine whether the censorship or stopping of letters, because of complaints they contain, is justified under Article 8 (2); for example, it has said of Articles 8 and 10 that their second paragraphs

---

[1] 646/59: 3 *Yearbook* 278 following 219/56 and a number of similar decisions.
[2] 1649/62: *Recueil* (1964) i (Polish national imprisoned in Belgium desiring to write to his family in Poland).
[3] 1753/63: *Recueil* (1965) i.

leave the Contracting Parties a certain margin of appreciation in determining
the limits that may be placed on the exercise of the rights in question ... in the
present case, it appears that the letters withheld by the prison administration
contained statements and accusations against their persons which, after a
careful enquiry, proved groundless:[1]

What the Commission can do is to insist there be no interference with
effective correspondence by prisoners with itself under Article 25.

It is doubtful whether the use by the authorities of correspondence
of prisoners for purposes of publicity is consistent with Article 8.[2]

The control of correspondence in prisons in the United Kingdom
has been subject to many applications to the Commission over the
years, and was brought to the Court in a case, involving seven applications together characterizing the main problems.[3] The Commission
report had been supported by massive documentation including
letters of prisoners that had been controlled or stopped. It would be
impractical to try to summarize the judgment of the Court, much of it
being concerned with the analysis of the particular applications and
findings on them, but its statements on the two terms, 'in evidence
with the law/prévue par le loi' (Article 8) and 'necessary in a democratic society' call for attention. It was common ground that the
control and restriction of prisoner's correspondence was based on the
Prison Act (1952) and the Prison Rules (1964), and that the measures
complained of were in conformity with English law.

The court then recalled the principles of accordance with the law. It
was 'adequately accessible' to the citizen: further, 'a norm cannot be
regarded as a "law" unless it is formulated with sufficient provision to
enable the citizen to regulate his conduct: he must be able if need be
with appropriate advice—to foresee, to a degree that is reasonable in
the circumstances, the consequences which a given action may entail.'

Coming then to discretion in control of prison correspondence the
Court said:

88–90. A law which confers a discretion must indicate the scope of that
discretion, however, the Court has already recognised the impossibility of

---

[1] 1628/62: *Recueil* (1963) iii. Compare 1037/63: *Recueil* (1962) i (letters stopped as
being 'defamatory and lying' and prisoner left free to write letters in place, omitting
those passages—full account of the matter supplied to Commission by the Prison
Director—held, no evidence that Article 8 (2) had been exceeded).

[2] 2742/66 (appearance of contents of letters by prisoner in a newspaper—mode of
communication of letter not established).

[3] *Silver et al.* (U.K.) Judgment No. 61 (25.3.1963).

attaining absolute certainty in the framing of laws and the risk that the search for certainty may entail excessive rigidity [in having to control in the present case ten million items of correspondence a year] ... The Orders and Directives established a practice which had to be followed save in exceptional circumstances ... In these conditions the Court considered that although those directives did not themselves have the force of law they may—to the admittedly limited extent to which those concerned were made sufficiently aware of their contents—be taken into account in assessing whether the criterion of foreseeability was satified in the application of the [statutory] rules ... However, the Court does not interpret the expression 'in accordance with the law' as meaning that the safeguards must be enshrined in the very text which authorises the imposition of restrictions. In fact, the question of safeguards against abuse is closely linked with the question of effective remedies: Article 13

The factors in Article 8 (2), which could make restrictions of correspondence necessary were in the view of the Court, the interest of public safety, and the prevention of disorder and crime. Examining the correspondence raised in the case, the Court found restriction necessary of seven letters, but the stopping of the 57 remaining letters to be not necessary, and that for the latter there were no effective remedies under Article 13.

prevention of disorder or crime/la défense de l'ordre et ... la prévention des infractions pénales

The notion of prevention is an inadequate basis for certain measures affecting correspondence and private life: thus, while letters to witnesses might be stopped, as being likely to influence them,[1] the seizure of correspondence for production in evidence, or wire-tapping in certain cases, could not be excused under this clause. Further, it is not easy to see under what part of Article 8 (2) investigation of private life can be brought, in the prosecution of crime, however necessary it may in particular cases be.

ARTICLE 9

(1) Everyone has the right to freedom of thought, conscience and religion; this right includes freedom to change his religion or belief and freedom, either alone or in community with others

[1] 2566/65.

and in public or private, to manifest his religion or belief, in worship, teaching, practice and observance.

(2) Freedom to manifest one's religion or belief shall be subject only to such limitations as are prescribed by law and are necessary in a democratic society in the interests of public safety, for the protection of public order, health or morals, or for the protection of the rights and freedoms of others.

1. Toute personne a droit à la liberté de pensée, de conscience et de religion; ce droit implique la liberté de changer de religion ou de conviction, ainsi que la liberté de manifester sa religion ou sa conviction individuellement ou collectivement, en public ou en privé, par le culte, l'enseignement, les pratiques et l'accomplissement des rites.

2. La liberté de manifester sa religion ou ses convictions ne peut faire l'objet d'autres restrictions que celles qui, prévues par la loi, constituent de mesures nécessaires, dans une société démocratique, à la sécurité publique, à la protection de l'ordre, de la santé ou de la morale publiques, ou à la protection des droits et libertés d'autrui.

The first paragraph reproduces Article 18 of the universal Declaration. The preparatory work revolved largely around the formulation of the second paragraph. One version would have perpetuated certain restrictions, rooted in history or custom: thus it was proposed[1] that the first paragraph should be

subject to reservations as regards the measures required for ensuring security and public order, as well as those restrictions which, for reasons of history, it has been considered necessary, by the States signatory to this Convention, to place on the exercise of this right.

This proposal was adapted in the form of the following proviso to Article 9 (2) of Alternative A:

Provided that nothing in this Convention may be considered as derogating from already existing national rules as regards religious institutions and foundations, or membership of certain confessions.[2]

[1] In the Committee of Experts (2–8.2.1950): *T.P.* ii. 358.
[2] *T.P.* ii. 452, 457.

and a similar clause as Article 7 (*b*) in Alternative B.

These were explained by the Committee as being

intended to cover those reasonable restrictions on the eligibility for public office of members of certain religious faiths which are prescribed in the constitutions of certain States and which it was recognised could not be removed immediately.[1] It is also intended to cover similar regulations regarding the membership and activity of certain religious institutions.[2]

The language used in both Alternative A and B were certainly wider than was necessary to meet the stated intention, and the whole exception was finally abandoned, the second paragraph being brought into line generally with the second paragraphs of Articles 8, 10, and 11.

What is *necessary in a democratic society*, is justifiable for one of the purposes set out in the second paragraphs of Articles 8–11, has to be left in great part to the margin of appreciation of the national authority concerned, subject to convention supervision. But there are differences between the stated purposes, which are not always clear.

Common purposes that can justify the restriction of rights and freedoms under the second paragraphs are:[3] national security—not in 3 (2); public safety; prevention of disorder or crime—'crime' is not mentioned in 3 (2); the protection of health and morals/de la santé ou de la morale publiques in 9 (2); the protection of the rights and freedoms of others.

Additional recognized purposes are the protection of the 'economic well-being of the country': 8 (2); territorial integrity: 10 (2); and protection of the reputation or rights of others, for preventing the disclosure of information received in confidence or 'for maintaining the authority and impartiality of the judiciary'; 10 (2).

Traditional restrictions imposed on certain religious faiths and orders have created difficulties for some countries under the Convention. Norway, in accepting it, declared that

whereas Article 2 of the Norwegian Constitution of 17th May 1814 contains a provision under which Jesuits are not tolerated, a corresponding reservation is made with regard to the application of Article 9 of the Convention.

---

[1] *T.P.* ii. 452, 457.

[2] Compare Act of Settlement 1700, s. 30: '. . . whosoever shall hereafter come to the possession of this Crown shall join in communion with the Church of England as by law established'.

[3] The statute and proceedings, prohibiting the reorganization from the dissolved fascist party in Italy were declared to be justified under all the second paragraphs of Article 9–11. See 1747/62 (Austria): imprisonment for neo-Nazi activities.

However, Norway was able to withdraw this reservation on 4 December 1956, the offending provision having been abrogated.

The First U.N. Covenant, Article 18, is cast in broadly the same form as Article 9 of the Convention; but for the reference to change or religion or belief there is substituted 'freedom to have or to adopt a religion or belief of his choice'.

Belief is then distinguished in both Articles from religion, and, as its French equivalent 'conviction' in Article 9 implies, is an attitude determined primarily by thought and conscience.

freedom of thought, conscience and religion/liberté de pensée, de conscience et de religion

A distinction is made in Article 9 between freedom of thought, religion, or belief, and their expression or manifestation. The freedoms set out appear to be absolute[1] and not subject to any interference by public authority, which is confined in paragraph 2 to manifestations of religion or belief; further, freedom of expression has separate consideration in Article 10. The distinction is essential for, while it is true that the manifestation of religion or belief is vital to them and demands protection in society, the internal freedom for religious experience or the construction of belief is not less vital; so of what became Articles 9 and 10 the Commission on Legal and Administrative Questions said

> It should be added that in recommending a collective guarantee not only of freedom to express convictions, but also of thought, conscience, religion and opinion, the Committee wished to protect all nations of any Member State, not only from breaches of obligations for so-called reasons of State, but also from those abominable methods of policy enquiry or judicial process which rob the suspected or accused person of his intellectual facilities and conscience.[2]

But the line to be drawn between thought and belief and their manifestation is not always easy to draw in practice. It might perhaps be said that thought or belief is being mainly forced by action or

---

[1] Compare *State of Bombay* v. *Narasu Appa Mali* [1951] A.I.R. Bombay 775, importing the same distinction into Indian Constitution Article 25. For discussion of freedom of religion in India see J. D. M. Derrett, 'Freedom of Religion under the Indian Constitution', 12 *I.C.L.Q.* [1963] 693, and C. H. Alexandrowicz, 'La Liberté religieuse dans la Constitution de l'Inde', *Revue intern. de droit comparé* [1964] no. 2. See also *Cantwell* v. *Connecticut* [1940] 310 U.S. 296 for the same distinction.

[2] Report (5.9.1949) § 12: *T.P.* 91.

behaviour that has both some social impact and the purpose of demonstrating that thought or belief. So:

Marriage is not considered simply as a form of expresion of thought, conscience or religion, but is governed by Article 12.[1]

In other words, its prime purpose is a human union, and hopefully the founding of a family, and not the expression of thought and belief under Article 9.

Again, while pacifism is a belief under Article 9 (1), the distribution of leaflets to soldiers urging them to avoid or refuse service in the armed forces in Northern Ireland cannot be said to be manifesting that belief.[2]

A subtle failure to be manifesting religious belief appeared in an advertisement published in Sweden by the Church of Scientology.[3] The advertisement described a device called an E-metre as 'an invaluable aid to measuring man's mental state and changes in it', and as a 'religious artifact' used to measure the 'static field' around the human body, as an indicator of the degree of 'relief from the spiritual impediment of sins'. Following complaints, the Consumer ombudsman granted an injunction under the Marketing Improper Practices Act (1970), prohibiting certain passages in the advertisement. The Supreme Court on appeal maintained the injunction. On the application to the Commission by the Church of Scientology, claiming breaches of the convention, it decided first that:

A church body is capable of possessing and exercising rights contained in Article 9 (1) in its own capacity as a representation of its ministers.

It distinguished an earlier decision, that a *legal person* does not possess rights under Article 9 (1).[4] It then considered that advertisements may be informational or descriptive or may have direct commercial objective; and that the passage about the E-metre was 'more the manifestation of a desire to market goods for profit' and was declared inadmissible.

---

[1] 6167/79 (F.R.G.) 1 D.R. 64.

[2] *Arrowsmith* (U.K.) 7450/75 19 D.R. 5: see below.

[3] 7805/77 (Sweden) 16 D.R. 68.

[4] 3798/66: 29 *Recueil* 70: Further explained as being directed to 'profit-making corporate bodies': 7245/77 (Switzerland) 10 D.R. 85. Distinguish the right to take participation (All First Protocol, Article 3) which is not accorded to a *political party*: 6850/75 5 DR. 90.

conscience/conscience

A prime issue of conscience is objection to military service, which came before the Commission in the *Grandrath Case*.[1]

The applicant, a German citizen born in 1938 and a Bible study leader (*Buchstudienleiter*) in the congregation of Jehovah's Witnesses, had been recognized by the Düsseldorf District Office for Substitute Military Service (Kreiswehrersatzamt) as a conscientious objector. He was then required by the competent Minister (*Bundesminister für Arbeit und Sozialordnung*) to perform substitute civilian service,[2] but was given an opportunity to apply for exemption or postponement. The Minister rejected his claim for exemption, and this rejection was upheld by the administrative courts. As a result of his continued refusal to perform substitute civilian service proceedings were instituted against him under the Substitute Civilian Service Act (Gesetz über den zivilen Ersatzdienst); he was convicted and sentenced to eight months' imprisonment, reduced on appeal to six months. His appeal against conviction was rejected as was his constitutional appeal (*Verfassungsbeschwerde*) to the Bundesverfassungsgericht. All domestic remedies were then exhausted, and he served his sentence from October 1964 to April 1965. The applicant alleged breaches of the Convention in two respects: of Article 9, in that he had not been exempted from substitute civilian service though his objections to its performance were based on his conscience and religion; and of Article 14, in that he was, as a Bible study leader in the congregation of Jehovah's Witnesses, a minister in the sense of Article 11 (3) of the Compulsory Military Service Act and that in being

---

[1] 2299/64: Report of the Commission (12.12.1966) Doc. 4624/06. 2. /31.

[2] *Compulsory Military Service Act 1956*, as amended in 1962 (Wehrpflichtgesetz), Article 25 provides that persons, who for reasons of conscience refuse to perform war service as armed combatants, shall perform civilian service outside the armed forces in substitution for compulsory military service; Article 11 exempts for compulsory military service (1) ordained ministers of Evangelical faith; (2) ministers of Roman Catholic faith, being sub-deacons or above; (3) ministers of other faiths, whose principal occupation is their ministry and whose function is equivalent to that of the ministers in the other categories (hauptamtlich tätige Geistliche anderer Bekenntnisse, deren Amt dem eines ordinierten Geistlichen evangelischen oder eines Geistlichen römisch-katholischen Bekenntnisses, der die Subdiakonatsweihe empfangen hat, entspricht). The Substitute Civilian Service Act 1960, Article 9 (3), accords exemptions from civilian service to the same categories of minister; Article 1 provides that substitute service shall be of public utility; Article 18 permits such outside work as does not interfere with the substitute service required.

refused exemption he had been subject to discrimination as compared with Evangelical or Roman Catholic ministers.

The Commission distinguished under Article 9 the issues of religion and of conscience. It found that the applicant had not claimed that the substitute civilian service would have interfered with the private and personal practice of his religion; and that it would not in fact have interfered with this duties, as a Bible study leader to his religious community, since his situation would not, regard being had to Article 18 of the Substitute Civilian Service Act, have been greately different from that in which he normally lived.[1]

On the issue of conscience the Commission observed that, since in Article 4 (3) *b* of the Convention

it is expressly recognized that civilian service may be imposed on conscientious objectors as a substitute for military service, it must be concluded that objections of conscience do not, under the Convention, entitle a person to exemption from such service.

The reasoning may be put in this way: had there been no reference in Article 4 (3) *b* to conscientious objection to compulsory military service, it could have been argued that, while such service is not forced labour contrary to Article 4, it is still contrary to Article 9 (1) if imposed on conscientious objectors. But since Article 4 (3) *b* refers to conscientious objection in terms, which plainly imply that contracting States are not bound to recognize it, compulsory military service is an exception to Article 9 (1) as well as Article 4. It follows *a fortiori* that substititute civilian service is also an exception.[2]

The Commission found no breach of the Convention under Article 14 either in conjunction with Article 4 or with Article 9, on the grounds that Article 11 of the Compulsory Military Service Act introduced

a differentiation which must be considered to be reasonable and relevant, having regard on the one hand to the necessity of maintaining the effectiveness of the legislation regarding compulsory service and on the other hand the need of assuring proper ministerial service in religious communities

that the applicant's ministry in the congregation of Jehovah's Witnesses was not his principal function in the sense of Article 11 (3)

---

[1] The applicant had stated that he worked as a painter's assistant 43 hours a week during the material period and that his 'ministerial' duties were performed largely in his spare time, but occupied 120–150 hours a month.

[2] 7705/76 (F.R.G.) 9 D.R. 196: no right to be exempted from substitute service.

of the Act, since on his own statement it was exercised largely in his spare time; and that in any case his functions differed in important respects from those of ministers referred to in Article 11 (1) and (2) of the Act. The test of ministry under Article 11 of the Act is therefore different from that considered by the U.S. Supreme Court in three decisions cited by the applicant, on the entitlement to exemption from service of Jehovah's Witnesses. The only test of entitlement of a minister to exemption under the equivalent United States Act and Regulations was that

the ministry be his vocation, not an incidental thing in his life[1]

or again

not whether a minister is paid for his ministry but whether, as a vocation, regularly not occasionally, he teaches and preaches the principles of his religion

Therefore neither lack of payment in money or in kind for his ministry, nor part-time secular work by him, which might indeed be necessitated by that lack, could deprive him of his status as a minister if he satisifed the sole test of vocation. In Article 11 of the Geman Act there is a double test: that the ministry be his principal function, and that it correspond to that of ordained ministers in the Evangelical and Roman Catholic churches: to qualify then he must wear at least some of the 'garments of orthodoxy'. The application of Article 14 in this case will be discussed further below under that Article.

A curious manifestation of freedom of conscience was the refusal of an Austrian citizen to vote in the national elections, in contravention of a local regulation making voting compulsory, subject to penalties which he incurred. He invoked both Article 9 and Article 3 of the Protocol before the Commission. The Commission rejected the application saying:

Qu'en ce qui concerne notamment l'article 9 de la Convention, l'exigence sujette à sanction, selon laquelle toute personne ayant le droit de vote doit, dans une élection, passer par la procédure électorale, n'est pas une exigence qui constitue une interférence dans la liberté de conscience, parce qu'elle n'exige pas que l'électeur vote d'une certaine façon, mais le laisse, en fait, libre de rendre un bulletin blanc; que cette exigence a trait à la procédure et ne concerne pas l'action même du choix électoral.[2]

---

[1] The Supreme Court stressed that given this single test, the local draft boards must not fit the governments of orthodoxy on a pioneer minister of Jehovah's Witnesses.

[2] 1718/62: 16 Collection 30.

freedom to change/la liberté de changer

This obvious corollary of the freedoms already stated is aimed perhaps against any compulsion[1] to follow a particular religion or maintain a particular belief. The idea is more clearly expressed in the C.P.R. Covenant, Article 18 (2):

no one shall be subject to coercion which would impair his freedom to have or to adopt a religion or belief of his choice.

In communities where a particular religious faith is dominant, or certain beliefs are strongly held, departure from them may be costly to the individual in a number of ways. It may be asked then whether public authority should compel an individual to declare his religion, or lack of it, in such contexts as the registration of births and marriage,[2] or in school practices.[3]

in public or private/en public ou en privé

In a case concerning a religious procession in the public highway, to which we shall return later, the Netherlands Hoge Raad rejected the argument on appeal of the Public Prosecutor that these words in Article 9 (1) are designed to protect religious worship or observance in public only in the sense that 'such worship need not be in secret and that it is not necessary to conceal churches'. The court held that there was ground either in the text of the Convention itself or in the preparatory work for such a limitation of the scope of religious freedom under Article 9.[4]

to manifest his religion or belief in worship, teaching, practice, and to observance/de manifester sa religion ou sa conviction ... par le culte, l'enseignement, les pratiques et l'accomplissement des rites

To manifest means essentially to show by overt act, to demonstrate an attitude to the eyes or minds of others. The Commission has had to consider this clause largely in the context of limitations under

---

[1] The absence of any power of civil or judicial authorities in Iceland to annul the act of baptism was held by the Commission not to involve a breach of Article 9 (1): 2525/65: *Recueil* 22.
[2] This question is raised in 2854/66.
[3] See under Article 2 of the Protocol below.
[4] Hoge Raad (19.1.1962): 4 *Yearbook* 644.

Article 9 (2), both negative and positive. Negative limitations here are those by which the State insists on the observance of a particular law or regulation, although it is challenged on grounds of religion or conscience by an individual or group; positive limitations are those which are imposed by public authority on the conduct of religious activities, usually in the interest of public order.[1]

The first kind of limitation was in issue in applications to the Commission by members of the Dutch Reformed Church. In one the applicant was a dairy farmer and member of the Dutch Reformed Church, who had refused to participate in the Health Service for cattle as required by an Act of 1952 for the prevention of tuberculosis among cattle. The applicant was fined by the District Court for breach of the regulations in his refusal to join the Health Service; he appealed up to the Supreme Court, challenging the regulations on both technical and religious grounds. His appeal was dismissed. The Commission said, rejecting the application under Article 9:

> ... the Applicant alleges that Article 4 of the 1952 Act, by compelling him to sign an application for membership of the Health Service as a condition for the owning of cattle, places him in a situation in which his religious conscience as a member of the Dutch Reformed Church was opposed to the general legal obligations imposed upon dairy farmers and that the above Act therefore violates Article 9 of the Convention. . . . The obligation placed upon the Applicant was duly based on valid law. . . . The 1952 Act was considered by the Netherlands Parliament to be necessary to prevent tuberculosis among cattle; . . . it appears to the Commission that the term 'protection of health' used in paragraph (2) of Article 9 may reasonably be extended to cover such schemes . . .[2]

In the second case the applicants were a parish of the Dutch Reformed Church, represented by their pastor and secretary. They objected on religious grounds to the Old Age Insurance Act (Algemene Ouderdomswet), which had established a compulsory insurance scheme covering the whole population. Section 36 of the Act, recognizing this form of conscientious objection among members of the Dutch Reform Church, authorized the Minister to make appropriate regulations for conscientious objectors; these regulations in fact provided that objectors might, in lieu of contributions to the insurance

---

[1] For some restrictions on the practices of a Buddhist convert in prison, including growth of a beard, use of a prayer chain, and yoga exercises, see 1753/63: 16 Collection 20.   [2] 1068/61: 5 *Yearbook* 284.

scheme, make direct payment by way of tax. The applicants, though not opposed to insurance as such,[1] objected to the scheme on the ground that it overrode their religious duty to care themselves for the old, and refused to take advantage of the regulations under Section 36 of the Act on the ground that payments by way of tax would indirectly contribute to the maintenance of the scheme. The pastor, being ordered by the District Court to pay his annual contribution to the insurance scheme under the Act, and the Minister having ruled that ministers of religion were not exempt, appealed up to the Supreme Court, which dismissed the appeal in an elaborate judgment,[2] interpreting the Old Age Insurance Act, and dealing with its compatibility with the Netherlands Constitution and with Article 9 of the Convention. As regards its compatibility with Article 9 the Commission noted

first, that the Act does not oblige a person to apply for a pension and, secondly, that section 36 of the Act expressly provides that conscientious objectors are exempt from paying direct contributions to the scheme, and may in lieu make equivalent payments by way of tax; ... the Netherlands Parliament when passing the Act thereby made express provisions aimed at solving the religious problem which the Act might create for *inter alios* adherents to the Dutch Reform Church

and concluded that there was no breach of Article 9 (1).[3] The position was essentially like that in the *Grandrath Case*. The Commission in effect recognized that contribution to the scheme created a conflict of obligations, civic and religious, but considered that the conflict was resolved by the legislator in provision of exemption for conscientious objectors with a substitute tax, and that therefore objection to payment of that tax would not be an exercise of religious freedom, which has been expressly protected, but an evasion of civic obligations.[4] Thus the Commission, having no recourse to a provision similar to Article 4 (3) *b* in the *Grandrath Case*, at the same time did not invoke Article 9 (2).

[1] Compare 2065/63: *Recueil* (1965) ii (member of Dutch Reform Church who objected to any form of insurance).

[2] See p. 204, note 3, above.

[3] Nor of Article 8, nor, in respect of the imposition of the substitute tax, of Article 1 of the First Protocol: 1497/62: 5 *Yearbook* 286, 298.

[4] So, in finding the imposition of the substitute consistent with Article 1 of the First Protocol, the Commission said that it was levied 'in the public interest, as defined by the Netherlands Parliament and Government, to preserve equality and prevent evasion': 5 *Yearbook* 300. See further under Article 1 of the Protocol below.

The *Hoge Raad* arrived at the conclusion that there was no breach of Article 9 (1), also without reliance on Article 9 (2), but by different reasoning. It rejected the idea that the 'practice' of religion in the sense of Article 9 (1) was in issue at all:

... the freedom to manifest one's religion or beliefs herein [Article 9] guaranteed is not the same thing as freedom to oppose one's own religious ideas or beliefs to the provisions of the law, ... the provision of the Convention under which the appeal is lodged does not mean that anyone may be free to evade the enforcement of laws ... by alleging the nullity or irrelevance of such laws because of religious ideas or beliefs that do not accord with them;

further the terms 'practice/les pratiques' in Article 9 (1)

do not mean 'the application of religious rules in everyday life' as the appellant suggests but, in view of the context and the use of the plural in the French text, indicate acts which in any form are the expression of a religion or belief.

The court concluded that the compulsory old-age pensions scheme did not come within the scope of the exercise of religious freedom under Article 9 (1) at all, that the invocation of Article 9 (2) was therefore unnecessary, and that

the possibility of exemption [under section 36]: ... was not intended by the legislator to constitute the fulfilment of obligations undertaken in pursuance of Article 9 of the Convention, but was a concession of a general order in favour of those who for religious reasons could not accept the idea of applying for or accepting insurance.[1]

The meaning of 'practice' and 'observance' was further analysed by a Netherlands court in The Hague and its conclusions affirmed by the Supreme Court.[2]

The court pointed out that 'observance/l'accomplissement des rites' had been misrepresented in the unofficial Dutch translation of Article 9 as 'the maintenance of commands and prescripts' (*het onderhouden van de geboden en voorschriften*); that practice and observance were closely related and refer

to the performance of acts which, as for instance the administration of the Sacraments, by their nature give expression in some form to religion or belief,

---

[1] 3 *Yearbook* 668–70.
[2] Judgments of 22.11.1961 and 13.3.1963, officially translated in Council of Europe.

and cannot be extended to acts and decisions in the ordinary course of life, and especially those contrary to law.[1]

Turning now to the positive limitations based on provisions of Article 9 (2), we may note that what is perhaps the central provision is formulated differently from the equivalent paragraphs of Articles 8, 10, and 11. Article 9 (2) speaks of 'the protection of public order/la protection de l'ordre' while the other paragraphs use the expression 'the prevention of disorder/le défense de l'ordre'. The French term suggest that too much importance must not be attributed to the difference, and that the expression as a whole is directed to the prevention of local breaches of the peace rather than maintenance of the national social and political order which is covered rather by 'public safety/la sécurité publique'.[2]

The protection of public order in the sense of Article 9 (2) was considered by the Netherlands Supreme Court to be served by the regulation of religious services or observances conducted elsewhere than in enclosed premises;

... it should be brought out that in a country such as the Netherlands with a mixed population from the point of view of religious beliefs, public religious services may give rise to tension, agitation and disorder by the very fact that they are held on the public highway, where they will inevitably come to the notice of persons holding different beliefs; and ... thus, at least in principle, a law limiting in some way the right to hold such services, may be considered as a measure necessary for the protection of public order.[3]

---

[1] Compare, as a perhaps marginal case, the interpretation of a Canadian statute, providing that no school pupil should be required 'to join in any exercise of devotion or religion objected to by his parent or guardian'. A parent had religious objections to his child taking part in a salute to the flag, and the court said: 'It is difficult to understand how any well-disposed person could offer objection to join in such a salute on religious or other grounds. . . . [But] for the court to take to itself the right to say that the exercises here in question had no religious or devotional significance might well be for the court to deny that very religious freedom which the Statute is intended to provide': *Donald* v. *Hamilton Board of Education* [1945] 3 D.L.R. 424, Ontario Court of Appeal.

[2] 'la Sûreté publique' in Articles 8, 10, and 11. For the distinction see *India*: *Ramesh Thapper* v. *State of Madras* [1950] A.I.R.: Supreme Court 594: distinguishing between 'serious and aggravated forms of public disorder, which are calculated to endanger the security of the state, and the relatively minor breaches of the peace of a purely local significance'.

For an analogous distinction between the 'public interest' and the 'national interest' see *Iswarri Prasad* v. *N. R. Sen* [1952] A.I.R. Calcutta 273.

[3] Hoge Raad (19.1.1962): 4 *Yearbook* 646. Compare *Greece*: Arios Pagos (Supreme Court) 1955: 2 *Yearbook* 606 (regulation of use of buildings for religious purposes not contrary to Article 9). For the constitutional right of religious assembly in *Italy*, subject to notification to the authorities only where it is in a public place, see Annarosa Pizzi, 'Italian Constitutional Practice', *Journal of I.C.J.* (Summer 1963) 294, 308.

The observance of Sunday or Sabbath may lead to conflicts of interests between different groups, which may be resolved by measures justifiable under Article 9 (2) as protecting the rights and freedoms of others. The United States Supreme Court has observed that legislation prohibiting shop sales on a Sunday had a religious origin but that its function was to provide 'a Sunday atmosphere of recreation, cheerfulness, repose and enjoyment', and there was a practical necessity of having a common day of rest.[1] But administrative practice, based on the observance of a common day, may work against the interest of those who observe a different day of rest or religious observance. So the Complaints Board of the Brussels National Employment Office held[2] that to apply a rule, requiring unemployed to report for control on six consecutive days, so as to exclude a Jew from unemployment benefit because he did not report on Saturday, and could not on Sunday, the Office being closed, was contrary to Article 9. The Board held that

as a result of the decision of the Regional Office the complainant was placed under moral pressure obliging him to choose between the categorical obligations of his religion and the fear of losing his eligibility for unemployment benefits.[3]

Is wearing a turban a manifestation of religious belief? An Indian citizen living in the United Kingdom, was a Sikh required under his religion to wear a turban. Between 1973 and 1976 he was prosecuted and fined twenty times for failing to wear a crash helmet while riding his motor-cycle. At the end of 1976 the applicable statute was amended to exempt Sikhs from wearing crash helmets. The Commission reported his application briefly under Article 9, considering that: 'the compulsory wearing of crash helmets is a necessary safety measure of motor cyclists, that any resulting interference with the applicants freedom of religion was justified for the protection of health' under Article 9 (2), and that 'the later grant of exemption did

---

[1] *McGowan* v. *Maryland* [1961] 366 U.S. 420.

[2] Affirmed on appeal to the Appeals Commission: 5 *Yearbook* 364.

[3] Compare a view of legislation as a 'clog upon the exercise of religion' since the appellants 'could not simultaneously practise their religion and their trade, without being hampered by a substantial competitive disadvantage': per Brennan J. dissenting in *Braunfield* v. *Brown* [1961] 366 U.S. 399. See also *Sherbert* v. *Verner* [1963] 374 U.S. 398 (refusal of unemployment benefits to Seventh Day Adventist, who could not obtain work owing to his refusal to work on Saturday, the Adventist Sabbath, held unconstitutional).

not initiate the valid health considerations on which the regulations are based'. The reasoning is doubtful, for it is not shown how the wearing of a turban actually expresses the belief invoked, and in any case how the wearing of crash helmets protects 'public health' as distinct from the safety of the individual; for the protection of 'public health' must be limited, in the control of individual conduct, to that which endangers the health of others.[1] It may however be that the 'rights and freedoms of others' come into account as justification of the compulsory wearing of crash-helmets.[2] Finally, it is not explained how the regulations were 'necessary' under Article 9 (2), if exemption was granted in 1976.

The conflict may arise often in prison administration. The claims of prisoners to certain religious practice may have to be denied or restricted, because they go beyond what the practices can be said to demand,[3] or to maintain equality of treatment in the prison, or to preserve order.[4]

A perhaps surprising example of religious authority comes from the State church (Folkekirchen) of Denmark.[5] The applicant was a minister in the church and the incumbent of a parish. He made it a condition for christening a child that the parents attend five periods of religious instruction. The church Ministry, being of the opinion that he had no right to impose such conditions, advised him to abandon the practice or resign. On his refusal, the Ministry set up a consistory court with an advising function, which postponed its examination of the case pending the decision of the Commission on the admissibility of the application. As to Article 9 the Commission said:

A church is an organised religious community based on identical or at least substantially similar views. Through the rights granted to its members under Article 9, the church is itself protected in its right to manifest its religion, to organise and carry out worship, teaching practice and observance and is free to act out and enforce uniformity in these matters. Further, in a State church system its servants are employed for the purpose of applying and teaching a

[1] 'Health' in Article 9 (2) is qualified by 'public', as the French text makes clear.
[2] My wife points out that it can avoid injury, for which others in the community have to pay, through the national health service.
[3] In general 1753/63 8 *Yearbook* 174: 5442/72 (U.K.) 1 D.R. 41 (not necessary to religious practice in prison to publish articles in a Buddhist magazine).
[4] 6886/75 (U.K.) 5 D.R. 100 (Tao Buddhist book on 'Choreography for Body and Mind' refused to Sikh prisoner, on ground that it contained a section on martial arts and self-defence).
[5] 7374/76 (Denmark) 5 D.R. 157.

specific religion. Their individual freedom of thought, conscience or religion to exercise at the moment they accept or refuse employment as clergymen, and their right to leave the church guarantees their freedom of religion in case they oppose its teachngs ... Article 9 (1) does not include the right of a clergyman in his capacity of a civil servant in a State church system to set up conditions for baptising, which are contrary to the directives of the highest administrative authority within that church ...

The manifestation of religion or belief may collide in one way or another with legislation, administrative practices, or social policy. It would not be disputed that Article 9 does not sanction manifestation of religion or belief contrary to the ordinary criminal law; but there can be conflict between conscience and social policy, expressed in law or practice.

ARTICLE 10

(1) Everyone has the right to freedom of expression. This right shall include freedom to hold opinions and to receive and impart information and ideas without interference by public authority and regardless of frontiers. This Article shall not prevent States from requiring the licensing of broadcasting, television or cinema enterprises.

(2) The exercise of these freedoms, since it carries with it duties and responsibilities, may be subject to such formalities, conditions, restrictions or penalties as are prescribed by law and are necessary in a democratic society, in the interests of national security, territorial integrity or public safety, for the prevention of disorder or crime, for the protection of health or morals, for the protection of the reputation or rights of others, for preventing the disclosure of information received in confidence, or for maintaining the authority and impartiality of the judiciary.

1. Toute personne a droit à la liberté d'expression. Ce droit comprend la liberté d'opinion et la liberté de recevoir ou de communiquer des informations ou des idées sans qu'il puisse y avoir ingérence d'autorités publiques et sans considération de frontière. Le présent article n'empêche pas les États de

soumettre les enterprises de radio-diffusion, de cinéma ou de télévision à un régime d'autorisations.

2. L'exercice de ces libertés comportant des devoirs et des responsabilités peut être soumis à certaines formalités, conditions, restrictions ou sanctions, prévues par la loi, qui constituent des mesures nécessaires, dans une société démocratique, à la sécurité nationale, à l'intégrité territoriale ou à la sûreté publique, à la défense de l'ordre et à la prévention du crime, à la protection de la santé ou de la morale, à la protection de la réputation ou des droits d'autrui, pour empêcher la divulgation d'informations confidentielles ou pour garantir l'autorité et l'impartialité du pouvoir judiciaire.

This Article was modelled in its first two sentences on Article 19 of the Universal Declaration, but the whole Article has a more restricted form than either Article 19 or Article 19 of the C.P.R. Convenant. In the preparatory work an amendment that would have expressly permitted restriction on ther diffusion of 'extremist ideas' was rejected, and there was some hesitation over the inclusion of 'territorial integrity' as a ground for restrictions.[1] The form, which Alternative A, the first paragraph, had reached in the Committee of Experts,[2] was

> Everyone shall have the right to freedom of expression without governmental interference; this right shall include freedom to hold opinions and to receive and impart information and ideas without governmental interference, regardless of frontiers, either orally, in writing or in print, in the form of art or by duly licensed visual or auditory devices.

This form has been largely retained in Article 19 (1) and (2) of the C.P.R. Covenant,[3] though it has no reference to licensing. The change made in the final version of Article 10 (1) of the Convention is not

[1] Its purpose is obscure unless it is the discouragement of irredentist movements.

[2] (16.3.1950): *J.P.* ii. 518. Alternative B followed Article 19 of the Universal Declaration.

[3] 1. Everyone shall have the right to hold opinions without interference.

2. 'Everyone shall have the right to freedom of expression, this right shall include freedom to seek, receive and impart information and ideas of all kinds, regardless of frontiers, either orally, in writing or in print, in the form of art, or through any other media of his choice.'

explained in the preparatory work, but was probably due to a desire to clarify the notion of licensing, and to extend it only to enterprises and not to the 'devices' themselves.

Freedom of expression/la liberté d'expression. The term concerns 'mainly the expression of opinion and receiving and imparting information and ideas;[1] and Article 10 does not therefore guarantee a right to vote.[2]

The inherent limitations on the freedom of expression in the profession and the public service are normally matters of domestic law. The Commission has taken note of 'the general duty of civil servants, especially high-ranking officials, to observe a certain degree of discretion',[3] no direct invocation of Article 10 (2) being necessary. So where a civil servant in Nord-Rhein-Westfalen declared his intent to publish an article in the magazine *Der Spiegel* on his functions in the public administration, he was subjected to a disciplinary censure, confirmed by the courts, for taking the official recourse of making any complaint against his superiors, and for dishonourable behaviour in the exclusion of his functions. The Commission found that the disciplinary measures were prescribed in the applicable German legislation, and that the applicant had himself admitted that the intended article contained facts which he knew to be qualified as official secrets (*Amtsgeheimnis*); the disciplinary measures were then fully justified to prevent 'the disclosure of information, which the applicant had received in confidence, within the meaning of Article 10 (2)'.[4]

It is not clear:

(*a*) why, if the article had been in fact published, disclosing an official secret, it would not have constituted an offence under the domestic law;

(*b*) why then the Commission did not invoke 'the prevention of crime' as the justification of the measures under Article 10 (2);

(*c*) whether the conclusion reached, that it was the receipt of the official information in 'confidence' that characterized it, implied that all information received by civil servants is governed by Article 10 (2).

---

[1] 7215/75 (U.K.) 19 D.R. 66 (Report): Consequently it 'cannot encompass any action of the physical expression of feelings' as in a sexual relationship.

[2] 6573/74 (Netherlands) 1 D.R. 87; 7036/75 (U.K.) 3 D.R. 165. It is implied in First Protocol Article 2.

[3] 9401/81 (Norway) 27 D.R. 226.   [4] 4274/69 (F.R.G.) 35 *Recueil* 158.

Conditions may be imposed on professional instruction given in school in so far as it may embody opinions. A teacher in a State secondary non-denominational school was in charge of English and Mathematics, but used time in class hours to give religious instruction, and also held 'evangelical clubs' in the school. He wore stickers carrying religious and anti-abortion slogans. After numerous interviews and exchanges of notes with the headmaster, who found this practice objectionable and warned him of its consequences, he was finally dismissed for refusal to comply with the specific instructions given him. His appeals to the Industrial Tribunal and Employment Appeals Tribunal were unsuccessful.[1]

There is a line to be drawn between his freedom of thought and belief, which was not in itself infringed either by the institution or the dismissal, and the freedom of expression, which was justifiably restricted under Article 10 (2). The Commission was of the opinion that:

... schoolteachers in non-denominational schools should have regard to the rights of parents so as to respect their religious and philosophical convictions in the education of their children. This requirement assumes particular importance in a non-denominational school where the governing legislation provides that parents can seek to have their children excused from attendance at religious instruction, and further that any religious instruction given shall not include 'any catechism or formulary which is distinctive of any particular religious denomination': Education (1944) ss. 25, 26.

The Commission, without mentioning Article 2 of the First Protocol found the action taken as justified under Article 10 (2) for the protection of the rights of others.

As regards 'morals' in Article 10 (2) the Commission has said:

The view taken by municipal law of the requirements of morals varies from time to time and from place to place. By reason of their contact with the vital forces of their countries, state authorities are in a better position than the international judge to give an opinion on the exact content of these requirements as well as on the 'necessity' of a 'restriction' intended to meet them.

So the Commission, reciting its opinion and the judgment of the Court in the Handyside case, to be reviewed below, invoked the principle of a margin of appreciation.[2]

What is the range of 'morals' in Article 10 (2)?

---

[1] 8010/77 (U.K.) 16 D.R. 101.
[2] 6782–6784/74 (Belgium) 9 D.R. 19.

This question is posed by the texts of Articles 3 (2) and Articles 10 (2). The former refers to 'the protection of public order, health or morals/la protection de l'ordre, de la santé ou de la morale publique', while the latter speaks of 'the protection of health or morals/la protection de la santé ou de la morale'. So in Article 9 (2) the French text qualifies order, health, and morals as public, and, while 'public order' in English might be read as a distinct notion, separate from health and morals, it is possible to treat 'public' as qualifying all three. But in Article 10 (2) health and morals are not only kept separate from 'the prevention of disorder/la défense de l'ordre', but are not qualified as public in either the English or French texts. It might have been supposed that, if the prosecution of *public* morals is to permit restrictions, it would have been a purpose of Article 10 (2) rather than Article 9 (2); the reverse appears to be the case. What is really being asked here is how far freedom of information expressed in private—poetry reading, exhibition of pictures, showing of films—can be restricted under Article 10 (2), or whether only its public manifestation or impact can come into account, as for example, in the Indecent Displays (Control) Act (1981). This has not yet been clearly answered in applications under the Convention.

A leading case is that of 'the Little Red School Book'. The publisher Richard Handyside had first published it in Denmark, it being then translated and published with certain adaptations in a number of European countries and non-European countries, and in the United Kingdom in April 1971. It circulated freely in Austria and Luxembourg. A revised edition was published in November 1971. Prosecuted under the Obscene Publications acts (1959/1964) for possession of copies of the book, he was convicted and fined, and his appeal to the Inner London Quarter Sessions was dismissed. There followed the forfeiture and destruction of copies of the book that had been seized.

The Court said that:

[its] supervision would generally prove illusory if it did no more than examine [the decisions of national courts] in isolation: it must view them in the light of the case as a whole, including the publication in question and the arguments and evidence adduced by the applicant in the domestic legal system and then at the international level. The Court must decide, on the basis of the different data available to it, whether the reasons given by the national authorities to justify the actual measures of 'interference' they take are relevant and sufficient under Article 10 (2).

The Court then observed that the book was 'aimed above all at children and adolescents aged from twelve to eighteen'; and the applicant had made it clear that he planned a widespread circulation. The book contained:

... purely factual information that was generally correct and often used, as the [Inner London] Quarter Sessions recognised. However it also included, above all in the section on sex[1] and in the 'Be Yourself' chapter on pupils, sentences or paragraphs[2] that young people at a critical stage of their development could have interpreted as an encouragement to indulge in precocious activities harmful for them or even to commit criminal offences.

The Court had nevertheless to consider arguments advanced by the applicant that the book was not made the object of proceedings in Northern Ireland,[3] the Isle of Man or the Channel Islands; that in the United Kingdom 'a host of publications dedicated to hard core pornography and devoid of intellectual or artistic merit allegedly profit by an extreme degree of tolerance', and that most of the Convention countries had decided to allow the work to be distributed.

The reference by the Court to these arguments is inadequate. So in § 54 it said:

The competent authorities in Northern Ireland, the Isle of Man and the Channel Islands may, in the light of local conditions, have had plausible reasons for not taking action against the book and its publisher ... Their failure to act—into which the Court does not have to enquire and which did not prevent the measures taken in England from leading to revision of the Schoolbook—does not prove that the judgment of 29 October 1971 was not a response to a real necessity, bearing in mind the national authorities margin of appreciation.

No evidence was adduced, or sought by the Court, to show why there were 'plausible reasons' for non-action, and 'real necessity' for action, in different parts of a single Convention country. Further, if the Court relies on the margin of appreciation, and to the 'different views prevailing'—not only in the 'retrospective territories' of the contracting states, but even under 'local conditions', about 'the demands of the

---

[1] Including contraceptives, intercourse, homosexuality, methods of abortion, venereal diseases, pornography; and addresses for help and advice on general matters.

[2] Three passages, quoted from the book in the judgment of the Inner London Quarter Sessions, are taken to illustrate: § 32.

[3] The Obscene Publications Act (1959/1964) was not extended to Scotland or Northern Ireland, but prosecution was possible under local law. Proceedings brought in Scotland against the book did not succeed. § 19.

protection of morals in a democratic society',[1] how can even 'the first steps for the collective enforcement'[2] of Article 10 (2) be taken?

As regards the second argument, the Court had recourse only to the Government statement that:

... the Director of Public Prosecutions does not remain inactive nor does the police, despite scanty manpower resources of the squad specialising in this field. Moreover, they claim that, in addition to proceedings so called, seizures were frequently made at the relevant time under the 'disclaimer/caution' procedure.

This procedure was plainly ineffective on a broad scale, and, as stated in § 26, it was discontinued in 1979, a fact to which the Court does not refer; nor does it question the situation described in the second argument.[3]

Language may be a vehicle of free expresssion or an obstacle to it. In countries where two or more languages are spoken, nationally or regionally, the legislature may find itself compelled to regulate their use in such contexts as public education, the courts, and the public administration. The Belgian linguistic cases raised the issue under the first head. The applicants argued that the freedom of thought and expression in Articles 9 and 10 entail linguistic freedom, or free choice of the language in which thought may be expressed, and that this linguistic freedom should be exercised in choice of the language of instruction for their children. The Commission said:[4]

... neither the texts quoted [Articles 9 (1) and 10 (1)] nor any other Article of the Convention or first Protocol explicitly guarantees 'linguistic freedom' as such; ... the only clauses of the Convention that deal with the use of languages, namely Articles 5 (2) and 6 (3) a and e, are limited in scope and irrelevant to the case in point;

... freedom of religion is not in question ... this is also true of the freedom of thought, conscience and expression of the Applicants themselves, since nothing prevents them from expressing their thoughts freely in the language of their choice;

[1] See §§ 54, 57. The Commission also found it 'undesirable and impracticable to apply a moral double standard according to whether the publication is intended for a domestic or foreign audience': 9615/21 (U.K.) 32 D.R. 231.

[2] Convention Preamble.

[3] For the transfrontier trade in pornography see 5777/72 (Austria) 45 *Recueil* 87; and the European Court of Justice ruling in *R.* v. *Honn and Darby* [1980] 27 C.M.L.R. 246.

[4] 1474/62: 6 *Yearbook* 342; see also 1769/62: 6 *Yearbook* 454–6.

... the problem presents a different aspect as regards the Applicants' children; the Applicants claim ... that although their children can freely use their mother tongue [sc. French], at least out of school, they nevertheless risk permanent harm to the development and exercise of their intellectual faculties through being obliged to study in a language other than that of their family [sc. Flemish]; ... the Convention observes that the manner in which human thought is formed and expressed is perforce determined by a concatenation of circumstances over which the individual has virtually no control (time and place, social environment, divers events and influences) without any threat to freedom of thought and expression as such, resulting *ipso facto* therefrom ...[1]

... the Applicants are claiming the right to have the imprint of their own personality and of the culture they acknowlege as their own take first place among the factors conditioning the education of their children, in order that their childrens' thinking should not become alien to their own; ... however it appears that the guarantee of this right is outside the scope of Article 9 and 10.

The Commission has taken the same view of the regulation of the use of languages for administrative purposes. A group of Belgian applicants complained that

par la loi du 24 juillet 1960, Article 3, ordonnant l'exécution d'un recensement, suivi de son arrêté royal d'exécution du 3 novembre 1961, le législateur a supprimé le volet linguistique du recensement général qu'il a exécuté le 31 décembre 1961 et a même interdit la distribution des formulaires du recensement bilingues, craignant que ceux-ci ne permettent un recensement linguistique indirecte. Un recensement linguistique aurait révélé à Leeuw-St. Pierre le nombre important de francophones.

The Commission found that

en dernière analyse, les requérants revendiquent le droit de pouvoir se servir de la langue de leur choix, ou de leur maternelle ou usuelle, dans leurs rapports avec l'administration ... il appert, toutefois, que la garantie de droit sort du cadre de la Convention, et notamment des Articles 9 et 10[2]

and invoking its decisions in the cases just described, rejected the application.[3] The reasoning appears to rest upon a distinction between form and content, between the mode or vehicle of expression and the ideas expressed, and upon a view of Article 10 as being designed for the protection of the second and being concerned only

---

[1] For some support for this approach see R. B. Le Page, *The National Language Question* (O.U.P., 1964), ch. ii.

[2] See for a similar view *Belgium*, Tribunal de Police, Aubel (21.6.1962): 5 *Yearbook* 369.   [3] 2333/64: *Recueil* (1965) ii.

incidentally with the first. In other words, opinions, information, and ideas are, whatever their character, to be freely communicated and exchanged though subject to possible restrictions under paragraph 2. Regulation of the mode or vehicle of expression, including language, will then only be contrary to paragraph 1 if it interferes substantively with freedom of opinions, information, or ideas.

A German court has held that Article 10 (1) confers a right upon any person attacked in an article in the press to have a reply inserted in the journal concerned.[1] In Belgium the Law of 23 June 1961 confers such a right of reply on certain conditions. An applicant to the Commission claimed[2] that a number of newspapers had written accounts of his trial by the Brussels Criminal Court (Tribunal Correctionnel), which he said were defamatory of him, and that they had refused to publish replies by him. The Commission observed that

la question pourrait se poser de savoir si le droit de répouse ou de retification s'analyse, au moins en Belgique, en un 'droit de caractère civil' au sens de l'Article 6 (1) . . . et s'il constitue un corollaire de la liberté d'expression, telle que la consacre l'Article 10 . . . dans l'affirmative il faudrait se demander si les autorités des États contractants, au premier chef les tribunaux, n'ont pas l'obligation de veiller au respect de ce droit dans les rapports entre particuliers

but that, the applicant having failed to take to the courts, under the Law of 23 June 1961 itself, the issue of the refusal of the papers to print his replies, he had failed to exhaust domestic remedies.

It is plain that complaint against the newspaper editors for refusing to print his replies would be incompatible with the Convention *ratione personae*. From the point of view of the legislator there is here under Article 10 a conflict of rights, the right of the newspaper editor subject to law to print, or refuse to print, any article he pleases, and the right of any person, subject of the article, to contradict it or give his version of the facts. While a statutory right of reply, of the kind to be found in the Belgian Law of 23 June 1961, would in so far as it interfered with the freedom of expression of the newspaper be consistent with the Convention, as a measure for the protection of the rights and freedoms of others under Article 10 (2). But it is very doubtful whether a contracting State could be held to be in breach of Article 10, if it gave no

---

[1] Landgericht, Mannehim (12.8.1955): *N.J.W.* [1956] 384.
[2] 1906/63: *Recueil* (1963) iii.

such statutory right of reply, being content to leave the conflict to be resolved in proceedings for defamation.[1]

A similar line may be drawn in libel between the expression of a personal opinion and an objective presentation of facts, that affect the reputation of another person. So in the assessment of a press notice, which had been the subject of a private prosecution for libel for alleging that a Member of Parliament, Central Secretary of the Austrian Socialist Party, had invented an untrue story against the Association of Austrian Manufacturers, the Commission said:

The applicants' article indeed went beyond the expression of such a suspicion in that it presented the personal conclusion which the applicants had drawn from the incomplete information available in such a way as if it were established matter of fact.

This comes close to the question whether it is sufficient in libel that a publication is objectively defamatory or whether there must also be an intention to defame.[2]

The licensing of broadcasting, permitted by Article 10 (1), necessarily implies its regulation. The term 'enterprises', being expressed in the plural, does not mean that the practice of many convention countries to establish monopoly enterprises for radio and TV is contrary to Article 10.[3] There is then no unfettered right to access to broadcasting by way of participation in programmes:

It is evident that the freedom 'to impart information or ideas' . . . cannot be taken to include a general or unfettered right to any private citizen or organisation in access to broadcasting time on radio or television in order to forward its opinion. On the other hand, the Commission considers that the denial of broadcasting time to one or more specific groups or persons, may in particular circumstances, raise an issue under Article 10 alone or in conjunction with Article 14 . . .[4]

In the same application, declared inadmissible, the Commission referred to the practice of exclusion or control of advertisements in

[1] See, for example, *Germany*: Bundesverfassungsgericht (25.1.1961): *Journal of I.C.J.* (Winter 1965) 317.

[2] Considered in *Whitehouse* v. *Gay News Ltd* [1979] 2 W.L.R. 281: the House of Lords (3–2) adopted the first alternative.

[3] 3071 (67) (Sweden) 11 *Yearbook* 456; 4750/71 (U.K.) 40 *Recueil* 29 (no Convention right to set up a commercial radio station); 6452/74 (Italy) 5 D.R. 43.

[4] 4515/70 (U.K.) 35 Collection 86, 14 *Yearbook* 538; 9237/81 (Sweden) 28 D.R. 204. Radio and TV programmes constitute 'information' under Article 10: 5178/71 (Netherlands) 8 D.R. 5.

broadcast programmes:[1] for example, the statute in question, Television Act (1964) schedule 2 excluded advertisements from 'any body the object where of are wholly or mainly of a religious origin or political nature' and are 'directed towards any religious or political object and or have any relation to any industrial dispute'. Penal measures may then be taken against those that avoid obtaining a licence to broadcast, and those who promote or encourage 'pirate broadcasting stations'.[2]

The publication of broadcasting programmes raised issued of general interest in an application by De Geillustreerde Pers N.V., a Netherlands company publishing a 'general interest magazine'. This company wished to publish, in this weekly magazine, a complete list of radio and television programmes. However, under the Broadcasting Act (1967) and Decree (1969), the eight broadcasting organizations are co-ordinated by the Netherlands Broadcasting Foundation, but determine the form and content of their transmissions themselves, and depend in part on sales of programme magazines, and licence fees, since they are not wholly financed from public funds. Under Articles 22 and 23 of the Broadcasting Act, the lists of programmes, published in the programme magazine with approval of the Netherlands Broadcasting Foundation, were subject to copyright; the broadcasting organization shared a monopoly of publication. The application invoked Articles 10 and 14.

The Commission began with a general interpretation of Article 10:

84. The Commission considers that the freedom under Article 10 to impart information of the kind described above[3] is only granted to the person or body who produces, provides or organises it. ... It follows that any right which the applicant company itself may have under Article 10 of the Convention has not been interfered with where it is prevented from publishing information not yet in its possession.

---

[1] The Independent Broadcasting Authority has a Code of Advertising Standards and Practice, paragraphs 9 and 10 of which respect the provisions of the Television Act (1964) quoted above.

[2] 8255/78 (U.K.) 16 D.R. 190 (windscreen sticker saying 'Sound of the nation, Radio Caroline, tune in to 259 metres').

[3] '83 ... list of programme data are not simple facts, or views in the proper sense of the word ... The characteristic feature of such information is that it can only be produced and provided by the broadcasting organisations being charged with the production of the programmes themselves.' Note that the phrase 'regardless of frontiers' in Article 10 (1) does not embody a right of intervention by the State in respect of the acts of a non-contracting State for which the contracting State is in no way responsible: Bertrand Russell Peace Foundation (U.K.) 7597/76 14 D.R. 117.

85. Furthermore, in the area of 'information' i.e. in the area of facts and views as opposed to 'ideas' and 'opinions' the protection which Aricle 10 ... seeks to secure concerns the free flow of such information to the public in general.

freedom to hold opinions/la liberté d'opinion

It is difficult to distinguish this freedom from freedom of thought in Article 9, and as will have been seen, the Commission tends to bring them together. In an application, already considered under Article 6 (3) *a*, the Commission found that

the Applicant's rights to freedom of thought and expression, as guaranteed in Article 9 and 10 ... were not violated by his conviction and sentence, which ... were in pursuance of provisions of penal law; ... further, having regard to the Applicant being duly convicted for activities aimed at the reintroduction into Austria of National-Socialist activities ... that these restrictions were necessary in a democratic society in the interests of public safety and national security and for the protection of the rights and freedoms of others.[1]

to receive and impart information and ideas/de recevoir ou de communiquer des informations et des idées

The *exchange* of ideas essential here has been well described by the Federal Constitutional Court in Germany:

Only free public discussion of subjects of general importance assures the free formation of public opinion that in a free democratic country is achieved 'pluralistically' in the dispute between different concepts, which may be maintained from varying motives, but at least are put forward freely, above all by means of arguments and counter-arguments.[2]

But the free formation of public opinion may be affected by the licensing system (*régimes d'autorisations*) for broadcasting, television, or cinema enterprises, which are expressly permitted under Article 10 (1) and may raise issues of public control as against private enterprise, of monopoly and indepenence.

It is not easy to accord the freedom to impart the information as a right only of the producer of it—the principle of copyright—and at the same time to maintain that Article 10 (1) seeks to secure a free flow of information to the public in general. If the information is imparted to

---

[1] 1747/62: 6 *Yearbook* 442 (consideration of Article 17 held not to be necessary).
[2] Ibid. 318.

the public in a programme magazine, why under Article 10 (1) cannot the general interest magazine reproduce it?

Have the Commission recognized the commercial disadvantages for the applicant company in being prevented from publishing the lists of programmes? Further,

87 ... The Commission has noted the applicant company's submissions that, although the legislation in question imposed various restrictions on the contents and presentation of the 'programme magazines' so as to prevent them from being competitive with the 'general interest magazines' these legislative restrictions were not in fact complied with, and consequently the 'programme magazines' were real competitors of the 'general interest magazines' ...

88 Be that as it may, the Commission considers that the protection of the commercial interests of particular newspapers or groups of newspapers is not as such as contemplated by the terms of Article 10 ...

But is not the copyright, accorded under Article 10 (1) to the producer of the programmes for the publication of lists of them, a commercial interest?

Restrictions of detainees, serving sentence, of access to newspapers or radio, may be justifiable as a penalty under Article 10 (2).[1]

Access to information in possession of State agencies may come into account.

The United States Freedom of Information Act (1967), as amended in 1974, is impressive in that it provides that, if a State agency refuse access of information, the reference may be reviewed by a district court, which under s. 558(*a*):

... may examine the contents of such agency records *in camera* to determine whether such records or any part thereof shall be withheld under any of the exceptions set forth, in subsection (b), and the burden is on the agency to sustain its action.

Under s. 558(*b*) public access to the recorded information shall be excluded on matters that are:

A. specifically authorized under criteria established by an Executive Order to be kept secret in the interest of national defense or foreign policy; and
B. are in fact properly classified pursuant to such Executive order.

These provisions clearly would meet the criterion of 'prescribed by law', and secure the freedom of information in practice until its restriction can be independently shown to be necessary.

[1] *McFeeley et al.* 8317/78 (U.K.) 20 D.R. 44.

The requirement of independent control is also to be found in the Data Act (1974) in Sweden, which provides that personal data registers may be established only on licence by the Data Inspection Board, which issue instructions on methods of obtaining information and its scope, has powers of inspection of data registers, and can receive complaints.

formalities, conditions, restrictions or penalties/formalités, conditions, restrictions ou sanctions

This being the only Article in the convention to refer to concomitant duties and responsibilities in the exercise of rights and freedoms, the limits that may be set to that exercise are described more elaborately than in other Articles. Given that the Contracting States have a margin of appreciation in determining those limits,

in exercising supervision the Commission must always bear in mind not only the extent of such limits, which mut not exceed the margin of appreciation, but also the aim of these limits, since under Article 18 . . . such restrictions shall not be applied for any purpose other than those for which they have been prescribed . . .[1]

The Commission was occupied with several aspects of such limits in the *de Becker Case*.[2] Raymond de Becker, a Belgian journalist, was condemned to death in July 1946 by the Brussels Conseil de Guerre on the ground that he had collaborated with the German authorities, during their occupation of Belgium, principally in the exercise of functions as editor of the Belgian newspaper *Le Soir*. The judgment also entailed forfeiture by him of rights as set out in Article 123 (b) of the Belgian Penal Code. In June 1947 the Brussels Military Court commuted the death sentence to life-imprisonment but confirmed the forfeiture of rights under Article 123 (b).

At the time of his application to the Commission in September 1956 de Becker was deprived for life under paragraphs (e), (f), and (g) of that Article of the rights

to have a proprietary interest in or to take part in any capacity whatsoever in the administration, editing, printing or distribution of a newspaper or any other publication;

to take part in organizing or managing any cultural, philanthropic or sporting activity or any public entertainment;

[1] 735/60: 3 *Yearbook* 318.   [2] 214/56.

to have a proprietary interest in or to be associated with the administration or any other aspect of the activity of any undertaking concerned with theatrical production, film or broadcasting.

From the submissions of de Becker and the Belgian Government three questions emerged of the place of these manifest restrictions on freedom of expression under the Convention: were they, as the Belgian Government argued, justifiable under Articles 2 to 7; if not, were they restrictions covered by one or more of the exceptions set out in Article 10 (2); and if so, were they 'necessary in a democratic society'.

After reviewing Articles 2 to 7, the Commission said:[1]

It is true that Articles 2, 5 and 4 deal with three of the most important forms of penal sanction, while Articles 3 and 7 lay down two important general principles in regard to penal sanction. This does not however mean that these Articles can be regarded as dealing exhaustively with the question of penal sanctions in their relation to human rights and fundamental freedoms.[2] ... The method adopted by the framers of the Convention was to state and define each right and freedom in separate Articles and to insert in each Article the exceptions and reservations that were considered appropriate to the particular right or freedom. ... Accordingly, where the penal sanction in question involves a deprivation or restriction of the right to freedom of expression, it runs counter to the whole plan and method of the Convention to seek its justification in Articles 2, 5 and 4 ... rather than in Article 10. ... The fact that Articles 2 and 5 authorize those forms of penal sanction with all their automatic consequences cannot be interpreted as implying that these Aricles at the same time authorize deprivation or restriction of the right of freedom of expression as an independent penal sanction, regardless of the provisions of Article 10.

As regards the applicability of Article 10 (2), the Commission observed that:

The authors of this paragraph no doubt had in mind primarily the conditions, restrictions and penalties to which freedom of expression is commonly subject in a democratic society as being necessary to prevent seditious, libellous, blasphemous and obscene publications, to ensure the proper administration of justice, to protect the secrecy of confidential information etc. The restrictions ... contained in paragraphs (*e*), (*f*) and (*g*) of Article 124 (b) are however of a somewhat different kind. They are imposed as penal sanctions

---

[1] Report of the Commission (8.1.1960) § 263: *C.E.D.H.* Series B, 1962, pp., 124, 125.
[2] The Commission noted that Article 10 (2) itself and Article 1 of the First Protocol also refer to penalties.

and deterrent measures on persons convicted of certain crimes committed in time of war which do not necessarily involve misuses of the right to freedom of expression. .... The Commission considers that to impose on persons convicted in time of war a total incapacity for life to publish their political opinions may be justifiable under Article 10 (2) as a deterrent sanction and a preventive measure of public security. But Article 123 sexies goes beyond the imposition of incapacities in regard to the publication of political opinions and includes incapacities which have no direct relation to the offence committed. Even so, the Commission believes that the imposition of the incapacities contained in paragraphs (*e*), (*f*) and (*g*) . . . may be justifiable in time of war and for such periods as may be necessary after the conclusion of a war.[1]

Nevertheless, such necessity cannot continue as public order comes to be re-established, and the Commission concluded that these incapacities were

not justifiable insofar as the deprivation of freedom of expression in regard to non-political matters, which they contain, is imposed inflexibly for life without any provision for its relaxation when with the passage of time public morale and public order have been re-established and the continued imposition of that particular incapacity has ceased to be a measure 'necessary in a democratic society' . . .[2]

While the case was before the European Court of Human Rights, an enactment in Belgium on 30 June 1961 of a law on 'l'épuration civique' amended Article 123 (b) of the Belgian Penal Code. In particular, Article 4 (7) and (8) of the law had the effect of reinstating de Becker in the rights which he had forfeited under paragraphs (*e*), (*f*), and (*g*), except in so far as his participation in activities there enumerated might be of a political character; and Article 4 (4) provided that persons in the cateogory of de Becker might apply to the courts for restitution of all rights, except that of the right to vote, to be elected, or to stand for election. It was in these circumstances that de Becker withdraw his application in October 1961 on the ground that it had been 'satisfaite par le vote par le Parlement belge de la loi du 30 Juin 1961'. The Belgian Government asked the court 'to strike the case off the list; or failing that to declare that no incompatibility exists between the provisions of the Convention and Article 123 (b) . . . as amended and supplemented by the Act of June 30, 1961, and as applicable at the present time to Mr. de Becker'.[3]

---

[1] Ibid., pp. 126, 127.
[2] Ibid., p. 128.   [3] 5 *Yearbook* 330.

The Commission did not oppose this solution 'since it considers the provisions of the Belgian Penal Code now applicable to Mr. de Becker to be in conformity with the Convention'; but suggested that, if the court thought it desirable to pronounce on the general issues of the interpretation of the Convention, it should decide whether the compatibility with the Convention of Article 123 (b), as amended, should be determined in relation to Articles 2 to 7, or to Article 10; and whether it was in fact compatible with Article 10. The Commission invited the court, if it so proceeded, to confirm the opinion of the Commission that it is by reference to Article 10 that such compatibility must be determined, and that the limitations maintained in the Act of 30 June 1961 do not go beyond the 'formalities, conditions, restrictions or penalties' authorized by Article 10 (2).

The court did not so proceed and struck the case off the list by seven votes to one (Judge A. Ross).[1]

In two later cases, based on similar facts to that of de Becker, the Commission developed its view and also explained certain of its obervations in the *de Becker Case*. It noted that:

il en résulte que si la Cour n'a point expressément confirmé l'avis de la Commission sur la licéité d'une déchéance perpétuelle de la liberté d'expression politique, elle ne l'a pas non plus infirmé;

la Commission, de son côté, persiste à penser que les limitations maintenues par l'article 4 de la loi du 30 juin 1961 dans le domaine de la liberté d'expression, à l'encontre de personnes reconnues coupables de trahison en temps de guerre, ne sortent point du cadre tracé par l'article 10 § 2 de la Convention; que l'argumentation de X ne contient rien, ai cet égard, qui puisse justifier unrevirement de la jurisprudence de la Commission'[2]

further that

il appartient, au premier chef, aux autorités compétentes des États contractants d'apprécier à partir de quel moment certaines restrictions exceptionnelles aux droits et libertés fondamentaux, introduites pour faire face à une crise nationale d'une ampleur et d'une acuité particulières, cessent de constituer 'une mesure nécessaire dans une société démocratique' au sens de

---

[1] Ibid. 332–6 (27.3.1962). The court considered that 'la radiation de l'affaire . . . n'est pas nature à porter préjudice aux libertés fondamentales de l'auteur de la requête initiale' and that it was not called upon 'à statuer d'office . . . sur un problème abstrait touchant la compatibilité de cette loi avec des dispositions de la convention': *C.E.D.H.* Series A, pp. 26, 27.

[2] 924/60: 6 *Yearbook* 169.

l'article 10 § 2 de la Convention; que les États contractants conservent, à cet égard, un pouvoir d'appréciation étendu.[1]

and that

la Commission ne se prononçait pas sur le point de savoir si, à date du 8 janvier 1960, la restauration du moral de la nation et de l'ordre public était telle, en Belgique, que les déchéances litigieuses entraînaient d'ores et déjà une violation concrète de la Convention au détriment de M. de Becker . . . en l'état actuel du dossier, du moins, la Commission ne discerne aucun élément tendant à établir que la Belgique a indûment tardé à modifier l'Article 123 (b) de son Code Pénal . . .[2]

In sum, it may be said that the view of the Commission, which has not been either confirmed or contradicted by the court, is that a perpetual restriction,[3] on freedom of expression on political matters may be imposed if it is necessary at least in the interests of national security or public safety; and that the point at which this necessity ceases to operate falls within the margin of appreciation of a contracting State, subject to the right and duty of ultimate supervision in terms of the Convention by the bodies established under it.

In its conclusions submitted to the court in the *de Becker Case*, the Commission stressed that what is political action cannot be defined *in abstracto* but must be determined on the facts of each case.

in the interests of

This expression has no equivalent in the French text and, in so far as it might be read as widening the field of exceptional measures, should be ignored. It is in any case governed by the requirement of necessity, and the powers in the armoury of a modern state must be kept in mind

---

[1] 724/60: *Recueil* (1964) i. Decision delayed by repeated requests for adjournment by the applicant.

[2] 924/60: 6 *Yearbook* 180.

[3] Compare *India*—Supreme Court: *Virendra* v. *State of Punjab* [1957] A.I.R.: SC (statutory provisions prohibiting publication in, or introduction into, the State of certain newspapers must satisfy three conditions of constitutionality that prohibition be limited in duration, be confined to prescribed subject-matters, and be subject to representations by persons affected). For the requirement that restrictions be imposed in terms of subject-matter and not of named persons see *Australian Communist Party* v. *The Commonwealth* [1950] 83 C.I.R. 1 (Communist Party Dissolution Act 1950 held *ultra vires* since its provisions did not proscribe specific acts or omissions as being dangerous or subversive, but only named persons and bodies, so that Parliament was itself purporting to determine, or seeking to empower the Executive to determine, the facts upon the existence of which the exercise of the constitutional power must depend).

before extreme measures are accepted as consistent with Article
10 (2).¹

national security/la sécurité nationale

The limits of judicial control of decision by the Executive of what is or
is not necessary for national security has been discussed in England
over activities of supporters for the Campaign for Nuclear Disarma-
ment, in a case raising fundamental issues.²

the protection of health or morals/la protection de la santé ou de la morale

The question whether public authorities have acted within the margin
of their appreciation of the necessity to protect morals was raised in an
application by wholesale newsagent and a trade organization, of which
he was a member. He had delivered to his regular customers,
including several kiosks, an issue of a journal devoted to photographs
and activities of film stars. He was convicted of circulating a publication likely to corrupt the young. The Commission rejected the application on the ground that neither the provision of the statute itself nor
their application by the courts in the present case exceeded the margin
of appreciation or were contrary to Article 10.³ The Commission did
not state its reasons for these conclusions, but possible factors were
the common form of the statute, and the careful investigation by the
courts of the particular case, including consideration of any aesthetic
merits the publication might have and the hearing of an expert
witness⁴ called by the court.⁵

---

¹ The expression has been held in *India*—Supreme Court: *Ramji Lal* v. *State of Uttar
Pradesh* [1957] A.I.R. SC 620 to be wider than 'for the maintenance of' so as to cover
restrictions on statements or utterances, tending to cause public disorder, though they
may not actually lead to a breach.

² *Regina* v. *Chandler* [1962] 2 A.E.R. 314.

³ See petition of the Rhodesian Guild of Journalists on the suppression of the
[Rhodesian] *Daily News* in September 1964: 'If the Government considers that the
newspaper has transgressed the laws of the country, there are many processes within
those laws to which the Government has recourse before punitive action of this nature':
Bulletin of I.C.J. no. 21 (December 1964) 7.

⁴ The report does not say in what this expertise consisted. The Commission recalled
its earlier constructions of Article 6 (3) *d* to hold that refusal by the courts to hear a
priest and a child psychologist as witnesses for the defence was not inconsistent with
Article 6: see under Article 6 (3) *d* above.

⁵ 1167/61: 6 *Yearbook* 218. See above on Handyside.

for preventing the disclosure of information received in confidence/pour empêcher la divulgation d'informations confidentielles

If the accent is on prevention, as the place of the clause among the permitted restrictions might suggest, it is to be confined perhaps to one form or another of official secrets legislation. But again this it might be said that the references to national security and public safety in paragraph 2 already sufficiently protect official secrets.

The development of computers and sophisticated techiques for obtaining information has led to concern for data protection.[1] The European Convention on Data Protection was drafted in January 1981, but it has received only five ratifications and is not yet in force. It requires[2] that data be 'adequate, relevant and accurate' and that, in particular:

(a) information shall be obtained and processed fairly and lawfully for a specified and legitimate purpose;
(b) the data subject shall have access to information held about him and be entitled to its conviction where the legal data provisions have not been compiled with.

Obvious questions, which the text does not answer, are: What is meant by 'lawfully' and 'legitimate'? Must the data subject be told that there is recorded data about him, or does he merely have access to it if he finds that it exists?

Information from the press or broadcasting media, which may be regarded as subject, in the terms of Article 10, to 'formalities, conditions or restrictions' or as confidential, has been subject since 1912 to the D notice system.

It implements in practice, but not in law, the provisions of the Official Secrets Act (1911), which states:

5.1 it is an offence for any person to obtain or communicate any document or information, for a purpose 'prejudicial to the safety or interests of the state', which is 'calculated to be or might be or is intended to be directly or indirectly useful to an enemy';

---

[1] See in the United Kingdom the Lindop Committee Report (1979): Cmnd 7341 on computer systems holding personal information; the Law Commission Report (1981) on Breach of Confidence: Cmnd 6388; and the H.M.G. proposals on data protection: Cmnd 8539. [2] Articles 5, 7, and 8.

5.2 it is an offence for any person to communicate official information without authority.

There are at present twelve D notices covering defence plans, details of weapons systems, the intelligence services and so on. Notices issued in confidence to the recipients are advisory, the arrangement being administrative without legal sanction,[1] and voluntary for the recipient, who may accept or report the view given in the Notice on the communication of information.

for maintaining the authority and impartiality of the judiciary/pour garantier l'autorité et l'impartialité du pouvoir judiciaire

Publications or statements may impair the authority of a court, if they disturb the conduct of a trial itself or criticize unfairly findings or judgments of the courts in general or in a particular case; they may threaten its impartiality if they are designed to influence the outcome of a trial. These ideas have been illuminated by the Judicial Committee of the Privy Council:

... whether the authority and position of an individual judge, or the due administration of justice is concerned, no wrong is committed by any member of the public who exercises the ordinary right of criticising, in good faith, in private or public, the public act done in the seat of justice. The path of criticism is a public way; the wrong-headed are permitted to err therein: provided that members of the public abstain from imputing improper[2] motives to those taking part in the administration of justice, and are genuinely exercising a right of criticism, and not acting in malice or attempting to impair the administration of justice, they are immune.[3]

The prohibition of press articles or other statements, which constitute a 'contempt of court' in the English system, raised major issues in the *Sunday Times* case, of what is 'prescribed by law' and what is 'necessary', in Article 10 (2). Major, because the disagreement about the justifiability of the injunction imposed on the *Sunday Times* was widespread. The Court of Appeal discharged the injunction, stressing

---

[1] It is not an offence in itself to publish D notices that have been received.

[2] The expression 'improper motives' is ambiguous here: it might mean motives improper in the judge or motives improper for a member of the public to impute; the general sense of the passage implies that it means the second.

[3] *Ambard* v. *Attorney-General for Trinidad and Tobago* [1936] A.C. 322 PC; see also *Vidyasagara* v. *The Queen* [1963] A.C. 589 PC.

that the litigation was dormant and not being pursued, that the subject of the *Sunday Times* articles had been covered by Parliamentary proceedings and other publications, and that freedom of information for the public on a matter of public concern must prevail. The House of Lords reversed the judgment of the Court of Appeal, in five individual speeches relying in great part on the 'prejudgment test'. In the application of the Convention, the conclusion that the injunction was in breach of Article 10 was reached by eight votes to five in the Commission and by eleven votes to nine in the Court.[1] It is not therefore possible to treat the whole process as an organic, let alone authoritative, application of the Convention. But certain features may be mentioned. First, the 'impartiality of the judiciary, as being infringed by a press publication, was not put in issue by the respondent Government, or considered *ex officio* by the Court. It was then the authority of the judiciary that could, contrary to Article 10 (1), be compromised by the *Sunday Times* article, by the presence they put on Distillers as litigants or by the prejudgment of the trials they embodied. The English judges had recourse to both the principles of pressure and prejudgment, but the latter appears to have prevailed. For the House of Lords remitted the cause to the Divisional Court with a direction that an injunction be granted to restrain the publication of the *Sunday Times* of 'any article or matter which prejudges the issues of negligence, breach of contract or breach of duty . . .'

The Court declared that:

. . . the authority of that machinery [of justice] will not be maintained unless protection is afforded to all those involved in or having recourse ot it.[2]

But it did not characterize the actions that weaken that authority, accepting the reasons why the House of Lords found the proposed article objectionable, as 'falling within the aim of maintaining the authority of the judiciary'.[3] In short, there is no conclusive answer, either in the judgments of the English courts or of the Court, to the question how far press publications may be restricted in law as contempt of court—weakening the authority of the judiciary.

This leads naturally to the requirement that any restriction be 'prescribed by law'. The Court was here, it said, 'confronted with versions of a law-making treaty which was equally authentic but not

---

[1] *Sunday Times* (U.K.) 6538/74: Report of Commission (18.5.1977): Judgment No. 30 (26.4.1979).   [2] Ibid. § 55.
[3] § 57, spelling out the reasoning of the House of Lords, set out in §§ 29–33.

exactly the same', namely, the true English equivalents to 'prévues par la loi', in Articles 8 (2), Article 1 of the First Protocol, and Article 2 of the Fourth Protocol. However, it found as a matter of interpretation that there are two requirements that flow from the expression 'prescribed by law' in Article 10:

Firstly the law must be adequately accessible: the citizen must be able to have an indication that is adequate in the circumstances of the legal rules applicable to a given case. Secondly, a norm cannot be regarded as a 'law' unless it is formulated with sufficient precision to enable the citizen to regulate his conduct: he must be able—if need be with appropriate advice—to foresee, to a degree that is reasonable in the circumstances, the consequences which one given action may entail.

But the consequences need not be foreseeable with absolute certainty.

... whilst certainty is highly desirable, it may bring in its train excessive rigidity, and the law must be able to keep pace with changing circumstances. Accordingly, many laws are inevitably couched in terms which, to a greater or lesser extent, are vague and whose interpretation and application are questions of practice.[1]

The Court found the question, whether the requirements of accessibility and foreseeability of the law had been met in the present case, was complicated by the principles of foresight and prejudgment being both adopted by English courts. But, while describing these two principles in detail and finding that the applicants had in the circumstances 'adequate indications' of each, it did not say which 'prescribed' the law or whether the law was constituted by a combination of both.

The judgment of the Court is then as ambiguous as that of the House of Lords. It is absurd to describe the rules governing contempt of court as foreseeable or accessible, and so 'prescribed by law' when they have no statutory base and have, as common law, been disputed throughout the English courts both in formulation and application.

It is not surprising that the United Kingdom was moved to enact a statute to regulate contempt of court. The Contempt of Court Act (1981)[2] is like all modern legislation, lengthy in its textual provisions and supported by a number of schedules. Two features may be noticed that relate to Article 10 of the Convention; the element of intent in a publication, and the impact of the publication on court proceedings.

---

[1] §§ 48, 49.
[2] See A. E. Boyle, 'Contempt of Court Act 1981' *Human Rights Review* (1981) 2, 148.

The exclusion of intent as a factor in liability—the strict liability rule—is confined in the statute to publications, and to those which create a risk that the course of justice would be seriously impeded or prejudiced in particular progress; and there are elaborate provisions for determining the periods, in which proceedings are to be treated as active for this purpose. Further, the strict liability rule is limited by the creation of the defence for a publication, which contained a discussion in good faith of public affairs if risk or prejuduce to particular proceedings is incidental, or which is a fair and accurate report of legal proceeding held in public,[1] published contemptoraneously and in good faith.[2]

How publications may impede or prejudice the course of justice is not described, but it is a contempt of court to publish information about the deliberation of a jury, in such way as to identify the case or any juror, or to disclose or solicit the disclosure of such information with a view to publication.

These provisions of the statute can be said to be obliged in effect to maintain the authority and impartiality of the judiciary; and consequential restrictions on the freedom of publication do not then have to be justified under Article 10 (2), though Article 18 requires that they be reasonable and proportionate to the stated purpose.

Finally, the crude assumption that the enactment of the Contempt of Court Act was simply an extension of the judgment of the Court would misunderstand the function of the convention. There were at least several factors at work in the United Kingdom: the recognition of the uncertainty of the law governing contempt of court; the policy, in absence of a written constitution, of giving the development of the law on civil rights specific statutory forms; the psychological impact of the judgment of the Court, finding a breach of the Convention, that judgment being not directly unforeseeable but, at the least, an excuse for legislation that some interests might oppose.

ARTICLE 11

(1) Everyone has the right to freedom of peaceful assembly and to freedom of association with others, including the right to form and to join trade unions for the protection of his interests.

---

[1] A tape recorder may not be used without leave of the court, subject to conditions.
[2] The nature of intent in a case of blasphemous libel was considered in *Whitehouse* v. *Gay News Ltd* (1979) 2 W.L.R. 281.

(2) No restrictions shall be placed on the exercise of these rights other than such as are prescribed by law and are necessary in a democratic society in the interests of national security or public safety, for the prevention of disorder or crime, for the protection of health or morals or for the protection of the rights and freedoms of others. This Article shall not prevent the imposition of lawful restrictions on the exercise of these rights by members of the armed forces, of the police or of the adminsitration of the State.

1. Toute personne a droit à la liberté de réunion pacifique et à la liberté d'association, y compris le droit de fonder avec d'autres des syndicats et de s'affilier à des syndicats pour la défense de ses intérêts.

2. L'exercice de ces droits ne peut faire l'objet d'autres restrictions que celles que, prévues par la loi, constituent des mesures nécessaires, dans une société democratique, à la sécurité nationale, à la sûreté publique, à la défense de l'ordre et à la prévention du crime, à la protection de la santé ou de la morale, ou à la protection des droits et libertés d'autrui. Le présent article n'interdit pas que des restrictions légitimes soient imposées à l'exercice de ces droits par les membres des forces armées, de la police et de l'administration de l'État.

The Universal Declaration, Article 20 (1), affirms the right of peaceful assembly and association, while paragraph (2) adds that no one may be compelled to belong to an association. In the earlier drafts of Article 11 the freedoms of peaceful assembly and of association were dealt with, as they logically should be, in separate articles in both alternatives of the Convention.[1] They were unified in a draft prepared by the Drafting Committee,[2] and this with the addition of the reference to trade unions became in substance the final version. The Committee of Experts emphasized that the freedom of association included the right to join trade unions.[3] But the Conference of Senior Officials 'on account of the difficulties raised by the "closed shop system" in

[1] *T.P.* ii. 388, 429. Alternative was a United Kingdom draft.
[2] *T.P.* ii. 433.
[3] The Universal Declaration deals with it as a right distinct from right of association in general: Article 23 (4).

certain countries ... considered that it was undesirable to introduce into the Convention a rule under which "no one may be compelled to belong to an association" ', as under Article 20 (2) of the Universal Declaration.

The C.P.R. Covenant, Article 22, is identical with Article 11 of the Convention, save that 'public order ("ordre public")' appears in place of 'the prevention of disorder or crime', and the reference to 'the administration of the State' at the end of Article 11 is omitted.

Freedom of peaceful assembly. The Commission has spoken of peaceful assembly as a foundation of a democratic society, and 'as such the right covers both private meetings and meetings in public thorough-fares'. But public assembly can take many forms, and it is processions and demonstrations that can have a purpose that may need action by the authorities to prevent disorder; and 'the problem of freedom of expression cannot in this case be separated from that of freedom of assembly, as guaranteed by Article 11, and it is the latter freedom which is primarily involved'.

The simple priority given here to Article 11 evades the question whether it is not the motives of demonstrators and counter-demonstrators, who may together create disorder, that should determine, which assembly should be banned. So where the Commissioner of Police in London considered that:

... by reason of particular circumstances existing in any police area [the statutory police powers] will not be sufficient to enable to prevent serious public disorder being occasioned by the holding of public processions in the Metropolitant Police District. I ... prohibit for the period of two months ... the holding of the following class of public processions, that is to say, all public processions other than those of a religious educational, festive or ceremonial character customarily held within the Metropolitan Police District.

The ban was imposed for the immediate purpose of preventing a procession organized by the National Front, a racist organization, to take place three days later. The ban, also, given its duration, prevented the holding of a public meeting or demonstration by C.A.R.A.F. (Christians against Racism and Fascism), a body constituted by several church organizations. Among its declared objectives were:

v. to encourage church leaders to oppose at national level, the divisive poli-cies and activities of organisations such as the National Front and the National Party;

vi. to cooperate with other initiatives aimed at promoting racial justice and
   opposing fascism.

The Commission said:

Whilst it was clear that the applicant association [C.A.R.A.F.] had wholly
peaceful intentions it is nevertheless true that its statutory purposes were
expressly directed against the National Front policies, and it could therefore
not be excluded that the proposed procession could also give rise to disorder.[1]

If the reasoning here is that the National Front might counter-
demonstrate, causing disorder, it should alone be banned under
Article 17.

Freedom of association with others. This has been invoked by students and
by professional associations, also in the context of elections, and of
litigation over industrial contracts.

The Commission has held that Article 11 (1) protects private
institutions and trade unions, and consequently a student union in
Sweden was not to be regarded as a trade union, and was, given its
base, a public institution; the Statute for Swedish Universities
(universitatsstadgan) obliges all students to be members of a student
union and pay a subscription to it; further, the Rector's office may
exclude students from teaching and examinations, if they do not
comply. The Commission

... does not see the [student union] as a professional organisation which
upholds ethics and discipline within the profession or defends its members'
interests in outside disputes; ... [but as] a formal way of organising student
participation in the administration of the university.[2]

In the Netherlands an association was formed for safeguarding the
interests of conscript servicemen (V.V.D.M.); it was recognized by the
Government for negotiations in this field, and its membership comprised about two-thirds of the conscripts. The Court held that
disciplinary punishment, imposed by the Supreme Military Court, for
participation in the publication and distribution of material likely to
undermine military discipline, was not in itself an interference with
their freedom of association.[3]

The distribution between professional associations as public or as

---

[1] 2440/78 (U.K.) 21 D.R. 138.
[2] *Association x* (6094/73) (Sweden) 9 D.R. 5.
[3] *Engel et al.* (Judgment No. 22 23.11.1976) p. 14. The applicants were Dona and
Schul.

private institutions was also made in determination of the status and rights under Article 11 of the Ordre des Médecins in Belgium under Royal Decree No. 79 (10.11.1967)

the *Ordre des Médecins* shall include all physicians, surgeons, and obstetricians, who are permanently resident in Belgium and entered on the register of the *Ordre* for the Province where they have their permanent residence.

and,

in order to practise medicine in Belgium, every medical practitioner must be entered on the register of the *Ordre*.

In addition to the *Ordre*, there exist private medical associations formed to protect professional interests, and these are recognized for the purpose of collective negotiations.

The *Ordre* is divided into Provincial Councils, Appeals Councils, and the National Council. In addition to administrative functions, the Councils are to be 'responsible for disciplinary misconduct committed by their registered members in or in connection with the practice of the profession, and serious misconduct committed outside the realm of professional authority, whenever such conduct is liable to damage the reputation or dignity of the profession'. The Court held[1] that the *Ordre* was a 'public-law institution', pursuing

an aim which is in the general interest, namely the protecting of health by exercising under the relevant legislation a form of public control over the practice of medicine ... it is legally invested with administrative as well as rule-making and disciplinary prerogatives out of the orbit of the ordinary law (prérogatives exorbitantes du droit commun) and, in this capacity, employs process of a public authority ...

further, the establishment of the *Order* 'must not prevent practitioners from forming together or joining profesional associations'. There was consequently no interference with the freedom of association protected by Article 11 (1).[2]

the right to form and to join trade unions for the protection of his interests

This is another illustration of the difficulties of setting out in a single, short clause the range of recognized social rights and needs, and the

---

[1] *le Compte, van Leuven, de Meyere* Judgment No. 43 (23.6.1981) §§ 65, 65.
[2] The reasoning was repeated in *Albert, Le Compte* (Belgium) Judgment No. 58 (10.2.1984) and applied on *Barthold* 8734/79 (F.R.G.) 26 D.R. 145, to the Veterinary Surgeons Council in the Federal Republic of Germany: 8734/79 (F.R.G.) 26 D.R. 145.

implied conflicts between them. The Legal Affairs Committee of the Council of Europe Parliamentary Assembly included, in its extensive recommendations on widening the scope of the Convention,[1] the right to choose or accept paid work freely, to have access to free employment services, occupational guidance and training, and to an adequate standard of living in the event of involuntary unemployment. The Committee stressed in its report that, under Article 11, the rights of trade unions are 'protected only in so far as they are essential for the exercise of the rights of individuals'; and that:

In relation to some of these rights, the correlative obligations are not obligations of the state but of the employer and the obligations of the state (insofar as the state is not also the employer) are limited to securing that legislation imposes the necessary obligations on employers and provides the necessary remedies for employees.

On the often complicated question of the extent to which the Government may be held responsible for actions of a State enterprise, the Commission has distinguished at least general policy and day-to-day administration. So, of the Electricity Supply Board in Ireland, a statutory body performing a public service on public funds, it said:

... while the Government exercises, at least, general supervision over the policy of the Board, the day-to-day administration is solely in the hands of the Board; ... the acts alleged by the applicant [a shop steward subjected, to disciplinary and other employment measures] clearly fall within the domain of such day-to-day administration for which the Government is not directly responsible.[2]

Collective action is the heart of industrial relations, for the individual employee can hardly act alone. While strikes and lock-outs and working-to-rule express conflict, collective bargaining over wages and conditions of employment is of prime interest to trade unions and employers;[3] and it may be extended into collective agreements between a group of trade unions and an employers' association or a State agency. The Court has held that Article 11:

safeguards freedom to protect the occupational interests of trade union members by trade-union action, the conduct and development of which the Contracting States must both permit and make possible.

[1] C.E. Document 4213 (27.9.1978).
[2] 4125/69 (Ireland) 37 *Recueil* 42.
[3] I.L.O. Convention No. 98 (Right to Organise and Collective Bargaining) (1949).

but nevertheless the Article,

does not secure any particular treatment of trade unions, or their members by
the State, such as the right that the State should conclude any collective agreement with them. Not only is this latter right not mentioned in Article 11 (1),
but neither can it be said that all the Contracting States incorporate it in their
national law or practice, or that it is indispensable for the effective enjoyment
of trade union freedom.[1]

It was then in view of the Court, sufficient that the Lokmannaför-
bundet was free 'to present claims, to make representations for the
protection of the interests of its members', and to negotiate with the
National Collective Bargaining Office. It followed that the fact that
this office

prefers as a general rule to sign collective agreements only with the most
representative organisations; it is anxious not to find itself faced with an
excessive number of negotiating partners.

expresses a legitimate aim, there being no other purpose involved.[2]

The voluntary character of collective bargaining is confirmed in the
European Social Charter, in which the contracting undertake:

to promote, where necessary and appropriate, machinery for voluntary negotiations between employers and employers' organisations and workers'
organisations, with a view to the regulation of terms and conditions of employment by means of collective agreements: Aricle 6 (2).

But Article 11 (1), the Court tells us, leaves to each State a 'free choice;
in limiting the means used to protect the occupational interests of
trade union members by trade union action: for example:

the grant of a right to strike represents without any doubt one of the most
important of these means, but there are others. Such a right, which is not
expressly enshrined in Article 11, may be subject under national law to regulation of a kind that limits its exercise in certain intances.[3]

The conformity of 'closed shop' agreements with Article 11 has
been much questioned, and has been denied by the Convention
organs. In a leading case[4] United Kingdom legislation was in issue.

---

[1] *Swedish Engine Drivers' Union* (*Svenska Lokmanna Förbundet*). Judgment No. 20
(6.2.1976) §§ 39, 40, repeating the reasoning in *Syndicat National de la Police Belge* Judgment No. 19 (27.10.1975), was followed in 7361/76 (Belgium) (8.5.1978) 14 D.R. 40.
[2] S.E.D.U. § 46. The criteria of representativity were considered in the Belgian
police case.
[3] *Schmidt and Dahlström* (Sweden) Judgment (6.2.1976) § 36.
[4] *Young, James and Webster* (U.K.) Judgment No. 44 (13.8.1981).

The Trade Union and Labour Relations Act (1974), repealed the Industrial Relations Act (1971), and so removed the prohibition of closed shops, and the right of an employee not to belong to union. As amended by the Amendment Act (1976) the Act provides that:

Dismissal of an employee by an employer shall be regarded as fair if . . . it is the practice in accordance with a union membership agreement for all employees of that employer or all employees of the same class as the dismissed employee to belong to a specified independent trade union, or to one of a number of specified trade unions: unless the employee genuinely objects on the grounds of religious belief to being a member of any trade union whatsoever . . . in which case the dismissal shall be regarded as unfair.

Subsequent legislation led to the Employment Act (1980), which altered the rule as to unfair dismissal, providing that such dismissal is to be regarded as unfair if:

(a) the employee objects on grounds of conscience or other deeply-held personal conviction to being a member of any or a particular union; or

(b) the employee belonged, before the closed shop agreement or arrangement came into effect to the class of employees covered thereby and has not been a member of a union in accordance therewith; or

(c) in the case of a closed shop agreement or arrangement taking effect after 15 August 1980, either it has not been approved by the vote in a ballot of not less than 80 per cent of the employees affected or, although it is so approved, the employee has not since the balloting been a member of a union in accordance therewith.

A Code of Practice, issued with the approval of Parliament and coming into effect on 17 December 1980, recommended, *inter alia*, that closed shop agreements should protect basic individual rights and be applied flexibly and tolerantly and with due regard to the interests of individuals as well as unions and employers. The Code is admissible in evidence, but imposes no legal obligations in law.

The Employment Act maintained the right to claim compensation for dismissal for non-membership of the union, where 'closed shop' operates, but 'closed shop' itself was not rendered unlawful. Claims remained available to industrial tribunals under the Industrial Relations Act (1971).

British rail had concluded in 1970, a 'closed shop' agreement with the N.U.R. (National Union of Railwaymen), T.S.S.A. (Transport Salaried Staffs' Association), and A.S.L.E.F. (Associated Society of Locomotive Engineers and Firemen); but this agreement was not put in effect, in face of the Industrial Relations Act (1971). However, in 1975 a 'closed shop' agreement was concluded with the unions, coming into effect on 1 August.

The applicants were not eligible for membership in A.S.L.E.F., but Young and James were requested, on the conclusion of the 'closed shop' agreement in 1975, to join the T.S.S.A. or the N.U.R., and Webster to join the N.U.R. Young and Webster had objections to certain trade union policies and activities, coupled by Young with objections to the political affiliations of the special unions. All the applicants considered the membership condition to be interference with freedom of association. On refusal to join the specified unions, the employment of the applicants was terminated.

The Commission expressed the opinion, in its report under Article 31 by 14 to 3 that there had been a breach of Article 11. The Court, holding also that there had been a breach by 18 to 3, started with the question whether the guarantee of freedom of association in Article 11 necessarily entails as a 'negative right' in freedom not to associate. The Court rejected this polarity as determinative of the issues:

Assuming for the sake of argument that, for the reasons given [in a passage cited from the *travaux preparatoires*][1] a general rule such as that in Article 20 (2) the U.D.H.R. was deliberately omitted from and so cannot be regarded as itself enshrined in the Convention, it does not follow that the negative aspect of a person's freedom of association falls completely outside the ambit of Article 11, and that each and every compulsion to join a particular trade union is compatible with the intention of the provision. To construe Article 11 as permitting every kind of compulsion in the field of trade union membership would strike at the very substance of the freedom it is designed to guarantee.[2]

On the other hand, it follows from the conclusion that Article 11 does not formally express the 'negative right', not to associate that:

[1] 'On account of the difficulties raised by the "closed shop" system in certain countries, the Conference [of Senior Officials] in this connection considered that it was undesirable to introduce into the Convention a rule under which "no one may be compelled to belong to an association", which features in [Article 20 (2) of] the Universal Declaration of Human Rights': *Report of the Conference* (19.6.1950).
[2] See also *Belgian Linguistic Case* Judgment No. 6 (23.7.1968) § 5; *Winterwerp* (Netherlands) Judgment No. 33 (24.10.1979) § 60.

Assuming that Article 11 does not guarantee the negative aspect of that freedom on the same footing as the positive aspect, compulsion to join a particular trade union may not always be contrary to the Convention. However, a threat of dismissal involving loss of livelihood is a most serious form of compulsion and, in the present instance, it was directed against persons engaged by British Rail before the introduction of any obligation to join a particular trade union.

Moreover, the protection of personal opinion and convictions comes also into account:

... notwithstanding its autonomous role and particular sphere of application, Article 11 must, in the present case, also be considered in the light of Articles 3 and 10[1] ... The protection of personal opinion afforded by Article 3 and 10 in the shape of freedom of the right, conscience and religion and of freedom of expression, is also one of the purposes of freedom of association as guaranteed by Article 11. Accordingly, it strikes at the very substance of this Article to exert pressures of the kind applied to the applicants, in order to compel someone to form an association contrary to his convictions.

In concluding that there had been an interference with the rights of the applicants under Article 11, the Court had to consider whether it was justified as being 'necessary in a democratic society' in the senses of Article 11 (2). The Court reverted to its criteria of necessity, elaborated in the *Handyside case*,[2] and applied them to the present case.[3]

Firstly, 'necessary' in this context does not have the flexibility of such expressions as 'useful' or 'desirable'. The fact that British Rail's closed shop agreement may in a general way have produced certain advantages is, therefore, not of itself conclusive as to the necessity of the interference complained of.

Secondly, pluralism, tolerance, and broadmindedness are hallmarks of a 'democratic society'. Although individual interests must on all occasion be subordinated to those of a group, democracy does not simply mean that the views of a majority must always prevail; a balance must be achieved which ensures the fair and proper treatment of minorities and avoids any abuse of a dominant position. Accordingly, the mere fact that the applicants' standpoint was adopted by very few of their colleagues was again not conclusive of the issue now before the Court.

---

[1] Citing *Kjeldsen, Busk Madsen, Pedersen* (Denmark) Judgment No. 23 (7.12.1976) § 52.
[2] Judgment No. 24 (7.12.1976).
[3] § 63.

Thirdly, any restriction imposed on a Convention right must be proportionate to the legitimate aim pursued.

The Court stressed that it was not placing the 'closed shop' system under any general review, and that its task was the assessment of the rights of the applicants under Article 11; nevertheless in its recourse to Article 11 (2) for the determination of what is 'necessary', it did not explain how the British Rail 'closed shop' arrangements might be protecting the 'rights and freedoms of others', the other British Rail employees, and British Rail as the employer, which was not in fact wholly disadvantaged by the 'closed shop'. Further, it might be asked how the dismissal of 54 employees out of a total staff of 250,000 could be disproportionate to the aim pursued.

The Employment Act (1982), amending the Employment Protection (Consolidation) Act (1978) ss. 58, 58A, provides that dismissal by an employer, relating to trade union membership, shall be unfair, if the reason was that the employee:

(*a*) was, or proposed to become a member of an independent trade union, or

(*b*) had taken part, or proposed to take part, in the activities of an independent trade union, or

(*c*) was not a member of any trade union, or of a particular trade union, or of one of a number of particular trade unions, or had refused or proposed to refuse to become or remain a member: s. 58(1)

shall be fair[1] if:

(*a*) it is the practice, in accordance with a union membership agreement, for employees of the employer who are of the same class as the dismissed employee to belong to a specified independent trade union or to one of a number of specified independent trade unions and;

(*b*) the reason (or if more than one, the principal reason) for the dismissal was that the employee was not, or had refused or proposed to refuse to become or remain, a member of a union in accordance with the agreement; and

(*c*) the union membership agreement had been approved in relation to employees of that act in accordance with s. 58A through a ballot

---

[1] Subject to exceptions under s. 58(6)(7).

held within the period of five years ending with the time of dismissal: 5.58(3).

The meaning of peaceful assembly has not been put in issue in any application to the Commission. But it has held that freedom of association does not extend to participation in a profession. Speaking of the restrictions imposed under Article 123 sexies of the Belgian Penal Code, already considered under Article 10, the Commission said that

le droit de participer à l'administration, la gérance ou la direction d'une association professionnelle ou d'une association sans but lucratif [covered by Article 123 sexies, para. i] ne figure pas, en tant que tel, parmi, les droits garantis par la Convention et que, spécialement, il ne rentre pas dans le concept traditionnel de la liberté d'association, consacré à l'Article 11; . . . on peut en dire autant du droit de se livrer aux activités du'énumérait l'alinéa h [the exercise of any number of listed professions].[1]

The rights to form and join trade unions and associations is restated in the European Social Charter, Article 5;[2] and, as in Article 11, the extent to which these rights may be exercised by the police, and by members of the armed forces, is restricted, but the formulation of this exception is not identical. Article 11 (2) of the Convention speaks of the imposition of 'lawful restrictions on the exercise of these rights/ des restrictions légitimes . . . à l'exercise de ces droits'. This implies, first, that 'trade union' is not to be understood in a narrow sense, but includes any association of workers or employees for their mutual protection in their employment; and, secondly, that the restrictions, since their character is not in any way delimited, may in effect nullify the right to form or join a trade union. It would certainly be unusual to have trade unions in the armed forces. The formulation in the European Social Charter makes a distinction between the police and members of the armed forces,[3] which prompts a different approach. The principle of the application of the guarantees is raised only with respect to the armed forces, which suggest that the police have the

---

[1] 1028/61: *Recueil* (1961) ii. See also 764/60: *Recueil* (1964) i.

[2] 'Freedom of workers and employers to form local, national or international organizations for the protection of their economic and social interests, and so join these organizations.'

[3] 'The extent to which the guarantees provided for in this Article shall apply to the police shall be determined by national laws and regulations. The principle governing the application (*le principe de l'application*) to the members of the armed forces of these guarantees, and the extent to which they shall apply to persons in this category, shall equally be determined by national laws or regulations.'

right to form or join trade unions, though the way in which it is exercised may be regulated by special rules of law. Since the right to form or join a trade union is a right common to Article 11 of the Convention and Article 5 of the European Social Charter, Article 60 of the Convention would require that, if the construction suggested of Article 5 of the Charter is correct, Article 11 be interpreted in like manner, in respect of any country party to both instruments. The same considerations would apply to civil servants, as members of the administration of the State; it may be noted that, neither under the European Social Charter nor the C.P.R. Covenant, can they be subject to special restrictions on their forming or joining trade unions.

ARTICLE 12

Men and women of marriageable age have the right to marry and to found a family, according to the national laws governing the exercise of this right.

A partier de l'âge nubile, l'homme et la femme ont le droit de se marier et de fonder une famille selon les lois nationales régissant l'exercice de ce droit.

This Article appears to have been uncontroversial and was not substantially altered in the course of the preparatory work. It is limited in its scope, as compared with the Universal Declaration, Article 16, which has been taken over with little alteration into the C.P.R. Covenant, Article 23. These provisions also require full and free consent to the marriage of the intending spouses; equality of rights and responsibilities of the spouses 'as to marrriage, during marriage, and at its dissolution; and the necessary protection of children of the marriage in case of dissolution'.

The seemingly uncontroversial character of Article 12 may also have been a cause of its poor drafting. National laws are said to govern the exercise of 'this right', but in fact two distinct rights are involved, not one. Further, if these rights are to be exercised wholly according to national law, then the sentence is circular; if, however, national laws do not define the rights, but only regulate their exercise, then the question is posed as to what elements in Article 12 are independent of national laws. The expression 'national laws' is itself ambiguous in the context. If it refers primarily to the domestic laws of the contracting States, how far may it be extended to cover the *lex domicilii* or *lex patriae* of the parties to a marriage, as far as capacity is concerned?[1]

At least the notion of marriageable age must, it seems, be determined by the law of the contracting State where a marriage is to take place, and in the practice of contracting States it varies.[2] It also may be presumed from the practice of contracting States that under their domestic laws requirements of parental or other consent and certain impediments to marriage may be imposed, consistently with Article 12.

Marriage is created in law by the observance of the procedure described, which does not normally recognize a religious ritual as creating the status of marriage. The law may raise issues of private international law.[3]

The failure to recognize a medically confirmed change of sex by refusal of amendment of the birth certificate is an infringement of the right to marry under Article 12.[4]

The claim of the right to marry has been naturally made often by those in prison. In an early application the Commission took a rather negative approach, though the decision of inadmissibility rested in large part on the circumstances, in particular, the applicant was serving a long term imprisonment and there was no indication that he and his proposed spouse were planning to find a home in partnership; the Commission also accepted the suggestion that the performance of a ceremony of marriage in prison would make difficult the maintenance of order.[5] However, in a later case the Commission held that it must consider the issue in the light of present-day conditions:

In this respect it is relevant to note the general tendency in European penal systems in recent years towards reduction of the differences between prison life and life at liberty and the increasing emphasis laid on rehabilitation.

---

[1] Issues under Article 12 could arise in cases of immigrants to Europe from societies where polygamous marriages are lawful.

[2] e.g. for males, sixteen in *United Kingdom*: Age of Marriage Act 1929, and *Italy*: Codice Civile, Art. 144, and eighteen in *Germany*—Ehegesetz 1946, s. 1 (2); and for females, fourteen in *Italy*, sixteen in *Germany* and *United Kingdom*.

[3] 3898/68 (U.K.) 35 *Recueil* 102, Rules of public law were considered in 6167/73 (F.R.G.) 1 D.R. 64 as prevailing.

[4] *von Oosterwijk* 7654/76 (Belgium). This was the opinion of the Commission. The Court found a failure to exhaust domestic remedies and took no cognizance of the merits of the case.

[5] 892/60 (U.K.) 6 *Recueil* 7.

An applicant had been sentenced to five years' imprisonment, and he more than once from October 1974 to October 1975, petitioned the prison authorities for permission to marry the woman with whom he had been living before arrest.[1] At one stage his petition was brought to the Home Secretary, who replied:

The Secretary of State has fully considered your petition but points out that in accordance with the regulations it is not possible to allow you temporary release for the purpose of marriage as consent is only given if there is a child to legitimate.

The Commission examined the domestic law, including the Marriage Act (1949), and the Prison Act (1952) and Prison Rules (1964). As regards the celebration of marriage it concluded that:

Despite the theoretical possibility for a prisoner to obtain a special licence[2] . . . the effect of the provisions outlined above [of the Marriage Act [1949]] is thus that it is only possible in practice for a prisoner to marry if he is able to leave prison and have the marriage solemnised in a prescribed place outside.

As regards the Prison Act (1952) and the Prison Rules, made under it, the Commission found no right to temporary release, under Rule 6 but only a *discretion* of the prison authority to allow a release.

The Commission concluded that:

Personal liberty is not a necessary precondition to the exercise of the right to marry. The practice of States in allowing prisoners to marry, either within prison or on temporary release under escort, show that no specially onerous or complex arrangements are necessary. The exercise of the right, particularly within a prison, does not . . . involve the prisoner escaping from the supervision and control of the prison authorities . . . the imposition by the state of any substantial period of delay on the exercise of this right must in general be seen as an injury to its substance.

The opinion was unanimous that Article 12 had been breached.[3] In August 1977 the practice was changed so that, in general, prisoners serving determinate sentence and having over twelve months of their

---

[1] She married another man in early 1976.

[2] Granted by the Archbishop of Canterbury, under the Ecclesiastical Licences Act (1533), only for a marriage celebrated under the rites of the Church of England; or by the Registrar General, under Marriage (Registrar Generals Licence) Act (1970) in certain cases of serious illness.

[3] *Hamer* (U.K.) 7114/75 24 D.R. 5; *Draper* (U.K.) 8186/78 24 D.R. 72.

sentence still to serve, would be allowed temporary release in order to marry; and the period of twelve months is now reduced to six.[1]

The right to found a family may be distinguished from the right to marry in two ways. First, the right of a married couple to have children may call for affirmation and protection, not only in extreme situations,[2] but, in a world preoccupied with the control of population growth, where family limitation is sought by public measures of taxation, withdrawal of social security benefits, or the like. This situation has not yet been reached in Europe, but it is doubtful whether Article 12 as drafted would give much protection against such measures.

Secondly, it may be asked whether, if 'family life' in Article 8 embraces an unmarried couple and their children, at least if they are together, an unmarried couple may claim a right to found a family under Article 12. It is probable that by the close conjunction of the two rights, in which the right to marry and to found a family may be envisaged as a single process, the drafters intended that only married couples have the right under Article 12.

While it is probable that the drafters of Article 12 envisage the right to marry and to found a family as a single process, so that only married couples would have the right to found a family under Article 12, the concept of marriage has been widened to include the unmarried couple.[3] Adoption by a 'married couple' can also be the founding of a family.[4] Another feature of marriage is that the surname of the husband and father has to be taken by the wife and children, this being a 'suitable measure, proportionate to the aim it is sought to realise'.[5]

Article 12, as it stands, does not, in the view of the Commission, extend to the dissolution of marriage or its consequences;[6] nor, in the opinion of the Bundesverwaltungsgericht in Germany does it cover contracts in restraint in marriage since the restraint is voluntary and not imposed by law.[7]

---

[1] 6564/74 (U.K.) 2 D.R. 105 is now out of date.
[2] Genocide Convention, Article 2: 'genocide' includes '(d) imposing measures intended to prevent births within the group'.
[3] 7289/75 (Switzerland) 9 D.R. 57.
[4] 8896/80 (Netherlands) 24 D.R. 176.
[5] 8042/77 (Switzerland) 12 D.R. 202.
[6] 1783/63: *Recueil* (1964) i.
[7] (22.2.1962): *N.J.W.* [1962] 1532 (clause (*Zölibatsklausel*) in the contract of engagement to serve in the police force forbidding marriage for two years).

ARTICLE 13

Everyone whose rights and freedoms as set forth in this Convention are violated shall have an effective remedy before a national authority notwithstanding that the violation has been committed by persons acting in an official capacity.

Toute personne dont les droits et libertés reconnus dans la présente Convention ont été violés, a droit à l'octroi d'un recours effectif devant une instance nationale, alors même que la violation aurait été commise par des personnes agissant dans l'exercice de leurs fonctions officielles.

With Article 12 the enumeration of substantive rights and freedoms is concluded,[1] and the remaining provisions of Section I are largely concerned with certain modalities and conditions of their exercise and enjoyment.

Article 13 is an unsatisfactory Article, difficult both to construe and to place in the Convention system, lying as it does on the frontier between the international supervision and enforcement of the Convention by the bodies established under it, and its observance in the national and domestic law and practice of contracting States.

In recommending to the Committee of Ministers that they prepare a Convention, the Consultative Assembly distinguished between the observance by States, that accepted the Convention, of its provisions, and the collective guarantee of that observance, in the following way:

4—Subject to the provisions laid down in Articles 5, 6 and 7, every Member State, signatory to the Convention, shall be entitled to establish the rules by which the guaranteed rights and freedoms shall be organised and protected within its territory.

5—The fundamental rights and freedoms enumerated above shall be guaranteed without any distinction based on race, colour, sex, language, religion, political or other opinion, national or social origin, affiliation to a national minority, fortune or birth.

6—In the exercise of these rights, and in the enjoyment of the freedoms guaranteed by the Convention, no limitations shall be imposed except those established by the law, with the sole object of ensuring the recognition and respect

---

[1] For the question how far Article 14 embodies rights independent of the others enumerated in Section I, see under that Article.

for the rights and freedoms of others, or with the purpose of satisfying the just
requirements of public morality, order and security in a democratic society.

7—The object of this collective guarantee shall be to ensure that the laws of
each State in which are embodied the guaranteed rights and freedoms as well
as the application of these laws are in accordane with 'the general principles of
law as recognised by civilised nations' and referred to in Article 38 (c) of the
Statute of the International Court of Justice.[1]

In the Committee of Experts, meeting in February and March 1950,
the United Kingdom proposed that Articles 4–7 in this Recommendation be replaced by three Articles, which after adaptations finally
emerged as Articles 1, 13, 57, and 15 respectively. The first proposed
Article read as follows:

(1) Each State party hereto undertakes to ensure to all individuals within its
jurisdiction the rights defined in this Convention. Every deposit of an instrument of access shall be accompanied by a solemn declaration made by the
Government of the State concerned with full and complete effect as given by
the law of that State of the provisions of the Convention.

(2) Each State party hereto undertakes to ensure:
(a) that any person whose rights or freedoms as herein defined are violated
    shall have an effective remedy notwithstanding that the violation has
    been committed by persons acting in an official capacity;
(b) that any person claiming such a remedy shall have his rights thereto
    determined by national tribunals whose independence is secured; and
(c) that the police and executive authorities shall enforce such remedies
    when granted.

The States party hereto declare that they recognise the rights and freedoms
set forth in Article 2 hereof, as being among the Human Rights and fundamental freedoms founded on the general principles of law recognised by
civilised nations.[2]

Paragraph (1) first sentence and paragraph (2) were taken into Alternative A of the draft Convention, and paragraph (2) a in substance
into Alternative B.[3] But it is not clear from the remainder of the
preparatory work what determined the choice of paragraph (2) a alone
as the nucleus of Article 13, and no direct discussion of the provisions
is recorded.

The central question presented by Article 13 is whether it is concerned with the international or the domestic implementation of the

---

[1] Recommendation (8.9.1949): Consultative Assembly, first Session: *T.P.* i. 224.
[2] Ibid. ii. 354.
[3] Ibid. ii. 448, 458/9.

Convention, with the collective guarantee, or with internal remedies. It could mean in effect that, where a breach of the Convention has already taken place, an effective remedy must then be provided. But strictly, a breach of the Convention can only be found either by the Committee of Ministers, or by the court, or by a national court before which the material provision of the Convention has been invoked as part of the domestic law. If, then, a finding of a breach of the Convention is a necessary precondition of any claim to an effective remedy under Article 13, the Article is only applicable after one of these three findings; and it then provides the framework for the 'measures required' in Article 32 (4) and the 'reparation' envisaged in Article 50. Only if the remedy proves ineffective, in that the measures are inadequate, or the reparation is only partial, that the Committee of Ministers can take further action under Article 32 or the court under Article 50.

In the unlikely event that, in the third case, the national courts held that there had been a breach of the Convention, but that there was no effective remedy, application could be made to the Commission claiming a breach of Article 13.

This view of Article 13, as part of the collective guarantee of enforcement of the Convention, may be called the collective view. Against this is the interpretation adopted by the Commission and the Court, which is an *individualist* view: in effect, the term 'allegedly' is inserted before 'violated' so that, whether the provisions of the Convention have been incorporated in domestic law or not, the individual must be entitled to domestic remedies, if he claims that there has been a substantive breach of any of these provisions in his regard. In short, it is a part of the 'remedy/reviewing' called for by Article 13 to have that very issue determined.[1]

whose rights and freedoms as set forth in the Convention are violated/dont les droits et libertes reconnus dans la convention présente ont été violés.

Though it is now decisive, the individualist view is not without its difficulties now expressly resolved by the Convention organs.

---

[1] In the Court's view, Article 13 requires that where an individual considers himself to have been prejudiced by a measure allegedly in breach of the Convention, he should have a remedy before a national authority in order both to have his claim decided and, if appropriate, to obtain redress: *Klass* (F.R.G.) Judgment No. 28 (6.9.1978) § 64.

In the first place, the English expression 'are violated' is ambiguous in that it can mean either 'if they are violated' or 'have been violated', while the French equivalent, supported by the term 'l'octroi' not represented in the English text, has clearly the second sense. In short, Article 13 covers a violation established and not merely asserted. Secondly, the Commission has in earlier decisions suggested that Article 13 is applicable only to a violation found of a Convention right. So, as a first step,

an application or part of an application alleging a violation of Article 13 can be considered only so far as the Commission has declared the Application admissible in respect of one of the Articles of Section I . . .[1]

then,

the effective remedy before a national authority, which is guaranteed to everyone under Article 13 of the Convention, relates exclusively to a remedy in respect of a violation of one of the rights and freedoms set forth in the Convention; and . . . the Applicant not having established any violation of the right there is a basis for the application of Article 13 . . .[2]

However, the Court has said that Article 13 guarantees an effective remedy

à quiconque *allègue* une violation de ses droits et libertés garanties par la Convention.[3]

The provisions of Article 13 may in some degree coincide with other provisions of the Convention. The Court found:

Since Article 13 and 6 (1) overlap in this particular case, the Court does not deem it necessary to determine whether there has been a failure to observe the requirements of the former Article; these requirements are less strict than, and here entirely absorbed by, those of the latter Article![4]

So the remedy prescribed in Article 5 (4) both in form, proceedings before a court, and in purpose, is more specific than in Article 13; it is a *lex specialis* as distinct from *les generalis*.[5]

---

[1] 768/60.
[2] 472/53 2 *Yearbook* 212; 1092/61 5 *Yearbook* 212; 1167/61 6 *Yearbook* 22D.
[3] *Klass* (F.R.G.) n. 2.
[4] *Airey* (Ireland): Judgment No. 27 (9.10.1079) § 35.
[5] *Eggs* (Switzerland) 7341/76 6 D.R. 170.

effective remedy/un recours effectif

A German court has held that this does not include, as of right, a process of constitutional appeal;[1] and the Commission has also said that such a right is not accorded by the Convention, without making particular reference to Article 13.[2] An Austrian court has also said that the expression refers to remedies already provided by domestic law, but that the clause does not create additional remedies.[3] In particular, it could not be invoked to reopen a decision that had become *res judicata*.[4] 'National authority' is, it seems, to be taken as being not limited to courts and tribunals.

Article 13 does not require several degrees of jurisdiction;[5] but the process of appeal for example, from the adjudicator to an Immigration Appeal Tribunal against a deportation order in the United Kingdom, is an effective remedy.[6] However, Article 13 cannot itself be invoked in regard to the law of proceedings before the 'highest court in the domestic legal system', there being a manifest limit.[7]

The Commission has also held in a number of contexts that Article 13 does not accord as of right a judicial review of other assessment of legislation.[8]

notwithstanding that the violation has been committed by persons acting in an official capacity/alors que même la violation aurait été commise par des personnes agissant dans l'exercice de leurs fonctions officielles

This clause fits the 'individualist' view of the Article, since for the bodies established under the Convention it is meaningless; for their competence extends *ratione personae* only to acts of persons exercising public authority.

---

[1] Decision cited in p. 124,n. 1.

[2] 436/58: 2 *Yearbook* 386; 778/69: *Recueil* (1961) i.

[3] Administrative Court (Verwaltungsgerichtshof) 11.12.1958. For a similar view see in *Netherlands*: Hoge Raad (24.2.1960): Article 13 creates an obligation for the legislature to provide remedies, if they do not yet exist, not a remedy in itself: *Ned. Jur.* (1960) 1121.

[4] *Germany*: Bundesgerichtshof (20.7.1964): *N.J.W.* (1964) 2119: 1552/62: is to the same effect.

[5] 5849/72 (Austria) 1 D.R. 46.

[6] *Uppal Singh et al.* 8244/78 (U.K.) 17 D.R. 149.

[7] *Crociani et al.* 8603/79 (Italy).

[8] *Young, James, Webster* (U.K.) 7601/76, 7806/77 Report (14.12.1979); *Kaplan* (U.K.) 7598/76 21 D.R. 5; 5297/81 (Sweden) 28 D.R. 204.

The fact is that there is a basic confusion of thought as to the real purpose and function of the Article.

ARTICLE 14

The enjoyment of the rights and freedoms set forth in this Convention shall be secured without discrimination on any ground such as sex, race, colour, language, religion, political or other opinion, national or social origin, association with a national minority, property, birth or other status.

La jouissance des droits et libertés reconnus dans la présente Convention doit être assurée, sans distinction aucune, fondée notamment sur le sexe, la race, la couleur, la langue, la religion, les opinions politiques ou toutes autres opinions, l'origine nationale ou sociale, l'appartenance à une minorité nationale, la fortune, la naissance ou toute autre situation.

The first formulation of this Article, based on Article 2 of the Universal Declaration, is to be found in the Recommendation of the Consultative Assembly, already set out under Article 13. Although there were drafting changes—between 'guaranteed' and 'secured', and 'distinction' and 'discrimination' in the English text—and the important addition of association with a national minority was made[1]—the Article retained substantially the same form throughout. Further, the Drafting Committee proposed at one point to add, as a separate paragraph: 'All are equal before the law',[2] and the Conference of Senior Officials added to the Article what later became Article 18.

The draft Article was not, it appears, given any extended discussion, and the only indication of its purpose is the statement of Mr. Teitgen, as *rapporteur* of the Committee of Legal and Administrative Affairs, that it was to prevent 'the indirect destruction' of the freedoms guaranteed under the Convention.[3]

---

[1] *T.P.* ii. 433. Adopted in C.P.R. Covenant, Article 26, which otherwise is the same as Article 14.

[2] C.P.R. Covenant, Article 27.

[3] *T.P.* i. 130.

The enjoyment of the rights and freedoms set forth in this Convention shall be secured/La jouissance des droits et libertés reconnus dans la présente Convention doit être assurée . . .

The problem is posed whether Article 14 is auxiliary to these rights and freedoms, or whether it establishes a right to non-discrimination independent of them. It has then to be asked whether there can be a breach of Article 14 found where the decision of action of which the applicant complains:

(*a*) is on the face of it discriminatory, but no right or freedom, guaranteed by other provisions of the Convention, is involved, or

(*b*) involves one of these rights or freedoms, appears in the facts not to be an infringement of it; or

(*c*) has been taken in exercise of one of the restrictions expressly permitted by the Convention of the rights and freedoms.

The Convention organs have given a negative answer to (*a*) from the beginning:

. . . Article 14 de la Convention . . . ne consacre le principe de non-discrimination . . . que dans la jouissance des droits et libertes reconnus; . . . seule la violation prétendue d'un de ces droits et libertés par une des Parties contractantes peut faire l'objet d'un requête.[1]

This principle has been repeated so many times by the Commission and the Court that it is not necessary to cite further applications.

The answer to (*b*) is also negative, though the Commission used language in an early application[2] suggesting the opposite:

. . . the Commission has already held above that such right [to fair hearing under Article 6 (1)] is not violated in the present case, . . . it follows that Article 14 has no application in the circumstances of the present case.

It is possible that the Commission was following the reasoning of its Report on the *Pfunders/Fundres* case,[3] which turned on the same issue, the use of minority languages in the courts. The Commission was

---

[1] 85/55: 1 *Yearbook* 199. See for example, *Belgian Linguistic Cases* Report §§ 400, 401 for a reasoned analysis.

[2] 808/60: 5 *Yearbook* 108. This decision was cited in dissenting opinions in the *Belgian Linguistic Cases*.

[3] *Austria* v. *Italy* (788/60). Report No. 209.

taking account of the fact that the principle of non-discrimination may be expressed in provisions of the Convention other than Article 14:

An examination of the case-record does not enable the Commission to find any discrimination contrary to Article 14. In this connection, the Commission points out that two of the provisions invoked by the Applicant Government, Article 6 (1) ('a fair hearing') and Article 6 (3) *d in fine* ('under the same conditions'), convey to some extent in their special field an idea of equality very similar to the principle of non-discrimination laid down in Article 14. The Commission has already expressed the opinion that these provisions were complied with.

So, if the principle of equality in fair hearing has been observed, Article 14 need not be brought in. The *lex specialis* applies, as under Article 13.

The negative answer to (*b*) has been stated by the Court and the Commission:

Despite finding no breach of Article 11, the Court must ascertain whether the difference of treatment, characterised by the applicants as discriminatory, infringed Articles 11 and 14 taken together.[1]

The Commission, recalling that Article 14 embodies the principle of non-discrimination only in the enjoyment of the rights and freedoms set forth in the Convention, said:

This does not mean, however, that it is necessary first to find a violation of one of those rights and freedoms before Article 14 becomes operative. ... A measure which is in itself in conformity with the requirements of the Article enshrining the right or freedom in question may ... infringe this Article when read in conjunction with Article 14 for the reason that it is of a discriminatory nature.[2]

This reply to (*c*) is to be found in the Commission Report on the *Belgian Linguistic Cases*, where it said:

Afin de déterminer les cas ou une discrimination peut constituer l'élément décisif d'une violation de la Convention, il faut tenir compte des différentes méthodes dont la Convention se sert pour definir les droits et libertées reconnus par elle.

En premier lieu, on trouve des dispositions qui définissent d'une manière précise et exhaustive les droits en question, et par consequent les obligations

---

[1] *Schmidt/Dahlström* (Sweden): Judgment No. (6.2.1976).

[2] *Müller* 5843/72 (Austria): 3 D.R. 32. The second sentence is quoted from the Judgment of the Court in the *Belgian Linguistic Cases* § 9.

des États contractants. Si une mesure de l'État porte atteinte à un tel droit à l'égard d'un groupe d'individus mais non a l'égard d'autres, son aspect discriminatoire demeure sans importance independante: ainsi qu'on l'a indiqué ci-dessus, la discrimination pourrait constituer une circonstance aggravante, mais la Convention serait enfreinte du seul fait que le droit dont il s'agit n'a pas été intégralement respecté.

D'autres dispositions, cependant, ne définissent pas avec précision les droits qu'elles ont pour objet de garantir. Parfois, en effet, la Convention emploie des expressions ou notions qui n'ont pas en elles-mêmes de portée exacte et généralement admise et auxquelles on ne saurait en attribuer une par voie d'interprétation. Ces dispositions laissent aux États une certaine marge d'appréciation en ce qui concerne l'accomplissement de leurs engagements. Si une mesure étatique reste en dedans de cette marge, elle est en principe conforme a la Convention; si elle la dépasse, il y a violation. Une certaine marge d'appréciation est également concédée aux États contractants par plusieurs articles qui autorisent des restrictions ou exceptions aux droits garantis. Il est enfin des dispositions qui abandonnent aux États, jusqu'à un certain point, le choix des moyens propres à réaliser un droit protégé, par exemple celles qui renvoient expressément à la legislation nationale.

Or, l'article 14 revêt une importance particulière par rapport aux clauses de la Convention qui, tout en consacrant un droit ou une liberté, laissent aux États un pouvoir discrétionnaire quant aux mesures à adopter en vue d'en assurer la jouissance. Il ne s'analyse pas en une disposition normative de la même nature que l'article 8 de la Convention ou l'article 2 du Protocole: il a trait aux modalités ou à l'étendue de la jouissance de droits et libertés déjà énumérés dans d'autres textes. Il se peut que des mésures différentes prises par un État envers différentes parties de son territoire ou de sa population n'entraînent aucun manquement à l'article de la Convention qui définit le droit considéré, mais que semblable différenciation comporte une violation si l'on apprécie la conduite de l'État sous l'angle de l'article 14. Il s'agirait alors de la violation non du seul article 14 mais du droit en question, tel qu'il est énoncé par l'article pertinent en combinaison avec l'article 14: l'individu au détriment duquel un État enfreint l'article 14 ne jouit pas, en fait, de pareil droit ou liberté selon les modalités ou le degré que prescrit la Convention, envisagée dans son ensemble.

In substance then, Article 14 is not equivalent in function to the second paragraph of Articles 8–11, and other permitted restrictions, but is auxiliary in that it adds a separate control of the exercise of rights and freedoms.

without discrimination/sans distinction

No definition of this word is offered in the Convention, but various definitions are to be found in contemporary conventions. So discrimination is in employment and occupation is described as including

> any distinction, exclusion or preference ... which has the effect of nullifying or impairing equality of opportunity or treatment in employment or occupation.[1]

This formulation is taken over into the U.N. Convention on Racial Discrimination,[2] Article 1 of which provides that:

> In this Convention, the term 'racial discrimination' shall mean any distinction, exclusion, restriction or preference based on race, colour, descent or national or ethnic origin, which has the purpose or effect of nullifying or impairing the recognition, enjoyment or exercise on an equal footing, of human rights and fundamental freedoms in the political, economic, social, cultural or any other field of public life.[3]

In the U.N.E.S.C.O. Convention against Discrimination in Education 1960, Article 1, discrimination

> includes any distinction, exclusion, limitation or preference which being based on race, colour, sex, language, religion, political or other opinion, national or social origin, economic condition or birth, has the purpose or effect of nullifying or impairing equality of treatment and in particular ...

These definitions, adopted as they are by a large number of States including most if not all the contracting parties to the Convention, must be of persuasive authority in interpreting Article 14.

A number of important elements may be noticed in them. First, they all define discrimination in terms of exclusion and preference, these

---

[1] I.L.O. Convention No. 111 (Discrimination in respect of Employment and Occupation) Article 1 (*a*).

[2] Adopted by U.N. General Assembly Resolution 2106: xx (19.1.1966) to enter into force after twenty-seven ratifications. See also the earlier Declaration in General Assembly Resolution 1904: xviii (20.11.1963).

[3] Article 1 (*b*) of the draft Convention prepared by the U.N. Commission of Human Rights, on the Elimination of all Forms of Religious Intolerance, is, apart from the reference to religion, identical: *Commission Report*, E/4322 (March 1967). U.N.E.S.C.O. declarations on race and racism were adopted from 1950 to 1967; and the Convention on Racial Discrimination had 108 parties by 1982. A Convention on the Suppresion and Punishment of the Crime of Apartheid was adopted in the U.N. General Assembly in 1973.

being its two essential forms, the presence of one entailing the presence of the other. So in an English case, it was said:

The Railways Clauses Consolidation Act 1845, used the terms 'prejudicing' or 'favouring', and the Railway and Canal Traffic Act 1854 . . . used the terms 'preference and advantage' and 'prejudice and disadvantage' and in no case, so far as I have observed, have these expressions been regarded as other than expressions of the same thing from different points of view.[1]

Secondly, the definitions set equality of rights or of treatment opposite to discrimination, so that non-discrimination and equality of treatment *are* equivalent. So in the I.L.O. Convention on Equal Remuneration 1951[2]

the term 'equal remuneration for men and women workers for work of equal value' refers to rates of remuneration established without discrimination based on sex.

Thus discrimination and non-discrimination are relational terms, so that whether we speak of disadvantage, equality, or advantage,[3] we are speaking of treatment of one person or group as measured by the treatment, or the standard of treatment, of another person or group. So

The word 'equal' implies that the right so enjoyed must be equal in measure to the right enjoyed by somebody else. . . . A right which is unconditional and independent of that enjoyed by other people cannot with accuracy be described as an 'equal right'. 'Equality' necessarily implies the existence of some extraneous criterion by reference to which the content is to be determined.[4]

The court developed the notion of equality further:[5]

It is perhaps not easy to define the distinction between the notions of equality in fact and equality in law; nevertheless it may be said that the former notion excludes the idea of a merely formal equality; that is, indeed what the

[1] *South of Scotland Electricity Board* v. *British Oxygen Co. Ltd.* [1959] 2 A.E.R. 225 (HL) *per* Lord Reid at 248.

[2] No. 100, Article 1 (6).

[3] In what follows 'disadvantage' is to be understood to comprise exclusion, restriction, hardship, denial, while 'advantage' comprises preference, privilege, and benefit.

[4] *Minority Schools in Albania* [1935] P.C.I.J.: A/B 64 at 25 *per* Judges Sir Cecil Hurst, Rostworowski, and Negulesco: in Joint dissenting opinion.

[5] P.C.I.J.: A/B 64 at 19. The court was considering the clause 'minorities will enjoy the same treatment and security in law and in fact as other Albanian nationals' in Article 5 (1) of the Albanian Declaration of 2 October 1921.

Court laid down in its Advisory Opinion of September 10, 1923[1] . . . in which it said that: 'There must be equality in fact (égalité de fait) as well as ostensible legal equality (égalité formelle on droit) in the sense of absence of discrimination in the words of the law.'

Equality in law precludes discrimination of any kind; whereas equality in fact may involve the necessity of different treatment (traitements différents) in order to attain a result which establishes an equilibrium between diferent situations.

The court has in later cases used the expresssion 'different treatment/ traitement différentiel' to describe the factual rather than the legal element in discrimination.[2]

In the *South West Africa Cases* (*Second Phase*) Judge Tanaka devoted a large part of his dissenting opinion to a forceful analysis of the notions of discrimination and equality. In conclusion he said:

The principle of equality does not mean absolute equality, but recognizes relative equality, namely different treatment proportionate to concrete individual circumstances. Different treatment must not be given arbitrarily; it requires reasonableness, or must be in conformity with justice, as in the treatment of minorities, different treatment of the sexes regarding public conveniences, etc. In these cases the differentiation is aimed at the protection of those concerned, and it is not detrimental and therefore not against their will. . . . [The practice of apartheid is fundamentally unreasonable and unjust. The unreasonableness and injustice do not depend upon the intention or motive of the Mandatory, namely, its *mala fides*. Distinction on a racial basis is in itself contrary to the principle of equality, which is of the character of natural law, and accordingly illegal.]

The third element to be noticed in the definitions is that of aim, expressed in two of them and implied by the term 'based on' in all of them. It is perhaps this element which most often characterizes discrimination, though, as Judge Tanaka has shown, it is not essential; differentiation between individuals or groups may be necessary in many social policies which serve the community, but where the differentiation is aimed against an individual or group then there is discrimination.

The point at which different treatment becomes discrimination

---

[1] *German Settlers in Poland* [1923] P.C.I.J.: B 6 at 24. Compare *Oscar Chinn Case* [1934] P.C.I.J.: A/B 63 at 110 *per* judge Anzilotti: 'Quid juris, s'il agit d'une impossibilité de fait et qui laisse subsister le droit, pour les tiers, d'exercer l'industrie dont il s'agit, mais qui toutefois est la conséquence nécessaire et directe d'un acte du gouvernement.'

[2] Ibid. at 87; *U.S. Nationals in Morocco Case* [1952] I.C.J. Rep. 185.

must be determined in the light of the social situation. So in interpreting a non-discrimination clause in the Constitution of Ceylon,[1] the Judicial Committee of the Privy Council said:

> Standards of literacy, of property, of birth, or of residence are . . . standards which a legislature may think it right to adopt in legislation on citizenship, and it is clear that such standards though they may operate to exclude the illiterate, the poor and the immigrant to a greater degree than they exclude other people, do not create disabilities in a community as such, since the community is not bound together as a community by its illiteracy, its poverty or its migratory character, but by its race or its religion.[2]

In India the Supreme Court has investigated differentiation in a number of social contexts in order to see whether it was contrary to Article 14 of the Constitution; and it has found differentiation reasonable, which was based on geography,[3] the character of a particular trade or calling,[4] the need to introduce a reform gradually,[5] the necessity of preventing only the aggravated forms of a mischief,[6] or on a balance of costs and benefit in administration.[7]

Social policies, serve the community, but where the differentiation is aimed against an individual or group then there is discrimination.

The point at which different treatment becomes discrimination must then be determined in the light of the social situation and the measures adopted or action taken. So:

> . . . the Court following the principles, which may be extracted from the legal practice of a large number of domestic states, holds that the principle of

---

[1] *Ceylon (Constitution and Independence) Order in Council 1946*, s. 29 (2): 'No law shall . . . (*b*) make persons of any community . . . liable to disabilities or restrictions to which persons of other communities . . . are not made liable.' The *Indian and Pakistani Residents (Citizenship) Act 1949* was held not *ultra vires* the Constitution, though its residence requirements were in conflict with the migratory habits of the Indian Tamils. . . . For the notion of a 'community' see the *Greco-Bulgarian Communities Case* [1930] P.C.I.J.: B 17; and *Keren Kayemeth Leisrael Ltd.* v. *Members of the Arab Mazareeb Tribe* [1942] 2 A.E.R. 570 P.C.: a 'fluctuating body' of nomads held capable exercising rights of occupation of land.

[2] *Pillai* v. *Mudanayake* [1953] A.C. 514 PC.

[3] *State of Punjab* v. *Ajaib Singh* [1953] S.C.R. 254.

[4] *State of Bombay* v. *Barbara* [1951] S.C.R. 682.

[5] *Biswambhar* v. *State of Orissa* [1954] S.C.R. 842.

[6] *Sakhwant* v. *State of Orissa* [1955] 1 S.C.R. 1004.

[7] *State of Bombay* v. *United Motors* [1953] A.I.R.: SC 252 (tax exemption of small group of individuals justified on ground that the tax recoverable would not be worth the cost of its collection).

equality of treatment is violated if the distinction has *no objective or reasonable justification*. The existence of such a justification must be assessed in relation to the *aim and effects of the measure* under consideration, regard being had to the principles that normally prevail in democratic societies. A difference of treatment in the exercise of a right laid down in the Convention must not only pursue a legitimate aim: Article 14 is likewise violated when it is clearly established that there is no reasonable relationship of *proportionality between the means employed and the aim* sought to be realised.

In attempting to find out in a given case whether or not there has been an arbitrary distinction, the Court cannot disregard those legal and factual features which characterise the life of the society in the State which as a Contracting Party, has to answer for the measure in dispute.[1]

The Commission has had to consider complaints of discrimination in many applications, often manifestly ill-founded. But at least those based on grounds of sex, religion, property, and language demand consideration here, though the grounds enumerated in Article 14 are not exhaustive.

Sex. Issue of discrimination against women in relation to men have been seldom raised under the Convention, and have not in any reported case involved its interpretation. Differentiation between married and unmarried or divorced women, in contributions required and benefits obtained under the Netherlands pensions statute, was found not to be discriminatory:

The distinction is made in a legitimate interest taking into account the general family pattern of the society, and is not out of proportion to the general purpose of the legislation concerned, namely to provide for an adequate standard of living for old people and survivors.[2]

The penalization of homosexual relations has already been described under Article 8. The differentiation between male and female homosexuality was considered rather evasively by the Commission,[3] and wholly avoided by the Court.[4] The Commission had before it the law and practice in the Federal Republic of Germany, and a most interesting explanation by the Government for its reasons:

a. it is generally admitted that there are comparatively few female homosexuals compared with males.

---

[1] *Belgian Linguistic Cases* Judgment (23.7.1965) § 10.
[2] 4130/69 (Netherlands): 38 *Recueil* 9.
[3] 5935/72 (F.R.G.) 3 D.R. 46.
[4] *Dudgeon* (U.K.): Judgment No. 45 (22.10.1981) § 69.

b. Experience shows that adult female homosexuals prefer partners of their own age.
c. It is generally admitted that these women seldom change their partners.
d. It follows that homosexual relationships between an adult woman and a girl under age are very rare.
e. In the rare cases of the seduction of a girl by an adult woman experience shows that the girl's personal development and the insertion in society are not generally affected because female homosexuality does not usually show itself in public.

The situation was fundamentally different as regards male homosexuality.
a. This was much more frequent.
b. Male homosexuals prefer young partners.
c. These homosexuals frequently change their partner.
d. It follows that young men are much more exposed to the risk of homosexual relations with adults than girls.
e. On account of the tendency of masculine homosexual couples to show themselves in public, a young man or adolescent is much more exposed to social isolation and conflicts with society.

The Commission, combining Article 14 with Article 8, held that the differentiation was justified by the need to prevent social danger:

In the distinction which it draws between the two forms of homosexuality German law is based on the principle that the serious interference with private life constituted by criminal proceedings for a sexual offence is only justified by a clearly established need for social protection.

The necessity of social protection or the existence of a corresponding danger thus constitute the criteria justifying the difference of treatment.

In the Commission's opinion this is a reasonable criterion. Does it however constitute an objective criterion in the sense that it can be used with certainty without being subject to variable or arbitrary interpretation?

The establishment of the existence of a danger making it necessary to protect a social category must be based on various concordant analyses of the position, and particularly in the instant case, those of psychologists, sociologists and specialists in social protection. It is certain that such studies have been made on several occasions in the Federal Republic of Germany both on adult homosexual behaviour and on the effects on the personality of adolescents of homosexual relationships with adults. They have lead to convincing conclusions as to the existence of a specific social danger in the case of masculine homosexuality. This danger results from the fact that masculine homosexuals often constitute a distinct socio-cultural group with a clear tendency to proselytise adolescents and that the social isolation in which it involves the latter is particularly marked.

The Commission therefore considers that the criterion of the need for social protection is, in the field in question, an objective criterion.

The threat and employment of criminal sanctions constitute moreover means which are not disproportionate to the object pursued, i.e. that of protection.

The Commission concludes that the difference in treatment is prima facie objective and reasonable and that there is accordingly no appearance of discrimination in an interference with private life.

The Commission has had to consider complaints of discrimination on grounds of sex, religion, property, and language; and it may be observed here that the grounds enumerated in Article 14 are not exhaustive.

The element of aim or purpose which characterizes discrimination as opposed to different treatment and which links Articles 14 and 18 of the Convention may be illustrated from applications to the Commission concerning taxation, the language of instruction used in schools, and the exemption of ministers of religion from military service.

Taxation. In 1957 Law No. 44 was enacted in Iceland, which provided for taxation on capital assets of both individuals and corporations. The applicants, who had been assessed for tax under this law, alleged before the Commission that it was an expropriation of property contrary to Article 1 of the Protocol,[1] but that its incidence was discriminatory in that the law contained certain exemptions, in particular for co-operative societies, and preferential treatment for particular forms of enterprise. The Commission held that:

...with regard to the complaint that Law No. 44 of 1957 violates Article 14 of the Convention in that it accords different treatment to co-operative societies and joint stock companies, it is to be observed that this is a common incident of taxation laws that they apply in different ways or in different degrees to different persons or entities in the community; whereas, accordingly, the mere fact that Law No. 44 may not act upon co-operative societies and joint stock companies in exactly the same way, does not afford any sufficient basis for calling in question its character as a legitimate means of taxation for the purposes of Article 1 of the Protocol.[2]

---

[1] See below under that Article.
[2] 511/59: 3 *Yearbook* 424. The property rights of individuals and corporate bodies were distinguished in 7742(76) (F.R.G.) 14 D.R. 146.

In other words, the tax differential between co-operative societies and companies was a necessary component of the whole taxation scheme and was not aimed against the companies as such.

Language. The use of the French and Flemish languages as vehicles of instruction in Belgian schools and universities was considered by the Commission at length in the *Belgian Linguistic Cases*. Having made the general observations, already quoted above, on the place and function of Article 14 in the Convention, the Commission went on to say:

De l'avis de la majorité de la Commission, un régime linguistique de l'enseignement organisé sur un base territorialiste ne serait pas nécessairement contraire à la Convention. Un tel système pourrait se justifier par des considérations majeures d'ordre administratif, financier ou autre. La Commission ne croit pourtant pas devoir entrer dans la discussion de la légitimité des différentes conceptions sur lesquelles un régime linguistique peut être édifié. En effet, il lui incombe seulement d'examiner si et dans quelle mesure pareil régime—quelle que soit la conception générale dont il se réclame—respecte les droits et libertés garantis. . . .[1]

But, the Commission said that different treatment, creating disadvantages for some groups and advantages for others, was not the sole criterion

. . . il ne suffit pas de constater que la législation litigieuse, si on la considère dans son ensemble, a pour but et pour effet de favoriser en région flamande, quant à la jouissance de certains droits garantis par la Convention, les habitants d'expression néerlandaise et de défavoriser dans la même région les habitants francophones, ainsi que d'ailleurs les Flamands qui désireraient faire donner à leurs enfants une instruction en française. Il ne découle pas de cette seule constatation que toutes les distinctions introduites par la dite législation soient nécessairement incompatibles avec l'Article 14 de la Convention.

Il faudra encore rechercher si ces distinctions s'analysent, uniquement en des faveurs ou des privilèges accordés à la population d'expression néerlandaise ou si, au contraire, elles imposent à la population francophone des rigueurs, des inégalités ou des désavantages. Dans le premier cas, la Commission ne serait pas en mesure de conclure à l'existence d'une violation de l'Article 14. D'autre part, dans la seconde hypothèse, on devra se demander si les rigueurs inégalités ou désavantages en question peuvent se justifier par des nécessités d'ordre administratif, financier ou autre ou si, au contraire, ils sont délibérément imposés à la population francophone dans le but de léser ses intérêts ou d'affaiblir sa position dans la communauté.[2]

---

[1] Report of the Commission (24.6.1965) § 405.   [2] Ibid., § 425.

Religious duties. The application by the Jehovah's Witness, already
considered under Article 9, raised issues of discrimination under
Article 14.[1] The question was whether the legislation had a discriminatory effect on him, which exempted from compulsory military
service ministers of the Catholic and Evangelical churches and 'ministers of other religions, whose principal occupation is their ministry
and whose function is equivalent' to that of the ministers already
described. The applicant maintained that 'as a minister of Jehovah's
Witnesses' he had been denied the benefit of this exemption.

The Commission, by a majority, stated the opinion, already quoted
from the *Belgian Linguistic Cases*, that

> In certain cases, Article 14 may be violated in a field dealt with by another
> Article of the Convention, although there is no violation of that Article. . . . [I]f
> a restriction which is in itself permissible under paragraph (2) of one of the
> above Articles [8 to 11] is imposed in a discriminatory manner, there would be
> a violation of Article 14 in conjunction with the other Article concerned. The
> situation under Article 4 is similar.

The Commission went on to conclude unanimously that there had
been no breach of Article 14 in conjunction with Article 4, since:

> The significance of the German law is that the real basis of the distinction
> made by it is in the function performed by different categories of ministers and
> not according to the religious community to which they belong. For these
> reasons, the criteria adopted in Article 11 of the German Act are not discri-
> minatory within the meaning of Article 14. They constitute a differentiation
> which must be considered to be reasonable and relevant . . . on the one hand,
> to the necessity of maintaining the effectiveness of the legislation regarding
> compulsory service and, on the other hand, the need of assuring proper
> ministerial service in religious communities.

There was differentiation then not between religious faiths[2] to the
disadvantage of one of them, but between the social functions of
ministers of religion.

---

[1] 2299/64: Report of the Commission (12.12.1966) § 40.
[2] In *Germany* an interesting decision of the Landgericht, Fulda, is reported in A.D.
1950, No. 29. The Civil Procedure Code (Zivilprozessordnung) §§ 383 (1) and 385 provide that a clergyman may refuse to give evidence in court of matters communicated to
him in the exercise of his religious functions, unless the person communicating has
released him from the obligation of secrecy. The Concordat of July 1933, Article 9, had
given Catholic priests an absolute exemption from the duty to testify. The court held
that, while the Concordat was a treaty which was part of municipal law and prevailed
over the provisions of the code, the right to refuse to testify which is accorded could, on
the principles of equality, and of the religious neutrality of the State, be claimed by
Protestant clergy also.

ARTICLE 15

(1) In time of war or other public emergency threatening the life of the nation any High Contracting Party may take measures derogating from its obligations under this Convention to the extent strictly required by the exigencies of the situation, provided that such measures are not inconsistent with its other obligations under international law.

(2) No derogation from Article 2, except in respect of deaths resulting from lawful acts of war, or from Articles 3, 4 (paragraph 1) and 7 shall be made under this provision.

(3) Any High Contracting Party availing itself of this right of derogation shall keep the Secretary-General of the Council of Europe fully informed of the measures which it has taken and the reasons therefor. It shall also inform the Secretary-General of the Council of Europe when such measures have ceased to operate and the provisions of the Convention are again being fully executed.

1. En cas de guerre ou en cas d'autre danger public menaçant la vie de la nation, toute Haute Partie Contractante peut prendre des mesures dérogeant aux obligations prévues par la présente Convention, dans la stricte mesure où la situation l'exige et à la condition que ces mesures ne soient pas en contradiction avec les autres obligations découlant du droit international.

2. La disposition précédente n'autorise aucune dérogation à l'article 2, sauf pour le cas de décès résultant d'actes licites de guerre, et aux articles 3, 4 (paragraphe 1) et 7.

3. Toute Haute Partie Contractante qui exerce ce droit de dérogation tient la Secrétaire Général du Conseil de l'Europe pleinement informé des mesures prises et des motifs qui les ont inspirées. Elle doit également informer le Secrétaire Général du Conseil de l'Europe de la date à laquelle ces mesures ont cessé d'être en vigueur et les dispositions de la Convention reçoivent de nouveau pleine application.

This Article, based upon a United Kingdom draft amendment[1] to the original Consultative Assembly Recommendations, underwent no substantive change in the preparatory work, save for the addition of Article 7 in paragraph (2).

It appears in almost identical form in the European Social Charter, 1961, Article 30.[2]

public emergency threatening the life of the nation/ danger public menaçant la vie de la nation

In the *Lawless Case*, the court said:[3]

... in the general context of Article 15 ... the natural and customary meaning of the words 'other public emergency threatening the life of the nation' is sufficiently clear; ... they refer to an exceptional situation of crisis or emergency (*une situation de crise ou de danger exceptionnel et imminent*) which affects the whole population[4] and constitutes a threat to the organized life (*une menace pour la vie organisée*) of the community of which the State is composed.

The court stresses two elements in particular. First, the emergency must be nation-wide in its effects, so that however severe the local impact of an emergency may be, it will not, in the absence of that condition, be a 'public emergency' in the sense of paragraph (1). Secondly, the threat must be to organized life, which suggests that the emergency does not have to be one in which 'the life of the nation' as such is threatened with extinction, but one in which there is such a breakdown of order or communications[5] that organized life cannot, for the time being, be maintained.

---

[1] *T.P.* ii. 355, 424–5.

[2] Compare also European Convention on Establishment 1955, Article 28.

[3] 4 *Yearbook* 472–5.

[4] Compare Report of the Commission, § 90: 'exceptional and imminent danger or crisis affecting the general public, as distinct from particular groups': *C.E.D.H.* Ser. B (1960–1) at 82. The first version of Article 15 (1) had the expression 'the interests of the people' instead of 'the life of the nation'.

[5] Compare the descriptoin of the position shortly before the last factor which precipitated the Proclamation: '... despite the gravity of the situation, the Government had succeeded, by using means available under ordinary legislation, in keeping public institutions functioning more or less normally': 4 *Yearbook* 474. Compare *United Kingdom*: Emergency Powers Act 1964, s. 1, providing that a state of emergency may be declared 'if at any time it appears to Her Majesty that there have occurred, or are about to occur, events of such a nature as to be calculated, by interfering with the supply and distribution of food, water, fuel or light, or with the means of locomotion, to deprive the community, or any substantial portion of the community, of the essentials of life.'

In applying this construction to the factual situation in the case before it, the court enumerated four factors from which it found that the Irish Governments had 'reasonably deduced the state of public emergency, which it proclaimed: the existence in the Republic of Ireland of a secret army engaged in unconstitutional activities and using violence to attain its purposes; its operations outside the territory of the Republic, which seriously jeopardized the relations of the Republic with the United Kingdom; the steady increase in terrorist activities from the autumn of 1956 and, finally, the homicidal ambush on the night of July 3/4[1] near the border but in the territory of Northern Ireland, and not long before 12 July (the anniversary, well remembered in Ireland, of the Battle of the Boyne, 1690).'

to the extent strictly required by the exigencies of the situation/dans la stricte mesure où la situation l'exige

Given the large sense in which 'public emergency' is to be understood in Article 15 (1), this limitation is difficult to construe and apply in any given emergency. The measures in question are *ex hypothesi* measures restricting or stopping the exercise or enjoyment of rights or freedoms guaranteed.

The Commission found that the evidence offered by the regime of 'the colonels' in Greece did not show the existence of a public emergency threatening the life of the nation in April 1967;[2] in particular, there was no demonstration of an imminent threat of political instability or disorder, or of the Communist take-over by force of arms; and the work stoppages were on a scale comparable to those being experienced in other European Countries.

The Commission has stated that, where there is a critical situation in the country concerned, it will not take Article 15 into consideration if it has not been relied on by the respondent Government.[3] But it will consider it, in its determination of whether the application is incompatible or manifestly ill founded, if it has been invoked.[4]

---

[1] The Commission had also named these factors in the emergency, and described them more fully: in particular under the third factor it found that the Irish Government was 'entitled to give substantial weight to its obligation under international law to prevent its territory from being used as a base for attacks upon a neighbouring territory': *C.E.D.H.* Ser. B (1960–1) at 88.

[2] *Denmark, Norway, Sweden and Netherlands* v. *Greece* 3321–3/67: 3344/67 Report (5.11.1969).

[3] *McVeigh et al.* 8022/77 (U.K.) 25 D.R. 15.

[4] 5727/72 (U.K.) 14 D.R. 5.

The Commission considered in the first *Cyprus Case*[1] that it was competent to pronounce:

on the existence of a public danger which under Article 15 . . . would grant to the Contracting Party concerned the right to derogate from the obligations laid down in the Convention,

and that, while

the Government should be able to exercise a certain measure of discretion,[2] in assessing the extent strictly required by the exigencies of the situation

the Commission was also competent to pronounce whether the measures in fact met that requirement.

In the *Lawless Case* the court assumed the same principle:

it is for the Court to determine whether the conditions laid down in Article 15 for the exercise of the exceptional right of derogation have been fulfilled in the present case.[3]

but, in adjudicating on the state of emergency and on the necessity for the measures in issue, it did not invoke the notion of a margin of appreciation by the government in any form, but proceeded directly to an assessment of the facts before it in the light of the provisions of the Convention.

The notion of a margin of appreciation is to be found expressed in only one provision of the Convention, Article 1 (2) of the Protocol, under which a State may take certain measures which 'it deems necessary'. The other conditions, on which there may be restrictions or derogation of rights, and, in particular, what is necessary in a democratic society or what is strictly required by the exigencies of the situation, are capable of more than one interpretation. The first might be interpreted as meaning what the State considers to be necessary, or what the citizens in a democratic society would consider or accept as being necessary, or what is objectively necessary, to attain the end permitted; again what is strictly required may be determined by the State or by an objective criteria.

The notion of a margin of appreciation occupies a middle position in these approaches, and in using it the Commission comes nearest

---

[1] 176/56: 2 *Yearbook* 177.

[2] For further applications of the notion of a margin of appreciation see 735/60: 3 *Yearbook* 319; 911/60: 4 *Yearbook* 219; 1068/61: 5 *Yearbook* 285; 1167/61 *Yearbook* 220; 1329/62: 5 *Yearbook* 208; 1449/62: 6 *Yearbook* 26 and 1628/62: *Recueil* (1963) iii.

[3] 4 *Yearbook* 472.

perhaps to the second suggested interpretation of what is necessary. The Commission, in considering whether a particular restriction or derogation is necessary or strictly required, does not, as of course, accept the judgment of the respondent government as conclusive; but it rather places itself in the position of the citizens in a democracy who, because they have accorded to their legislature and executive the responsibility for their government and the means of discharging it, will accept restrictions and derogations which appear, within the limits of reasonableness and good faith, necessary to government. These limits are set for the Commission by Article 18,[1] and the notion of the margin of appreciation, which covers in particular the knowledge of the relevant facts, and the judgment of what measures may be effective.

It would, it is believed, be mistaken to draw any inference from the fact that the court did not in the *Lawless Case* expressly adopt this notion. Its judgment is consistent both with the notion having been a factor and not having been a factor in it.

Since the determination of what is strictly required must turn on the facts of the particular case, it serves no purpose to quote in detail here the full examination given by the court to the circumstances surrounding the detention of Lawless.[2] However, two lines of thought in the judgment may be picked out as pointing to general criteria of what measures may be strictly required under Article 15: first that

in the judgment of the Court . . . in 1957 the application of the ordinary law had proved unable to check the growing danger which threatened the Republic of Ireland; . . . the ordinary criminal courts, or even the special criminal courts or military courts, could not suffice to restore peace and order; . . . therefore the Administrative detention—as instituted under the Act (Amendment) of 1940—of individuals suspected of intending to take part in terrorist activities, appeared, despite its gravity, to be a measure required by the circumstances,[3]

and, secondly, that the Act

---

[1] It may be observed that the Irish Government argued before the court in the *Lawless Case* that, provided measures taken under Article 15 are not contrary to Article 18, they are outside the control of the Convention bodies.

[2] The Commission had held by eight votes to six votes that the measures in the case of Lawless were strictly required in the ssense of Article 15 and a number of separate opinions were set out in the Report: *C.E.D.H.* Ser. B (1960–1) 114–56.

[3] 4 *Yearbook* 476–8.

was subject to a number of safeguards designed to prevent the abuses in the operation of the system of administrative detention.

These comprised constant supervision by Parliament, and the possibility of reference of cases of detention to a Detention Commission with power to order release. Further, the Irish Government had made a public declaration that it would release any detainee prepared to give an undertaking not to engage in the illegal activities in question. The court concluded that the measures neither went beyond what was strictly required under Article 15 nor offended against Article 18.

Two criteria at least are then indicated: that measures derogating from rights under Articles 5 and 6 may be regarded as strictly required if there is a proved inadequacy[1] or breakdown of the ordinary means of law enforcement, and if there are safeguards in some form against abuse of the powers taken.

It is plain, as was stated by the Commission in the *de Becker Case*,[2] that the continuing derogation of rights will not be justifiable under the Convention after the emergency has ceased.

not inconsistent with its other obligations under international law/pas en contradiction avec les autres obligations découlant du droit international

It is not easy to see in what circumstances this clause could be applied so as to invalidate a derogation of rights under Article 15. It must include obligations under treaty and under customary international law, and introduces a purely legal restriction on the right to derogate, which is in rather odd contrast to the other factual criteria in the Article. It was not invoked on behalf either of the Irish Government or Lawless in the *Lawless Case*, but the court considered that it had a duty to determine *ex officio* whether the condition imposed by the clause had been satisfied; it stated that no facts had come to its knowledge to suggest that the condition had not.[3]

The second paragraph of Article 15 forbids the derogation even in time of war or public emergency of certain enumerated rights. Since certain of these rights are themselves qualified in the Articles setting them out, that is to say, in Articles 2 and 7, the inference could be

---

[1] 214/56: Report of the Commission, 155–8.
[2] e.g. 'Psychological and political obstacles to their effective use': Report of the Commission at 115, *per* Sir Humphrey Waldock, President.
[3] 214/56: Report of the Commission, 480–2.

drawn that the only rights under the Convention, which can be strictly described as fundamental and inalienable are those guaranteed by Articles 3 and 4 (1).

shall keep the Secretary General of the Council of Europe fully informed/tient le Secrétaire Générale ... pleinement informé

That this clause does not require *prior* notification of derogation of rights under Article 15 is shown by the finding of the court that the notice in the *Lawless Case* by the Irish Government to the Secretary General twelve days after the measures were taken had been given 'without delay'. The court added that Article 15 did not require a contracting State to promulgate the notice in its own territory.[1]

ARTICLE 16

Nothing in Articles 10, 11 and 14 shall be regarded as preventing the High Contracting Parties from imposing restrictions on the political activity of aliens.

Aucune des dispositions des articles 10, 11 et 14 ne peut être considérée comme interdisant aux Hautes Parties Contractantes d'imposer des restrictions à l'activité politique des étrangers.

Originally limited to Article 10 and 11, this Article was introduced in the Committee of Experts, and extended to Article 14, as necessary to avoid any claim of discrimination.

The political activity of aliens may be internally directed, and here it must be presumably taken to cover participation by vote, or otherwise, in the elections envisaged in Article 3 of the Protocol, or externally to their own or other countries, and might in certain cases engage the responsibility of the State of residence.

The Article has not been invoked in any application before the Commission.

---

[1] 4 *Yearbook* 484–6. Here again the Convention fails to provide publicity to individuals of their rights under it. However, Committee of Ministers Resolution (56) 16 requires the Secretary General to circulate notifications. For examples of notifications under Article 15 (3) see 1 *Yearbook* 47–8; 2 *Yearbook* 48–51.

ARTICLE 17

Nothing in this Convention may be interpreted as implying for any state, group or person any right to engage in any activity or perform any act aimed at the destruction of any of the rights and freedoms set forth herein or at their limitation to a greater extent than is provided for in the Convention.

Aucune des dispositions de la présente Convention ne peut être interprétée comme impliquant pour un État, un groupement ou un individu, un droit quelconque de se livrer à une activité ou d'accomplir un acte visant à la destruction des droits ou libertés reconnus dans la présente Convention ou à des limitations plus amples de ces droits et libertés que celles prévues à la dite Convention.

This Article was introduced in the Committee of Experts, at the instance of the Turkish representative, to give effect to an intention expressed in the Consultative Assembly.[1] We have first to ask what are the relations between it and other provisions of the Convention, and then to survey on the one hand State action and on the other action of individuals or groups, contrary to it.

The relation between Article 17 and the particular rights and freedoms, upon which it depends, has not been sufficiently explained in decisions of the Commission and Court. It remains unclear whether Article 17 introduces a new rule, in that, given that a Convention right or freedom is involved, Article 17 may be invoked and applied separately; or whether it is auxiliary only, the position of the given right or freedom having priority. The Commission, has said that Article 17 may be invoked in relation to a Convention right or freedom, if domestic remedies have been exhausted in regard to the latter;[2] and

---

[1] '... d'empêcher que les groupments totalitaires puissent exploiter en leur faveur les principes poses par la Convention, c'est à dire invoquer les droits de liberté pour supprimer les Droits de l'Homme': *First Session (1949)* pp. 1235–9. The C.P.R. Covenant Article 5 (1) is virtually identical.

[2] *Le Compte* 6878/75 (Belgium) 6 D.R. 79. Similarly, Articles 9–11 invoked by two former members of the Communist Party on its dissolution, considered to be not applicable since Article 17 was overriding and 'l'organisation et ce fonctionnement du parti ... constituent, dans les circonstances de la cause, une activité ou sens de l'Article 17': 250/57 (F.R.G.) 1 *Yearbook* 222.5.

again, where the imposition of a lawful penalty is seen as justified under Article 10 (2), there is no appearance of violation of Article 17 or 13.[1] But the Court has said that the 'absence of any interference with the rights of the applicants under Article 11 (1), releases the Court from having to consider Article 11 (2) or Articles 14, 17, or 18 and where there is a breach of a Convention provision found, it is not necessary to examine the case under Articles 17 or 18'.[2]

As regards action by the State, the Article is declaring that nothing in the Convention may be interpreted as implying a right of the State to perform any act, aimed at limiting the rights or freedoms guaranteed to a greater extent then is provided primarily in Articles 8 (2)–11 (2) and in Article 15. So, since the words 'Nothing in this Convention' must extend to Article 17 itself, it follows that the State, in countering the activities of those who are exercising Convention rights undermine it, may still not transgress those limitations.[3]

In the activities of individuals and groups, it has to be asked whether they are aimed at the destruction of the rights or freedoms of others; and, if so, is the activity the exercise of a Convention right or freedom, which is then invoked to defend it; and finally what is the extent of the authority of the State to punish or counter it.

We are in great part facing here the activities of the irregular fighters,[4] the terrorists or freedom fighters as they may be called. They use armed force and other violence for political ends, ranging from casual incidents of shooting, bombing, and arson to guerrilla warfare; or campaign in different ways for the establishment of totalitarian or discriminatory regimes. It may be said that the first of these activities are aimed at, and bring about the destruction of the rights and freedoms of others, and are in themselves a violation of Article 17, which is here autonomous. Campaigning may be defended by the invocation of Convention rights, particularly under Articles 9–11, and their applicability will depend on an assessment of the aims and political consequences of the capaign. As noted above, the Commission, in considering the dissolution of the Communist Party in the Federal

---

[1] 6782/74 (Belgium) 9 D.R. 13 (prosecution of pornographic publication).
[2] *Engel et al.* (Netherlands) Judgment No. 22 (8.6.1976) § 108; *Sporrong/Lönnroth* (Sweden) Judgment No. 52 (23.9.1982) § 76. In all these applications, Article 17 had been invoked by the applicants.
[3] Universal Declaration of Human Rights, Article 30, in substance the same as Article 17 does not have the final clause, and so could accord the State wider power.
[4] So named by Colonel G. I. A. D. Draper.

Republic of Germany, made no assessment in terms of Articles 9–11, but, simply resting on the judgment of the Constitutional Court,[1] concluded that:

le recours à dictature pour l'instauration d'un régime est incompatible avec la Convention de qu'il comporte la destruction de nombre des droits et libertés consacrés par la Convention . . .

However, in examining the application of members of a racist group in the Netherlands, the Commission went into Article 10, and Article 3 of the First Protocol, in detail, in regard in particular to spreading of racially discriminatory ideas and to the right of members of the group to be candidates in municipal elections.[2] It respected both provisions as defending in the circumstances the activities of the applicants:

The general purpose of Article 17 is to prevent totalitarian groups from exploiting in their own interests the principles enunciated by the Convention. To achieve that purpose, it is not necessary to take away every one of the rights and freedoms guaranteed from persons found to be engaged in activities aimed at the destruction of any of those rights and freedoms. Article 17 covers essentially those rights which, if invoked, will facilitate the attempt to derive therefrom a right to engage personally in activities aimed a the destruction of any of the rights and freedoms set forth in the Convention.

In countering activities aimed at the destruction of the rights and freedoms of others, the State is limited, under the interpretation of the Convention in two ways. First, past and no longer continuing activities cannot be taken into account:

Accordingly, Article 17 cannot be used to deprive an individual of his rights and freedoms permanently merely because at some given moment he expressed totalitarian convictions and acted consequently. Certainly Mr. de

---

[1] In confirming the dissolution of the Party, the Constitutional Court had held:
(1) Le Parti communiste d'Allemagne est anti-constitutionnel.
(2) Le Parti communiste d'Allemagne sera dissous.
(3) La création d'organismes de remplacement du Parti communiste d'Allemagne ou la continuation d'organismes déja existants, en tant qu'organismes de remplacement sont interdites.
(4) Les biens du Parti communiste d'Allemagne serait confisqués par la Republique Federale d'Allemagne et utilisés aux fins d'interéts communs.
[2] It left open the question whether Article 3 of the First Protocol in fact embraces municipal elections: *Glimmerveen/Hagenbeek* (Netherlands) 8348/76 and 8406/78: 18 D.R. 187.

Becker's past conduct may be considered as being within the meaning of Article 17 of the Convention, even though it occurred before the Convention came into force. This does not mean however that the Applicant is today stopped by the provision of that Article unless he tries to abuse the freedom of expression which he claims.[1]

Secondly, Articles 5 and 6, being the prime provisions governing countering measures, are not to be overridden by Article 17, given its final clause. So, when the Irish Government maintained that I.R.A. activities, in which Lawless was said to be engaged, were aimed at the destruction of rights and freedoms, the Court interpreted this as in effect a plea in bar, and first summarized the opinion of the Commission on the application:

... le but général de l'Article 17 est d'empêcher que des groupements totalitaires puissent exploiter en leur faveur les principes posés par la Convention; ... pour atteindre ce but il ne fallait cependant pas priver de tous les droits et libertés garantis par la Convention les individus dont on constate qu'ils se livrent a des activités visant à détruire l'un quelconque de ces droits et libertés; ... si on les invoquait, d'essayer d'en tirer le droit de se livrer effectivement a des activities visant a la destruction ... en ce qui concerne le cas présent, la Commission a estimé que, même si G. R. Lawless participait effectivement, au moment de son arrestation, aux activities de l'I.R.A., Article 17 ne l'empêchait pas de revendiquer la protection des articles 5 et 6 de la Convention, pas plus qu'il ne dispensait le Gouvernement irlandais de respecter des dispositions de ces articles ...

The court adopted this criterion, that Convention rights are overridden by Article 17 only in so far as they are being specifically exercised or relied on to further the prohibited purpose and said:

... cette disposition [Article 17] qui a une portée négative, ne saurait être interprétée a contrario comme purant une personne physique des droits individuals fondamentaux garantis aux articles 5 et 6; ... en l'espèce, G. R. Lawless ne se prévaut pas de la Convention en vue de justifier ou d'accomplir des actes contraires aux droits et libertés y reconnus, mais il a porté plainte pour privé des garanties accordées par les articles 5 et 6; ... par consequent la cour ne peut retenir, sur ce chef, les conclusions présentées par la Gouvernement irlandaise;[2]

---

[1] de Becker 214/56 (Belgium) Report No. 279: Judgment (27.3.1962).
[2] Lawless (Ireland) 332/57: Judgment No. 1 (1.7.1961): 4 Yearbook 451. As to the distinction between disciplinary and criminal sanctions: 5916/72 (U.K.) 42 Recueil 165.

The dilemma has been graphically expressed by the composer Arnold Schoenberg:

... a code of human rights lacks the capacity of defending itself against attacks and annihilation to the same extent as does democracy. Everything which one might undertake in their name would violate the human rights of the attackers—that as everything is undemocratic which might protect democracy. The last resort is only persuasion.[1]

In the last decade steps have been taken, internationally and in this and other countries in Europe, to cope with the irregular fighter. A number of United Kingdom statutes may be described.

The Hijacking Act (1971) implemented the Hague Convention for the Suppression of Unlawful Seizure of Aircraft, in force in October 1971.[2] Under it whoever 'unlawfully by the use of force or by threats of any kind, seizes the aircraft or exercises control of it 'may be sentenced to imprisonment for life; and the offence is added to the Extradition Act (1870) and Fugitive Offences Act (1967). Aircraft in military, customs, or police service are excluded, unless the taking is by a British national. The Suppression of Terrorism Act (1978) was enacted to enable the United Kingdom to ratify the European Convention on the Suppression of Terrorism,[3] which aims at collaboration in the handling of the irregular fighters. An important step is to deny them political status. Article 1 of this Convention states that an offence within the scope of the Convention 'shall not be regarded as a political offence or as an offence connected with a political offence or as an offence inspired by political motives'. Offences within the scope of the Convention are set out in an annex and include offences under the Convention on aircraft and on internationally protected persons, murder, and manslaughter, and offences

involving kidnapping, the taking of a hostage, serious unlawful detention, or involving the use of a bomb, grenade, rocket, automatic firearm, or letter or parcel bomb, if this use endangers persons.

It is also an offence within the Convention to attempt to commit any of these offences. However, reservations may be made to Article 1: Article 13. As regards extradition, Article 1 offences are to be listed in

---

[1] In Los Angeles in July 1947, and published in *Style and Idea* (1951) § 204.
[2] See also Convention for the Suppression of Unlawful Acts against the Safety of Civil Aviation, adopted in Montreal in September 1971.
[3] In force on 4.6.1978. Ratified by the United Kingdom on 24.7.1978.

extradiction agreements between the convention countries, if they are not already included: Article 3; and there is an obligation to prosecute an offender, who is for some reason not extradited: Article 7.

The Suppression of Terrorism Act (1978) implements this Convention effectively. Schedule 1 lists the offences covered, whether committed in the United Kingdom or abroad, and includes common law offences and under the Offences against the Person Act (1861); abduction; offences under the Firearms Act (1965), and Criminal Damage Act (1971); and offences under the Hijacking Act (1971); Protection of Aircraft Act (1973): 5.1. Further, an act committed in another convention country, which constitutes murder, manslaughter, kidnapping, false imprisonment, abduction, use of explosives or firearms, and is an offence within the Convention, is liable in the United Kingdom: 5.4.

Further, limits are set to extradition. The Extradition Act (1870) s. 3(1) prohibits the surrender of a criminal:

... if he proves that the requisition for his surrender has in fact been made with a view to try or punish him for an offence of a political character.

and to this the new Act adds:

or ... on acount of his race, religion, nationality, or political opinions, or that he might, if surrendered, be prejudiced at his trial, or punished, detained, or retricted in his personal liberty, by reason of his race, religion, nationality, or political opinions: s. 2(1).

The Taking of Hostages Act (1982) implements the International Convention against the Taking of Hostages.[1]

These Conventions, and the United Kingdom Statutes, go far in their working definitions of irregular fighting, and their policy is reflected in the statement in the Seven Nations Summit Meeting in Venice (22.6.1980)[2] that it is a duty of States under international law:

to refrain from organising, instigating, assisting or participating in terrorist acts in another State, or acquiescing in organised activities within its territory towards the commission of such acts.

But the dilemma remains unresolved. The irregular fighter, though an outlaw, is to be accorded the same Convention rights as the ordinary citizen, including the practice of limiting extradition. Is this not 'acquiescence', condemned in the statement quoted?

---

[1] Adopted by the U.N. General Assembly (17.12.1979): UN 34/46; and analysed by Sami Shubber 'The International Convention against the Taking of Hostages', *B.Y.I.L.* (1981) 205.　　　　　　　　　　　　　　　　　　　　　[2] *B.Y.I.L.* (1980) 466.

ARTICLE 18

The restrictions permitted under this Convention to the said rights and freedoms shall not be applied for any purpose other than those for which they have been prescribed.

Les restrictions qui, aux termes de la présente Convention, sont apportées auxdits droits et libertés ne peuvent être appliquées que dans le but pour lequel elles on été prévenues.

This expression of the rule against *détournement de pouvoir* has its origin in the Recommendation of the Consultative Assembly to the Committee of Ministers.[1]

The restrictions, which may be imposed under the Convention, fall within a margin of appreciation of the State, acting through its legislature, executive or judiciary, but remain subject to supervision by the bodies established under the Convention. Article 18 then supplies one of the standards by which this supervision may be exercised. In this respect the standards are closely parallel to that of necessity in the second paragraphs in Articles 8–11, to the strict requirements exacted by the situation in Article 15, and to the control of State action in Article 17. Indeed, it is not always easy to distinguish on the facts between a restriction imposed for a purpose other than that permitted under the Convention and one which is not, or is no longer, necessary for the purpose or strictly required by the situation.

So the Commission has said that:

... in exercising supervision [it] must always bear in mind not only the extent of such limits, which must not exceed the margin of appreciation granted to the States, but also the aim of the said limits, since under Article 18 of the Convention such restrictions shall not be applied for any purpose other than those for which they have been prescribed. ...[2]

Where an applicant, complaining of detention in Ireland under the offences against the State (Amendment) Act 1940, alleged that the

---

[1] *T.P.* i. 224.

[2] 753/60: 3 *Yearbook* 318. Compare *United Kingdom*: *Pillai* v. *Mudanayake* [1953] A.C. 14 PC, where the Judicial Committee observed that, while the legislature may not do indirectly what it cannot do directly, 'the Court will not be astute to attribute to any legislature motives or purposes or objects, which are, beyond its power'; the legislative plan must be looked at as a whole to see what is 'the pith or substance'.

order was made, not because it was necessary to the preservation of public order, but in order to remove a political opponent of the Government, the Commission said:

... with respect to the Applicant's complaint that the Respondent Government detained him without trial for the improper purpose of ridding itself of a political opponent, application to the Detention Commission was a domestic remedy which, under the generally recognized rules of international law, it was incumbent upon him to exhaust....[1]

The application is on this point to be distinguished from the *Lawless Case*, since Lawless had not challenged the *bona fides* of the Irish Government in making an order of detention against him, and therefore had not put Article 18 in issue. The rejection of the application by the Commission for non-exhaustion of remedies implies that *détournement de pouvoir* under Article 18 may, in addition to being a standard of supervision of the Convention, be also a matter of application to the Commission under Articles 24 or 25. In other words, the Commission will have a duty *ex officio* to consider the consistency of restrictions with Article 18, if it is not directly invoked in an application.

In the *Lawless Case* the court distinguished between purpose of restriction under Article 18 and exigencies of the situation requiring them under Article 15, saying

... there is nothing to show that the powers of detention conferred upon the Irish Government by the Offences against the State (Amendment) Act 1940, were employed against him, either within the meaning of Article 18 of the Convention, for a purpose other than that for which they were granted, or within the meaning of Article 15 of the Convention, by virtue of a measure going beyond what was strictly required by the situation at that time.

The court pointed out under these two heads that first, Lawless had been detained on the demonstrably well-founded suspicion that he was engaged in unlawful activities contrary to the Offences against the State Act 1939; and secondly, that release from detention was offered to him on condition that he give a written undertaking to respect the Constitution and Laws of Ireland, and to desist from these unlawful activities, and was immediately granted upon his giving this undertaking.[2]

---

[1] 493/59: 4 *Yearbook* 322: for the character of the domestic remedies involved in this case, see below under Article 26.

[2] 4 *Yearbook* 480; *Kamma* (Netherlands).

We may distinguish then in the Convention between the object or purpose of restrictions or limitations on the rights and freedoms guaranteed, the permitted purposes being enumerated,[2] and the conformity of a particular restriction to one or more of those purposes. It may fail to conform in being imposed for a purpose other than those enumerated or in going beyond, either in duration, scope, or severity, what is strictly necessary.

Measures may be disproportionate given their purpose. The Commission has examined *ex officio* solitary confinement imposed on a detainee on remand, under both Articles 17 and 18;[3] and disciplinary measures in prison.[4]

---

[2] See Articles 4, 8–11 (second paragraphs), 15, 16, and Article 1 of the Protocol.
[3] 6038/73 (F.R.G.) 44 *Recueil* 115.
[4] *McFeeley et al.* 8317/78 (U.K.) 20 D.R. 44, 102.

SECTION II

ARTICLE 19

To ensure the observance of the engagements undertaken by the High Contracting Parties in the present Convention, there shall be set up:

(1) A European Commission of Human Rights hereinafter referred to as 'the Commission';

(2) A European Court of Human Rights, hereinafter referred to as 'the Court'.

Afin d'assurer le respect des engagements résultant pour les Hautes Parties Contractantes de la présente Convention, il est institué:

(*a*) une Commission européenne des Droits de l'homme ci-dessous nommée 'la Commission';

(*b*) une Cour européenne des Droits de l'homme, ci-dessous nommée 'la Cour'.

To ensure the observance of the engagements/afin d'assurer le respect des engagements

This provision defines the task of the Commission and the court, which is elaborated under succeeding Articles and will be further discussed under them. But there is place here for an examination in general of the character and limits of the competence of the Commission and in particular the line of demarcation between it and that of national authorities in contracting States. The functions of the court will be examined under particular provisions of Section IV.

General functions. The task of the Commission is to receive applications, by contracting States under Article 24 or by individuals under Article 25; to determine whether such an application is admisible on criteria expressly set out in Articles 26 and 27; to examine with the parties the merits (*fond*) of the application; to stand ready to assist the parties, as far as is practicable, to reach a friendly settlement within the framework of the Convention; and to draw up a report, containing a brief statement of the facts and the solution reached or, failing a friendly settlement, a statement of the facts and of the *opinion* of the Commission as to whether or not those facts disclose a breach of the Convention. Only the Committee of Ministers or the court can take a binding decision on the merits of an application.

The Commission may be broadly described then as a commission of inquiry, with certain limited advisory and mediatory functions; advisory, in that it provides the Committee of Ministers with what is in effect an advisory opinion on the application of the Convention, and mediatory, in that the parties may use it as a medium of settlement. But its task could not be properly described as mediation or conciliation in the usual international sense, and the term 'friendly settlement' was deliberately chosen for that reason.[1]

Certain features of the competence of the Commission to receive and deal with applications, and of its exercise, which are not expressly covered by Section III of the Convention, must now be described.

Provisional measures. The Commission is not competent to order provisional measures to be taken by the parties in an application before it,[2] nor is a contracting State under any obligation to refrain from taking any particular action, either administrative or judicial, by reason only that an application has been made to the Commission.[3] However, in some cases, where as in proceedings for extradition or deportation or the custody of a child, a decisive change in the position of an individual is to be made, government authorities have, voluntarily and in their discretion, stayed administrative action pending action by the Commission.

Relation to national courts. The relation of the Commission to national courts turns mainly around the question whether there can be any conflict of jurisdiction between them. In particular, it may be asked whether the procedure for application to the Commission can exclude the invocation of provisions of the Convention before national courts,

---

[1] 'étant donné que ce premier terme [conciliaton] est surtout employé en cas de conflits entre États, alors que la Convention s'occupe également des conflits entre États et particuliers': *T.P.* ii. 417, 489.

[2] e.g. 1584/62: *Recueil* (1963) iii (no competence to order psychiatric examination of an applicant). This does not, however, prevent the Commission from requiring that applications conform, in their presentation, to certain standards before they are accepted for consideration: see under Article 27 (2) below.

[3] 297/57: 2 *Yearbook* 212; 1420/62: 6 *Yearbook* 590, 626.

and how far the Commission can scrutinize and control the decisions of national courts.

An affirmative answer was given to the first question by the Tribunal Correctionel of Luxembourg.[1] The appellant had been fined by the Minister of Economic Affairs, in exercise of powers conferred on the Minister by a Grand-Ducal Decree of 8 November 1944, relating to price control. Article 6 of the Decree provided for prepayment in full of the fine imposed as a precondition of any appeal against it. The appellant contended, *inter alia*, that this condition was in conflict both with Article 11 (3) of the Luxembourg Constitution, as infringing natural rights, and also with Article 6 of the Convention, though in what precise respect the report of the judgment does not say. The court rejected the first contention on the ground that it was not, under the Law of Luxembourg, competent to examine the constitutionality of the decree, being *une véritable loi*. The basis of the rejection of the second contention is not wholly clear but appears to be twofold: that the provisions of Article 6 of the Convention were not self-executing in Luxembourg so as to create direct rights for individuals, and that therefore to determine the compatibility of Article 6 the Decree with Article 6 of the Convention would be analogous to judicial control of its constitutionality, not permitted to the court. The court said:

Attendu que ce principe,[2] s'il était admis, permettrait au Tribunal d'examiner le moyen ci-avant déclaré irrecevable, comme impliquant un contrôle juridictionnel de la constitutionnalité d'une loi, en ce sens que le Tribunal pourrait examiner si le principe posé dans l'Article 6 de l'Arrêt . . . est ou non contraire à l'Article 6 de la Convention. . . .

Attendu qu'il faudrait cependant encore, même dans ce cas, que les deux règles en conflit fussent des normes de même nature et ayant le même domaine d'application, c'est-à-dire en l'espèce des règles conférant des droits ou imposant des obligations directement aux sujets du droit ou gouvernés; . . .

Attendu que l'idée mise en avant de garantie collective [in the Convention] exclut déjà à elle seule l'intention de créer des effets juridiques directement dans la personne des gouvernés. . . .

Attendu qu'il résulte de l'ensemble des considérants qui précèdent que les droits et principes énoncés dans la Convention ne peuvent . . . pas être opposés ou invoqués directement devant les juridictions nationales internes, mais peuvent seulement fonder les recours internationaux établis et réglementés par la Convention.

---

[1] 24.10.1960; 4 *Yearbook* 622.
[2] Viz. that the Convention takes precedence over any national law.

Nevertheless while as appears from Article 1 above, the Convention does not oblige contracting States to incorporate the provisions of Section I into domestic law, it certainly does not exclude incorporation; and the establishment of *recours internationaux* under Articles 19, 24, and 25 cannot of itself preclude a national court from applying provisions of the Convention to a case before it, where the domestic law permits their invocation; nor, it seems, can it enable the court to refuse judgment on the applicability of a provision of the Convention, which is part of domestic law, and refer the complainant to the Commission, for that would defeat the rule of exhaustion of local remedies.[1]

The Commission has many times stated that it does not sit as an 'instance' above or addition to the normal national instances of trial and appeal, for it

was not set up as a higher court to examine alleged errors of law or fact committed by the domestic courts of the Contracting Parties acting wholly within their jurisdiction but, in accordance with Article 19 ... to ensure, observance of the obligations undertaken by the Parties in the Convention,[2]

so that

... at the stage of considering the admissibility of Applications under Article 25, [it] cannot deal with any errors of fact or law imputed rightly or wrongly to the domestic courts of Contracting States, save if and in so far as such errors appear to it to have involved violation of any of the rights and freedoms guaranteed by the Convention;[3]

The reference to the stage of admissibility does not imply that, at the later stage of consideration of the merits, the requirement that the error alleged must involve a breach of the Convention is no longer applicable; on the contrary it means that an application, which complains only of such errors without disclosing any facts which might involve a breach of the Convention, must be rejected out of hand as inadmissible. So, in consideration of the merits:

The Commission ... is not competent to substitute its own assessment of the evidence for that of the national courts, but can only pronounce as to

---

[1] Compare 1420/62: 6 *Yearbook* 626, '... far from obliging national courts to wait for the Commission to complete its work before they complete theirs, the Convention, in principle, provides for the opposite solution (Article 26) and assigns a mainly subsidiary role to the collective guarantee machinery set up by it.'

[2] 254/57: 1 *Yearbook* 152.

[3] 1103/61: 5 *Yearbook* 190.

whether the domestic courts have committed any abuse or procedural irregularity.[1]

For example:

> The task under the Convention is to decide whether the evidence for and against the accused has been presented in such a manner, and the proceedings have been conducted in such a way that he has had a fair trial [within the meaning of Article 6 (1)].[2]

Again, as regards domestic law,

> ... it should be stressed that it is not for the Commission to give a ruling on the application and the interpretation of domestic law by national courts unless the law itself constitutes a violation of the Convention or the domestic courts have committed such violation in the application or interpretation of this law;[3]

this statement embodies the principle laid down by the Permanent Court when it said:

> Le fait que les autorités judiciaires auraient commis une erreur dans le choix de la disposition légale, applicable en l'espèce et compatible avec le droit international, ne concerne que le droit interne et ne pourrait intéresser le droit international que dans la mesure ou une règle conventionnelle ou la possibilité d'un déni de justice entrerait en ligne de compte.[4]

Further, even where an application alleges a breach of the Convention in the interpretation or application of domestic law, the primary role of national courts must be recognized, and the Commission has pointed out that

> it is primarily for the domestic courts to interpret the legislation of the Contracting Parties, even in fields where the non-observance of such legislation constitutes a violation of the Convention; ... the Commission exercises in this respect a purely supervisory function and must carry out its task with caution.[5]

---

[1] 788/60 (*Austria* v. Italy): Report of the Commission (30.3.1963), para. 181; 899/60; 5 *Yearbook* 136; 8417/78 (Belgium) 16 D.R. 200.

[2] 343/57: 4 *Yearbook* 568. Similarly, the Commission may examine decisions of East German courts, which are outside the scope of the Convention *ratione loci*, 'to investigate whether, by agreeing to enforce them on its own territory, the Federal Republic of Germany did or did not act in accordance with the Convention': 448/59: 3 *Yearbook* 264.

[3] 458/59: 3 *Yearbook* 232. Compare 1140/61: *Recueil* [8] 57.

[4] *The Lotus* [1927] P.C.I.J.: ser. A, no. 10 at 24.

[5] 1852/63: *Recueil* (1965) i. See also 1169/61: 6 *Yearbook* 588–90.

This principle is also extended to applications where the constitutionality of a statute or order is challenged, and so

proceedings before the domestic courts of the Contracting Parties, including those relating to the question of the constitutionality of legislation, . . . concern the Commission, during its examination of the admissibility of an application, only in so far as they appear to involve a possible violation of any of the rights and freedoms limitatively listed in the Convention.[1]

However, the Commission is not precluded from examining provisions of domestic law and must do so where the Convention, as it does in a number of instances, makes express reference to domestic law. So in the application just cited,[2] the Commission said:

. . . under Article 7 the application of a provision of municipal penal law to an act not covered by the provision in question directly results in a conflict with the Convention, so that the Commission can and must take cognisance of allegations and of such false interpretation of municipal law;

Similarly, the Commission may have to consider whether a particular rule or regulation is a 'law', or whether a rule or a procedure has been duly 'prescribed by law', where provisions of the Convention require a basis of 'law' or a procedure 'prescribed by law'.[3]

However, the Commission has held that it is not enabled by Article 19 to consider or apply general principles of international law in isolation from provisions of the Convention: for example, the principle of compensation for a public act of expropriation of foreign property cannot be applied by the Commission because the Convention does not recognize it.[4]

Further, the Convention does not confer on the Commission,[5] or the Court:

any competence to declare invalid an Act passed by a national parliament, or to declare invalid an administrative order issued by a competent national authority, or to give a decision that a judgment of a national court cannot be enforced.

---

[1] 511/59: 3 *Yearbook* 394; 1466/62: *Recueil* (1963) ii; 1658/62: *Recueil* (1964) ii.
[2] 1852/63.
[3] In the *Netherlands*, the Hoge Raad (25.6.1963) held that 'law' in Article 9 (2) of the Convention included subordinate or delegated legislation: *Ned. Jur.* (1964) 595.
[4] *A. S. Company et al.* (F.R.G.) 7742/76 14 D.R. 146.
[5] *Iversen* (Norway) 1468/62 12 *Recueil* 80, 105.

It may be out of place to point out two interesting resemblances between the administration of the Convention and the function of the Judicial Committee of the Privy Council in the United Kingdom. First, the Judicial Committee has in criminal matters less the task of revision than that of maintaining standards of justice in the courts which are within its jurisdiction; so it has been observed by the Judicial Committee itself that

... it is the inherent prerogative right and, on all proper occasions, the duty, of the Queen in Council to exercise an appellate jurisdiction with a view not only to ensure as far as may be the due administration of justice in the individual case, but also to preserve the due course of procedure generally ... but the exercise of this prerogative is to be regulated by a consideration of circumstances and consequences; and interference by H.M. in Council in criminal cases is likely in so many instances to lead to mischief and inconvenience, that in them the Crown will be slow to entertain an appeal by its officers on behalf of itself or by individuals.[1]

So, the limitations which it imposes upon itself have been explained in terms which are apt to describe those under which the Commission deals with issues of fact, already passed on by national courts:

The Judicial Committee is not a revising court of criminal appeal: that is to say, it is not prepared or required to retry a criminal case, and does not concern itself with the weight of evidence, or the conflict of evidence or with inferences drawn from evidence, or with questions as to corroboration or contradiction of testimony, or whether there was sufficient evidence to satisfy the burden of proof. Neither it is concerned to review the exercise by the previous tribunal of its discretion as to permitting cross-examination of a witness as hostile or in awarding particular punishment.[2]

Secondly, although the Judicial Committee operates to all intents and purposes as a court, its conclusions are technically not judicial decisions, but advices to the Crown in its prerogative exercise of jurisdiction, and a separate order is made by the Queen in Council to give judicial effect to that advice. Similarly, the report of the Commission to the Committee of Ministers under Article 31 will contain an opinion, on the application of the Convention to the case in issue, a form of advice which the Committee of Ministers are not as a matter of law bound to accept, though it is to be expected that they would not without good reason reject it.

[1] *Regina* v. *Bertrand* [1867] .R. 1 PC 520, 530.
[2] *Muhammad Nawaz* v. *King-Emperor* [1941] L.R. 68 IA 126, 127.

Ex officio action. In performing its part in ensuring that engagements under the Convention are observed, the Commission may in certain cases have wider interests to protect than those of the particular applicant. The Commission has said:

que les obligations souscrites par les États contractants dans la Convention ont essentiellement un caractère objectif, du fait qu'elles visent à protéger les droits fondamentaux des particuliers contre les empiètements des États contractants plutôt qu'à créer des drots subjectifs et réciproques entre ces derniers; ... que le caractère objectif des dits engagements apparait également dans le mécanisme érigé dans la Convention pour en garantir le respect . . .; qu'un État contractant, lorsqu'il saisit la Commission en vertu de l'Article 24, ne doit . . . pas être considéré comme agissant pour faire respecter ses droits propres mais plutôt comme soumettant à la Commission une question qui touche à l'ordre public de l'Europe (an alleged violation of the public order of Europe).[1]

The notion of 'l'ordre public de l'Europe' was invoked more than once in the drafting of the Convention. The rapporteur M. Teitgen spoke of the Convention as creating 'un ordre juridique européen et un système de droit européen' and again as forming 'le dénominateur commun de nos institutions politiques'.[2]

The notion may be understood in one of several ways. *Ordre public* might be taken in the narrow sense, given it in judical usage as

l'ensemble des institutions et des règles destinées à maintenir dans un pays le bon fonctionnement des services publics, la sécurité et la moralité des rapports entre les particuliers et dont ceux-ci ne peuvent en principe écouter l'application dans leurs convention.[3]

Provisions of the Convention might then be seen as declaratory of standards of *ordre public* common to all the contracting States in Europe. But, apart from the fact that the content of *ordre public* must be variable from country to country, obstacles appear in the Convention itself to this view of 'l'ordre public de l'Europe'. First, while some provisions such as Articles 11, 12, or 14 might be characterized as a part of

---

[1] 788/60: 4 *Yearbook* 139. The English expression 'public order' is rather the opposite of 'public disorder' and is only approximately equivalent to *ordre public* in its normal sense.

[2] *T.P.* v (5–8.9.1949) 1164, 1299. For an extended study see G. van der Meersch, 'La Convention Européenne a-t-elle dans le cadre du droit interne une valeur d'ordre public;' *Vienna Colloquium*, 1965.

[3] H. Capitant, *Vocabulaire Juridique*, v°, cited op. cit.

ordre public in the narrow sense, others are positive rules of law, which could not be so characterized with bringing the whole function of *ordre public* into confusion. Secondly, in the Convention itself there is a distinction between those provisions which express rules of law and those which refer to the *ordre public* of contracting States: for the conditions, on which they may, consistently with the Convention, impose restrictions on rights and freedoms, are set out in terms which embody many of the commonly accepted elements of *ordre public*.[1]

At what is perhaps another extreme, 'l'ordre public de l'Europe' might be accorded a large, teleological meaning, recourse being had again to some of the language of the Preamble:

Considering that the aim of the Council of Europe is the achievement of greater unity ('une union plus étroite') between its Members and that one of the methods by which that aim is to be pursued is the maintenance and further realisation of Human Rights and Fundamental Freedoms.

But to fix our gaze upon the ideal of 'a more perfect union' could lead to a view of the Convention as a kind of instrument of unification of law and practice in Europe, placed in the hands of the Commission and the court. While it may well be that, as the result of the work of these two bodies, the contracting States will be moved to harmonize their law and practice in particular fields covered by the Convention, its provisions which prescribe the tasks and competence of the Commission and the court nowhere suggest that the unification or harmonization of law are to be the prime objectives they must set before themselves.

The meaning to be given then to 'l'ordre public de l'Europe', which is both effective and conformable to the Convention, lies somewhere between the other two, having some features of both. Broader than *ordre public* in its strict sense, it would describe certain characteristic elements of European order, which are built into the Convention and which may form part of an emergent international *ordre public*, in so far as they contain generally recognized principles governing the relations of State and individual. These are common social values, a number of rights and freedoms already acknowledged and established in legal form, and means of enforcement of these rights, which is

---

[1] See, for example, the second paragraph of Articles 8–11. The Fourth Protocol goes further in making express reference in Article 2 to *ordre public*, which appears in both French and English texts.

collective because there is a common interest in their maintenance; for no country is now an island. So the contracting States resolved:[1]

as the Governments of European countries which are like-minded and have a common heritage of political traditions, ideals, freedom and the rule of law, to take the first steps for the collective enforcement of certain of the Rights stated in the Universal Declaration.

and, in the words of the Commission,[2] their purpose was

not to concede to each other reciprocal rights and obligations in pursuance of their individual national interests but to realise the aims and ideals of the Council of Europe ... and to establish a common public order[3] ('un ordre public communautaire') of the free democracies of Europe.

But that part of 'l'ordre public de l'Europe' which is embodied in the Convention is not static, for it marks only 'the first steps'. Further steps continue to be taken not only in the conclusion of such instruments as the European Social Charter, and the European Conventions on Establishment, and on Extradition, and in the drafting of additional protocols to the Convention, but in the manifold work of the Council of Europe and other European institutions.[4] The conception and application of the provisions of the Convention must also move forward over time, as, for example, in the progressive abolition of the death penalty, for

it is of the very nature of a free society to advance in its standards of what is deemed reasonable and right. Representing as it does a living principle, due process is not confined within a permanent catalogue of what may at a given time be deemed the limits of fundamental rights.[5]

We can now perhaps see the ways in which the Commission may seek to protect the wider interests of the Convention, sometimes by *ex officio* action, and also the limitations upon that action.

First, the invocation of *ordre public* by a contracting State is, as will

---

[1] Preamble, fifth paragraph, echoing the words of Vattel, *the Law of Nations* (1758), cited by F. H. Hinsley, *Sovereignty* (C. A. Watts & Co., 1966), 194: 'Europe forms a political system in which the nations are bound together by their relations and their various interests into a single body ... a sort of republic, whose members—each independent but all bound together by a common interest—unite for the maintenance of order and the preservation of liberty.'

[2] 788/60: 4 *Yearbook* 138.

[3] Compare the second sense assigned to *ordre public* by Judge Sir Hersch Lauterpacht as embracing 'fundamental national conceptions of law, decency and morality': *Case concerning the Guardianship of Infants Convention (1902)* [1958] I.C.J. Rep. 61 at 90.

[4] See A. H. Robertson, *Human Rights in Europe*, 231 and generally.

[5] *Wolf* v. *Colorado* [1949] 338 U.S. 25, *per* Frankfurter J.

be seen below under particular Articles, subject to a measure of control by the Commission; for when a State

is bound by a treaty in relation to a particular subject-matter it can invoke public order only if, in case its action is challenged, it is prepared to submit the legality of its action to impartial decision. It is that jurisdiction which removes the notion of and recourse to *ordre public* from the orbit of uncertainty, pure discretion and arbitrariness, and which endows the treaty with the character of an effective legal obligation.[1]

But the Commission cannot exercise a general and unsolicited supervison of national authorities, whether executive or legislative, and it cannot, of its motion, initiate any general inquiry into the conditions of Convention rights and freedoms in a contracting State, a task assigned to the Secretary General under Article 57.[2] The Commission can only act on applications made to it under Articles 24 and 25; and even so it will not examine *in abstracto* the conformity of domestic legislation with the provisions of the Convention in a case where the applicant does not or cannot claim to be a 'victim', in the sense of Article 25, of its operation.[3]

On the other hand, the Commission is not, in dealing with an application, confined by this reasoning, or the formulation of the complaints, to be found in it. The Commission must of course satisfy itself that it has jurisdiction under the Convention to entertain the application; in particular, it must *ex officio* determine whether the applicant has observed the rule of exhausting local remedies.[4] But

la Commission a été instituée afin de veiller au respect des engagements assumés par les Parties Contractantes en vertu de la Convention et du Protocole additionnel. Chargée d'assurer la sauvegarde des droits de l'homme, elle interprète sa tâche comme impliquant le pouvoir, lorsqu'elle se trouve régulièrement saisie, d'examiner d'office l'ensemble du dossier, indépendamment de l'argumentation présenté par le requérant. Cette notion d'examen d'office domine toute sa jurisprudence.[5]

---

[1] *Per* Judge Sir Hersch Lauterpacht, 4 *Yearbook* 100.

[2] It needs hardly to be said, perhaps, that the Commission cannot itself initiate proceedings, by way of constitutional appeal or otherwise, in national courts on behalf of individuals, see 1516/62: *Recueil* (1963) ii.

[3] 290/57: 3 *Yearbook* 214; 867/60: 4 *Yearbook* 270: 'The Commission is competent to examine the compatibiity of domestic legislation with the Convention only with respect to its application to a person.' See also 2290/64: *Recueil* 22.

[4] See under Article 26.

[5] 261/57: 1 *Yearbook* 255: and numerous later decisions: 7604/76 (Italy) 14 D.R. 134; 7721/76 (Netherlands) 11 D.R. 209.

and

la Commission procède d'office à cette recherche afin de déterminer si l'objet de la plainte tombe de par sa nature même dans le champ de l'application de la Convention, sans que le requérant doive nécessairement se prévaloir d'un article de la Convention nommément désigné. . . .[1]

Here the Commission acts both for the protection of the applicant and to ensure observance of the Convention. Unless he has the assistance of a lawyer, the applicant is unlikely to follow the lines of the Convention clearly, or even to have read it; he may not have directly invoked any provision of it, or he may invoke provisions that are inapposite; here the Commission may *ex officio* place the facts, of which he complains, in their right context within the Convention. In this way too, possible breaches of the Convention, of which he does not directly complain, may be brought under review; but here it is to be observed that these must be breaches, of which he could be seen, on the facts of which he does complain, to be a 'victim' in the sense of Article 25.

So, where an applicant seeks to withdraw an application which he had made to the Commission, it must *ex officio* consider whether there are interests involved wider than those of the applicant himself, which would lead the Commission to retain the application; for example, the applicant may have complained of the operation of a statute or a rule of practice, which must inevitably affect others than himself or the application may raise an issue of the interpretation or application of the Convention, affecting law or practice in several or even all of the contracting States. Such factors will have the greater weight, if withdrawal is sought *after* the Commission has declared the application admissible. Other factors, which the Commission may have to take into account here are, on the one hand, the reasons for the withdrawal, and in particular the extent to which an individual may compromise his rights under the Convention.[2] and, on the other, the fact that, if the applicant refuses to pursue his application further, the Commission may have difficulty, if it retains it, in obtaining necessary evidence and generally in proceeding under Article 28. The task of the Commission

---

[1] 202/56: 1 *Yearbook* 192; 261/57: ibid. 257.

[2] Compare Article 28 (*b*) which requires that any friendly settlement must be based 'on respect for human rights as defined in this Convention'. For a case where the withdrawal of the application was a condition made by the government of a settlement, which the applicant found satisfactory, see 2339/64: *Recueil* 22. The Commission saw no reason to refuse the withdrawal.

then is to protect, so far as it can in every application to it, the common interest of all members of the Council of Europe in respect for and enforcement of Convention provisions, and therefore, when the Commission appears before the court, it is to perform that task rather than to defend the interests of the individual applicant.[1]

But, while in the *ex officio* action that the Commission may take there is some analogy between its role and that of a Prokurator-general or Ministère Public, in their responsibility for the 'protection of the law', the analogy must not be pressed too far, for the *ex officio* powers and duties of the Commission are only those that can be necessarily implied, but are also limited, by the provisions of the Convention defining its tasks.

An allied question arises here whether, and if so to what extent, the Convention can be said to permit waiver by individuals of rights and freedoms guaranteed. It is hardly to be denied that the individual cannot waive those rights under Articles 2, 3, and 4 (1), derogation from which the Convention forbids even in time of national emergency under Article 15. Though Article 7 is linked in Article 15 with them, it is less obvious that waiver of one or more of its provisions is inadmissible. Of other provisions of the Convention it might be necessary to make a distinction between those in which the rights guaranteed may be regarded as essentially personal to the individual in a given case, and those in the maintenance of which there is a public interest: for example, the individual may voluntarily forgo legal assistance for his defence without touching any principle of fair trial, but if he forgoes the right to a public trial[2] the consistency of the proceedings with Article 6 is not so clear, for it may be argued that the very notion of 'public hearing' in Article 6 (1) embodies a public as well as an individual right.

Construing the Convention. The Convention is interpreted in the strict sense either by a reasoned judgment of the court or by a decision of the Committee of Ministers. However, the Commission could not do its work without construing the provisions of the Convention and reaching conclusions as to their meaning and field of application, and its methods may be seen in the decisions cited under the Articles which follow.

---

[1] See statements before the court by Sir Humphrey Waldock, President of the Commission, in *Lawless* v. *Government of Ireland* [1960–1] C.E.D.H. ser. B. 32–3, 244–5.
[2] See, for example, *United States* v. *Sorrentino* [1949] 338 U.S. 868, 896.

As far as the texts of the Convention go, the Commission bases itself on the English and French texts which are equally authentic.[1] But a number of questions arise in construing and interpreting provisions of the Convention: for example, how far is the Convention to be treated exclusively as an international agreement? Are particular terms that have a technical meaning in some systems of law to be assigned that meaning or given a more general sense? In the determination of the standard set by a particular provision of the Convention, is the practice in a majority of the contracting States decisive or is some other standard to be looked for and applied? Are there any circumstances in which the decisions of national courts, on the application of the Convention under domestic law, could be binding on the Commissioner the court?

there shall be set up/il est institué

Though established by the contracting States, which were all members of, but not collectively identical with, the Council of Europe, it appears that the Commission is to be regarded as structurally at least part of the Council of Europe. The issue came before the Court of Appeal in England on the interpretation of the International Organisations (Immunities and Privileges) Act 1950, s. 1.[2] The plaintiff had commenced proceedings against the former President, and the Secretary, of the Commission, alleging mismanagement by them of his application to the Commission. The defendants invoked their immunity from judicial process, conferred by the Council of Europe (Immunities and Privileges) Order 1960, made under s. 1 of the Act of 1950. S. 1 applied

(1) ... to any organisation declared by Order in Council to be an organisation of which the United Kingdom or H.M. Government therein and one or more foreign sovereign powers or the government or governments thereof are members.

Further

(2) His Majesty may by Order in Council ...
    (b) confer upon—
      (i) any persons who are representatives (whether of government or not) on any organ of the organisation or are members of any committee

---

[1] 222/56: 2 *Yearbook* 351. However, where the Convention forms part of internal law the text of the national language will be authentic there.

[2] *Zoernsch* v. *Waldock and McNulty* [1964] 1 W.L.R. 675.

of the organisation or of any organ thereof . . . to such extent as may be specified in the Order the immunites and privileges set out in Part II of the Schedule of this Act.

The first Defendant, as former President of the Commission, relied upon s. 12 of the Order,[1] and the second Defendant, as Secretary, on s. 11. The plaintiff appealed against an order of the court upholding the claims of immunity and dismissing his action with costs. With regard to s. 12 of the Order he argued that it was *ultra vires* the Act on the ground that the Commission was not an 'organ' of the Council of Europe and that there was therefore no power under s. 1 (2) *b* of the Act to extend immunities or privileges to its members. The Court of Appeal was unanimously of the opinion that the Commission is an 'organ' of the Council of Europe. Lord Justice Diplock said:

In the context in which the expression is used in the Act of 1950 it is plain that 'organ' means a body of persons; and 'organs' of an 'organisation' means, in my view, a body of persons whose function is to do acts for the purpose of carrying out the aims or objects of the organisation. The only argument against the Commission being an organ of the Council of Europe is that it was constituted by a separate agreement providing for common action in the maintenance and future realisation of human rights and fundamental freedoms. But this is a method of achieving the aim of the Council of Europe which is expressly contemplated by Article 1 of the Statute of the Council of Europe. The achievement of this aim of the Council of Europe is expressed to be the purpose of the Convention for the Protection of Human Rights and Fundamental Freedoms, by which the Commission was established, and participation in the Convention is limited to members of the Council of Europe. The members of the Commission are elected not by the signatories of the Convention, but by the Committee of Ministers of the Council of Europe. They report not to the signatories of the Convention but to the Committee of Ministers who prescribe the action to be taken unless the question is referred to the Court. The expenses of the Commission are borne by the Council of Europe and its secretariat provided by the Council of Europe. I am clearly of the opinion that the Commission is an organ of the Council of Europe in the sense in which that expression is used in the Act of 1950.[2]

---

[1] S.I., no. 422/1960, conferring on members of the Commission '(*a*) in respect of words spoken or written and all acts done by them in their official capacity, the like immunity from legal process as is accorded to an envoy of a foreign sovereign power accredited to Her Majesty'.

[2] Compare Report of Committee of Experts (16.3.1950): 'It does seem in fact advisable to attach the Commission from an administrative point of view, to the Council of Europe.' *T.P.* ii. 497.

SECTION III

ARTICLE 20

The Commission shall consist of a number of members equal to that of the High Contracting Parties. No two members of the Commission may be nationals of the same State.

La Commission se compose d'un nombre de membres égal à celui des Hautes Parties Contractantes. La Commission ne peut comprendre plus d'un ressortissant du même État.

ARTICLE 21

(1) The members of the Commission shall be elected by the Committee of Ministers by an absolute majority of votes, from a list of names drawn up by the Bureau of the Consultative Assembly; each group of the Representatives of the High Contracting Parties in the Consultative Assembly shall put forward three candidates, of whom two at least shall be its nationals.

(2) As far as applicable, the same procedure shall be followed to complete the Commission in the event of other States subsequently becoming Parties to this Convention, and in filling casual vacancies.

1. Les membres de la Commission sont élus par le Comité des Ministres à la majorité absolue des voix, sur une liste de noms dressée par le Bureau de l'Assemblée Consultative; chaque groupe de représentants des Hautes Parties Contractantes à l'Assemblée Consultative présente trois candidats dont deux au moins seront de sa nationalité.

2. Dans la mesure où elle est applicable, la même procédure est suivie pour compléter la Commission au cas où d'autres États deviendraient ultérieurement Parties à la présente Convention, et pour pourvoir aux sièges de devenus vacants.

The size of the membership of the Commission and of the court may differ since one is equal to the number of contracting States and the other to the number of members of the Council of Europe. Both are at present 21.

The provisions of Articles 20 and 21 (1), relating to the nationality of members of the Commission, appear to imply that a member need not of necessity be a national of a State member of the Council of Europe,[1] though normally he or she will be such.

ARTICLE 22

(1) The members of the Commission shall be elected for a period of six years. They may be re-elected. However, of the members elected at the first election, the terms of seven members shall expire at the end of three years.

(2) The members whose terms are to expire at the end of the initial period of three years shall be chosen by lot by the Secretary-General of the Council of Europe immediately after the first election has been completed.

(3) In order to ensure that, as far as possible, one half of the membership of the Commission shall be renewed every three years, the Committee of Ministers may decide, before proceeding to any subsequent election that the term or terms of office of one or more members to be elected shall be for a period of over six years but not more than nine and not less than three years.

(4) In cases where more than one term of office is involved and the Committee of Ministers applies the preceding paragraph, the allocation of the terms of office shall be effected by the drawing of lots by the Secretary General, immediately after the election.

(5) A member of the Commission elected to replace a member whose term of office has not expired shall hold office for the remainder of his predecessor's term.

---

[1] See generally on the composition and election of the Commission: F. Monconduit, *La Commission européenne des droits de l'homme* (1956) 54–69.

(6) The members of the Commission shall hold office until replaced. After having been replaced, they shall continue to deal with such cases as they already have under consideration.

1. Les membres de la Commission sont élus pour une durée de six ans. Ils sont rééligibles. Toutefois, en ce quie concerne les membres désignés à la première élection, les fonctions de sept membres prendront fin au bout de trois ans.

2. Les membres dont les fonctions prendront fin au terme de la période initiale de trois ans, sont désignés par tirage au sort effectué par le Secrétaire Général du Conseil de l'Europe immédiatement après qu'il aura été procédé à la première election.

3. Le membre de la Commission élu en remplacement d'un membre dont le mandat n'est pas expiré achève le terme du mandat de son prédécesseur.

4. Les membres de la Commission restent en fonctions jusqu'à leur remplacement. Après ce remplacement, ils continuent de connaître des affaires dont ils sont déjà saisis.

The Fifth Protocol to the Convention, drawn up in 1966, is designed to rationalize the procedure of election of members both of the Commission and the Court. It came into force on 20.12.1971.

The fourth paragraph, which in its second sentence creates a continuing limited membership for a member, who has been replaced, can be inconvenient to administer, and in a body of the size of the Commission appears hardly to be necessary as a mandatory rule.

ARTICLE 23

The members of the Commission shall sit on the Commission in their individual capacity.

Les membres de la Commission siègent à la Commission à titre individuel.

The Commission expressed the primary object of this fundamental provision by saying that it was 'de marquer l'indépendance des membres de la Commission envers les États dont ils sont ressortissants'.[1] Its application where a member is appointed to a sub-commission by a respondent government under Article 29 (2), or where a member desires to express a separate or dissenting opinion under Article 31 (1), will be considered under those provisions.

ARTICLE 24

Any High Contracting Party may refer to the Commission, through the Secretary-General of the Council of Europe, any alleged breach of the provisions of the Convention by another High Contracting Party.

Toute Partie Contractante peut saisir la Commission, par l'intermédiaire du Secrétaire Général du Conseil de l'Europe, de tout manquement aux dispositions de la présente Convention qu'elle croira pouvoir être imputé à une autre Partie Contractante.

The objective character of the rights and freedoms, established in the Convention, and of their collective guarantee, described in the Preamble, can be shown from the decision of the Commission on the admissibility of the *Pfunders/Fundres Case: Austria* v. *Italy*.[2] Italy had objected that Austria could not file an application against her under Article 24 in respect of facts or events prior to 3 September 1958, the date of acceptance of the Convention by Austria. Italy herself had accepted the Convention on 26 October 1955, and based her contentions on two grounds: first, that in the intervening period there was no mutality of obligation between her and Austria under the Convention; and second, that it would be inequitable to admit the Austrian application, since Italy would be precluded from bringing any counter-claim against Austria in respect of facts or events in the intervening period, when Austria was not yet bound by the Convention. The Commission answered the objection by saying that since the purpose of the contracting States was not to establish a collective guarantee, an applicant State under Article 24

---

[1] First plenary session: Doc. DH (54) 3, p. 6.
[2] 788/60: 4 *Yearbook* 139, 142. See under Article 19.

is not to be regarded as exercising a right of action for the purpose of enforcing its own rights, but rather as bringing before the Commission an alleged violation of the public order of Europe;

therefore neither reciprocity, nor equivalence of rights, was a condition of application, and Austria was not debarred from making an application, in respect of facts and events in the intervening period, by reason only of the fact that her right of application under Article 24 was after-acquired. When, therefore, a State refers an alleged breach of the Convention to the Commission under Article 24, it does so primarily by way of application of that collective guarantee and not of the protection of its national interest. Two cases have been referred in addition to the *Pfunders/Fundres Case*, both by Greece against the United Kingdom concerning observance of the Convention in Cyprus before its independence in 1960.[1] On the first application, members of the Sub-commission visited Cyprus in January 1958 in order to investigate the position on the spot, and the Commission reported to the Committee of Ministers in October 1958.[2] The Committee of Ministers decided in April 1959 that, in face of the Zurich and London Agreements reached by the States principally concerned on the future status of the island, 'no further action was called for'. While the second application, alleging forty-nine cases of 'torture or maltreatment amounting to torture', was still in the Sub-commission, the Zurich and London Agreements were concluded, and both Greece and the United Kingdom jointly invited the Commission to terminate the proceedings. The Commission asserted that the principle governing withdrawal of an application must be observed also in case of an application brought by contracting State under Article 24:

the withdrawal of the application was a matter which concerned the Commission as well as the Parties, and the Commission must satisfy itself that the termination of the proceedings was calculated to serve, and not to defeat, the purposes of the Convention.

In June 1967 the Standing Committee of the Consultative Assembly[3] affirmed the collective guarantee, upon which the Convention rests,

---

[1] 176/56 and 299/57. See 1 *Yearbook* 139 and 2 *Yearbook* 177.

[2] During the proceedings before the Commission a number of the regulations complained of were revoked or relaxed by the Government of Cyprus.

[3] The Standing Committee acts on behalf of the Consultative Assembly outside its regular sessions.

in a resolution[1] concerning the situation in Greece,[2] which reads in part:

The Assembly, . . .

5. Considers that respect for the Statute of the Council of Europe and for the European Convention of Human Rights constitutes the very foundation of the Council of Europe's existence and must therefore admit of no exception . . .

8. Having been informed of the notice of derogation addressed to the Secretary General of the Council of Europe by the Greek Government under Article 15 of the European Convention on Human Rights:

9. Considering that such a derogation may only be made in time of war or other public emergency threatening the life of the nation and only to the extent strictly required by the exigencies of the situation, provided that such matters are not inconsistent with other obligations under international law and that the Greek Government has not shown that these conditions are satisfied;

10. Believing that an important and serious case of this kind the Contracting Parties to the Convention have a duty to act under Article 24 of the Convention and that, if they do not act as requested, the mechanism of collective guarantee of human rights set up by the Convention runs the risk of becoming meaningless;

11. Expresses the wish that the Governments of the Contracting parties to the European Convention on Human Rights refer to the Greek case, either separately or jointly, to the European Commission of Human Rights in accordance with Article 24 of the Convention;

12. Calls upon the Bureau to appoint a Rapporteur with a view to reporting at the next January Session on the reported violations of the fundamental human rights and democratic freedoms committed by the Greek Government so that action could be taken, if necessary, in terms of the Statute whether or not a member Government presents the Greek case to the European Commission of Human Rights.

This resolution, an initiative without precedent in the Council of Europe, was followed by the submission of applications under Article 24, jointly by Norway, Sweden, and Denmark, and by the Netherlands separately, in September 1967. The governments of

---

[1] Doc. B (67) 37.

[2] By Royal Decree no. 280 of 21 April 1967 the Martial Law Act 1912 as amended by Legislative Decrees of 1922 and 1962, and an Act of 1941, was brought into force throughout Greek territory, and a number of Articles of the Constitution were suspended.

Belgium, Iceland, and Luxembourg associated themselves with the applications though not as parties.

The application of Cyprus against Turkey posed questions of the role of State recognition and of constitutional defects in the *locus standi* of the applicant government.

In the first case[1] the Commission found that the applicant government had been internationally recognized in a number of contexts of diplomatic and treaty relatives: in particular by Security Council Resolution 364 (13.12.1974) on the prolongation of service of the U.N. Peace-keeping force in Cyprus (U.N.F.I.C.Y.P.) with the approval of its government, by the participation of representative of the government in the Committee of Ministers of the Council of Europe, and by its ratification without objection by any other contracting party, including Turkey, of Protocols 2, 3, and 5 to the Convention. In the second case[2] the Commission stressed that Article 24 is a means of collective enforcement of Convention obligations by interstate application; but it is the enforcement not of interstate allegations but of the obligations of a Convention contracting party to persons within its jurisdiction; consequently, an application under Article 24 does not create a relationship between the applicant government and the government against which the application is brought therefore,

to accept that a government may avoid 'collective enforcement' the Convention under Article 24, by asserting that they do not recognise the government of the applicant State, would defeat the purpose of the Convention.[3]

ARTICLE 25

(1) The Commission may receive petitions addressed to the Secretary-General of the Council of Europe from any person, non-governmental organisation or group of individuals claiming to be the victim of a violation by one of the High Contracting Parties of the rights set forth in this Convention, provided that the High Contracting Party against which the complaint has been lodged has declared that it recognises the

---

[1] 6780/74 and 6950/75, declared admissible on 26.5.1975: 2 D.R. 125.

[2] 8007/77 declared admissible on 10.7.1978: 13 D.R. 85.

[3] 8007/77: 13 D.R. 147.

competence of the Commission to receive sucn petitions. Those of the High Contracting Parties who have made such a declaration undertake not to hinder in any way the effective exercise of this right.

(2) Such declarations may be made for a specific period.

(3) The declarations shall be deposited with the Secretary-General of the Council of Europe who shall transmit copies thereof to the High Contracting Parties and publish them.

(4) The Commission shall only exercise the powers provided for in this Article when at least six High Contracing Parties are bound by declarations made in accordance with the preceding paragraphs.

1. La Commission peut être saisie d'une requête adressée au Secrétaire Général du Conseil de l'Europe par toute personne physique, toute organisation non gouvernementale ou tout groupe de particuliers, qui se prétend victime d'une violation par l'une des Hautes Parties Contractantes des droits reconnus dans la présente Convention, dans le cas où la Haute Partie Contractante mise en cause a déclaré reconnaître la compétence de la Commission dans cette matière. Les Hautes Parties Contractantes ayant souscrit une telle déclaration s'engagent à n'entraver par aucune mesure l'exercice efficace de ce droit.

2. Ces déclarations peuvent être faites pour une durée déterminée.

3. Elles sont remises au Secrétaire Général du Conseil de l'Europe, qui en transmet copies aux Hautes Parties Contractantes et en assure la publication.

4. La Commission n'exercera la compétence qui lui est attribuée par le présent article que lorsque six Hautes Parties Contractantes au moins se trouveront liées par la déclaration prévue aux paragraphes précédents.

The first paragraph embodies the vital and remarkable right of individual petition,[1] vital because the efficacy of the Convention depends in great part upon it, and remarkable because it carries the individual beyond the traditional limits upon his status in international law. No longer dependent for the protection of his Convention rights upon diplomatic intervention by the State, of which he is a national, the individual may bring an application against any contracting State, which has made the necessary declaration, even if he is a national of that State, and even if he is not a national of any contracting State; and, in doing so, he exercises not only a procedural right, such as been granted by other treaties to individuals, but acts in his own behalf to vindicate his own rights and freedoms.

petitions ... from any person, non-governmental organisation or group of individuals/une requête ... par toute personne physique, toute organisation non-gouvernementale ou tout groupe de particuliers

In the practice of the Commission the term 'petition' has been largely replaced by 'application' as the equivalent of the French 'requête'. That it is more than a petition in the strict sense is indicated by the fact that it institutes a procedure, which requires an initial decision to be taken on its admissibility by the Commission, and, failing a friendly settlement, a binding decision on its merits by either the Committee of Ministers or the court.[2]

The personality or past conduct of an applicant does not qualify the right of petition. So Ilse Koch, 'imprisoned in execution of a sentence imposed on her for crimes against the most elementary rights of men', was still entitled to exercise here right of petition.[3]

The formal requirements, which must be met by an application, are simple and are largely contained in Rules 37–42 of the Commission Rules of Procedure. As to its material content,[4] an applicant is not

[1] See generally on the origin and function of this Article, Monconduit, *La Commission européenne des droits de l'homme* (1956) 176–91.

[2] So Monconduit, op. cit. 184–6, who develops this argument, summing it up in the words: 'Il exerce donc un droit d'action, qui oblige l'organe saisi à statuer.'

[3] But her application was held to be manifestly ill founded and, since it neither in terms or by any reasonable implication even alleged any actual breach of the Convention, abusive: 1270/61: 5 *Yearbook* 134.

[4] The admissibility of additions to an application, after it has been registered by the Commission, in the form of new statements of fact or new complaints, and the problem of defamatory or offensive statements in an application, will be considered below under Article 27 (2).

bound to invoke any specific provision of the Convention. Where the applicant invokes no specific provision, or invokes some but not others, which may on the facts come into issue, or invokes obviously inapplicable provisions, the Commission will determine *ex officio* under what provisions of the Convention the application as a whole properly falls.[1] In considering under what provisions of the Convention the application is in whole or in part admissible, the Commission will normally confine itself to those facts or events of which the applicant actually complains; and it will investigate matters, which are contained in the application but of which the applicant makes no issue, only if they are of general concern in the implementation of the Convention.[2] Article 25 imposes no obligation upon the contracting States to publicize the Convention or to inform individuals of their rights of petition under it.[3]

The principle on which the Commission may consent to the withdrawal of an application has been described under Article 19.[4] It has said that it

doit passer outre à une déclaration de retrait si elle a lieu de penser que cette déclaration ne reflète pas la libre volonté de son auteur (comp., *mutatis mutandis*, Cour européenne des Droits de l'Homme, affaire De Becker, arrêt du 27 mars 1962, Série A, p. 25, § 13 *in fine*), ou si la requête soulève un grave problème de principe dominant la personne et les intérêts du requérant, ou encore si l'attitude du demandeur trahit un manque délibéré de respect envers la Convention et les organes chargés de veiller à son application'.[5]

So where an applicant arrives at an agreement with the respondent Government for a settlement of his complaints before his application has been admitted by the Commission, it will examine the form of the settlement under these criteria.[6] Where an application has been

---

[1] See for example 1468/62: 6 *Yearbook* 278.

[2] See above under Article 19.

[3] 1789/63: *Recueil* (1963) iii. The Commission stated that Article 25 (3) made the Secretary-General responsible for publication of declarations recognizing the right of individual petitions. In contrast to the meagre arrangements for publicity for the Convention are those in the Geneva Conventions 1949. See also 1814/63.

[4] The death of the applicant does not itself terminate the application, which may be continued by legal successors: 6166/73 (F.R.G.) 2 D.R. 58 or by a family member as 'indirect victim': 7467/76 (Belgium) 3 D.R. 72.

[5] 2169/64, 2204/64, 2326/64: *Recueil* (1964) ii (three applications by the same person, the first two being withdrawn; she had been declared a vexatious litigant in two countries).

[6] 1470/60. See also 865/60 (withdrawal after acquittal by national courts, implying that the application would have been inadmissible for non-exhaustion); and in contrast

admitted by the Commission, its withdrawal may need stronger justification. So in a case where an applicant complained of prolonged detention pending trial in West Berlin contrary to Article 5 (3), and the application had been admitted on this point and was before a subcommission, the remainder of the application being adjourned,[1] the Commission did not consent to withdrawal on the ground that it 'raises problems of individual freedom involved in the application of Article 5 (3) . . . which may extend beyond the interests of the particular Applicants'. However, at a later stage the Commission adopted its report on another application closely analogous, which was referred to the court, and found no reason to retain the application in question. It made a short report on the facts of the application, the Commission proceedings on it, and its withdrawal, to the Committee of Ministers.[2] It stated that, while the application had been admitted and would normally be governed by Articles 28–31, the situation created by the request for withdrawal did not fall exactly under either Article 30 or 31, but was similar to that which had arisen in the second Cyprus case. It had therefore followed the same procedure.[3] This poses the theoretical question whether, once an application has been admitted by the Commission, the Committee of Ministers can be said to be indirectly seised of it so that the Commission reports its proposed withdrawal to the Committee for action rather than for information; there is nothing in Articles 28–31 pointing to such a conclusion, and the Committee of Ministers in fact simply took note of the Report, and no further action.

The character of non-governmental organizations and of groups may raise questions of status and overlap. Local government councils or organizations are not non-governmental organizations under Article 25, given their specifically public function, though councillors or individual members are free to bring applications on their own behalf.[4] Political parties however rank as non-governmental organizations or groups.[5] Applications may be lodged in combination by a

---

2004/64 (statement of withdrawal of application alleging ill-treatment in prison not accepted by Commission, which, however, went on to find non-exhaustion of remedies), and 2294/64.

[1] Involving complaints of the wife of the applicant arising out of his detention.
[2] 2294/64: *Recueil* 20.
[3] 299/57, where the Commission decided that 'proceedings . . . should be terminated' and that a 'summary Report of the proceedings in the case' should be transmitted to the Committee of Ministers.
[4] 5767/72 *Sixteen Austrian communes et al.* (Austria) 46 *Recueil* 118.
[5] 8765/78 (U.K.) 21 D.R. 211 (Liberal Party).

corporate body, a group, and an individual, as in the *Sunday Times* application.[1] Here Times Newspaper Ltd, a registered corporation, a group of journalists working on the *Sunday Times*, and the editor of the paper, were applicants together. All were found by the Commission to be applicants under Article 25, claiming breach of Article 10. However, the Commission observed that the *Sunday Times* itself, as distinct from its group of journalists;

as a printing product, owned and published by the first applicant, does not as such fall within any of the categories of petitioners set forth in Article 25 . . . nor can it claim such to be a victim a victim of a breach of Article 10.

The Commission also held that it was not necessary that the complaints of the applicants under Article 10 be independent of each other.[2]

addressed to the Secretary-General of the Council of Europe/adressée au Secrétaire Général du Conseil de l'Europe

The fact that applications must at least initially be made in writing raises the question of the right of an applicant to appear in person before the Commission.

After an application has been admitted, Articles 28 and 29 are governing and call for its examination by the Sub-commission 'together with the representatives of the parties'. This is an expression[3] which would be more appropriate to interstate than to individual applications, but the Commission has not read into it the condition that an individual must be represented before the Commission. Rule 36 (2) of its Rules of Procedure provides that 'The persons, non-governmental organisations and groups of individuals referred to in Article 25 . . . may represent their case in person before the Commission ('peuvent défendre eux-mêmes leur cause devant la Commission'), or may be represented by a lawyer. But this rule, which is in fact operative at all stages of an application, cannot be read as according an automatic right of personal appearance before the Commission, for not only do the inclusion of organizations and the French text imply

---

[1] 6538/74 (U.K.) 2 D.R. 90.
[2] Compare *Nielsen* 342/57 (Denmark) 2 *Yearbook* 444 on time-limits.
[3] In an earlier version it appears as 'with the representative of either party': *T.P.* ii. 523.

the contrary, but the plain purpose of the rule is to show that representation by a lawyer is not essential, appearance in person being at the discretion of the Commission.[1]

claiming to be the victim of a violation . . . of the rights set forth/qui se prétend victime d'une violation . . . des droits reconnus

The meaning of the word 'victim' has already been considered under Article 5 (5). But there the subject is 'Everyone who has been a victim' ('Toute personne victime'), and the three possible constructions suggested of that expression do not necessarily apply to 'claiming to be a victim'.

It is clear at least that the word 'victim' entails the presence of some link between the violation and the claimant; in other words, an applicant cannot be heard to complain of a violation to which he is a 'stranger'. We have then to see how the Commission has interpreted these notions of a link and a 'stranger'.[2]

The cases must first be distinguished in which the application is brought by a representative of the victim. These will include representation under a power of attorney by a lawyer or some other designated person,[3] or where the applicant is a corporation or other body of persons. Since a right of petition is under Article 25 vested in every person, whatever their age or condition, application may be made by or on behalf of minors, and of persons of unsound mind. In the former case the Commission will receive an application direct or be prepared to treat a parent or guardian as representative for purposes of application; in the latter the Commission has shown itself reluctant to insist on representation, even where the applicant has been placed by court order under partial or complete legal disability,[4] or has been committed to an asylum.

---

[1] An applicant might be called also as a witness to facts within his particular knowledge: Rule 54.

[2] Compare the term 'person aggrieved': *Buxton* v. *Minister of Housing* [1961] 1 Q.B. 278; *Simpson* v. *Edinburgh Corporation* [1960] S.C. 313.

[3] 1800/63: *Receuil* (1964) i (fiancée).

[4] 1527/62: 5 *Yearbook* 246 (the applicant, placed under partial incapacity with a guardian (*Entmündigungsordnung*), has nevertheless 'the right, of his own accord and without being represented by his guardian, to refer to an application to the Commission'). The logic of this was followed out in 993/61: *Receuil* (1961) ii (failure by applicant placed under guardianship by Danish court order to appeal against the order held to be non-exhaustion of domestic remedies). For applicants suffering from *paranoia querulantoria* see, for example, 412/58: *Receuil* (1959) and 996/61: *Receuil* (1961) ii.

There may also be representation by succession, though a mere legatee of the victim will not as such be entitled to present an application.[1]

Distinct from these forms of representation is the link of personal interest where the applicant claims to be a victim of an alleged violation of the Convention in respect of another person. The Commission has found this personal interest to exist within the family:

under the terms of Article 25, paragraph (1), of the Convention, the Commission may only receive an application from an individual where that individual claims to be himself the victim of a violation by one of the High Contracting Parties of the rights set forth in the Convention; . . . this does not exclude the possibility of a near relative of the victim submitting, on his own initiative, an application to the Commission to the extent that the alleged violation is prejudicial to him or he had a genuine personal interest in the termination of the violation: . . . the present Applicant is a near relative, namely the mother, of the alleged victim who, after signing the first letter addressed to the Commission, has moved from the Federal Republic of Germany to Leipzig in the Soviet-occupied zone of Germany; and whereas the Commission finds that the Applicant has a genuine personal interest in the termination of the violations alleged, in particular, in regard to the decision of the District Court of Hamburg by which, on 4th October 1957, her daughter was acquitted in criminal proceedings on the ground that she had been temporarily irresponsible for her acts; whereas it follows that the Commission is competent to receive this Application *ratione personae*.[2]

The Commission made three earlier decision, in which the same principle is asserted.[3] There may also be a claim for consequential damage by the wife or children of the victim.[4]

The Commission has had no hesitation in treating an applicant as a 'stranger', who was not a party to a judgment of which he complains,[5]

---

[1] 282/57: 1 *Yearbook* 166. 439/58.

[2] 1109/61: *Recueil* (1962) i. For shareholders in a company see under Article 1 of the Protocol below.

[3] In these cases the relationship of the applicant to the actual 'victims' was respectively: brother and brother-in-law (100/55); brother (113/55); father (155/56); 1 *Yearbook* 161–4. See also 898/60: *Recueil* (1961) ii (mother) and 1133/61 and 1218/61: *Recueil* (1962) ii (application by widow—issue of representation or interest not raised).

[4] 1478/62: 6 *Yearbook* 621. See also 2294/64: *Recueil* 20 (effect of prolonged detention pending trial upon the wife and children of the detainee not investigated owing to withdrawal of application).

[5] 436/58: 2 *Yearbook* 390.

or who impugns legislation as contrary to the Convention without showing that it has been applied to him to his detriment,[1] for

the Commission is competent to examine the compatibility of domestic legislation with the Convention only with respect to its application to a person, nongovernmental organization or group of individuals, and only insofar as its application is alleged to constitute a violation of the Convention in regard to the person, organisation or group in question. . . .

The distinction made between individuals, non-governmental organizations, and groups of individuals in Article 25 is, nevertheless, important, for it contemplates three possible forms of individual application: by an individual on his own behalf, by an organization of individuals, and by a group of individuals claiming to be victims of a Convention breach by reason of their membership of the group.

The third form of application will commonly involve Article 14 which is itself based upon 'association with a national minority' and other social group concepts. Further, the second and third forms of application will tend to coalesce where an organization has been formed for protecting the interests of a particular social group. This is illustrated by a holding of the United States Supreme Court that the National Association for the advancement of Coloured Peoples (N.A.A.C.P.) may assert and maintain in its own name the rights to freedom of expression and of association under the First and Fourteenth Amendments.[2]

The individual ceases to be a victim, for purposes of maintaining an application, when the convention breach of which he complains must be taken to have been rectified by a domestic remedy,[3] but there may be still a question whether the reparation is complete.[4]

not to hinder in any way the effective exercise of this right/à n'entraver par aucune mesure l'exercice efficace de ce droit

The Commission has held that with this undertaking it does not establish rights for the individual of the same character as those set out in Section I. Therefore, while an individual may refer to the Commis-

---

[1] 290/57: 3 *Yearbook* 220; 867/60: 4 *Yearbook* 276. No *actio popularis* can be brought by an individual applicant.

[2] *N.A.A.C.P.* v. *Button* [1963] 371 U.S. 415.

[3] 986/61.

[4] See under Article 50 below.

sion, either with or without allegations of a breach of Section I of the
Convention, alleged interference with the exercise of his right of petition, this reference is not an application to which the normal rules as
to admissibility apply, including in particular that of the exhaustion of
domestic remedies; nor will the reference be dealt with by the Commission under the application procedure.[1] The issue, being one of
effective administration of the Convention, lies primarily between the
Commission and the contracting State to which the alleged interference is imputed; the complainant will, however, be given an opportunity to reply to any observations that the State may make.

Correspondence with the Commission. In practice the issue arises for the
most part over communications with the Commission of individuals,
who are in some kind of detention.

The Commission has taken the view that not all control of correspondence of prisoners constitutes interference, and has not claimed
that communications between them and the Commission be sent
unopened by prison or other authorities,[2] though it has said

> it would be more in accord with the spirit of the Convention that letters
> addressed to the Secretary should not first be submitted unsealed to the
> prison authorities; . . . nevertheless, it recognises that Governments may have
> reasonable grounds for making this requirement.[3]

But control, in the form of reading the correspondence of prisoners
before dispatch, is distinct from interference in the form of censorship, stopping or delay of letters,[4] and punishment for their contents.
Interference will contravene Article 25 (1) only if it effectively prevents
an applicant in a particular case 'de présenter ses griefs à la Commission d'une manière complète et détaillée', and the Commission from
forming an opinion on it.[5] Most difficult are the cases where the applicant makes charges of ill-treatment against the prison authorities
themselves, or uses language which may be regarded as defamatory of

---

[1] Viz. Rules 45 and 46 of the Commission Rules of Procedure.

[2] 793/60: 3 *Yearbook* 448; 833/60: ibid. 442; 1649/62: *Recueil* (1964) i.

[3] 1593/62: *Recueil* (1964) i.

[4] e.g. through censorship; rationing of writing paper; prohibition of use of a foreign
language. The authorities are not bound to supply copies of documents in a case-file to
which the applicant has access: 997/61. For delay see 369/58: 2 *Yearbook* 380.

[5] 188/56: 1 *Yearbook* 179: 1273/61: *Recueil* (1962) ii. See also 1174/61: *Recueil* (1962) ii
1405/62: *Recueil* (1963) ii and 1628/62: *Recueil* (1963) ii. The Federal Republic of
Germany has, after consultation by the Commission, adjusted its prison regulations to
avoid contraventions of Article 25 (1) in this respect.

particular officials, or makes scurrilous attacks on the respondent Government or its administration, or on the courts or judges. What is scurrilous must vary with time, place, and occasion, and should not be viewed too severely[1] in applications. The Commission has said:

the right of individual petition could be seriously impaired if an Applicant were deterred by punishment from proceeding further with his Application, or if others were deterred by the threat of punishment from making statements in their Application which they believed to be justified;

nevertheless, the Commission also recognises that it is no part of the effective exercise of the right of petition to make unnecessary or irrelevant offensive statements in an Application; ... the Commission believes that in the case of X the punishment imposed might be considered as a violation of Article 25, paragraph (1), because of its general deterrent effects as indicated above; whereas, however, it does not consider that X's Application was in fact frustrated and therefore decides in this case to take no further steps.[2]

Punishment of a prisoner for sending letters secretly to the Commission would not, it appears, contravene Article 25 (1).[3]

Where an applicant is informed that a recommendation for pardon (*Begnadigung*) or mitigation of sentence (*Strafmilderung*), is a matter of grace, will depend upon the withdrawal of his application to the Commission, such a condition is not an interference with the right of petition in so far as its acceptance is the free act of the applicant.[4]

There is no interference with the right of petition where the authorities

n'autorisent pas d'une manière générale les détenus, d'une part, à recevoir des visites supplémentaires de leurs parents ou amis pour discuter avec eux les modalités d'introduction, d'une requête devant la Commission et, d'autre

---

[1] See, for example, *India: Kartar Singh* v. *State of Punjab* [1956] A.I.R. SC 541 (the appellants had attacked the proposals of the Punjab Government to rationalize motor transport, using abusive slogans. The Supreme Court considered that they belonged to 'a stratum of society where such vulgar abuse is so freely indulged in' that it could have hardly any effect on the people hearing them).

[2] 1593/62. Compare 833/60: 3 *Yearbook* 442 and 1765/63: *Recueil* (1965) i (concerning an Order of the Austrian Minister of Justice 9.10.1963: ZI 46187/63) in which 'it expressly stated that disciplinary punishments are also permissible in respect of gross untruths or insulting statements contained in applications addressed to the European Commission of Human Rights.' The Commission found that there was no interference in fact with the application in question, but repeated its statement quoted from 1593/62. See further below under Article 27 (2).

[3] 1899/63: *Recueil* (1965) i.

[4] 2618/65: *Recueil* (1965) ii.

part, à addresser à la Commission les dossiers les concernant par l'inter-mediaire d'un simple particulier, alors qu'ils ont le droit de la faire soit directement, soit par l'intermediaire d'un avocat.[1]

ARTICLE 26

The Commission may only deal with the matter after all domestic remedies have been exhausted, according to the generally recognised rules of international law, and within a period of six months from the date on which the final decision was taken.

La Commission ne peut être saisie qu'après l'épuisement des voies de recours internes, tel qu'il est entendu selon les principes de droit international généralement reconnus et dans le délai de six mois, à partier de la date de la décision interne définitive.

That the rule of the exhaustion of domestic remedies is a large and necessary limitation on the competence of the Convention bodies to deal with alleged breaches of it, hardly needs demonstration. The rule is expressed at an early stage in the Consultative Assembly draft,[2] and it can hardly be imagined that the principle of individual petition would have been accepted without it.

The rule of exhaustion of domestic remedies was declared to be a well-established rule of customary international law by the International Court of Justice;[3] and it is sufficient here to point to the provisions of the Civil and Political Rights Covenant and its optional Protocol. The Human Rights Committee:

... shall deal with a matter referred to it only after it has ascertained that all available domestic remedies have been invoked and exhausted in the matter, in conformity with the generally recognised principles of international law ...
Article 41 (1) c

Further, under the Optional Protocol:

... individuals who claim that any of their rights enumerated in the Covenant have been violated and who have exhausted all available domestic remedies

---

[1] 499/59: 2 *Yearbook* 400.
[2] *T.P.* ii. 436.
[3] *Interhandel Case* (*Switzerland* v. *U.S.A.*) Judgment 21.3.1959.

may submit a written communication to the Committee for consideration: Article 2

The Commission has stressed the principle of State responsibility obtained in the rule:

... the rule requiring the exhaustion of domestic remedies as a condition of the presentation of an international claim is found upon the principle that the Respondent State must first have an opportunity to redress by its own means within the framework of its own domestic legal system the wrong alleged to be done to the individual.[1]

The wording is not perfect, for it could be read as saying that the respondent state is entitled, in what is in effect a litigious process, to invoke domestic remedies as a defence. But this is not the situation under the Convention. The respondent state has under the Convention obligations to guarantee its rights and freedoms to all those within its jurisdiction, and these obligations can be effectively implemented only by the domestic law and process; it follows that the exhaustion of domestic remedies is not simply a procedural condition, but is a means of enforcing the Convention, as Articles 13 and 50 envisage, and, through Article 26, making the pursuit of an international claim unnecessary.

may only deal with the matter/ne peut être saisie que

This is a peremptory condition, which is underlined in Article 27 (3). It refers not to the receipt of an application, as in Article 25, but to its admissibility.

after all domestic remedies have been exhausted, according to the generally recognized rules of international law/après l'épuisement des voies de recours internes, tel qu'il est entendu selon les principes de droit international generalement reconnus

We have to consider in turn the kinds of remedies that come within the rule; the effectiveness of remedies; special circumstances limiting the application of the rule; and finally the role of the six-months rule.

---

[1] *Nielsen* (Denmark) 2 *Yearbook* 436 343/57: The Commission considered at length the implication of the reference in Article 26 for the generally recognized rules of international law and included in particular that Article 26 applied to interstate applications under Article 24: 788/60 4 *Yearbook* 150.

Kinds of remedies. A remedy may be afforded by judicial process, by administrative authority, or as an act of grace or discretion. Article 26 is not regarded as covering the last acts: so as a petition to Parliament[1] or other political authority, an appeal for clemency,[2] or a request for the wholly discretionary exercise of a public function, are not remedies that must be exhausted under Article 26.3

While the Convention does not guarantee any right of appeal in civil or criminal proceedings, or right of retrial for the accused, the individual must under Article 26 exhaust them as remedies, to the extent that they are available under the domestic law. So the appellate court must examine the appeal in substance, including all the relevant facts.[4] The remedy must have the finality of decision, to meet the requirements of Article 26.

The expression of a doubt as to whether a remedy is available at all, or whether an indicated remedy can be effective, is not easy to resolve. Is it sufficient that an applicant has acted on legal advice in not pursuing a remedy, or must court proceedings be taken, it being in the end for the courts to decide? It will depend on the circumstances. If there is a line of judicial decisions, to which the legal adviser points, which indicate a line of reasoning or interpretation rejecting the suggested remedy, that can be the end of the matter. If however it is shown that an essential question is still open for decision by a higher court, proceedings must be taken under Article 26 to have it resolved.[5]

Given the obligation of the respondent state to redress, through its national authorities, any violation of the Convention, the burden of proof is seen to rest upon it, to demonstrate the availability of domestic remedies.[6] So the burden of proof of the failure of the

---

[1] 97/55.

[2] 458/59: 3 *Yearbook* 234.

[3] In Austria the Prokurator General may, on request and at his discretion, introduce a plea of nullity for the maintenance of the law (*Nichtigkeitsbeschwerde zur Wahrung des Gesetzes*). It is not a remedy in the sense of Article 26: 1159/61 and 1552/67.

[4] *Colozza/Rubinat* (Italy) 9024/81: 28 D.R. 138; *van Oosterwijk* (Belgium) 7654/76: 11 D.R. 194.

[5] 1661/62 (Belgium) 6 *Yearbook* 366. Where detention follows an order for deportation, it is necessary to see what separate remedies if any, possible for detention and deportation: see *Caprino* 6871/77 (U.K.) 12 D.R. 4: Report 22 D.R. 5; *Kaplan* 7598/76 (U.K.) 15 D.R. 120; *Zamir* 9174/80 (U.K.) 29 D.R. 153 (appeal to the Adjudicator limited to order for deportation).

[6] 788/60: Report (31.3.1963) § 75; 5575/72 (Austria) 1 D.R. 44; 6870/74 (*Cyprus* v. *Turkey*) 2 D.R. 125.

applicant to have failed to exhaust remedies falls upon the respondent state,[1] and it is free to waive the rule.[2]

This general rule does not however prevent the Commission from taking notice *ex officio* of domestic remedies that have become familiar to it in the course of its work; and it may find, on the particular facts presented and after questioning the applicant, that he has failed to exhaust remedies and that the rule in Article 26 must be applied; the application will then be declared inadmissible.[3]

The Commission may exceptionally join an issue of non-exhaustion of remedies to the merits of the application. So in the *Pfunders/Fundres Case*,[4] in which the applicability of Article 26 to interstate applications is also illustrated;

a link may exist between the question of an application and the question of substance raised thereby, making it impossible to separate one from the other . . . in such a case the Commission would be unable to carry out its tasks efficiently, unless there were a joinder of the verity and the questions of admissibility.

The Commission used the application to communicate general propositions about interstate applications. First, the rule of exhaustion of domestic remedies is, as a condition precedent to the making of a claim by a state in respect of injury to one of its nationals, limited to such national claims. Secondly, in the system of *collective* guarantee and protection of rights under the Convention, which extend to all persons within the jurisdiction of a party to the Convention, 'the rule applies *a fortiori* to the international protection under the Convention of a State's own nationals'.

Effectiveness of remedies. Procedurally, Article 26 does not require that a complaint be presented to the national authorities in terms of precise reference to Convention provisions or to domestic law, but it must be presented in *substance* to both fact and law.[5] Further, any doubt that may exist as to the prospects of success of a particular remedy does not relieve an applicant of the obligation to exhaust that remedy, it being left to the domestic courts to resolve the doubt.[6]

---

[1] 7456/79 (U.K.) 13 D.R. 40.
[2] 8919/80 (Belgium) 23 D.R. 144. In interpretation of the Convention the acceptance of this waiver appears questionable.
[3] 450/59: 3 *Yearbook* 232.
[4] 788/60 (*Austria* v. *Italy*) Report No. 89.
[5] 5574/42 (U.K.) 3 D.R. 10; 1103/61: 5 *Yearbook* 186.
[6] 712/60 (F.R.G.) 8 Collection 29.

Exhaustion of remedies may also be completed after an application has been submitted to the Commission.[1]

The Commission has said that the 'normal use' of remedies must be 'likely to be effective and adequate', to meet the requirements of Article 26.[2] So, while doubt about a remedy is one thing, *une jurisprudence constante* against the decision or order sought by the applicant makes Article 26 inapplicable;[3] current related decisions would have the same consequence.

Representations made to an advisory panel against an order of deportation, or to the Home Secretary to alter the decision, are not effective remedies;[4] nor are court proceedings concerning deportation, if the order to be made by the court is suspensive only.[5] There must then be a finality in the remedy; and a proceeding by way of remedy, which brings out an error in the infringed decision must, in order to be effective, lead to its annulment.[6]

Appeals on points of law, or pleas of nullity, to higher courts will normally rank as remedies for Article 26, but a distinction has to be made for the rule does not extend to:

complaints the object of which is to determine the compatibility with the Convention of legislative measures and administrative practices, except where a specific remedy against the legislation exists.[7]

Special circumstances limited the application of the rule. It has already been observed that the Convention does not oblige contracting States to give any publicity to the possibility of application to the Commission, but lack of knowledge or understanding of the Convention will not excuse non-compliance with Article 26.[8]

Closely allied is the question of legal aid and representation. Where, as in some systems, access to particular courts, generally appellate, may only be had through legal representation, failure to obtain legal representation, by grant if necessary of free legal assistance, may constitute non-exhaustion under Article 26.[9] But where

---

[1] *Luberti* (Italy) 9019/80: 27 D.R. 181.

[2] 839/50: 5 *Yearbook* 144.

[3] *Simon Herold* (Austria) 4330/69: 14 *Yearbook* 352; *Donnelly et al.* (U.K.) 5577/72: 4 D.R. 64, where the available remedies against assault of detainees are analysed at length.

[4] *Agee* (U.K.) 7729/76: 7 D.R. 164.

[5] 7011/75 (Denmark) 4 D.R. 215.

[6] 9362/81 (Netherlands) 28 D.R. 212.

[7] Seond *Corak Case*: 34 Collection 70; *Ireland* v. *U.K.* 5310/71: 41 *Recueil* 3,84.

[8] 1019/61: *Recueil* (1962) i.   [9] 1131/61: *Recueil* (1962) ii.

legal aid is refused, on the ground that the appeal or application proposed has no prospect of success, or the applicant has received legal advice to the same effect, the question may arise as to whether this is because the proceeding is not in fact an effective remedy, or simply because it is a case without merit. The Commission will generally, and in absence of evidence on the point, assume the latter[1] if the former is the case, Article 26 is satisfied.[2]

Where an applicant attributes his failure to exhaust domestic remedies to the negligence or incompetence of his lawyer,[3] the position under Article 26 is different from that under Article 6; that is to say, in so far as the applicant may have been denied his rights under Article 6 by the negligence or incompetence of his lawyer, his complaint under that Article will be inadmissible *ratione personae*, but the failure of the lawyer may, if proved, be a special circumstance excusing compliance with the rule in Article 26, provided that he has sought and failed to obtain *restitutio in integrum*.[4]

Deportation and extradition can pose a special problem of the effectiveness of domestic remedies for one who has been already removed from the country.[5]

The Commission has repeatedly said that lack of means does not in itself excuse from compliance with the rule of exhaustion of remedies at least where an application for free legal assistance can be made.[6] Similarly, ill health cannot in itself excuse compliance.[7]

It is sometimes said by an applicant that he did not seek remedies that were available for fear of repercussions.[8] This plea may in some cases call for close examination; for example, where a prisoner complains of ill-treatment in the sense of Article 3 at the hands of the

[1] 1812/63: *Recueil* (1964) i.
[2] 1008/61: *Recueil* (1962) i.
[3] 578/61: *Recueil* (1961) i.
[4] 495/59: *Recueil* (1959).
[5] See 1211/61: 5 *Yearbook* 226 (deportation from Netherlands to Germany, but evidence of sufficient means to take legal action in the Netherlands through legal representative). Compare 1008/61: *Recueil* (1962) i (applicant resident outside Austria); and 434/58: 2 *Yearbook* 372 (applicant denied entry to Sweden but entitled to obtain ruling on whether his personal appearance was necessary, in the interest of justice, in proceedings instituted there on his behalf).
[6] 1412/62: *Recueil* (1963) ii. Compare 1263/61: *Recueil* (1962) ii (failure both to appeal against refusal of grant of free legal assistance and to bring action for damages at own expense—non-exhaustion).
[7] 289/57: 1 *Yearbook* 149; nor advanced age, 568/59.
[8] e.g. 604/59: 3 *Yearbook* 240.

police or prison officers, and his complaint is in part at least corroborated,[1] the rule of exhaustion of remedies has to be applied with caution.

The Commission held that a detainee had a remedy before the Detention Commission, established in Iceland under the Offences against the State Act (1940); for, while this Commission was an administrative rather than judicial tribunal, and an application to it was an exceptional remedy in the conditions then prevailing, 'it could nevertheless examine the grounds of detention including their *bona fides*'. It then offered effective means of redress to the applicant, which he had not exhausted.[2]

Complaints of prison conditions, and the availability of remedies, can create many problems, which are surveyed in a group of applications by detainees in the Maze Prison in Northern Ireland.[3] As regards the imposition of disciplinary sanctions by the prison governor, the Commission held that an order of constraint would not be an effective remedy. It distinguished the disciplinary awards of a Board of Visitors, which are by statute subject to judicial review, and may be set aside, if they are not in accordance with the 'principles of natural justice';[4] further, it noted that two judges of the Court of Appeal had 'expressed reservations as to whether *certiorari* lies in respect of awards . . . by a prison governor. In any case, even if the remedy was available:

it could only be considered sufficient to redress their complaint . . . concerning the procedural propriety of the adjudications . . . and not the cumulative severity of the punishments awarded.

The Commission also found that the English law of tort could not in its present state be extended to cover general prison conditions or treatment by the prison authorities.[5]

It may be finally observed that, since the conduct of proceedings is the responsibility of the prosecuting and judicial authorities, there is no obligation on the accused to accelerate the proceedings in any way as an *exhaustion of remedies*.[6] But the situation is different on the merits

---

[1] e.g. 2004/64: *Recueil* 20 and 2686/65, Report of Commission: 4.10.1967.

[2] 493/59: 2 *Yearbook* 322. See also under Article 18, and *Retimag* (F.R.G.) 712/60: 4 *Yearbook* 384.

[3] *McFeeley et al.* (U.K.) 8317/78: 20 D.R. 44.71.75. Compare also 6562/79 (U.K.) 20 D.R. 184.

[4] *R.* v. *Board of Visitors, Hull Prison, ex pte German* [1979] 2 W.L.R. 42.

[5] Similar finding in 6840/74 (U.K.) 10 D.R. 5,20.

[6] *Kofler* (Italy) 8261/78: 25 D.R. 157.

where the behaviour of the accused can be relevant to the length of the proceedings.[1]

and within a period of six months from the date on which the final decision was taken/et dans un délai de six mois à partir de la date de la décision interne définitive

The period runs from the date, when the trial decision was taken to the date of introduction of the application, that is, the date of the receipt of the application by the Secretariat of the Commisison:[2] its registration may usually be later.

Decision comprises any act of public authority, which alters the position of the individual in law or fact: typical are the enactment of a statute, a court order or judgment, and characteristic acts of public administration. So, in the absence of domestic remedies, a statute taking away a proprietary interest in land is a decision on the date in which it comes into force;[3] the date of release of an individual from detention on remand is the beginning of the six-months limit; and so is the delivery of a spoken judgment in court, in presence of the counsel if there is no further pressure.[4] But a discretionary refusal of leave to appeal is not an element in the six-months period.[5] Where a number of district criminal proceedings are conducted on offences of a similar nature, the six-months rule will be applied to each one separately, even if a global sentence is finally imposed.[6]

Where a general regulation exists, or is brought into force, there being no particular decision made under it, and no means of challenging it, the critical date is that of the actual impact or effect upon an individual.[7]

The 'six months' rule is closely interrelated with the rule of exhaustion of remedies. So in the *de Becker Case* the Commission said:

... the two rules contained in Article 26 ... are closely interrelated since not only are they combined in the same Article, but they are also expressed in a single sentence whose grammatical construction implies such correlation; and

---

[1] 8435/78 (U.K.) 26 D.R. 18.
[2] 8299/78 (Ireland) 22 D.R. 51.
[3] 7379/76 (U.K.) 8 D.R. 211.
[4] 5759/72 (Austria) 6 D.R. 15.
[5] 9136/80 (Ireland) 26 D.R. 242.
[6] Eckle 8130/78 (F.R.G.) 16 D.R. 120.
[7] 8440/78 (U.K.) 21 D.R. 138 (regulation, issued under Public Order Act (1936), banning public processions).

... the term 'final decision' ... refers exclusively to the final decision con-cerned in the exhaustion[1] of all domestic remedies according to the generally recognized rules of international law, so that the six-months' rule is only operative in this context ...

In the same case the Commission remarked that the six-months' rule

... s'explique par le souci des Hautes Parties Contractantes d'empêcher la constante remise en cause du passé ...

But it follows that, though the rules are interrelated, the rule of exhaustion of remedies has logical priority; that is to say, Article 26 requires an applicant to exhaust all available remedies, and then to make his application to the Commission within six months of the final decision terminating that process. This is well illustrated by the following decision:[2]

... the Commission has considered the question whether the Applicant could have seised the Constitutional Court of a complaint against the decision of the Ministry of Internal Affairs [rejecting allegations by the Applicant of ill-treatment by the police]; ... on the basis that such a remedy was available, it appears that the Applicant failed to submit a complaint to the Constitutional Court within the time-limit laid down in Austrian law; ... if on the one hand, the decision of the Minister is to be considered as final, the Applicant failed to lodge his Application to the Commission within the time-limit of six months ...

In other words, there were two possible 'final decisions': that of the Constitutional Court, which the applicant had failed to obtain, and that of the Minister in rejecting the complaint. Since in either case there was a failure to comply with Article 26, it was unnecessary for the Commission to inquire further into the possibility of a constitutional appeal.

The date of the 'final decision' for purposes of Article 26 is that on which the applicant has had 'reasonable effective notice' of it,[3] where 'effective' means that the individual is given sufficient time and oppor-tunity to make his application to the Commission;[4] it has already been remarked that some initiative may be required of him here.

---

[1] The French text of the decision here reads: 'la décision définitive rendue *dans le cadre normal* de l'épuisement . . .'. See also 654/59: 4 *Yearbook* 276; 918/60: *Recueil* (1961) ii; and 1736/62.

[2] 1967/63: *Recueil* (1965) ii.

[3] 864/60.

[4] Six months run from introduction of application: 8299/78 (Ireland) 22 D.R. 51.

Various questions have arisen in the application of the six-months' rule: What is its relation to the inadmissibility of applications *ratione temporis*? Can the period of six months be interrupted? Are there continuing situations to which the rule cannot properly apply? How far does the rule exclude submission of additional facts or complaints by an applicant?

Inadmissibility ratione temporis. The practice of the Commission has been to distinguish this ground of inadmissibility from failure to observe the six-months rule, and to confine the latter to applications, which relate to matters arising before the Convention entered into force, or before the respondent government became a party to it, or in the case of individual petitions before the effective date of its declaration under Article 25. For practical purposes the first two of these dates are the same and may be called the 'Convention date'; the third may be called the 'individual petition date'.

On individual applications there are then four possible periods to be considered, varying with the dates operative for particular contracting States; to illustrate, the dates which are operative for the United Kingdom are given in brackets:

I. Subsequent to the individual petition date [after 13.1.1966]
II. Up to six calendar months prior to the individual petition date [14.7.1965–14.1.1966]
III. From the Convention date to the date six calendar months prior to the individual petition date [3.9.1953–14.7.1965]
IV. Prior to the Convention date.

Periods I and IV present no difficulty. For matters arising in Period I, Article 26 including the six-months rule governs applications under Article 25.[1] But applications on matters arising in Period IV are inadmissible *ratione temporis*. The second point is important, for the six-months rule is not here retroactive; that is to say, it does not operate to allow an application to be brought in respect of matters arising up to six months prior to the Convention date. Prior to that date no provision of the Convention is in operation at all. So in the *Nielsen Case*, where the period of detention, of which the applicant complained under Article 5 (3), extended over the Convention date for

---

[1] For applications under Article 24, the six-months rule begins to operate as from the Convention date.

Denmark, the Commission excluded from consideration that part of the detention which was prior to the Convention date.[1]

However, a problem arises for Periods II and III, for in these the Convention is in force. Since, even prior to the individual petition date, a contracting State is bound to observe and apply the provisions of the Convention, can applications be brought, as soon as the door to applications under Article 25 is opened, in respect of matters arising in Period II? The answer appears to be that, unless the declaration under Article 25 expressly excludes them,[2] that they can.

In the *de Becker Case* the Commission said that the decision of the Brussels Military Court on 14 June 1947 could not mark the beginning of the six-months' period, being prior to the Convention date for Belgium of 14 June 1955, and that:

> ... il importe en outre de souligner que jusqu'au 5 juillet 1955, date de l'acceptation du droit de recours individuel par la Belgique, le requérant n'avait pas la faculté de saisir la Commission; ... le délai de six mois ne lui était donc non plus opposable entre le 14 juin et le 5 juillet 1955; ... il s'ensuit que la question de ce délai ne peut surgir en l'espèce que pour la période postérieure au 5 juillet 1955 ...

The *de Becker Case* was, however, as we shall see below, one of a continuing situation, and the meaning of this passage becomes clearer in a later decision of the Commission in an application against the Netherlands, where the dates were these: Convention date, 31 August 1954; of final decision, 18 January 1960; individual petition date, 5 July 1960; and date of application, 8 August 1960. The final decision fell within Period II, but the application was more than six months later than the final decision. The Commission cited the passage just quoted, and observed that:

> entre le dit dépôt [declaration under Article 25] et celui de la requête il s'est écoulé moins de six mois; ...[3]

The facts of these two cases preclude any certain inference as to the position in Period III. The problem is best solved by express provision in the declaration under Article 25.

Interruption of six-month period. The running of the six-month period may be 'interrupted or suspended' by special circumstances[4] in a

---

[1] 343/57: 2 *Yearbook* 454.
[2] As does the United Kingdom declaration of 14.1.1966.
[3] 846/60: *Recueil* (1961) i.   [4] 1863/64: *Recueil* (1964) ii.

particular case. In general, an application for a new trial will not interrupt the period;[1] unless it appears that, because of the production of
new evidence, it is likely to constitute an effective remedy. An unsuccessful request to the Prokurator General in Austria to introduce an
appeal 'for the maintenance of the law'[2] does not interrupt the period.[3]

Continuing situation. On the particular facts of the *de Becker Case* the
Commission found that his loss of civil rights was derived from legislation, which had the effect of excluding any domestic remedy, and the
compatibility of which with the Convention was in issue. Since this
loss of civil rights was 'une situation continue et même perpétuelle,
contre laquelle il ne possède aucun recours interne', the period of six
months under Article 26 could only commence to run when this situation ceased to exist.[4] To the argument of the Belgian Government that

... en introduisant dans l'Article 26 ... la nécessité de respecter ce délai les
Parties Contractantes ont eu la volonté de couvrir le passé et que, si un doute
surgit quant à la portée précise de cette règle, c'est la *ratio legis* qui doit
prévaloir

the Commission replied that it could only be pertinent when the continuing situation was terminated, since the six-months rule could not
reasonably be extended to cover the present or *a fortiori* the future.
The Commission supported its conclusion by two wider considerations: that since the six-months rule may have the consequence that
the right of individual petition may lapse or be forfeited, it is an exception to Articles 24 and 25, which confer competence, and must therefore be restrictively interpreted;[5] and further that even if it were to be
argued that, since the *lex specialis* of Article 26 did not apply, the general rule that all international claims be brought within a reasonable
time must apply, the application had been so brought by de Becker.[6]

---

[1] 1736/62; 1971/63; 2245/64.
[2] 654/59 *Recueil* (1961) i; 1998/63: *Recueil* (1965) i.
[3] 1148/61: *Recueil* (1962) ii.
[4] Contrast 1028/61: 4 *Yearbook* 324, 334: (deprivation of civic rights in Belgium in
circumstances similar to those of de Becker—confirmation of deprivation, with certain
exceptions, by civil court—order of civil court a specific decision bringing Article 26
into operation).
[5] The Commission cited the *Nationality Decrees in Tunis and Morocco Case* [1923]
P.C.I.J.: B4 at 25, and the *German Interests in Polish Upper Silesia Case (Merits)* [1926]
P.C.I.J.: A7 at 76, and added that 'ces arguments de technique juridique acquièrent une
force particulière' in the field of human rights.
[6] 214/56: 2 *Yearbook* 244–6, Sporrong/Lönnroth 7151/75 (Sweden) 15 D.R. 15.

But the fact that, for example, detention in an asylum may be permanent does not make it a continuing situation, in the sense described above, where it depends upon an express and challengeable court order.[1]

Additional facts or complaints. Applicants to the Commission frequently send additional evidence or documents, connected with their application, or make new complaints. This may give rise to difficulties under the six-months rule. The practice of the Commission may be broadly described as follows:

Where an application is rejected for non-exhaustion of domestic remedies and the applicant proceeds to exhaust them, and then introduces a new application with regard to the same complaints, the proceedings in the first application will be treated as an integral part of the second;[2] however, the new application would still have to be introduced within six months of the final decision.

A statement of additional new facts grounding a new complaint under the Convention must generally be made the basis of a new application.

A statement of new facts relating to the initial complaint or a new complaint grounded on facts already set out in the application, may in general be accepted even though more than six months has elapsed.[3]

Renewal of application. Where an application has been rejected for non-exhaustion of domestic remedies, and the applicant proceeds to exhaust them without satisfaction, the application may be reinstated.[4]

ARTICLE 27

(1) The Commission shall not deal with any petition submitted under Article 25[5] which

    (*a*) is anonymous, or

    (*b*) is substantially the same as a matter which has already been examined by the Commission or had already been submitted to another procedure of international investigation or settlement and if it contains no relevant new information.

---

[1] 996/61: *Recueil* (1961) ii.
[2] 911/60: 4 *Yearbook* 24: the earlier application was 434/58: 2 *Yearbook* 362.
[3] See further under Article 27 (1) *b* below.
[4] 347/58: 2 *Yearbook* 407; 434/58: 2 *Yearbook* 362.
[5] Not applicable to interstate applications: 9007/77 (*Cyprus* v. *Turkey*) 13 D.R. 85, 155.

(2) The Commission shall consider inadmissible any petition submitted under Article 25 which it considers incompatible with the provisions of the present Convention, manifestly ill-founded, or an abuse of the right of petition.

An application is not abusive, even if motivated by a desire for publicity or having the character of propaganda, provided it is supported by evidence of relevant facts and is not outside the scope of the Convention.[1]

The notion of abuse cannot be extended to Article 24, given the language of Article 27 (2).[2]

(3) The Commission shall reject any petition referred to it which it considers inadmissible under Article 26.

1. La Commission ne retient aucune requête introduite par application de l'article 25, lorsque:
   (a) elle est anonyme;
   (b) elle est essentiellement la même qu'une requête précédemment examinée par la Commission ou déjà soumise à une autre instance internationale d'enquête ou de règlement et si elle ne contient pas de faits nouveaux.

2. La Commission déclare irrecevable toute requête introduite par application de l'article 25, lorsqu'elle estime la requête incompatible avec les dispositions de la présente Convention, manifestement mal fondée ou abusive.

3. La Commission rejette toute requête qu'elle considère comme irrecevable par application de l'article 26.

This crucial Article governs the decisions of the Commission upon the admissibility or inadmissibility of applications. The decision on admissibility is the one part of its work in which the Commission can be said to exercise a quasi-judicial function: it is independent, it examines the facts in the light of the Convention provisions which are applicable, hears both sides, in an *audience contradictoire* if necessary,

---

[1] *McFeeley* (U.K.) 8317/78: 20 D.R. 44; *Foti* (Italy) 7604/76: 14 D.R. 133.
[2] First *Cacok Case* 11 *Yearbook* 764; *Cyprus* v. *Turkey* 6780/74.

and renders a decision which is under the Convention a determination, which for certain purposes is final.[1]

The provisions of Article 27 are mandatory. However, two qualifications must be made here; first, paragraphs (1) and (2) are expressly limited to individual applications under Article 25, while paragraphs (3), relating to Article 26, covers both individual and interstate applications. In the second *Cyprus Case* the Commission said:

> ... in considering the admissibility of an application lodged pursuant to Article 24 ... it is not the Commission's task to ascertain whether the applicant Contracting Party establishes 'prima facie' proof of its allegations, since enquiry into such aspects relates to the merits of the case and cannot therefore be undertaken at the present stage of the proceedings ...[2]

The test under Article 27 (2) whether the application is manifestly ill founded is thus not applied.

The second qualification is that the Commission may in a proper case reserve questions of admissibility for consideration of the merits. Such a joinder of questions of admissibility with the merits has been made in a number of cases.[3]

Thus in the *Lawless Case* the Irish Government had invoked Articles 15 and 17. If the derogation under Article 15, notified by the Irish Government to the Secretary General, was effective, or if Lawless was, as the Irish Government maintained, a person engaged in activity aimed at the destruction of Convention rights and freedoms in the sense of Article 17, then his application alleging breaches of Articles 5 and 6 would have been inadmissible under the Convention in the sense of Article 27 (2). The Commission found that a determination of the issues of admissibility, raised under both Articles, turned on matters of fact, 'closely connected with matters arising upon the merits of the Applicant's claim', and therefore joined these issues to the merits.

In the *Pfunders/Fundres Case* the Commission stated the principle in the more general terms already quoted.[4]

---

[1] But see Third Protocol, Article 1 (2), which proposes a new Article 29. The proposed new Article is difficult to reconcile with the judgment of the court in the *Lawless Case*.

[2] 299/57: 2 *Yearbook* 190; 788/60: 4 *Yearbook* 180-2.

[3] *Lawless Case*: 332/57: 2 *Yearbook* 328-34; *Pfunders/Fundres Case* 788/60: Report of the Commission 64-5; 2122/64: *Recueil* (1964) ii; 2991/66. In 788/60 and 2991/66 the issue of admissibility was the exhaustion of domestic remedies.

[4] At p. 293 above.

substantially the same as a matter which has already been examined by the Commission/essentiellement la même qu'une requête précédemment examinée par la Commission

Renewal of applications to the Commission may take various forms. The applicant may adduce new facts[1] or arguments, or make additional complaints, or new parties may join.[2] Whether an application is substantially the same–the French text is here to be preferred to the vague word 'matter'–must be a question of fact in each case, but the Commission has indicated[3] that it should not be too strict:

> Considérant le domaine dans lequel elle exerce sa tâche et ses attributions, la Commission estime qu'elle ne doit pas, dans la matière de la sauvegarde des Droits de l'Homme, suivre des règles strictes qui aboutiraient à revêtir ses décisions de l'autorité de la chose jugée, comme il en est devant les Tribunaux de droit commun, lorsqu'il y a identité d'objet, de parties et de cause.

The reference to another procedure of international investigation or settlement is linked with Article 62.

Article 27 (2) contains the prime criteria for the determination of admissibility of individual applications. Since the provision is mandatory, the Commission applies each of the criteria *ex officio*.[4] No complete definition of these criteria is either possible or useful, nor is it always easy to distinguish between the first two, but their general function may be seen in the practice of the Commission.

incompatible with the provisions of the present Convention/incompatible avec les dispositions de la présente Convention

Without exclusion of other possibilities, an application may be said to be incompatible with the Convention, which

(1) claims a right or freedom, which is not protected or guaranteed by the Convention; or

---

[1] 434/58: 2 *Yearbook* 362, in relation to 172/56: 1 *Yearbook* 211; see for further proceedings 911/60, already considered under Article 26 above.

[2] 499/59: 2 *Yearbook* 397.

[3] 202/56: 1 *Yearbook* 191.

[4] 202/56: 1 *Yearbook* 192.

(2) falls outside the scope of the Convention *ratione temporis*,[1] *personae*, or *loci*; or

(3) falls within the scope of a reservation to the Convention under Article 64; or

(4) is made by an applicant engaged in activities described in Article 17.[2]

manifestly ill founded/ manifestement mal fondée

This seemingly simple phrase, derived from continental rather than English juridical usage, is by no means always easy to apply. The Commission has given it slightly different formulations, but in the same sense.

The Commission

declare an application inadmissible as being manifestly ill-founded only when an examination of the file does not disclose a prima facie violation (*l'apparence de semblable violation*),[3]

or again

only when a preliminary examination of the case does not disclose any appearance (*l'apparence même*) of a violation of the Convention;[4]

and so its task

is limited to determining whether a prima facie examination[5] of the facts of the case and the statements of the parties does or does not disclose any possible ground on which a breach of the Convention could ultimately be found to be established;[6]

and again[7]

. . . at the present stage of the proceedings [admissibility] the task of the Commission is not to determine whether an examination of the case . . . discloses the actual existence of a violation of one of the rights and freedoms guaranteed by the Convention but only to determine whether it excludes any possibility of the existence of such a violation.

---

[1] For a discussion of this head see M.-A. Eissen, 'La Compétence ratione temporis de la Commission', *Ann. Français de D.I.* (1963) 723.

[2] 250/57: 1 *Yearbook* 222.

[3] 214/56: 2 *Yearbook* 254. [4] 524/59: 3 *Yearbook* 338.

[5] 'Prima facie examination' and 'preliminary examination' appear both as 'un premier examen' in the French text.

[6] 332/57: 2 *Yearbook* 336. [7] 596/59: 3 *Yearbook* 368.

The most common phrase used by the Commission is 'no appearance of a violation',[1] and the general concept might be expressed in English terms as 'no prima facie case' or 'no case to answer'. What is manifestly ill founded then is a question of fact, or of the facts seen in the light of Convention provisions, which are in principle applicable to them. Here, in general, lies the distinction between what is manifestly ill founded and what is incompatible; if an application fairly raises the issue, whether or not there is a breach of a Convention provision, it is not incompatible.

Logical problems may arise of priority among the various grounds of inadmissibility. For example, in what order must the rule of exhaustion of domestic remedies and the criterion of manifestly ill founded be applied? It might be said that the criterion must be applied first, for if the application discloses on its facts no appearance of a breach of the Convention, then the rule is irrelevant; for, though for the facts complained of there may be a domestic remedy, that cannot involve the Convention. It might be added that, as it were, to invite the applicant to exhaust domestic remedies for a complaint which the Commission considers manifestly ill founded under the Convention is futile.

Another view would be that the complaint must be examined as it stands and as it is made,[2] and that domestic remedies must be exhausted in respect of it as such, before the Commission can consider its admissibility under Article 27. It could be said that this course is particularly called for where the Convention provisions in issue form part of the domestic law of the respondent State.

In practice, the Commission may, in declaring an application inadmissible, give more grounds than are strictly necessary or grounds that may appear not to be logically compatible: thus, it may reject an application for non-exhaustion of domestic remedies, but add that it is also manifestly ill founded. The purpose is here simply to show the applicant that his application has been fully considered.

abuse of the right of petition/abusive

The Commission is naturally hesitant to declare an application as an abuse of the right of petition. It has said that the fact that an applica-

---

[1] Compare also 'aucun commencement de preuve': 776/60: *Recueil* (1961) i; and no submission of 'material to substantiate allegations' 905/60: *Recueil* (1961) ii.

[2] Compare the principle followed in the *Finnish Ships Arbitration* [1934] 3 R.I.A.A. 1479, 1503, 1594.

tion is inspired by political motives, or is designed as propaganda or to seek publicity, does not itself make it an abuse. Offensive or scurrilous expressions in an application may also be an abuse of the right of petition, at least if they are aimed at individuals and do not serve in any way to support allegations of a breach of the Convention.[1] 'Persistent negligence' in responding to requests by the Commission for further information or documents,[2] and the repetition of baseless applications, have also been held an abuse.[3]

Two aspects of the procedure of the Commission, as far as it concerns the criterion of manifestly ill founded should be noted. First, it has become an established practice, on applications of substance, that the applicant and respondent government be given the opportunity of a hearing before the Commission, in addition to their written statements.[4] It is then sometimes difficult to restrict the proceedings to a mere preliminary examination; and the inquiry into the facts, and their analysis in light of the Convention provisions, for the purpose of deciding whether or not the application is 'manifestly ill founded', can come very close to an examination of the merits. Indeed, an officious bystander might ask how there can be extended argument about what is manifestly ill founded.

Secondly, there is no qualified majority prescribed by the Convention for decisions on admissibility, which are taken like all other of its decisions by a majority of the members present and voting. It can happen then that a substantial minority may not consider the application to be manifestly ill founded, but it must nevertheless be rejected. It would not be unreasonable to have a rule that if, say, a third of the members found the application not manifestly ill founded, it should be admitted.

ARTICLE 28

In the event of the Commission accepting a petition referred to it:

(*a*) it shall, with a view to ascertaining the facts, undertake together with the representatives of the parties an examination

---

[1] 2424/65: *Recueil* 21.
[2] 1297/61: *Recueil* (1963) ii following 26/55 and 244/57: 1 *Yearbook* 195, 197.
[3] 1080/61: *Recueil* (1962) i; 1307/61: 5 *Yearbook* 236.
[4] See Rule 46 (1) of the Commission Rules of Procedure.

of the petition and, if need be, an investigation, for the effective conduct of which the States concerned shall furnish all necessary facilities, after an exchange of views with the Commission:

(*b*) it shall place itself at the disposal of the parties concerned with a view to securing a friendly settlement of the matter on the basis of respect for Human Rights as defined in this Convention.

Dans le cas où la Commission retient la requête:

(*a*) afin d'établir les faits, elle procède à un examen contradictoire de la requête avec les représentants des parties et, s'il y a lieu, à une enquête pour la conduite efficace de laquelle les États intéressés fourniront toutes facilités nécessaires, après échange de vues avec la Commission;

(*b*) elle se met à la disposition des intéressés en vue de parvenir à un règlement amiable de l'affaire qui s'inspire du respect des Droits de l'homme, tel que les reconnaît la présent Convention.

This Article defines the essential functions of the Commission: to investigate the facts of an application, and to act as the medium of a friendly settlement of the matter, if that is possible.

accepting/retient

The English word should be 'admitting'.

an examination ... and, if need be, an investigation/un examen contradictoire ... et, s'il y a lieu, à une enquête

The French text underlines the point that in the examination not only must the principle *audi alteram partem* be observed, but the parties must each be given the opportunity to comment on or answer the statements or arguments of the other. The distinction made between examination and investigation suggests that the latter covers a visit of inquiry by the Commission or members of it to a particular place or to question particular persons.[1]

---

[1] As in the first Cyprus Case; see also 1850/63, 2178/64 and 2686/65 for investigations by the Commission away from Strasbourg. See Rule 58 of the Commission Rules by Procedure.

In the task of friendly settlement, the function of the Commission is to be a medium or channel of negotiation, rather than to take the initiative by proposing terms.[1] The requirement that any settlement be conformable to the Convention is, however, important, and imposes limits on the compromise of rights.

There is an analogy between friendly settlement in Article 28 (*a*) and preliminary negotiations between the parties in the regime of the International Court of Justice. The Permanent Court observed that

le règleme judiciaire des conflits internationaux, en vue duquel la Cour est instituée, n'est qu'un succédant au règlement direct et amiable des ces conflits entre les Parties; . . . dès lors, il appartient à la Cour de faciliter, dans toute la mesure compatible avec son statut, pareil règlement direct et amiable.[2]

and

La Cour se rend bien compte de toute l'importance de la règle suivant laquelle ne doivent être portées devant elle que des affairs qui ne sont susceptibles d'être réglées par négociations.[3]

However, the European Court of Human Rights has, in its own words,[4] a 'supervisory duty (*devoir du contrôle*)' in relation to the Convention, analogous to that indicated in the final clause of Article 28 (*b*); its relation to friendly settlement is therefore different from that of the International Court.

It is for the Sub-commission to decide whether in the exchanges directed towards a friendly settlement a solution appears possible. If a *point mort* is reached,[5] then Article 31 applies.

It is to be observed that Article 28, and the three Articles which follow it, govern the handling of all applications by the Commission, whether they are brought under Article 24 or 25. Some of the language, however, appears to be a survival from earlier drafts setting out a procedure for dealing with interstate applications; for example, the expresions 'States concerned', where 'State or States concerned' would be exact, in Articles 28 (*a*), 30, and 31, and even perhaps 'representative of the parties' in Article 28 (*a*) are apt for interstate rather than individual applications.

---

[1] For instances of friendly settlement see 1727/62: *Recueil* 15 and 2120/64: *Recueil* 21.
[2] *Free Zones of Upper Savoy and Gex Case* [1929] P.C.I.J.: A22 at 13.
[3] *Mavrommatis Palestine Concessions Case* [1924] P.C.I.J.: A2 at 15.
[4] *de Becker Case*: Judgment of 27.3.1962, §§ 11, 12.
[5] 'Si [la conversation] s'est heurtée finalement à un non possumus ou à un non volumus péremptoire de l'une des parties.' *Mavrommatis Palestine Concessions Case*, at 13.

ARTICLE 29

After it has accepted a petition submitted under Article 25, the Commission may nevertheless decide unanimously to reject the petition if, in the course of its examination, it finds that the existence of one of the grounds for non-acceptance provided for in Article 27 has been established.

In such a case, the decision shall be communicated to the parties.

Après avoir retenu une requête par l'application de l'Article 25, Commission peut néanmoins décider a l'unanimité de la rejeter si, en cours d'examen, elle constate l'existence d'un des motifs de non-recevabilite prévus a l'article 27. En pareil cas, la décision est communiquée au parties.

ARTICLE 30

If the Commission succeeds in effecting a friendly settlement in accordance with Article 28, it shall draw up a report which will be sent to the States concerned, to the Committee of Ministers, and to the Secretary General of the Council of Europe for publication. This report shall be confined to a brief statement of the facts and of the solution reached.

Si elle parvient à obtenir un règlement amiable, conformement a l'article 28, la Commission dresse un rapport qui est transmis aux États interessés, au Comité des Ministres et au Sécrétaire General de Conseil de l'Europe, aux fins de publication. Ce rapport se limite à un bref exposé des faits et de la solution adoptée.

Articles 29 and 30 were both amended by Protocol No. 3, which came into force on 21.9.1970. The phrase in Article 29, referring to grounds of inadmissibility, comprises all the grounds named, though it is hard to see how an admitted application could come to be seen as manifestly ill-founded.

ARTICLE 31

(1) If a solution is not reached, the Commission shall draw up a Report on the facts and state its opinion as to whether the facts found disclose a breach by the State concerned of its obligations under the Convention. The opinions of all the members of the Commission on this point may be stated in the Report.

(2) The Report shall be transmitted to the Committee of Ministers. It shall also be transmitted to the States concerned, who shall not be at liberty to publish it.

(3) In transmitting the Report to the Committee of Ministers the Commission may make such proposals as it thinks fit.

1. Si une solution n'a pu intervenir, la Commission rédige un rapport dans lequel elle constate les faits et formule un avis sur le point de savoir si les faits constatés révèlent, de la part de l'État intéressé, une violation des obligations qui lui incombent aux termes de la Convention. Les opionions de tous les membres de la Commission sur ce point peuvent être exprimées dans ce rapport.

2. Le rapport est transmis au Comité des Ministres; il est également communiqué aux États intéressés, qui n'ont pas la faculté de la publier.

3. En transmittant le rapport au Comité des Ministres, la Commission peut formuler les propositions qu'elle juge appropriées.

The Report of the Commission[1] may contain the opinions of individual members on the question whether there has or has not been a breach of the Convention in the case. Such opinions may be either separate or dissenting. The Report has in one instance set out a joint dissenting opinion in a decision declaring an application inadmissible.[2]

---

[1] For a list of Reports see Appendix 2.
[2] *Iversen Case*: 1468/62: *Recueil* (1963) ii.

The publication of the Report presents certain problems. Both the Commission and the Sub-commission conduct all their proceedings *in camera*,[1] and parties are always warned that they may not disclose matters arising during hearings before the Commission. Publication of the Report of a Sub-commission under Article 30 is prescribed because the case has met a satisfactory settlement and is therefore terminated. The Report of the Commission under Article 31 is not, however, the final stage; action has still to be taken by the Committee of Ministers or the case may be referrred to the court. Publication may therefore be withheld, until either the case has been referred to the court, or a decision taken by the Committee of Ministers under Article 32 (2) has not been satisfactorily complied with.[2] Where a case is referred to the court, the rule against publication is not to be understood as precluding the communication of the Report to the applicant[3] and other persons directly concerned. In the *Lawless Case* the Irish Government maintained before the court that the Commission had no authority to 'publish' the report to the applicant, that Rule 76 of the Rules of Procedure made by it was *ultra vires*, and that the comments of the applicant upon the Report were not admissible in the proceedings before the court.

The court answered these contentions saying:

it is true that the debates and the judgement alone are public and that other documents in the case can only be published, in accordance with Rule 52 . . . if the Court expressly authorises such publication; whereas however this provision cannot alter the fact that the proceedings take place in the presence of the Parties (le caractère contradictoire de la procédure),[4] nor does it prevent the communication of the documents in the case to the persons or bodies directly concluded, with the proviso, made either by the Commission or by one of the Parties, that they should not be published; . . . there is therefore a distinction between the publication of documents for which the authorization of the Court is required and the communication of the said documents to the Applicant, which requires no such authorization; . . . in communicating its

---

[1] Article 33; and see Commission Rules of Procedure, Rule 30.

[2] In the *Nielsen Case*, where the Committee of Ministers had confirmed the view of the Commission that there had been no breach of the Convention, the Committee authorized publication of the Report of the Commission at the request of the Danish Government with exception of the part dealing with attempts at friendly settlement.

[3] See Commission Rules of Procedure, Rule 76.

[4] The French text of the judgment is authentic.

Report to Lawless, the Commission did not fail to draw attention to its confidential character in expressly forbidding its publication.[1]

It is the practice of the Commission to issue press communiqués at various stages, including admissibility, on applications having a general importance or interest.[2]

The provision in Article 31 (3) authorizing the Commission to make proposals has given rise to some controversy. It might be read as meaning that the Commission is free to make any proposals that it thinks fit, without limitation: in support of this it may be pointed out, first, that the proposals may be submitted 'in transmitting the Report', which suggests that they are or may be collateral and separate from the conclusions of the Report itself; and secondly, that the expression 'such proposals as it thinks fit' is not qualified in any way, as to subject-matter or purpose, and appears to give the Commission a full discretion.

Against this, it might be said that the prime task of the Commission, as defined in Article 19, 'to ensure the observance of the engagements undertaken by the High Contracting Parties', limits proposals it may make under Article 31 (3) to cases where it is of the opinion that there has been a breach of the Convention; and that, where it is of the opinion that there has been no breach, there is no place for proposals, which could constitute an interference in the domestic affairs of a contracting State. The second view appears preferable.

ARTICLE 32

(1) If the question is not referred to the Court in accordance with Article 48 of this Convention within a period of three months from the date of the transmission of the Report to the Committee of Ministers, the Committee of Ministers shall decide by a majority of two-thirds of the members entitled to sit on the Committee whether there has been a violation of the Convention.[3]

---

[1] *Lawless Case*: Judgment of 14.11.1960: 3 *Yearbook* 510-12. Judge Maridakis dissented on this point. The court has now amended Rule 36 of its Rules of Procedure to authorize the Registrar to make public the Report of the Commission, excluding the part relating to the attempt to reach a friendly settlement, on the fixing of the date for the oral proceedings.

[2] See Doc. DH (61) 3 at 10.

[3] Absence of majority: 4626/70 *et al.* (U.K.) 13 D.R. 5.

(2) In the affirmative case the Committee of Ministers shall prescribe a period during which the High Contracting Party concerned must take the measures required by the decision of the Committee of Ministers.

(3) If the High Contracting Party concerned has not taken satisfactory measures within the prescribed period, the Committee of Ministers shall decide by the majority provided for in paragraph (1) above what effect shall be given to its original decision and shall publish the Report.

(4) The High Contracting Parties undertake to regard as binding on them any decision which the Committee of Ministers may take in application of the preceding paragraphs.

1. Si, dans un délai de trois mois à dater de la transmission au Comité des Ministres du rapport de la Commission, l'affaire n'es pas déférée à la Cour par application de l'article 48 de la présente Convention, le Comité des Ministres prend, par un vote à la majorité des deux tiers des représentants ayant le droit de siéger au Comité, une décision sur la question de savoir s'il y a eu ou non une violation de la Convention.

2. Dans l'affirmative, le Comité des Ministres fixe un délai dans lequel la Haute Partie Contractante intéressée doit prendre les mesures qu'entraîne la décision du Comité des Ministres.

3. Si la Haute Partie Contractante intéressée n'a pas adopté des mesures satisfaisantes dans le délai imparti, le Comité des Ministres donne à sa décision initiale, par la majorité prévue un paragraphe 1 ci-dessus, les suites qu'elle comporte et publie le rapport.

4. Les Hautes Parties Contractantes s'engagent à considérer comme obligatoire pour elles toute décision que le Comité des Ministres peut prendre en application des paragraphes précédents.

The Committee of Ministers has adopted from 1959 to 1966 certain rules of procedure[1] to govern its action under Article 32, and has those rules under consideration for possible extension and revision. Rule 4 suggests that the Committee of Ministers may itself carry out an investigation, in 'memorials, counter-memorials or other documents' which may be laid before it by the parties; but the reference in the Rule to 'the States Parties to the dispute', itself a not wholly apt description of applications under Articles 24 or 25, may mean that the Rule is limited to interstate applications.

The Committee of Ministers has not yet had occasion to take action under Articles 32 (2) or (3).[2] It has been held in Austria that a finding by the Committee of Ministers that the judgment or order of a national court is a breach of the Convention does not of itself annul that judgment or order.[3]

ARTICLE 33

The Commission shall meet *in camera*.

La Commission siège à huis clos.

ARTICLE 34

Subject to the provisions of Article 29, the Commission shall take its decisions by a majority of the Members present and voting.

Sous reserve des dispositions de l'Article 29, les décisions de la Commission sont prises à la majorité des membres présents et votant.

No precise rule governs the question what degree of participation in the handling of an application by the Commission entitles a particular member to vote in a decision. It is inevitable that in a body, which is not in permanent session, and the members of which have other duties beside the work of the Commission, not every member can be present

---

[1] See *Collected Texts*, 5th ed., section 4.
[2] For its decisions under Article 32 (1), see Appendix 2.
[3] Oberster Gerichtshof (29.1.1963): *Österr. Juristen-Zeitung* (1963) 328.

at every meeting. Rules 32 and 33 of the Commission Rules of Procedure direct how questions of participation are to be settled.

ARTICLE 35

The Commission shall meet as the circumstances require. The
meetings shall be convened by the Secretary-General of the
Council of Europe.

La Commission se réunit lorsque les circonstances l'exigent.
Elle est convoquée par le Secrétaire Général du Conseil de
l'Europe.

The Commission has adopted the practice of fixed sessions. These are
settled at the end of the year for the following year.

ARTICLE 36

The Commission shall draw up its own rules of procedure.

La Commission établit son règlement intérieur.

The court has made certain observations on the place of the Commission Rules of Procedure in the Convention system. In the *Lawless Case*
the Irish Government maintained, as already noted, that Rule 76 was
ultra vires the Commission. The court considered this first in general
and then in the applicability of the Rule in the particular case. Considering its own competence in general, the court said:

> ... the Court is not competent to take decisions such as that to delete a rule
> from the Commission's Rules of Procedure–a step which would affect all
> parties to the Convention–since this would amount to having power to make
> rulings on matters of procedure or to render advisory opinions; ... notwith-
> standing, it is the duty of the Court, in the exercise of its functions, to ensure
> that the Convention is respected and, if need be, to point to any irregularities
> and to refuse to apply in such a case any provisions or regulations which are
> contrary to the Convention. ...[1]

The Commission has undertaken, through a working group of four
members,[2] a complete revision of its Rules of Procedure.

---

[1] Judgment of 14.11.1960: 3 *Yearbook* 506-8.
[2] It began work in July 1967.

ARTICLE 37

The secretariat of the Commission shall be provided by the Secretary-General of the Council of Europe.

Le secrétariat de la Commission est assuré par le Secrétaire Général du Conseil de l'Europe.

The small Secretariat forms an integral part of the Commission. It conducts correspondence with applicants, prepares factual summaries, and assembles papers, on applications; it helps to systematize the jurisprudence of the Commission; and plays an important part in the preparation of draft decisions and reports.

The Secretary normally sits with the Commission at their meetings, which are also always attended by the member of the Secretariat who has worked on the application being considered. The Secretary also maintains contact with the authorties of a government respondent to an application at all stages, including friendly settlement.

SECTION IV

ARTICLE 38

The European Court of Human Rights shall consist of a number of judges equal to that of the Members of the Council of Europe. No two judges may be nationals of the same State.

La Court européenne des Droits de l'homme se compose d'un nombre de juges égal à celui des Membres du Conseil de l'Europe. Elle ne peut comprendre plus d'un ressortissant d'un même État.

ARTICLE 39

(1) The members of the Court shall be elected by the Consultative Assembly by a majority of the votes cast from a list of persons nominated by the Members of the Council of Europe; each Member shall nominate three candidates, of whom two at least shall be its nationals.

(2) As far as applicable, the same procedure shall be followed to complete the Court in the event of the admision of new Members of the Council of Europe, and in filling casual vacancies.

(3) The candidates shall be of high moral character and must either possess the qualifications required for appointment to high judicial office or be jurisconsults of recognised competence.

1. Les membres de la Cour sont élus par l'Assemblée Consultative à la majorité des voix exprimées sur une liste de personnes présentée par les Membres du Conseil de l'Europe, chacun de ceux-ci devant présenter trois candidats, dont deux au moins de sa nationalité.

2. Dans la mesure oú elle est applicable, la même procédure est suivie pour compléter la Cour en cas d'admission des

nouveaux Membres au Conseil de l'Europe, et pour pourvoir aux sièges devenus vacants.

3. Les candidats devront jouir de la plus haute considération morale et réunir les conditions requises pour l'exercice de hautes fonctions judiciaires ou être des jurisconsultes possédant une compétence notoire.

ARTICLE 40

(1) The members of the Court shall be elected for a period of nine years. They may be re-elected. However, of the members elected at the first election the terms of four members shall expire at the end of six years.

(2) The members whose terms are to expire at the end of the initial periods of three and six years shall be chosen by lot by the Secretary-General immediately after the first election has been completed.

(3) In order to ensure that, as far as possible, one third of the membership of the Court shall be renewed every three years, the Consultative Assembly may decide, before proceeding to any subsequent election, that the term or terms of office of one or more members to be elected shall be for a period other than nine years but not more than twelve and not less than six years.

(4) In cases where more than one term of office is involved and the Consultative Assembly applies the preceding paragraph, the allocation of their terms of office shall be effected by the drawing of lots by the Secretary General immediately after the election.

(5) A member of the Court elected to replace a member whose term of office has not expired shall hold office for the remainder of his predecessor's term.

(6) The members of the Court shall hold office until replaced. After having been replaced, they shall continue to deal with such cases as they already have under consideration.

1. Les membres de la Cour sont élus pour une durée de neuf ans. Ils sont rééligibles. Toutefois, en ce qui concerne les membres désignés à la première élection, les fonctions de quatre des membres prendront din au bout de trois ans, celles de quatre autres membres prendront fin au bout de six ans.

2. Les membres dont les fonctions prendront fin au terme des périodes initiales de trois et six ans, sont désignés par tirage au sort effectué par le Secrétaire Général du Conseil de l'Europe, immédiatement après qu'il aura été procédeu à la première élection.

3. Le membre de la Cour élu en remplacement d'un membre dont le mandat n'est pas expiré achève le terme du mandat de son prédécesseur.

4. Les membres de la Cour restent en fonctions jusqu'à leur remplacement. Après ce remplacement, ils continuent de connaître des affaires dont ils sont déjà saisis.

See the Fifth Protocol, Article 2, for amendments to this Article similar to those of Article 22.[1]

ARTICLE 41

The Court shall elect its President and Vice-President for a period of three years. They may be re-elected.

La Cour élit son Président et son Vice-Président pour une durée de trois ans. Ceux-ci sont rééligibles.

ARTICLE 42

The members of the Court shall receive for each day of duty a compensation to be determined by the Committee of Ministers.

---

[1] *Collected Texts*, 5th ed., section 5.

Les membres de la Cour reçoivent une indemnité par jour de fonctions, à fixer par le Comité des Ministres.

ARTICLE 43

For the consideration of each case brought before it the Court shall consist of a Chamber composed of seven judges. There shall sit as an ex officio member of the Chamber the judge who is a national of any State party concerned, or, if there is none, a person of its choice who shall sit in the capacity of judge; the names of the other judges shall be chosen by lot by the President before the opening of the case.

Pour l'examen de chaque affaire portée devant elle, la Cour est constituée en une Chambre composée de sept juges. En feront partie d'office le juge ressortissant de tout État intéressé ou, à défaut, une personne de son choix pour siéger en qualité de juge; les noms des autres juges sont tirés au sort, avant le début de l'examen de l'affaire, par les soins du Président.

ARTICLE 44

Only the High Contracting Parties and the Commission shall have the right to bring a case before the Court.

Seule les Hautes Parties Contractantes et la Commission ont qualité pour se présenter devant la Cour.

This Article, which is amplified by Article 48, precludes the bringing of a case to the court either by the Committee of Ministers or by an individual.

The first limitation would be reduced in part by the entry into force of the Second Protocol, drafted in May 1963, Article 1 of which would enable the court to give advisory opinions, at the request of the Committee of Ministers, on 'legal questions concerning the interpretation of the Convention'. However, Article 1 (2) imposes restrictions:

Such opinions shall not deal with any question relating to the content or scope of the rights of freedoms defined in Section I of the Convention and the

Protocols thereto, or with any other question which the Commission, the Court or the Committee of Ministers might have to consider in consequence of any such proceedings as could be instituted in accordance with the Convention.

It would take some ingenuity to formulate a legal question of interpretation of the Convention, which would be likely to arise before the Committee of Ministers, but would not also fall under one of these restrictions. A wider advisory competence for the court, than that given in the Protocol, could be of great use and value.

Since an individual cannot bring a case before the court, and cannot *a priori* be a respondent there, an applicant under Article 25 is not a party to the proceedings before the court, where his application has been referred to it. The court resolved the problem of the representation of an individual applicant before it in the *Lawless Case*. While recognizing the force of the precedents invoked by the Commission on the role of individuals before international tribunals,[1] the court found that none of them covered the case of an individual proceeding against his own Government, and that the solution to the problem must be looked for in the special nature of the procedure prescribed in the Convention:

la Cour doit avoir notamment égard au devoir lui incombant de sauvegarder les intérêts de l'individu qui ne peut être Partie devant elle; ... la procédure organisée devant la Cour, tant par la Convention que par le Règlement de la Cour, est tournée vers les fins qui concernent le requérant; ... il est dans l'intérêt d'une bonne administration de la justice que la Cour puisse connaître et, le cas échéant, prendre en considération le point de vue du requérant.

The court considered that the means it had at its disposal for this purpose were the Report of the Commission and observations made to the court, orally or in writing, by delegates of the Commission

qui en vertu de sa mission d'intérêt général, a le droit, même si elle ne les prend pas à son compte, de faire état, devant la Cour sous sa propre responsabilité, des considérations du requérant en tant qu'élément propre à éclairer celle-ci,

and finally evidence given by the applicant before the court as a witness under Rule 38 (1) of the Court Rules of Procedure.[2]

---

[1] See in particular, the *U.N. Administrative Tribunal Case* [1954] I.C.J. Rep. 47; and *Judgments of the Administrative Tribunal of the I.L.O.* [1956] I.C.J. Rep. 77.

[2] *Lawless Case*: Judgment of 14.11.1960: 3 *Yearbook* 514–16.

ARTICLE 45

The jurisdiction of the Court shall extend to all cases concerning the interpretation and application of the present Convention which the High Contracting Parties or the Commission shall refer to it in accordance with Article 48.

La compétence de la Cour s'étend à toutes les affaires concernant l'interprétation et l'application de la présente Convention que les Hautes Parties Contractantes ou la Commission lui soumettront, dans les conditions prévues par l'article 48.

In the *Belgium Linguistic Cases* the court dismissed the preliminary objection of the Belgian Government with a firm asseveration of Article 45:

> It follows from the very terms of Article 45 that the basis of the jurisdiction *ratione materiae* of the Court is established once the case raises a question of the interpretation or application of the Convention; and ... therefore the Court may decline jurisdiction only if the complaints of the Applicant are clearly outside the provisions of the Convention and the Protocol (étrangers aux dispositions de la Convention . . .).[1]

This passage is of interest for two further reasons. First, it implies that the court may not decline jurisdiction on grounds, such as judicial propriety, which may be material in the adjudication of disputes between States.[2] Secondly, it makes it clear that while a declaration by the Commission that an application is inadmissible for incompatibility with the Convention is conclusive, a declaration of admissibility does not preclude a subsequent finding by the court that the complaints of the applicant are in fact incompatible.

To return to the judgment, the court found that the interpretation and application of three Articles–Articles 8 and 14 of the Convention, and Article 2 of the Protocol–were plainly in issue, as appeared both from the Report of the Commission and the argumentation of the Belgian Government itself; it found further that the plea of the Belgian Government, based on the notion of reserved domain, was not to be regarded as a preliminary objection of incompetence.

---

[1] *Case relating to Certain Aspects of the Laws on the Use of languages in Education in Belgium (Preliminary Objection)*: Judgment of 9.2.1967 at 18.

[2] See *Northern Cameroons Case (Preliminary Objection)* [1963] I.C.J. Rep. at 37.

In deciding unanimously to proceed to the examination of the merits, the court said:

... in reaching this decision, which is of a procedural nature and which also disposes of the alternative submission of the Belgian Government that the objection should be joined to the merits, the Court in no way prejudges the merits of the dispute; ... the Government remains free to take up again and to develop on the merits its arguments on the scope of the rights and freedoms laid down in the Convention and the Protocol.[1]

This passage is again of interest for its firm categorization of the plea based on the notion of reserved domain. Though advanced as part of the preliminary objection of incompetence, the court refused to accord it the character in itself of a preliminary objection; it was part of the merits, that is to say, of the interpretation of the three Articles in issue, the issue raised by the plea being whether the scope of their application was in any way limited by the principle of the reserved domain. It would therefore be open to the Belgian Government to argue that issue on the merits.

ARTICLE 46

(1) Any of the High Contracting Parties may at any time declare that it recognises as compulsory *ipso facto* and without special agreement the jurisdiction of the Court in all matters concerning the interpretation and application of the present Convention.

(2) The declarations referred to above may be made unconditionally or on condition of reciprocity on the part of several or certain other High Contracting Parties or for a specified period.

(3) These declarations shall be deposited with the Secretary-General of the Council of Europe who shall transmit copies thereof to the High Contracting Parties.

1. Chacune des Hautes Parties Contractantes peut, à n'importe quel moment, déclarer reconnaître comme obligatoire de

---

[1] See *Northern Cameroons Case* (*Preliminary Objection*) [1963] I.C.J. Rep. at 19.

plein droit et sans convention spéciale, la juridiction de la Cour sur toutes les affaires concernant l'interprétation et l'application de la présente Convention.

2. Les déclarations ci-dessus visées pourront être faites purement et simplement ou sous condition de réciprocité de la part de plusiers ou de certaines autres Parties Contractantes ou pour une durée déterminée.

3. Ces déclarations seront remises au Secrétaire Général du Conseil de l'Europe qui en transmettra copie aux Hautes Parties Contractantes.

This Article is modelled on Article 36 (2) of the Statute of International Court. Where a declaration is made on conditions of reciprocity, it would appear to have the effect of giving the court jurisdiction only over cases which have been before the Commission in interstate applications between declarant States. Austria made her declaration on condition of reciprocity *vis-à-vis* any other contracting party making a similar declaration. However, when the Commission referred the *Neumeister Case*[1] to the court, Austria also referred it soon after as respondent State under Article 48 (*d*): since the court then had jurisdiction under Article 48 by reason either of the reference by Austria, or of the reference of the Commission with the consent of Austria, the reciprocity clause did not come into question.

ARTICLE 47

The Court may only deal with a case after the Commission has acknowledged the failure of efforts for a friendly settlement and within the period of three months provided for in Article 32.

La Cour ne peut être saisie d'une affaire qu'après la constatation, par la Commission, de l'échec du règlement amiable et dans le délai de trois mois prévu à l'article 32.

[1] 1936/63.

ARTICLE 48

The following may bring a case before the Court, provided that
the High Contracting Party concerned, if there is only one, or
the High Contracting Parties concerned, if there is more than
one, are subject to the compulsory jurisdiction of the Court or,
failing that, with the consent of the High Contracting Party
concerned, if there is only one, or of the High Contracting
Parties concerned if there is more than one:

  (*a*) the Commission;
  (*b*) a High Contracting Party whose national is alleged to be
       a victim;
  (*c*) a High Contracting Party which referred the case to the
       Commission;
  (*d*) a High Contracting Party against which the complaint
       has been lodged.

A la condition que la Haute Partie Contractante intéressée, s'il
n'y en a qu'une, ou les Hautes Parties Contractantes intéressées, s'il y en a plus d'une, soient soumises à la juridiction
obligatoire de la Cour ou, à défaut, avec le consentement ou
l'agrément de la Haute Partie Contractante intéressée, s'il n'y
en a qu'une, ou des Hautes Parties Contractantes intéressées,
s'il y en a plus d'une, la Court peut être saisie:

  (*a*) par la Commission;
  (*b*) par une Haute Partie Contractante dont la victime est le
       ressortissant;
  (*c*) par une Haute Partie Contractante qui a saisi la Com-
       mission;
  (*d*) par une Haute Partie Contractante mise en cause.

ARTICLE 49

In the event of dispute as to whether the Court has jurisdiction,
the matter shall be settled by the decision of the Court.

En cas de contestation sur le point de savoir si la Cour est
compétente, la Cour décide.

ARTICLE 50

If the Court finds that a decision or a measure taken by a legal authority or any other authority of a High Contracting Party is completely or partially in conflict with the obligations arising from the present Convention, and if the internal law of the said Party allows only partial reparation to be made for the consequences of this decision or measure, the decision of the Court shall, if necessary, afford just satisfaction to the injured party.

Si la décision de la Cour déclare qu'une décision prise ou une mesure ordonnée par une autorité judiciaire ou toute autre autorité d'une Partie Contractante se trouve entièrement ou partiellement en opposition avec des obligations découlant de la présente Convention, et si le droit interne de la dite Partie ne permet qu'imparfaitement d'effacer les conséquences de cette décision ou de cette mesure, la décision de la Cour accorde, s'il y a lieu, à la partie lésée une satisfaction équitable.

This Article provides for the order that the court may make in certain cases, in addition to its judgment, to remedy the breach of the Convention.[1]

if the internal law ... allows the only partial reparation to be made for the consequences of this decision/si le droit interne de la dite Partie ne permet qu'imparfaitement d'effacer les conséquences de cette décision

This clause poses a question of the relationship between Article 50 and Article 13. The expressions used in the two Articles are not exactly equivalent: 'remedy/recours'; 'reparation/d'effacer les conséquences', but the general purpose is clear that there shall be a remedy for a breach of the Convention. It is to be observed that the clause in question in Article 50 deals not with the failure of a national authority to accord an effective remedy, but with the situation in which the domestic law allows only partial reparation, that is to say, an ineffective remedy. This deficiency in the domestic law would have become

---

[1] For a discussion of the effects of a judgment of the court see T. Burgenthal, International Law Series No. 5 (B.I.I.C.L.), 94–106.

apparent to the court in the Report of the Commission dealing with the exhaustion of domestic remedies and probably also in submissions of the parties, or observations by the individual applicant presented to the court by the Commission.

But whatever view is taken of the precise sense and effect of Article 13,[1] it is difficult to see how such a deficiency would not itself be a breach of Article 13. The question could then arise whether the court could, in addition to making an order for 'just satisfaction' in the particular case, also order a correction of the deficiency in the domestic law.

The enforcement of any order made by the court is the responsibility of the Committee of Ministers under Article 54.

ARTICLE 51

(1) Reasons shall be given for the judgment of the Court.

(2) If the judgment does not represent in whole or in part the unanimous opinion of the judges, any shall be entitled to deliver a separate opinion.

1. L'arrêt de la Cour est motivé.

2. Si l'arrêt n'exprime pas en tout ou en partie l'opinion unanime des juges, tout juge aura le droit d'y joindre l'exposé de son opinion individuelle.

ARTICLE 52

The judgment of the Court shall be final.

L'arrêt de la Cour est définitif.

This provision does not, it appears,[2] exclude the possibility of proceedings for the interpretation or even in certain circumstances the revision, of a judgment. It is to be noted that a party or the Commission, but not the Committee of Ministers, may request an interpretation of a judgment.

---

[1] See discussion under that Article above, p. 289.
[2] Rules 53 and 54 of the Court Rules of Procedure.

ARTICLE 53

The High Contracting Parties undertake to abide by the decision of the Court in any case to which they are parties.[1]

Les Hautes Parties Contractantes s'engagent à se conformer aux décisions de la Cour dans les litiges auxquels elles sont parties.

ARTICLE 54

The judgment of the Court shall be transmitted to the Committee of Ministers which shall supervise its execution.

L'arrêt de la Cour est transmis au Comité des Ministres qui en surveille l'exécution.

ARTICLE 55

The Court shall draw up its own rules and shall determine its own procedure.

La Cour établit son règlement et fixe sa procédure.

ARTICLE 56

(1) The first election of the members of the Court shall take place after declarations by the High Contracting Parties mentioned in Article 46 have reached a total of eight.

(2) No can can be brought before the Court before this election.

1. La première élection des membres de la Cour aura lieu après que les déclarations des Hautes Parties Contractantes visées à l'article 46 auront atteint le nombre de huit.

2. La Cour ne peut être saisie avant cette élection.

---

[1] The principle of *res judicata* is binding only on the parties: 8778/79 (Switzerland) 20 D.R. 240.

SECTION V

ARTICLE 57

On receipt of a request from the Secretary-General of the Council of Europe any High Contracting Party shall furnish an explanation of the manner in which its internal law ensures the effective implementation of any of the provisions of this Convention.

Toute Haute Partie Contractante fournira sur demande du Secrétaire Général du Conseil de l'Europe les explications requises sur la manière dont son droit interne assure l'application effective de toutes les dispositions de cette Convention.

The general supervisory function assigned here to the Secretary-General is, on the one hand, limited by the fact that, in case a failure to implement one or more provisions effectively is disclosed, he cannot bring the issue before the Commission or the court. On the other hand, where no declaration under Article 25 is in force and no application made under Article 24, action under this Article could be useful; and the Secretary-General might in a particular case bring any failure disclosed under Article 57 to the attention of the Consultative Assembly[1] or to the Committee of Ministers for possible action under Article 8 of the Statute of the Council of Europe.

The Secretary-General addressed a letter in October 1964 to the then fifteen contracting States, which was the first application of Article 57. The letter invited them to

discharge the obligation devolving upon them under Article 57 by stating in their reports how their laws, their case-law and their administrative practice give effect to the fundamental rights and freedoms guaranteed by the Convention and its first Protocol. Texts of any relevant laws, administrative regulations or judicial decisions could be appended to the report concerning your country.[2]

---

[1] See Statute of Council of Europe, Articles 23 and 15; and see also Article 61 of the Convention.
[2] See Doc. H (66) 9 for the replies of eleven governments up to the end of May 1966.

ARTICLE 58

The expenses of the Commission and the Court shall be borne by the Council of Europe.

Les dépenses de la Commission et de la Cour sont à la charge du Conseil de l'Europe.

ARTICLE 59

The members of the Commission and of the Court shall be entitled, during the discharge of their functions, to the privileges and immunities provided for in Article 40 of the Statute of the Council of Europe and in the agreements made thereunder.

Les membres de la Commission et de la Cour jouissent, pendant l'exercice de leurs fonctions, des privilèges et immunités prévus à l'article 40 du Statut du Conseil de l'Europe et dans les Accords conclus en vertu de cet article.

It has been held in England that immunity from suit in respect of acts done in discharge of Commission functions continues after membership has ceased.[1]

ARTICLE 60

Nothing in this Convention shall be construed as limiting or derogating from any of the human rights and fundamental freedoms which may be ensured under the laws of any High Contracting Party or under any other agreement to which it is a Party.

Aucune des dispositions de la présente Convention ne sera interprétée comme limitant ou portant atteinte aux Droits de l'homme et aux libertés fondamentales qui pourraient être

The remaining four governments had replied by the summer of 1967. All the replies are in brief and summary form. Further requests were sent in 1970, 1975, and 1983.

[1] *Zoernsch* v. *Waldock and McNulty* 1 *WLR* 675 [1964]: see under Article 19 above at p. 336.

reconnus conformément aux lois de toute Partie Contractante ou à toute autre Convention à laquelle cette Partie Contractante est partie.

ARTICLE 61

Nothing in this Convention shall prejudice the powers conferred on the Committee of Ministers by the Statute of the Council of Europe.

Aucune disposition de la présente Convention ne porte atteinte aux pouvoirs conférés au Comité des Ministres par le Statut du Conseil de l'Europe.

ARTICLE 62

The High Contracting Parties agree that, except by special agreement, they will not avail themselves of treaties, conventions or declarations in force between them for the purpose of submitting, by way of petition, a dispute arising out of the interpretation or application of this Convention to a means of settlement other than those provided for in this Convention.

Les Hautes Parties Contractantes renoncement réciproquement, sauf compromis spécial, à se prèvaloir des traités, conventions ou déclarations existant entre elles, en vue de soummetre, par voie de requête, un différend né de l'interprétation ou de l'application de la présente Convention à un mode de règlement autre que ceux prévus par la dite Convention.

Since the provisions of this Article may, by its own terms, be set aside by special agreement, its scope is limited; but it would, in the absence of such agreement, bar objections to the competence of the Commission or the court on the ground that the complainant State was bound by treaty to submit the complaint to another mode of settlement. Article 62 could only operate, it seems, in regard to interstate applications under Article 24.

ARTICLE 63

(1) Any State may at the time of its ratification or at any time thereafter declare by notification addressed to the Secretary-General of the Council of Europe that the present Convention shall extend to all or any of the territories for whose international relations it is responsible.

(2) The Convention shall extend to the territory or territories named in the notification as from the thirtieth day after the receipt of this notification by the Secretary-General of the Council of Europe.

(3) The provisions of this Convention shall be applied in such territories with due regard, however, to local requirements.

(4) Any State which has made a declaration in accordance with paragraph 1 of this Article may at any time thereafter declare on behalf of one or more of the territories to which the declaration relates that it accepts the competence of the Commission to receive petitions from individuals, non-governmental organisations or groups of individuals in accordance with Article 25 of the present Convention.

1. Tout État peut, au moment de la ratification ou à tout autre moment par la suite, déclarer, par notification adressée au Secrétaire Général du Conseil de l'Europe, que la présente Convention s'appliquera à tous les territoires ou à l'un quelconque des territoires dont il assure les relations internationales.

2. La Convention s'appliquera au territoire ou aux territoires désignés dans la notification à partir du trentième jour qui suivra la date à laquelle le Secrétaire Général du Conseil de l'Europe aura reçu cette notification.

3. Dans les dits territoires les dispositions de la présente Convention seront appliquées en tenant compte des nécessités locales.

4. Tout État qui a fait une déclaration conformément au premier paragraphe et cet article, peut, à tout moment par la suite, déclarer relativement à un ou plusieurs des territoires visés dans cette déclaration qu'il accepte la compétence de la Commission pour connaître des requêtes de personnes physiques, d'organisations non gouvernementales ou de groupes de particuliers conformément à l'article 25 de la présente Convention.

The territorial extent of the Convention has already been discussed under Article 1, and the territories to which the Convention is extended under Article 63, there listed.[1]

Paragraph (3) introduces a rather large qualification, not easy to interpret. But practice under the Convention suggests at least that 'local requirements/nécessités locales' refers primarily to permanent or organic characteristics of a territory and would not extend to temporary features: thus the United Kingdom has, in face of temporary difficulties in territories covered by Article 63, always relied upon notice of derogation under Article 15.

The difficulties involved in deciding upon such an extension to overseas territories are shown in the hestitation of France over the acceptance of the Convention itself,[2] and the utility of such an extension is problematic.

ARTICLE 64

(1) Any State may, when signing this Convention or when depositing its instrument of ratification, make a reservation in respect of any particular provision of the Convention to the extent that any law then in force in its territory is not in conformity with the provision. Reservations of a general character shall not be permitted under this Article.

(2) Any reservation made under this Article shall contain a brief statement of the law concerned.

---

[1] See p. 20. For the position of the Belgian Congo before July 1960, to which the Convention had not been extended under Article 63, see 942/60: *Recueil* (1961) ii, and 1065/61: 4 *Yearbook* 266.

[2] See Ministerial statement in French National Assembly in 1960: 3 *Yearbook* 536.

1. Tout État peut, au moment de la signature de la présente Convention ou du dépôt de son instrument de ratification, formuler une réserve au sujet d'une disposition particulière de la Convention, dans la mesure où une loi alors en vigueur sur son territoire n'est pas conforme à cette disposition. Les réserves de caractère général ne sont pas autorisées aux termes du présent article.

2. Tout réserve émise conformément au présent article comporte un bref exposé de la loi en cause.

Reservations, which have come in issue in particular applications, are discussed under the relevant Articles.[1] Certain general remarks may be made here.

Of the reservations and similar declarations, which are still operative, the majority are statements of interpretation of Convention provisions, rather than reservations in the strict sense; they give notice of the meaning and effect, which the contracting State gives to the provision, rather than indicate that it cannot be effectively observed.

Certain principles emerge from decisions of the Commission on the effect of resrvations:

first, a reservation must be construed exclusively in terms of the language in which it has been expressed;[2]

second, a reservation, though limited in terms to a particular provision, must extend to other provisions of the Convention from which it cannot be dissociated with disregard to the plain intendment of the reservation;[3]

third, legislation or administrative action in the field directly covered by the reservation fall within it even though they are subsequent to the date of deposit of the instrument of reservation.[4]

---

[1] For texts of reservations still operative see *Collective Texts*, 5th ed., section 5.

[2] 1047/61: *Recueil* (1961) ii; 1452/62: 6 *Yearbook* 272.

[3] 1008/61: 6 *Yearbook* 86.

[4] 1731/62: *Recueil* (1964) i, and compare earlier decisions 473/59: 4 *Yearbook* 405 and decisions there cited. All these decisions concern the Austrian reservation in respect of Parts IV and V of the Austrian State Treaty. See also 2432/65: *Recueil* 22 for the effects of this Reservation. For the 'interpretative declaration' by Switzerland see Temeltasch (Switzerland) D116/80: 26 D.R. 217.

ARTICLE 65

(1) A High Contracting Party may denounce the present Convention only after the expiry of five years from the date on which it became a Party to it and after six months' notice contained in a notification addressed to the Secretary-General of the Council of Europe, who shall inform the other High Contracting Parties.[1]

(2) Such a denunciation shall not have the effect of releasing the High Contracting Party concerned from its obligations under this Convention in respect of any act which, being capable of constituting a violation of such obligations, may have been performed by it before the date at which the denunciation became effective.

(3) Any High Contracting Party which shall cease to be a Member of the Council of Europe shall cease to be a Party to this Convention under the same conditions.

(4) The Convention may be denounced in accordance with the provisions of the preceding paragraphs in respect of any territory to which it has been declared to extend under the terms of Article 63.

1. Une Haute Partie Contractante ne peut dénoncer la présente Convention qu'après l'expiration d'un délai de cinq ans à partir de la date d'entrée en vigueur de la Convention à son égard et moyennant un préavis de six mois, donné par une notification adressée au Secrétaire Général du Conseil de l'Europe, qui en informe les autres Parties Contractantes.

2. Cette dénonciation ne peut avoir pour effet de délier la Haute Partie Contractante intéressée des obligations contenues dans la présente Convention en ce qui concerne tout fait qui, pouvant constituer une violation de ces obligations, aurait été accompli par elle antérieurement à la date à laquelle la dénonciation produit effet.

---

[1] See the case of Greece: 34 *Recueil* 64.

3. Sous la même réserve cesserait d'être Partie à la présente Convention toute Partie Contractante qui cesserait d'être Membre du Conseil de l'Europe.

4. La Convention peut être dénoncée conformément aux dispositions des paragraphes précédents en ce qui concerne tout territoire auquel elle a été déclarée applicable aux termes de l'article 63.

No action under paragraph (4) has been found necessary in the case of territories to which the Convention has been extended under Article 63 and which have subsequently become independent States. As already observed under Article 1, membership[1] of the Council of Europe is a condition of participation by States in the Convention.

ARTICLE 66

(1) This Convention shall be open to the signature of the Members of the Council of Europe. It shall be ratified. Ratifications shall be deposited with the Secretary-General of the Council of Europe.

(2) The present Convention shall come into force after the deposit of ten instruments of ratification.

(3) As regards any signatory ratifying subsequently, the Convention shall come into force at the date of the deposit of its instrument of ratification.

(4) The Secretary-General of the Council of Europe shall notify all the Members of the Council of Europe of the entry into force of the Convention, the names of the High Contracting Parties who have ratified it, and the deposit of all instruments of ratification which may be effected subsequently.

1. La présente Convention est ouverte à la signature des Membres du Conseil de l'Europe. Elle sera ratifiée. Les ratifications seront déposées près le Secrétaire Général du Conseil de l'Europe.

---

[1] See under Article 66 below.

2. La présente Convention entrera en vigueur après le dépôt de dix instruments de ratification.

3. Pour tout signataire qui la ratifiera ultérieurement, la Convention entrera en vigueur dès le dépôt de l'instrument de ratification.

4. Le Secrétaire Général du Conseil de l'Europe notifiera à tous les Membres du Conseil de l'Europe l'entrée en vigueur de la Convention, les noms des Hautes Parties Contractantes qui l'auront ratifiée, ainsi que le dépôt de tout instrument de ratification intervenu ultérieurement.

The contracting States are now: Austria, Belgium, Cyprus, Denmark, Federal Republic of Germany, France, Greece, Iceland, Ireland, Italy, Lichtenstein, Luxembourg, Malta, Netherlands, Norway, Portugal, Spain, Sweden, Switzerland, Turkey, United Kingdom.

It appears that 'Member' in paragraph 1 is to be given the same meaning as in the Statute of the Council of Europe, where it includes Associate Members, save for purposes of representation on the Committee of Ministers.[1]

---

[1] Statute, Article 5 (*b*). The Saarland was an original party to the Convention having signed and ratified it on 14.1.1953. It ceases to be a party on its accession to the Federal Republic of Germany.

FIRST PROTOCOL

ARTICLE 1

Every natural or legal person is entitled to the peaceful enjoyment of his possessions. No one shall be deprived of his possessions except in the public interest and subject to the conditions provided for by law and by the general principles of international law.

The preceding provisions shall not, however, in any way impair the right of a State to enforce such laws as it deems necessary to control the use of property in accordance with the general interest or to secure the payment of taxes or other contributions or penalties.

Toute personne physique ou morale a droit au respect de ses biens. Nul ne peut être privé de sa propriété que pour cause d'utilité publique et dans les conditions prévues par la loi et les principes généraux du droit international.

Les dispositions précédentes ne portent pas atteinte au droit que possèdent les États de mettre en vigueur les lois qu'ils jugent nécessaires pour réglementer l'usage des biens conformément à l'intérêt général ou pour assurer le paiement des impôts ou d'autres contributions ou des amendes.

The concept of property is so vast and extended in its meanings and applications that it is not surprising either that the fathers of the Convention were hestitant to include it at all, or that the form of the Article finally agreed is of extreme generality. What is surprising is that the Article does not clearly enunciate a right to compensation for the taking of property, a principle which, though sometimes honoured in the breach, is recognized in the great part of the world, including those countries that seek to apply Communist doctrines of property ownership.[1] It is left to extract, if it is possible, a right to compensation out of

---

[1] See Alfred Drucker, 'Communist Compensation Treaties', 101 *C.L.Q.* [1961] 238, 904; and 'The Confiscation of Corporations and the Conflict of Laws': 234 *Law Times* (28 June 1963) 355.

the words 'no one shall be *deprived* of his possessions'; but the preparatory work is not helpful here.[1]

Three alternative approaches were considered at the meetings of the Committee of experts: to make an express requirement that there be compensation for the taking of property; to include a clause prohibiting 'arbitrary confiscation', from which, so it was argued, a right to compensation could be inferred; to omit any reference to compensation, either express or implied. The first approach had at one time the support of a majority in the Committee of Experts; the second approach was adopted by the Consultative Assembly in its original draft proposal for the Article, but it was the third approach, urged throughout by the United Kingdom, which appears in the end to have been taken. For if, as was pointed out in the preparatory discussion, 'arbitrary confiscation' is too vague a concept for the derivation of a precise right to compensation, the word 'deprived' is still feebler, and it is hard to see that a right compensation could be seriously implied by it.

Though the parts of the Article are laid out differently, it follows the pattern of Articles 8–11 of the Convention: a general right or freedom is enunciated, and then a number of conditions or circumstances are enumerated, in which derogation or restriction may be justified. However, Article 1 is unlike the earlier Articles in the extreme breadth and generality of the concepts with which the permitted exceptions are expressed: deprivation, control, and general interest are hardly capable, as they stand, of precise application.[2]

legal person/personne morale

The Commission has held that a shareholder in a company may, at least if he holds a substantial majority of the shares, be regarded as a 'victim' of alleged breaches of Article 1 in respect of the company:

... even if under Austrian law only the company as such would be entitled to take legal action in regard to the Applicant's complaints, ... the Applicant is to be considered a victim, within the meaning of Article 25 ..., of the alleged violations of Article 1 of the Protocol; ... in this respect the Commission has

---

[1] *T.P.* v.
[2] For a valuable discussion of the Article see K. H. Böckstiegel, *Die allgemeinen Grundsätze des Völkerrechts über Eigentumsentziehung* (de Gruyter, Berlin, 1963).

had particular regard to the fact that about 91% of the shares in the company were held by the Applicant.[1]

The principle of the 'corporate veil', that 'the corporation is a person and its ownership is a non-conductor that makes it impossible to attribute an interest in its property to its members',[2] is here rejected by the Commission.[3]

peaceful enjoyment/respect ... deprived of his possessions/privé de sa propriété

Article 1 in fact separates the ownership of property, and its deprivation, from the use of property, and its regulation. Its first sentence is then otiose, and 'peaceful enjoyment' could mean more than 'droit au respect'. But the Commission has not spent time over this picturesque phrase but has said simply that Article 1

se dirige essentiellement contre la confiscation arbitraire de la propriété.

reintroducing the expression in Article 17 (2) of the Universal Declaration, on the second approach already described. The drafters of Article 1 had not only considered but rejected this expression.

The Commission has given 'possessions/biens' a broad meaning, as covering any property right or interest recognized in domestic law. It has held that the deprivation of a right *in rem* is an instantaneous act or decision that does not produce a 'continuing situation', for purpose at least of the six months rule.[4] Further Article 1 does not create any obligation for the State to secure the value of property, as against inflation; nor does it extend to future earnings.[5]

Deprivation of possessions in the public interest includes taxation,[6] customs duties, imposition of fines, orders for attachment of unlawful

---

[1] 1706/62: *Recueil* 211. Compare 712/60: 4 *Yearbook* 394 for the converse situation; and for compulsory sale of minority shares 8588/79 (Sweden) 29.64.

[2] *Klein* v. *Board of Tax Supervisors* [1930] 282 U.S. 472.

[3] Compare *Czechoslovakia*: Law No. 100/1945 on nationalization of mines and certain industrial enterprises, s. 7 (3) of which provides that 'if compensation for the nationalized property is denied to the corporation, a proportionate part of the compensation is due to its members', not being German or Hungarian nationals or former collaborators with the enemy: cited by Alfred Drucker, op. cit., in n. 1.

[4] 7742/76 (F.R.G.) 14.140.

[5] 8724/78 (F.R.G.) 20 D.R. 226; 6776/74.

[6] 511/59 3 *Yearbook* 395.

property,[1] and redistribution of land in clearance schemes,[2] and compulsory contributions to social security schemes.[3] Taxation can raise many Convention issues: whether, for example, tax differentiation between the self-employed and other workers and employees is discriminating,[4] and whether a statutory rule limiting tax relief *retrospectively* to defeat tax evidence was wrong in principle.[5]

Compulsory contributions to social security may create a property right over a portion of the assets in the fund.[6] Consequently, pension rights may in certain circumstances be a property right for the purpose of Article 1. It does not of course guarantee any right to pension, but it can protect it; that is to say, the absence of a pension scheme, for example, State servants, is not inconsistent with the Convention, but if a scheme *is* established, it may create a property right for paricipants protected by Article 1.

Pensions schemes may be voluntary or compulsory, State or private, contributory or non-contributory. Without pursuing all the possible variations here (some combinations may create a property right, with which the State can be only very remotely concerned) but taking the case of a voluntary, contributory State scheme, we may then say that Article 1 gives protection since there is a *statutory obligation* on the State to pay the pension, since it is in consideration in part of the pension that the participant has worked and contributed; this obligation gives the participant what is in the nature of a contractual right.

Nevertheless, the State may, under Article 1 and in the 'public interest', alter the terms of a statutory pension and has a margin of appreciation as to what that interest requires. However, the Commission may 'control' the exercise of this judgment by satisfying itself that it is reasonable. So a rule denying pension to a participant as long as he obtains equivalent income from active work appears reasonable and in the public interest, since the purpose of a 'pension fund' is to provide income to those no longer working or able to work, and the rule protects the fund for the benefit of all participants.[7]

---

[1] *Handyside* (U.K.) Judgment No. 24.

[2] The effect of a clearance area scheme on established property rights under Articles 6, 8, and 13 of the Convention is reviewed in 9261/81 (U.K.) 28 D.R. 177.

[3] For example, under a collective labour agreement: 7669/76 (Netherlands) 15 D.R. 133.

[4] 6163/73 (Austria): 1 D.R. 60; 7995/77 (U.K.) 15 D.R. 198.

[5] 8531/79 (U.K.) 23 D.R. 203 (principle not extended in Convention to *civil* legislation).

[6] *Muller* (Austria) 5849/72 3 D.R. 25.

[7] 2207/64: *Recueil* (1965) ii.

in the public interest/pour cause d'utilité publique

The Commission has had no difficulty in finding measures, aimed at monetary and economic stability, to be in the public interest,[1] or, where this has been specifically questioned, to fall within the margin of appreciation by the legislature.[2]

It is possible that 'public interest' and 'general interest' in Article 1 are to be distinguished in the sense that the former is to be equated with the national interest, but the latter with the interest of the community, national or local, as opposed to that of the individual.[3]

But the question of compensation remains, how far the traditional principle of 'prompt, adequate and effective compensation'—ignored by the Convention, and the two U.N. Covenants—still be regarded as part of human rights. Earlier decisions of the Commission, where claims of compensation have come into account have not been precisely in print because any right to compensation has been submerged in the public interest. So it has repeated claims arising in devaluation of currency,[4] or for *indexation* of monetary value of savings accounts in face of inflation,[5] or in the case of a levy on capital gains, accruing to mortgages out of currency changes in Germany.[6]

However, in 1980 and 1981, surprisingly late in the history of the Commission, the scope of Article 1 (1) of the First Protocol was made a basic issue in a group of applications by United Kingdom companies, engaged in great part in aircraft and shipbuilding.[7] Under the Aircraft and Shipbuilding Industries Act (1977) two public corporations, British Aerospace and British Shipbuilders, were established, and the shares of a number of specified companies were to rest in the corporations. Compensation was to be paid on the basis of the actual

---

[1] See for example 511/59: 3 *Yearbook* 422.

[2] 2845/66 (compulsory acquisition of debentures held in steel companies taken into public ownership in the United Kingdom).

[3] Contrast 215/56 (eviction from house not fit for habitation); 496/59 (use of property contrary to interests of tenants); and 662/59 (eviction from illegally constructed house) with 673/59 (general rent control) and 1132/61 (town and country planning).

[4] 784/60; 1017/61; 2045/63 (revaluation of German mark in 1961 causing loss to an applicant resident in Germany and drawing pension from Austria).

[5] See n. 24.

[6] 673/59: 4 *Yearbook* 290.

[7] 9006/80: Sir William Lithgow, shipbuilder; 9262/81, Vosper P.L.C.; 9263/81 English Electric Co. and Vickers P.L.C.; 9265/81 Banstonian Co. and Northern Shipbuilding; 9266/81 Yarrow P.L.C.; 9405/81 Dawsett Securities Ltd, E.F.I. (U.K. Finance) P.L.C., and Prudential Assurance Ltd.

or hypothetical stock market valuation of the shares in 'acquired companies' during a six-months reference period.

The Commission report, adopted on 7.3.1984, on the manifold issues cannot be even summarized here, and we shall be confined to its statements on compensation, in which the cited reasoning of the Court and the conclusions of the Commission reveal two principles.

First, by recognizing the right to peaceful enjoyment of possessions, 'Article 1 is in substance guaranteeing the right of property'[1] for the

Convention is designed to safeguard the individual in a real and practical way as regards those areas with which it deals[2]

The language suggests that the right of property necessarily guarantees compensation for its taking. But this absolute principle, declared in Article 17 (2) of the Universal Declaration, is carefully avoided as it was in the drafting of the Convention and the Covenants.

The second and decisive principle is the balancing of interests called for in the second sentence of Article 1. The Commission explains this as follows in § 353 of its Report:

... the Court has held that it 'must determine whether a fair balance was struck between the demands of the general interest of the community and the requirements of the individual's fundamental rights': *Sporrong/Lonnroth Judgment* No. 52 § 69. One factor which the Court took into account in deciding whether such a balance had been struck was the absence of any provision for compensation for the interference in question: §§ 71, 73.

The Court thus treated a right to compensation for interference with property rights as being an inherent feature of the right of property set forth in Article 1, in so far as it might form a necessary ingredient in a fair balance between public and private rights.

The two principles expressed in Article 1 imply then that compensation for the taking of property is not an unqualified right but is a balancing of interests of the public and of the property holder.[3]

---

[1] *Marckx* Judgment No. 31 § 63.
[2] *Airey* Judgment No. 32 § 26.
[3] Compulsory contributions to a pension scheme create a property right over a portion of the assets, but no right to a particular account: n. 13.

the general principles of international law/les principes généraux du droit international

The Commission has said that this condition may not be invoked by an applicant against a contracting State of which he is a national. These principles referred to in Article 1

> have been established in general international law in relation to the confiscation of the property of foreigners; . . . it follows that measures taken by a State with respect to the property of its own nationals are not subject to these general principles of international law in the absence of a particular treaty clause specifically so providing.[1]

other contributions/autres contributions

These must include contributions or charges, similar to taxes,[2] and also in the view of the Commission to cover seizure of assets in execution of a court judgment,[3] and the payment of court costs.[4]

The sequestration of the money and effects of a prisoner serving sentence for the period of his detention has also been held to be consistent with Article 1.[5]

ARTICLE 2

No person shall be denied the right to education. In the exercise of any functions which it assumes in relation to education and to teaching, the State shall respect the right of parents to ensure such education and teaching in conformity with their own religious and philosophical convictions.

Nul ne peut se voir refuser le droit à l'instruction. L'État, dans l'exercice des fonctions qu'il assumera dans le domaine de l'éducation et de l'enseignement, respectera le droit des

---

[1] 511/59: 3 *Yearbook* 422. The Commission here invoked the preparatory work as confirming this construction: CM/WP (51) 3, 11, 20, 21, 29. The application concerned Law no. 44/1957 in Iceland imposing taxes on certain capital assets; the applicants were an Icelandic national and Icedlandic company. See also 1870/73: *Recueil* 18.

[2] So held in *Netherlands*: Hoge Raad (13.3.1963) (national insurance contributions).

[3] 1420/62 and 1477/62: 6 *Yearbook* 625–7.

[4] 323/57: 1 *Yearbook* 241.

[5] 1681/62: *Receuil* (1964) i. 8341/78 (Austria) 19 D.R. 230.

parents d'assurer cette éducation et cet enseignement conformément à leurs convictions religieuses et philsophiques.

The magnitude of the difficulty of formulating the right to education is
shown by its deferment to the First Protocol, by the length and complexity of the preparatory work, and by the reservations or declarations made in respect of the Article by the contracting States.

The Article was in its entirety in issue in the *Belgian Linguistic Cases*
before the Commission, and its interpretation, which is closely related
to that of Articles 8 and 14, must await the judgment of the court, to
which these cases have been referred. However, certain features of the
Article may be noted here.

No person shall be denied the right to education/Nul ne peut se voir refuser le droit à l'instruction

The original version of this clause, proposed by the Consultative
Assembly, was identical with Article 26 (1), first sentence, of the
Universal Declaration: 'Everyone has the right to education/Toute
personne a droit à l'instruction'. Supporters of the negative formulation considered that the Consultative Assembly draft would impose
positive obligations upon contracting States going beyond what they
could accept: in the words of the Secretary General, commenting on
the draft Protocol:[1]

Bien que l'État assure, comme il va de soi, l'instruction des enfants, dans
tous les pays membres, il est impossible à ces derniers de s'engager sans
restrictions à pourvoir à l'instruction, car cette clause pourrait être interprétée
comme s'appliquant aux adultes illettrés pour lesquels aucune facilité n'est
prévue, ou aux types ou aux degrés d'enseignement que l'État ne peut assurer
pour une raison ou pour une autre.

But whether the adoption of the negative formulation wholly solves
the problem, and whether there may not be still circumstances in
which the State must take action to prevent a denial of the right to
education, is an open question.

The second clause is addressed to social problems of great complexity, and its interpretation is correspondly difficult. Among the
'functions' which the State may assume, State aid to schools and State
establishment and management of schools must be distinguished; the

[1] Doc. AS/JA (5) 13 (18.9.1951): *T.P.* v. 1164–5.

extent of 'the right of parents' to establish private, including denominational, schools or other means of education, conforming with their convictions, is in question; in question too is the extent of the obligation of the State to 'respect' that right.[1]

Some of these issues were made matters of reservation. Thus Sweden

could not grant to parents the right to obtain, by reason of their philosophical convictions, dispensation for their children from the obligation of taking part in certain parts of the education in the public schools, and also . . . the dispensation from the obligation of taking part in the teaching of Christianity in these schools could only be granted for children of another faith than the Swedish Church, in respect of whom a satisfactory religious instruction had been arranged [Translation].[2]

Ireland declared that Article 2

is not sufficiently explicit in ensuring to parents the right to provide education for their children in their homes or in schools of the parents' own choice, whether or not such schools are private schools, or are schools recognised or established by the State.

The United Kingdom accepted the second clause

only so far as it is compatible with the provision of efficient instruction and training and the avoidance of unreasonable public expenditure.

The Netherlands, on the other hand, declared that the State should 'if need be, ensure the possibility [of parents] exercising these rights by appropriate financial measures'.

The meaning of the word 'philosophical' has given rise to much debate. The preparatory work shows that at least two senses were in the minds of the drafters: ideological and non-religious. In the first sense, philosophical convictions would in the second clause cover beliefs and attitudes opposed to totalitarian or other objectionable ideologies; in the second sense it would cover attitudes in which parents objected by lack of or hostility to religious belief any religious instruction being given to their children. The question whether

---

[1] This was one of the issues which for a time was an obstacle for France to ratification of the Convention; for a Ministerial Statement on the point in the National Assembly in December 1960, see 3 *Yearbook* 536.

[2] For a contrary solution of the problem in the United States see *McCallum* v. *Board of Education* [1948] 333 U.S. 203 (Supreme Court ruling that no person may be required to attend religious instruction in a State-recognized or State-aided institution).

'philosophical convictions' can also cover cultural attitudes, such as language preference, has been raised in the *Belgian Linguistic Cases*.

Similarly, in regard to opposition to religious instruction or practice in schools, we have seen the attitude of Sweden expressed in its reservation to the Protocol, under which it will not allow such opposition if based on other than religious convictions. The United States, while recognizing a right of parents to oppose religious instruction or practice in the schools on religious or philosophical grounds, does not facilitate it, while in the Federal Republic of Germany, the Constitutional Court of Land Hessen has carried the protection of the right to oppose to a point at which it might be thought that the rights and freedoms of others are infringed.[1]

Particular issues, arising under Article 1 and determined by the Commission, are that it is primarily concerned with elementary education,[2] that the right of a teacher to display particular more or religious belief in class hours, may be restricted if they fall within the regulation of Article 10 (2),[3] or that compulsory membership of a student association does not bar individual access to university, recognition of completed studies.[4] But there are three leading cases, in which the Commission and the Court both went in depth into the interpretation of Article 2; they involved the choice of language of instrution in the Belgian schools;[5] sex education introduced in the schools in Denmark;[6] use of corporal punishment in Scottish schools.[7]

Among the principles declared were:

The Contracting States do not recognise that such a right to education as would require them to establish at their own expense or to subsidise, education of any particular type or at any particular level[8]

---

[1] *Hoffman* v. *Land Hessen* [1966] Verfassungsgericht: *N.J.W.* [1966] No. 1/2, 31, in which the court observed that: 'The holding of classroom prayers in practice puts a strong degree of pressure upon the child to attend, in that his failure to do so marks him out as different and lays him open to the risk of being discriminated against.'

[2] 5962/72 (U.K.) 2 D.R. 50.

[3] 8010/77 (U.K.) 23 D.R. 228.

[4] 6094/73 (Sweden) 9 D.R. 5.

[5] The *Belgian Linguistic Cases*: Report of Commission (24.6.1965); Judgment No. 6 (23.7.1968) (brought from the districts of Alsemberg, Kraainem, Gand, Louvain, Vilvorde, and provoked in part by the Conflict between the French and the Flemish languages).

[6] *Kjeldsen, Busk Madsen, Pedersen* (Denmark): Report of Commission (21.3.1975): Judgment No. 23 (7.12.1976) (integrated programme of sex education in State schools).

[7] *Campbell and Cosans* (U.K.): Judgment No. 48 (25.2.1982). The cases are referred to as A, B and C. in the following notes.   [8] A. § 3.

In short, the State has no obligation under Article 2 to establish or subsidise private schooling.

Nevertheless, the State has clear responsibilities in education.

... the setting and planning of the curriculum fall in principle within the competence of the Contracting States. This mainly involves questions of expediency on which it is not for the Court to rule and whose solution may legitimately vary according to the country and the era. In particular, the second sentence of Article 2 of the Protocol does not prevent States from imparting through teaching or education information or knowledge of a directly or indirectly religious or philosophical kind ... The second sentence of Article 2 implies on the other hand that the State in fulfilling the functions assumed by it in regard to education and teaching, must take care that information or knowledge included in the curriculum is conveyed in an objective, critical and pluralistic manner.[1]

As regards the notion of philosophical convictions, there was some indicaton in the preparatory work that the term was added to non-religious or agnostic opinions,[2] but:

... it is not capable of exhaustive definition ... The Commission pointed out that the word 'philosophy' bears numerous meanings; it is used to allude to a fully-fledged system of thought, or rather loosely to views on more or less trivial matters. The Court agrees with the Commission that neither of these two extremes can be adopted for the purpose of interpreting Aricle 2 ... Having regard to the Convention as a whole, including Article 17, the expression 'philosophical convictions' in the present context ... denotes such convictions as are worthy of respect in a 'democratic society' and are not incompatible with human dignity: in addition, they must not conflict with the fundamental right of the child to education.[3]

This definition does not carry us very far, nor does it explain the distinction made in the context of language use where it is said[4] that Article 2:

does not require of States that they should, in the sphere of education or teaching respect parents' linguistic preferences, but only their religious and philosophical convictions.

The term 'legislature' has been understood by the Commission as the institution so described in the constitutional system of a given

---

[1] B. § 53.
[2] A. Report of Commission § 379.
[3] C. § 36.   [4] A. § 6.

country. In general, then, Article 3 is held as inapplicable to the election of local government organs, given that their legislative function is fixed by statute and is confined to the 'making of bye-laws applicable within their areas'.[1]

The rules governing elections are also matters of domestic law.

The Commission considers that, while Article 3 in principle recognizes proportional representation, it does not require its introduction. The recognition of political parties for participation in elections, and conditions to be met by candidates for election, have come in question in applications under Article 3. Of both these issues the Commission has said:

> ... conditions which are set up for political parties taking part in the elections serve the purpose of constituting the political process as a public one, of avoiding the confusions of the electorate by groups, which cannot assume political responsibility, because they do not propose candidates in accordance with the electoral law. The requirement of 500 signatures in Hamburg, and of 104 in Lower Saxony ... can easily be satisfied by parties, which have a real chance to have only the slightest success in the election ... the above conditions cannot therefore be said to hinder the free expression of the people in the choice of the legislature.

ARTICLE 3

The High Contracting Parties undertake to hold free elections at reasonable intervals by secret ballot, under conditions which will ensure the free expression of the opinion of the people in the choice of the legislature.

Les Hautes Parties Contractantes s'engagent à organiser, à des intervalles raisonnables, des élections libres au scrutin secret, dans les conditions qui assurent la libre expression de l'opinion du peuple sur le choix du corps législatif.

Free elections are often regarded as a cardinal principle of democracy.[2] Article 21 (3) of the Universal Declaration reads:

---

[1] 5155/71 (U.K.) 6 D.R. 13.
[2] As to free elections as a condition of recognition of new governments, see *Proceedings of the Crimea Conference, 1945*: Cmd. 7088 at 4.

The will of the people shall be the basis of the authority of government; this shall be expressed in periodic and genuine elections which shall be held by universal and equal suffrage, and shall be held by secret vote or by equivalent free voting procedures.

Certain elements in this paragraph throw light on the meaning of Article 3 of the Protocol: the will of the people is to be the basis of the authority of government; a distinction is made between genuine and free elections; and suffrage, that is the right to vote, is to be accorded without discrimination as to who exercises it or as to its effects.

The first two elements are to be found in Article 3, though there the will or opinion of the people is only expressed in the choice of the legislature. The distinction between genuine and free elections is made, though in slightly different language; thus an election could be said not to be genuine, or a free expression of opinion, if there was only one candidate, or, possibly, only one party, or if it was in some way 'rigged'; it would not be free if, for example, the voters were subjected to outside pressures or temptations to vote in a particular way.

It is in the third element that Article 3 presents a certain problem. Does it accord a right to vote to the individual citizen? The Commission has answered this in language which suggests that it does not:

... although, according to this Article, the contracting Parties undertake to hold free elections, it does not follow that they recognize the right of every individual (*reconnaissent à toute personne le droit*) to take part therein; ... in other words, an individual's right to vote is not guaranteed by Article 3. ...[1]

Again, where an applicant had had his right to vote suspended in Belgium, among other deprivations, for offences of collaboration during the Second World War,[2] the Commission said:

... Article 3 of the Protocol does not guarantee the right [set out in Penal Code, Article 31 (2)] but solely the right whereby the Contracting States hold 'free elections ... choice of the legislature'.[3]

Again, where Belgian citizens resident in the Congo complained of their exclusion from participation in elections in Belgium, the

---

[1] 530/59: 3 *Yearbook* 190: followed in 787/60: *Recueil* (1961) i (Article 3 provisions 'do not guarantee to an individual the right to participate in elections and to cast his vote').

[2] Under Penal Code, Article 123 sexies (*a*), referring to 'the right to vote, to stand for election or to be elected' set out in Penal Code, Article 31 (2).

[3] 1028/61: 4 *Yearbook* 338. See 778/60 *Recueil* (1961) i for the obligation to hold free elections as such.

Commission rejected the application as incompatible since the right to vote being not, as such, guaranteed,

the Contracting States may therefore exclude certain categories of citizen, such for example as overseas residents, from the vote, provided such exclusion does not prevent the free expression of the opinion of the people in the choice of the legislature.[1]

An examination of the facts in the four decisions of the Commission, cited on the point, will show that in each case there was a deprivation of the right to vote, or exclusion from participation in an election, for an individual or class of individuals. In short, the decisions are saying in effect, not that there is in general no right to vote recognized or guaranteed by Article 3, but that there is no right to vote, regardless of conditions or limitations which a contracting State may impose consistently with generally accepted practice and other provisions of the Convention, particularly Article 14.[2]

The opposite problem is posed by compulsion to vote, that is, a legislative requirement with penal sanctions that those having a right of vote exercise it in elections. The Commission has said that the notion of freedom used in Article 3 does not prohibit such a requirement:

le terme d' 'élection libres' signifie, non des élections où le vote n'est pas obligatoire, mais des élections où l'acte de faire un choix électoral est libre, et le système électoral en question est compatible avec cet article.[3]

Where there is a right to stand as a candidate in elections, which can be deduced from Article 3, is open.[4]

ARTICLE 4

Any High Contracting Party may at the time of signature or ratification or at any time thereafter communicate to the Secretary-General of the Council of Europe a declaration stating the extent to which it undertakes that the provisions of

[1] 1065/61: 4 *Yearbook* 268.
[2] See 2728/66 for a fuller formulation by the Commission; 6573/74 (Netherlands) 1 D.R. 87.
[3] 1718/62: *Recueil* 16. Compare *Mather* v. *Daniel* [1964] West Austrialian Rep. cited in *Annual Survey of Commonwealth Law 1965* at 106.
[4] 2366/65: *Recueil* 22 (right invoked by Communist in Federal Republic of Germany—application rejected for an exhaustion of constitutional remedies).

the present Protocol shall apply to such of the territories for the international relations of which it is responsible as are named therein.

Any High Contracting Party which has communicated a declaration in virtue of the preceding paragraph may from time to time communicate a further declaration modifying the terms of any former declaration or terminating the application of the provisions of this Protocol in respect of any territory.

A declaration made in accordance with this Article shall be deemed to have been made in accordance with Paragraph (1) of Article 63 of the Convention.

Toute Haute Partie Contractante peut, au moment de la signature ou de la ratification du présent Protocole ou à tout moment par la suite, communiquer au Secrétaire Général du Conseil de l'Europe une déclaration indiquant la mesure dans laquelle il s'engage à ce que les dispositions du présent Protocole s'appliquent à tels territoires qui sont désignés dans ladite déclaration et dont il assure les relations internationales.

Toute Haute Partie Contractante qui a communiqué une déclaration en vertu du paragraphe précédent peut, de temps à autre, communiquer une nouvelle déclaration modifiant les terms de toute déclaration antérieure ou mettant fin à l'application des dispositions du présent Protocole sur un territoire quelconque.

Une déclaration faite conformément au présent article sera considérée comme ayant été faite conformément au paragraphe 1 de l'article 63 de la Convention.

ARTICLE 5

As between the High Contracting Parties the provisions of Articles 1, 2, 3, and 4 of this Protocol shall be regarded as additional Articles to the Convention and all the provisions of the Convention shall apply accordingly.

Les Hautes Parties Contractantes considéreront les articles 1, 2, et 3 de ce Protocole comme des articles additionnels à la

Convention et toutes les dispositions de la Convention s'appliqueront en conséquence.

This article makes the First Protocol an integral part of the Convention, so that the two main instruments may be treated for all purposes of interpretation and application as one. Ratification of the Protocol is, however, distinct from ratification of the Convention.

Reservations have been made, by virtue of Article 64 of the Convention, to Article 1 of the Protocol by Austria and Luxembourg, and to Article 2 by Greece, Luxembourg, Sweden, Turkey, and the United Kingdom.

ARTICLE 6

This Protocol shall be open for signature by the Members of the Council of Europe, who are the signatories of the Convention; it shall be ratified at the same time as or after the ratification of the Convention. It shall enter into force after the deposit of ten instruments of ratification. As regards any signatory ratifying subsequently, the Protocol shall enter into force at the date of the deposit of its instrument of ratification.

The instruments of ratification shall be deposited with the Secretary-General of the Council of Europe, who will notify all Members of the names of those who have ratified.

Le présent Protocole est ouvert à la signature des Membres du Conseil de l'Europe, signataires de la Convention; il sera ratifié en même temps que la Convention ou après la ratification de celle-ci. Il entrera en vigueur après le dépôt de dix instruments de ratification. Pour tout signataire qui le ratifiera ultérieurement, le Protocole entrera en vigueur dès le dépôt de l'instrument de ratification.

Les instruments de ratification seront déposés près le Secrétaire Général du Conseil de l'Europe qui notifiera à tous les Membres les noms de ceux qui l'auront ratifié.

The Protocol has been ratified by all contracting States except Liechtenstein, Spain, and Switzerland.

Protocols 2 and 3 in force on 21 September 1970, cover the competence of the Court to give advisory opinions, and include amendments to the Convention; Protocol 5 in force on 20 December 1971, contains amendments to Articles 22 and 40.

Draft Protocols 7 and 8 containing amendments and additional Articles to the Convention are still in process.

Protocol 4 has not been adopted by Cyprus, Greece, Liechtenstein, Malta, Switzerland, Turkey, or the United Kingdom. Article 2 has been invoked unsuccessfully in three applications;[1] and in a different application concerning the repatriation of 199 Vietnamese children from Denmark the Commission gave a meaning to 'collective expulsion of aliens, in Article 4 as:

> ... any measure of the competent authority compelling aliens as a group to leave the country except where such a measure is taken after and on the basis of a reasonable and objective examination of the particular cases of each individual in the group. Since the respondent government will allow each individual case to be judged as far as practicable, on its merits and since it may be in the interests of some of the children to be repatriated rather than to remain in Denmark, no issue of collective expulsion can arise.[2]

---

[1] 8980I/80 (Belgium) 23 D.R. 237; 7680/76 (F.R.G.) 9 D.R. 190; 8988/80 (Belgium) 24 D.R. 198.

[2] Becker (Denmark) 70II/75: 4 D.R. 215.

FOURTH PROTOCOL

STRASBOURG, 16.9.1963

IN FORCE 2.5.1968

The Governments signatory hereto, being Members of the Council of Europe.

Being resolved to take steps to ensure the collective enforcement of certain rights and freedoms other than those already included in Section I of the Convention for the Protection of Human Rights and Fundamental Freedoms signed at Rome on 4th November 1950 (hereinafter referred to as 'the Convention') and in Articles 1 to 3 of the first Protocol to the Convention, signed at Paris on on 20th March 1952.

Have agreed as follows:

Les Gouvernements signataires, Membres du Conseil de l'Europe.

Résolus à prendre des mesures propres à assurer la garantie collective de droits et libertés autres que ceux qui figurent déjà le titre I de la Convention de sauvegarde des Droits de l'Homme et des libertés fondamentales, signée à Rome le 4 novembre 1950 (ci-après dénommée 'la Convention') et dans les articles 1er à 3 du premier Protocole additionnel à la Convention, signé à Paris le 20 mars 1952,

Sont convenus de ce qui suit:

ARTICLE 1

No one shall be deprived of his liberty merely on the ground of inability to fulfil a contractual obligation.

Nul ne peut être privé de sa liberté pour la seule raison qu'il n'est pas en mesure d'exécuter une obligation contractuelle.

ARTICLE 2

(1) Everyone lawfully within the territory of a State shall, within that territory, have the right to liberty of movement and freedom to choose his residence.

(2) Everyone shall be free to leave any country, including his own.

(3) No restrictions shall be placed on the exercise of these rights other than such as are in accordance with law and are necessary in a democratic society in the interests of national security or public safety, for the maintenance of *ordre public*, for the prevention of crime, for the protection of health or morals, or for the protection of the rights and freedoms of others.

(4) The rights set forth in paragraph 1 may also be subect, in particular areas, to restrictions imposed in accordance with law and justified by the public interest in a democratic society.

1. Quiconque se trouve régulièrement sur le territoire d'un État a le droit d'y circuler librement et d'y choisir librement sa résidence.

2. Toute personne est libre de quitter n'importe quel pays, y compris le sien.

3. L'exercice de ces droits ne peut faire l'objet d'autres restrictions que celles qui, prévues par la loi, constituent des mesures nécessaires, dans une société démocratique, à la sécurité nationale, à la sûreté, au maintien de l'ordre public, à la prévention des infractions pénales, à la protection de la santé ou de la morale, ou à la protection des droits et libertés d'autrui.

4. Les droits reconnus au paragraphe 1er peuvent également, dans certaines zones déterminées, faire l'objet de restrictions qui, prévues par la loi, sont justifiées par l'intérêt public dans une sociéte démocratique.

ARTICLE 3

(1) No one shall be expelled, by means of an individual or a collective measure, from the territory of the State of which he is a national.

(2) No one shall be deprived of the right to enter the territory of the State of which he is a national.

1. Nul ne peut être expulsé, par voie de mesure individuelle ou collective, du territoire de l'État dont il est le ressortissant.

2. Nul ne peut être privé du droit d'entrer sur le territoire de l'État dont il est le ressortissant.

ARTICLE 4

Collective expulsion of aliens is prohibited.

Les expulsions collectives d'étrangers sont intérdites.

ARTICLE 5

(1) Any High Contracting Party may, at the time of signature or ratification of this Protocol, or at any time thereafter, communicate to the Secretary General of the Council of Europe a declaration stating the extent to which it undertakes that the provisions of this Protocol shall apply to such of the territories for the international relations of which it is responsible as are named therein.

(2) Any High Contracting Party which has communicated a declaration in virtue of the preceding paragraph may, from time to time, communicate a further declaration modifying the terms of any former declaration or terminating the application of the provisions of this Protocol in respect of any territory.

(3) A declaration made in accordance with this article shall be deemed to have been made in accordance with paragraph 1 of Article 63 of the Convention.

(4) The territory of any State to which this Protocol applies by virtue of ratification or acceptance by that State, and each territory to which this Protocol is applied by virtue of a declaration by that State under this article, shall be treated as separate territories for the purpose of the references in Articles 2 and 3 to the territory of a State.

1. Toute Haute Partie Contractante peut, au moment de la signature ou de la ratification du présent Protocole ou à tout moment par la suite, communiquer au Secrétariat Général du Conseil de l'Europe une déclaration indiquant la mesure dans laquelle elle s'engage à ce que les dispositions du présent Protocole s'appliquent à tels territoires qui sont désignés dans ladite déclaration et dont elle assure les relations internationales.

2. Toute Haute Partie Contractante qui a communiqué une déclaration en vertu du paragraphe précédent peut, de temps à autre, communiquer une nouvelle déclaration modifiant les termes de toute déclaration antèrieure ou mettant fin à l'application des dispositions du présent Protocole sur un territoire quelconque.

3. Une déclaration faite conformément au présent article sera considérée comme ayant été faite conformément au paragraphe 1 de l'article 63 de la Convention.

4. Le territoire de tout État auquel le présent Protocole s'applique en vertu de sa ratification ou de son acceptation par ledit État, et chacun des territoires auxquels le Protocole s'applique en vertu d'une déclaration souscrite par ledit État conformément au présent article, seront considérés comme des territoires distincts aux fins des références au territoire d'un État faites par les articles 2 et 3.

ARTICLE 6

(1) As between the High Contracting Parties the provisions of Articles 1 to 5 of this Protocol shall be regarded as additional

articles to the Convention, and all the provisions of the Convention shall apply accordingly.

(2) Nevertheless, the right of individual recourse recognized by a declaration made under Article 25 of the Convention, or the acceptance of the compulsory jurisdiction of the Court by a declaration made under Article 46 of the Convention, shall not be effective in relation to this Protocol unless the High Contracting Party concerned has made a statement recognising such right, or accepting such jurisdiction, in respect of all or any of Articles 1 to 4 of the Protocol.

1. Les Hautes Parties Contractantes considéreront les articles 1er à 5 de ce Protocole comme des articles additionnels à la Convention et toutes les dispositions de la Convention s'appliqueront en conséquence.

2. Toutefois, le droit de recours individuel reconnu par une déclaration faite en vertu de l'article 25 de la Convention ou la reconnaissance de la juridiction obligatoire de la Cour faite par une déclaration en vertu de l'article 46 de la Convention ne s'exercera en ce qui concerne le présent Protocole que dans la mesure où la Haute Partie Contractante intéressée aura déclaré reconnaître ledit droit ou accepter ladite juridiction pour les articles 1er à 4 du Protocole ou pour certains de ces articles.

ARTICLE 7

(1) This Protocol shall be open for signature by the Members of the Council of Europe who are the signatories of the Convention; it shall be ratified at the same time as or after the ratification of the Convention. It shall enter into force after the deposit of five instruments of ratification. As regards any signatory ratifying subsequently, the Protocol shall enter into force at the date of the deposit of its instrument of ratification.

(2) The instruments of ratification shall be deposited with the Secretary General of the Council of Europe, who will notify all Members of the names of those who have ratified.

1. Le Présent Protocole est ouvert à la signature des Membres du Conseil de l'Europe, signataires de la Convention; il sera ratifié en même temps que la Convention ou après la ratification de celle-ci. Il entrera en vigueur après le dépôt de cinq instruments de ratification. Pour tout signataire qui le ratifiera ultérieurement, le Protocole entrera en vigueur dès le dépôt de l'instrument de ratification.

2. Les instruments de ratification seront déposés près le Secrétaire Général du Conseil de l'Europe qui notifiera à tous les Membres les noms de ceux qui l'auront ratifié.

SIXTH PROTOCOL

IN FORCE 1.3.1985

The member States of the Council of Europe, signatory to this Protocol to the Convention for the Protection of Human Rights and Fundamental Freedoms, signed at Rome on 4 November 1950 (hereinafter referred to as 'the Convention'),

Considering that the evolution that has occurred in several member States of the Council of Europe expresses a general tendency in favour of abolition of the death penalty;

Have agreed as follows:

Les États membres du Conseil de l'Europe, signataires du présent Protocole à la Convention de sauvegarde des Droits de l'Homme et des Libertés fondamentales, signée à Rome le 4 novembre 1950 (ci-après dénommée 'la Convention').

Considérant que les développements intervenus dans plusieurs États membres du Conseil de l'Europe expriment une tendance générale en faveur de l'abolition de la peine de mort;

Sont convenus de ce qui suit:

ARTICLE 1

The death penalty shall be abolished. No one shall be condemned to such penalty or executed.

La peine de mort est abolie. Nul ne peut être condamné à une telle peine ni exécuté.

ARTICLE 2

A State may make provision in its law for the death penalty in respect of acts committed in time of war or of imminent threat of war; such penalty shall be applied only in the instances laid down in the law and in accordance with its provisions. The

State shall communicate to the Secretary General of the Council of Europe the relevant provisions of that law.

Un État peut prévoir dans sa législation la peine de mort pour des actes commis en temps de guerre ou de danger imminent de guerre; une telle peine ne sera appliquée que dans les cas prévus par cette législation et comformément à ses dispositions. Ce État communiquera au Secrétaire Général du Conseil de l'Europe les dispositions afférentes de la législation en cause.

ARTICLE 3

No derogation from the provisions of this Protocol shall be made under Article 15 of the Convention.

Aucune dérogation n'est autorisée aux dispositions du présent Protocole au titre de l'article 15 de la Convention.

ARTICLE 4

No reservation may be made under Article 64 of the Convention in respect of the provisions of this Protocol.

Aucune réserve n'est admise aux dispositions du présent Protocole au titre de l'article 64 de la Convention.

ARTICLE 5

(1) Any State may at the time of signature or when depositing its instrument of ratification, acceptance or approval, specify the territory or territories to which this Protocol shall apply.

(2) Any State may at any later date, by a declaration addressed to the Secretary General of the Council of Europe, extend the application of this Protocol to any other territory specified in the declaration. In respect of such territory the Protocol shall enter into force on the first day of the month following the date of receipt of such declaration by the Secretary General.

(3) Any declaration made under the two preceding paragraphs may, in respect of any territory specified in such declaration, be withdrawn by a notification addressed to the Secretary General. The withdrawal shall become effective on the first day of the month following the date of receipt of such notification by the Secretary General.

1. Tout État peut, au moment de la signature ou au moment du dépôt de son instrument de ratification, d'acceptation ou d'approbation, désigner le ou les territoires auxquels s'appliquera le présent Protocle.

2. Tout État peut, à tout autre moment par la suite, par une déclaration adressée au Secrétaire Général du Conseil de l'Europe, étendre l'application du présent Protocole à tout autre territoire désigné dans la déclaration. Le Protocole entrera en vigueur à l'égard de ce territoire le premier jour du mois qui suit la date de réception de la déclaration par le Secrétaire Général.

3. Toute déclaration faite en vertu des deux paragraphes précédents pourra être retirée, en ce qui concerne tout territoire désigné dans cette déclaration, par notification adressée au Secrétaire Général. Le retrait prendra effet le premier jour du mois qui suit la date de réception de la notification par le Secrétaire Général.

ARTICLE 6

As between the State Parties the provisions of Articles 1 to 5 of this Protocol shall be regarded as additional articles to the Convention and all the provisions of the Convention shall apply accordingly.

Les États Parties considèrent les articles 1 à 5 du présent Protocole comme des articles additionnels à la Convention et toutes les dispositions de la Convention s'appliquent en conséquence.

APPENDIX 1

International Conventions and Declarations

These lists of leading conventions and declarations are divided into those which have a general coverage, and are global or regional, and those that are directed to particular rights and freedoms; and there is a separate list of ILO Conventions, and of instruments concerned with armed conflict.

References are made to:

Cmnd   Command Papers
U.N.T.S.   United Nations Treaty Series
G.A.   U.N. General Assembly Resolutions
I.L.M.   International Legal Materials
C.L.B.   Commonwealth Law Bulletin
Brownlie   I. Brownlie *Basic Documents on Human Rights* (Oxford, 1971)

The dates given are those of the entry into force of convention, or of the formal adoption of a declaration (in brackets); and of the ratification of a convention by the United Kingdom (to the left of the title).

GENERAL INSTRUMENTS

Universal Declaration of Human Rights (1948)	
1970 Genocide Convention (1951)	78 U.N.T.S. 277 Cmnd 4221
Convention for the Suppression of the Traffic in Persons and of the Exploitation of the Prostitution of Others (1951)	96 U.N.T.S. 271
1967 Convention on the Political Rights of Women (1954)	193 U.N.T.S. 135 Cmnd 3449
1951 European Convention on Human Rights (1953)	Brownlie pp. 358–88
1951 Protocol 1 (1952)	
Protocol 4 (1963)	
Protocol 6 (1985)	
Declaration on the Rights of the Child	G.A. 1386–XIV Brownlie p. 188
1962 Convention against Discrimination in Education (1962) (1968)	Cmnd 1760
Convention on the Nationality of Married Women (1958)	
Convention on the International Right of Correction (1962)	

1962 European Social Charter (1965)	6 I.L.M. 300
1969 Convention for Elimination of all Forms of	
Racial Discrimination (1969)	660 U.N.T.S. Cmnd 4108
Declaration on Principles of International Law	
concerning Friendly Relations and Cooperation	
among States	G.A. 2625–XXV
Convention on the Elimination of all Forms of	
Discrimination against Women (1981)	G.A. 34/180
	Brownlie p. 183
American Convention on Human Rights (1978)	6 I.L.M. 673
African Charter on Human and People's	
Rights	
1976 Civil and Political Rights Covenant (1976)	6 I.L.M. 383 Cmnd 6702
1976 Economic Social and Cultural Rights (1976)	6 I.L.M. 383 Cmnd 6702
Helsinki Conference: Final Act (1975)	Cmnd 6932
Universal Islamic Declaration of Human	
Rights (1981)	C.L.B. (Jan 1982) 232

PARTICULAR RIGHTS AND FREEDOMS

Slavery Convention (1927): amended by	
Protocol on Abolition of Slavery and Slave	
Trade (1957)	266 U.N.T.S. 3
1954 Status of Refugees (1954 Convention;	
1967 Protocol)	189 U.N.T.S. Cmnd 3906
	606 U.N.T.S. Cmnd 9171
Convention on Territorial Asylum	Organisation of American
Convention on Diplomatic Asylum	States: Treaty Series
	No. 34
1959 Convention on Status of Stateless Persons (1960)	360 U.N.T.S. 117 Cmnd 1098
Convention on Refugee Problems in Africa	14 U.N.T.S. 691 O.A.U.
Convention on Consent, Minimum Age and	
Registration of Marriage (1964)	
1961 Convention on Reduction of Statelessness (1975)	UN A/CONF/D15(1961)
	Cmnd 6364
Declaration on Territorial Asylum	G.A. 2312–XXII
1954 European Code of Social Security (1954)	European Treaty
	Series No. 10
Convention on Suppression and Punishment	
of the Crime of Apartheid (1976)	13 I.L.M. 30
1981 European Convention on Status of Children	
born out of Wedlock (1978)[1]	
Convention on Elimination of all Forms of	
Religious Intolerance	G.A. 36/55: C.L.B.
European Council of Ministers: Declaration	
on Freedom of Expression and Information	
(1982)	C.L.B. (April 1983) 630
Standard Minimum Rules for the Treatment	
of Prisoners	C.L.B. (October 1984) 1831

[1] See also Convention on Adoption of Children (1968), ratified by the United Kingdom (1967).

ILO CONVENTIONS

1949 Freedom of Association and Protection of the
      Right to Organise No. 87   68 U.N.T.S. 17
                                              Cmnd 7638

      Right to Organise and Bargain
            Collectively No. 98   96 U.N.T.S. Cmnd 7852
      Equal Remuneration for Equal Work for
            Men and Women No. 100 (1953)   165 U.N.T.S. 304
      Discrimination in respect of Employment and
            Occupation No. 111 (1960)   362 U.N.T.S. 31
      Equal Social Security Treatment
            No. 118 (1964)   494 U.N.T.S. 271

PROTOCOLS NOS 5–8 OF THE CONVENTION

Nos. 5, 6 and 8 entered into force on 20.2.1971,
   1.3.1985 and 19.3.1985; No. 7 has not entered
   into force.
No. 8 makes substantive changes in the structure
   and functions.

ARMED CONFLICT

1949 Geneva Conventions
      I Condition of wounded and sick in
        armed forces in the field
      II Condition of wounded, sick and ship
        wrecked members of armed forces at sea
      III Treatment of prisoners of war
      IV Protection of civilians in time of war
1978 European Convention on Suppression of
      Terrorism   15 I.L.M. 5272
1979 Convention against taking of hostages   G.A. 34/146
1970 Respect for human rights in
      armed conflicts   G.A. 2674–XXV

APPENDIX 2

United Kingdom Statutes related to Human Rights

Statutes have been selected, which are related to provisions of the European Countries or the International Covenants, and date from 1950. The formal title is given, the word 'Act' has been omitted.

1951 Common Informers
1952 Defamation
1955 Children and Young Persons (Harmful Publications)
1956 Sexual Offences: amendments in 1967 and 1976
1959 Restriction of Offensive Weapons
Obscene Publications (also 1964)
Mental Health
1960 Administrating Justice
Indecency with Children
1962 Commonwealth Immigrants (also 1968)
1965 Race Relations (also 1976)
1967 Fugitive Offenders
1969 Genocide
Immigration Appeals
Family Law Reform
1971 Hijacking of Aircraft
Recognition of Divorces and Legal Separation
1972 Legal Aid and Assistance

1973 Employment of Children
Guardianship
1974 Trade Union and Labour Relations
1975 Children
Social Security
1975 Sex Discrimination
Trade Union and Labour Relations: (Charter of Press Freedom)
1976 Domestic Violence
Race Relations
Prevention of Terrorism (Temporary Provision)
Legitimacy
Adoption
1978 Domestic Proceedings and Magistrates Courts
Suppression of Terrorism
1981 Indecent Displays (Control)
Contempt of Court
Education (special needs)
1982 Taking of Hostages
1984 Repatriation of Prisoners
Trade Union

APPENDIX 3

APPLICATION TO THE COMMISSION UNDER ARTICLE 25

1. An application to the European Commission of Human Rights may be made under Article 25 by any individual, group of individuals (including companies), or non-governmental organizations, by letter addressed to the *Secretary-General*, *Council of Europe*, *Strasbourg*, if the following conditions are satisfied:

(i) The applicant is a victim of the breach of the Convention alleged. A husband or wife or close relative may in certain cases be a victim. The Commission may, however, receive applications brought *on behalf of* a victim.

(*a*) in certain circumstances, by a husband or wife or close relative, or by a legal guardian,

(*b*) generally by any person, such as a lawyer, acting under a power of attorney.

(ii) The act or decision complained of is one of *public authority*: in general, of the central government, municipal authorities, or courts or tribunals established by law. No act or decision of a private person or body can be a breach of the Convention. Further, the act or decision must come within the meaning and scope of one of the provisions of the Convention; otherwise the application is *incompatible* in the sense of Article 27 (2).

(iii) The contracting State or government against which the application is brought has recognized the right of individual petition see Article 25. For application against the governments of dependent territories of Netherlands and the United Kingdom see Article 63.

(iv) Every reasonable effort has been made to get redress of the complaint in the country concerned, by proceedings in the courts or other action likely to secure an effective remedy.

(v) The application is brought *within six months* from the act or decision complained of, including the final decision on efforts to obtain redress.

2. There are no fees or charges imposed by the Commission or Council of Europe upon applications.

The Council of Europe has introduced a system of legal aid for applicants to the Commission, which is granted upon the conditions that are in general similar to those prevailing in countries where legal aid or assistance is available at public expense. Details can be obtained from the *Secretary of the Commission, Council of Europe, Strasbourg*.

APPENDIX 4

SELECTED SOURCES AND MATERIALS

Collected Texts, Fifth Edition—September 1966 (Council of Europe):
    European Convention on Human Rights (with reservations under
        Article 64)
    First Protocol (in force for all contracting States)
    Second Protocol conferring competence on Court to give certain
        advisory opinions (not in force)
    Third Protocol amending Articles 29, 30, and 34, to abolish Sub-
        commissions (not in force)
    Fourth Protocol adding certain rights and freedoms to the Conven-
        tion and First Protocol (in force for certain contracting States)
    Fifth Protocol amending Articles 22 and 40 (not in force)

Collection/Recueil: Decisions of the Commission 1955– .
CEDH: Judgments, Pleadings, and Documents of the Court.
Council of Europe, Human Rights in International Law: Basic Texts.
Yearbook of the European Convention on Human Rights:

1 1956–7
2 1958–9
3 1960
4 1961
5 1962
6 1963
7 1964
8 1965

[See also Bibliographies in the Yearbooks of the European Convention on Human Rights.]

1950

Sir Hersch LAUTERPACHT: *International Law and Human Rights* (Stevens).

1957

C. W. JENKS: *The International Protection of Trade Union Freedom*.

R. J. DUPUY: La Commission Européenne des Droits de l'Homme: *Ann. français de droit intern.* [1957] 449.

H. GOLSONG: The European Convention before Domestic Courts: 33 *B.Y.I.L.* [1957] 317.

C. EUSTATHIADES: Les recours individuels à la Commission Européenne des Droits de l'Homme: *Festschrift Spiropoulos* [1957] 111.

1958

Sir Humphrey WALDOCK: The European Convention for the Protection of Human Rights and Fundamental Freedoms: 34 *B.Y.I.L.* [1958] 356.

A. B. MCNULTY and M.-A. EISSEN: European Commission of Human Rights—Procedure and Jurisprudence: *Journal of I.C.J.*, vol. i, no. 198.

1959

H. WIEBRINGHAUS: *Die römische Konvention für Menschenrechte in der Praxis der Strassburger MRK* (Saarbrücken).

1960

P. O.'HIGGINS: The European Extradition Convention: 9 *I.C.L.Q.* 491.

C. W. JENKS: *Human Rights and International Labour Standards* (Stevens).

E. SCHWELB: International Conventions on Human Rights: 9 *I.C.L.Q.* 654.

M.-A. EISSEN: Procedural Aspects of the Lawless Case: *Ann. français de droit intern.* (1966) 444.

A. H. ROBERTSON: The First Case of the European Court of Human Rights: 28 *B.Y.I.L.* [1960] 343.

1961

A. H. ROBERTSON: Lawless *v.* Government of Ireland (second phase): 37 *B.Y.I.L.* [1961] 536.

W. MORVAY: Rechtssprechung nationaler Gerichte zur MRK: *Z. für A.Ö.R. und V.* Band 21, Nr. 1, 91.

1962

H. GOLSONG: The European Convention before Domestic Courts: 38 *B.Y.I.L.* 445.

G. Janssen-Pevtschin and J. Velu: La Convention et le fonctionnement des juridictions belges: 15. *Chronique de politique étrangère* 199.
D. G. Valentine: The Nielsen Case: 11 *I.C.L.Q.* 836.

1963

A. H. Robertson: *Human Rights in Europe* (Manchester U.P.).
R. B. Ellert: *NATO Fair Trial Safeguards* (Nijhoff).
F. Ermacora: *Handbuch der Grundfreiheiten und Menschenrechte* (Manz,
Wien).
H. Golsong: Implementation of International Protection of Human
Rights: 111 *Recueil des Cours* (Hague Academy) 7.
Gordon L. Weil: *The European Convention on Human Rights* (Sijthoff).

1964

U.N. Department of Economic and Social Affairs: Étude du droit en
vertu duquel nul ne peut être arbitrairement arrêté, détenu ou exilé:
E/CN. 4/826 Rev. 1.
K. Vasak: *La Convention européenne des droits de l'homme* (Pichon et
Durand-Anzias, Paris).
T. Burgenthal: Domestic Status of the European Convention on
Human Rights: 13 *Buffalo Law Review* (Winter 1964) 354.

1965

F. Monconduit: *La Commission Européenne des Droits de l'Homme* (Sijthoff).

1966

M. J. van Emde Boas: The Impact of the European Convention on
Human Rights on the Legal Order of the Netherlands: *Nederlands
Tijdschrift voor Internationaal Recht* (1966—IV) 337.
K. J. Partsch: *Die Rechte und Freiheiten der europäischen Menschenrechtskonvention* (Duncker und Humblot, Berlin).
D. J. Harris: The European Convention on Human Rights and English Criminal Law: *Criminal Law Review* (April 1966) 205; (May 1966)
266.
Geneviève Janssen: Les engagements des parties contractantes et la
mise en œuvre de la Charte Sociale Européenne: *Revue de l'Institut de
sociologie (Bruxelles)* [1966—I] 9.

1967

Henri ROLIN: Le contrôle international des juridictions nationales: *Revue belge de droit international* [1967–I]; [1968–I].

Edit. Evan LUARD: *The International Protection of Human Rights* (Thames and Hudson, London).

Clovis C. MORRISSON: *The Developing European Law of Human Rights* (Sijthoff).

N. ANTHONOPOULOS: *La Jurisprudence des organes de la Convention Européenne des Droits de l'Homme* (Sijthoff).

Edit. Asbjörn EIDE and August SCHOU: International Protection of Human Rights: *Nobel Symposium* 7 (Almqvist and Wiksell, Stockholm).

1968

Edit. A. H. ROBERTSON: *Human Rights in National and International Law* (Proceedings of Second Conference on the European Convention, October 1965) (Manchester University Press).

H. GURADZE: *Die europäisch Menschenrechtskonvention—Kommentar* (Verlag Franz Vahlen, Berlin u. Frankfurt).

Revue de droit international et comparé/Journal of International and Comparative Law: les droits de l'homme/Human Rights [1968] vol. i, no. 1 (Editor-in-Chief: K. VASAK).

1971

I. BROWNLIE: *Basic Documents on Human Rights* (Oxford).

1975

F. G. JACOBS: The European Convention on Human Rights (Oxford).

1979

Edit. F. E. DOWRICK: *Human Rights: Problems and Perspectives* (Saxon House).

H. PETZOLD: *The European Convention on Human Rights: Cases and Materials* (International Institute of Human Rights, Strasburg) 2 vols.

1981

COUNCIL OF EUROPE: *European Convention on Human Rights: Collected Texts*.

1982

Edit. K. VASAK: *The International Dimensions of Human Rights* (U.N.E.S.C.O.) 2 vols.

1983

A. DRZEMCZEWSKI: *The European Human Rights Convention in Domestic Law* (Oxford).
Paul SIEGHART: *The International Law of Human Rights* (Oxford).

1984

COUNCIL OF EUROPE: *Stocktaking on the European Convention on Human Rights*.

INDEX